Intellectuals in Action

Intellectuals in Action

The Origins of the New Left and
Radical Liberalism, 1945–1970

KEVIN MATTSON

The Pennsylvania State University Press • University Park, Pennsylvania

Library of Congress Cataloging-in-Publication Data

Mattson, Kevin, 1966–
  Intellectuals in action : the origins of the new left and radical liberalism, 1945–1970 /
Kevin Mattson.

      p.   cm.
  Includes bibliographical references and index.
  ISBN 0-271-02148-9 (cloth : alk. paper) — ISBN 0-271-02206-X (pbk. : alk. paper)
  1. New Left—United States.   2. Radicalism—United States.   3. Intellectuals—
United States—Political activity.   4. United States and government—1945–1989.
I. Title.

HN90.R3 M368   2002
320.51'3'092273—dc21

                                                                    2001055298

It is the policy of The Pennsylvania State University Press to use acid-free paper for the
first printing of all clothbound books. Publications on uncoated stock satisfy the minimum
requirements of American National Standard for Information Sciences—Permanence of
Paper for Printed Library Materials, ANSI Z39.48-1992.

For Vicky—and making a family together

In my own thinking and writing I have deliberately allowed certain implicit values which I hold to remain, because even though they are quite unrealizable in the immediate future, they still seem to me worth displaying. . . . One just has to wait, as others before one have, while remembering that what in one decade is utopian may in the next be implementable.
—C. Wright Mills, "Commentary on Our Country, Our Culture," 1952

Contents

Acknowledgments

It is always a pleasure to thank those who helped along the way. In my case, there were many. Thanks first of all to Taylor Stoehr. I contacted Taylor because of his immense knowledge about Paul Goodman's life, but he wound up giving more help than I deserved or expected—including plenty of editing and some fun, sharp debates about the overall project. Everyone I interviewed provided great insight and a willingness to answer pestering questions with grace. There were others who helped by reading the manuscript and providing remarkably astute advice: thanks to Robb Westbrook (for last time, this time, and more, I hope), Tom Bender (for a perfectly timed letter), John McMillian, Leon Fink, Mark Button, John Summers, David Sampliner (the best historian turned filmmaker that I know), Mark Schmitt (my anti-majoritarian friend), David Kallick (who keeps ideas like the ones explored here alive—and who suggested good titles), and Patrick Kavanagh (who read some drafts and drank a few with me). Penn State Press, as usual, provided wonderful assistance. Thanks especially go to Sandy Thatcher and Cherene Holland. Laura Reed-Morrisson did an amazingly astute job at editing and helped hone the book's arguments. The Press also lined up two great readers for this book: Paul Buhle (who sharpened my thinking) and Maurice Isserman (who shared his knowledge of the 1960s and something about why history actually matters). It goes without saying that all the readers I list here are not responsible for any errors in this book.

I would like to thank the following institutions and individuals for giving me permission to quote from unpublished papers and for providing me with assistance in my research endeavors: Yale University Library, Manuscripts and Archives, for permission to quote from the Dwight Macdonald Papers; the Center for American History at the University of Texas at Austin, for permission to quote from the C. Wright Mills Papers, 1934–1965 (with special thanks to Ralph Elder for so much assistance during my research at the Center); the Houghton Library, Harvard University, for allowing me to quote from the Paul Goodman Papers (bMS Am 2062 [174]; bMS Am 2062

[463]; bMS Am 2062 [177]; bMS Am 2062 [1143]; bMS Am 2062 [33]; bMS Am 2062 [34]; bMS Am 2062 [455]; bMS Am 2062 [6]; bMS Am 2062 [1218]: bMS Am 2062 [195]; bMS Am 2062 [185]; bMS Am 2062 [529]; bMS 2062 [1149]; bMS Am 2062 [165]; bMS Am 2062 [231]; bMS Am 2062 [205]; bMS Am 2062 [186]; bMS Am 2062 [148]; bMS Am 2062 [203]); Sally Goodman, for giving me permission to quote from the Paul Goodman Papers; the University of Oregon's Valley Library, for permission to quote from the William Appleman Williams Papers; and Elizabeth Kaufman, for permission to quote from the Arnold Kaufman Papers. Thanks are also due to the Bentley Historical Library at the University of Michigan for helping with my research into the Arnold Kaufman Papers and to the Wisconsin Historical Society for helping me with my research into the records of *Studies on the Left, Radical America,* and Students for a Democratic Society.

I presented this work and got helpful feedback at Indiana University (a special thanks to Jeff Isaac there) and the University of Maryland (thanks to Peter Levine). Another presentation at Ohio University to my colleagues— unbeknownst at the time—helped me think about some of the broader issues within the book. Without the support of Ben Barber and other folks at the Whitman Center, this book could not have been completed. My comrades have remained loyal throughout it all; Jeff is more like my brother than a friend, and Richard is not only a friend but also a *mensch.* Finally, there's my family: my mom has supported me in ways that are hard to imagine. And now there's Vicky, whose joy and exuberance at all of life makes me happier than she can ever know. I especially thank her for building a family together. For those I forgot: thanks, and *mea culpa.*

Introduction: Why Go Back?

The use of history . . . is to rescue from oblivion the lost causes of the past. History is especially important when those lost causes haunt us in the present as unfinished business.
—Paul Goodman, *Growing Up Absurd*, 1960

Lamenting the lack of an effective left in American politics is a venerable tradition. The title of Werner Sombart's classic work, *Why Is There No Socialism in the United States?* (1906), asked a formidable question—and Sombart did not need to justify asking it. Nearly one hundred years after he wrote, however, the words that best capture the state of the left in America are "dissolution" and "invisibility." Hanging on in a dwindling labor movement—itself not entirely trusted by left-leaning intellectuals who have increasingly gravitated toward the ivory tower—and a handful of politicians, the left is not simply small in number but also marginalized. It lacks any significant voice in the Democratic Party, having been displaced by the centrist (if not downright conservative) Democratic Leadership Council, which helped elect Bill Clinton as president. As a journalist wrote about the presidential election of 2000, "On big bread-and-butter issues, the triumph of market economics and the fear of a loaded label have left the [left-liberal] movement with neither a clear national champion nor a coherent agenda." This book hopes to address this deficit by examining a pivotal historical moment for the American left.[1]

I have confronted this political void in my personal life as well. I came of political age during the 1980s and worked within the remnants of organizations that had descended from the New Left of the 1960s, cutting my teeth in movements against the nuclear arms buildup and American foreign inter-

1. John Harwood, "Left Out: No Leader, No Real Candidate, Liberals Just Languish," *Wall Street Journal*, January 13, 2000 (I should note that I worked with an organization mentioned in this story); Werner Sombart, *Why Is There No Socialism in the United States?* (1906; reprint: White Plains, N.Y.: M. E. Sharpe, 1976). See also my own essays, "Where Are the Young Left Intellectuals?" *Social Policy* (Spring 1999): 53–58, and "Talking About My Generation (and the Left)," *Dissent* (Fall 1999): 58–63.

vention in Central America, especially El Salvador and Nicaragua. These movements called for America to decrease military spending in order to tackle the problems of rising social inequality. Organizations on the left had numerous strategic and reflective discussions in which political debate merged with action. I listened and took part in deliberations about whether peace movement organizations should concentrate on nonviolent direct action or more "legitimate" means of protest (and in D.C., my hometown, that meant a big march from the Washington Monument to the Capitol). A group that I helped organize constantly debated whether we should get our message across through the mass media (while potentially jeopardizing control over our ideas). My experiences within these movements and the debates they engendered also exposed me to the thinking of numerous political organizers who had come out of the struggles of the New Left—challenging the notion that all 1960s activists, such as Jerry Rubin, had "sold out" to become yuppies. Along with others in my generation, I heard a great deal about the heyday of the New Left during the 1960s. History, as it often does, spoke to me through my elders.[2]

In addition to this political activism, I happened to work in a used bookstore. (Activism, after all, was not a lucrative career.) In the store's back recesses, there were paperback copies of *Growing Up Absurd, The Power Elite, The Tragedy of American Diplomacy*—books I will discuss later. Reading these works confused me, because their assumptions and historical context seemed so terribly different from my own. It seemed that here was something completely off the map of my own time and era: public intellectuals on the left who addressed issues of political significance and who spoke to an active movement intent on changing America. Ideas seemed charged with political consequences rather than remaining purely academic. As a young activist growing up during the conservative decade of the 1980s, I did my best to reconstruct all of this; it seemed as though a different era haunted my own activism and political thinking. In becoming a historian, I believed that there was something to go back to in the New Left.

The history that will unfold in these pages focuses on the ideas that influ-

2. There is no comprehensive history of the political left during the 1980s, since it was overshadowed by Reaganism. But for some good sources, see *Reshaping the U.S. Left: Popular Struggles in the 1980s,* ed. Mike Davis and Michael Sprinker (London: Verso, 1988); Barbara Epstein, *Political Protest and Cultural Revolution: Nonviolent Direct Action in the 1970s and 1980s* (Berkeley and Los Angeles: University of California Press, 1991); and Lawrence Wittner, "Reagan and Nuclear Disarmament," posted at <http://bostonreview.mit.edu/BR25.2/wittner.html> and originally published in the April–May 2000 issue of *Boston Review.*

enced and sometimes oriented the New Left. This is *not* another book-on-the-1960s, for the New Left was only one feature of that peculiar decade (and perhaps less influential, some suggest, than the rise of the New Right at the time). I will not recount all of the events of the 1960s; they have been recounted elsewhere. Nor do I want to be sucked into the vortex of what many call the "culture wars"—battles over identity politics, countercultural lifestyles, and sexual liberation that, in some way or another, stem from the 1960s. And there are reasons not to address those issues here. First, in the New Left thinking that I will explore, we find few arguments about identity politics or celebrations of the counterculture. This, in and of itself, seems an important point to recall in any consideration of the legacy of New Left intellectuals. Second, I will not be defending or attacking everything that happened in the 1960s. If anything, I want to get out of the mind-set that has made the 1960s a booby trap. I do not want to write another *Destructive Generation* or *The Sixties Without Apology,* books with overly strident tones. Instead, I want to write a history that is concerned with the present but that also turns something of a dispassionate eye toward the past—specifically, toward the New Left.[3]

I am, by lack of birthright, incapable of writing a memoir about the 1960s. Memoir serves as our primary mode of 1960s history, but it is a genre that prizes personal experience over critical analysis (and it proliferates in our contemporary culture of narcissism). Baby boomers have spilled much ink coming to terms with what the 1960s meant for them. The generation that brought us the "politics of meaning" and a long period of soul search-ing churns out more memoirs than the publishing industry can handle. Ad-mittedly, some of these memoirs are good sources for historians trying to understand the past, but others reek of baby-boomer narcissism. Tom Hay-den, for instance, wrote, "We of the sixties accomplished more than most generations in American history." This sort of attitude becomes an impedi-ment to younger people who want to grapple with what the 1960s might mean for their own contemporary situation, their own standing in history. The culturally symbolic decade of the sixties has become the domain—indeed, the first-person, singular possession—of baby boomers and thus off-limits to those who happened to be born too late to witness it. So, too, with the New Left. In 1969, Staughton Lynd, a historian who would help canon-

---

3. See David Horowitz and Peter Collier, *Destructive Generation: Second Thoughts About the Sixties* (New York: Summit, 1989), and Sohnya Sayres et al., eds., *The Sixties Without Apology* (Minneapolis: University of Minnesota Press, 1984).

ize "bottom-up" histories told by participants, stated, "What Regis Debray says of the Cuban Revolution is also true of the American New Left, that its history 'can come to us only from those who organized and participated in it.'" Lynd's early inability to let go of his own history is reenacted today when I hear a presentation made by a younger historian about the New Left. Baby boomers in the room look askance at the young knave and break into a "well, I was *there*" declaration. Because the decade is not really past, in many people's minds, memoir substitutes for historical analysis.[4]

Though I want to do historical reconstruction here, my emphasis is on the ideas that inspired the New Left, some of which seem to live on today, even if they are not always recognized. This sort of intellectual history relates directly to contemporary concerns; in fact, one of the detrimental aspects of 1960s memoirs is that they make it too easy for members of my generation (so-called Generation X) to roll their eyes when listening to baby boomers recount their glory days. Gen X-ers laugh ironically at the innumerable memoirs about the 1960s, since they weigh like a tombstone on the lives of the young. That is one reason—along with the general historical amnesia from which all Americans suffer—why so many young adults do not know their past. Like it or not, the New Left did matter, and it continues to matter—especially for those of us (no matter what our age) concerned with the plight of American liberalism and progressivism today. The New Left promised a non-Marxist and democratic model of political change at a time of great historical possibilities. In order to explain the ideas of the New Left, I certainly pay attention to the events that informed them. Nonetheless, my emphasis here is not on the 1960s as a whole (indeed, my own historical focus goes beyond this one decade), but on the New Left and its ideas, some of which deserve pointed criticism and some of which could help enliven contemporary political discussions.

I believe, as a scholar, that the ideas examined here have been historically undervalued. In any history of the 1960s, we are served up a brief mention of writers like C. Wright Mills, Paul Goodman, and William Appleman Williams, who, we are told, provided the scaffolding of New Left activism. We might hear a bit about participatory democracy, criticisms of 1950s

4. Tom Hayden, *Reunion: A Memoir* (New York: Random House, 1988), xix; Staughton Lynd, "Toward a History of the New Left," in *The New Left,* ed. Priscilla Long (Boston: Extending Horizons, 1969), 2. For more on these issues, see Rick Perlstein, "Who Owns the Sixties?" *Lingua Franca* (May–June 1996): 30–37, and L. A. Kauffman, "Emerging from the Shadow of the Sixties," *Socialist Review* 18 (1990): 13.

conformity, anticommunism, or the development of a "new sensibility" in American culture. But the tumultuous events of the 1960s take their toll on the sustained analysis of ideas, for sooner rather than later, activism winds up displacing any mention of ideas in these histories. Instead of giving ideas short shrift, I think it is important to remain focused on them—even as they come into dialogue with activism—in order to understand the spirit of the New Left and its legacy. As Alan Brinkley has argued persuasively, "[t]he new radicals never developed the organizational or institutional skills necessary for building an enduring movement." Precisely for this reason, ideas seem that much more important: they have the capacity to endure more than fragile institutions can, and they can live on beyond the time in which they emerge. And I will argue that some of the ideas explored here deserve precisely this fate, while others do not.[5]

I also believe that this intellectual history will give us a much better sense of what the New Left was really about in historical terms. Too often, historians describe the New Left as a string of protest movements—originally appearing in the civil rights movement, then the anti-HUAC protests, the Free Speech Movement, the anti–Vietnam War protests, and finally the women's movement. In recounting this history, we frequently lose a sense of the political thought that transcended these specific movements and that formulated a wider conception of political change. Here we must pay attention to how the New Left defined itself against the Old Left, taking into account arguments against Marxism's failure to foresee capitalism's staying power. "Participatory democracy" and decentralization came to the fore when New Left intellectuals defined their own political theory. Politics was to be about more than just electoral activity; instead, it would relate directly to people's everyday lives. Intellectuals could play a central role in social and political change by confronting the power of what C. Wright Mills called the "cultural apparatus"—the mass media that seemed to have an increasingly pernicious control over America's public culture. All of these concepts (and many more, as we will see) were central to the New Left. Some have

5. Alan Brinkley, "The Therapeutic Radicalism of the New Left," in *Liberalism and Its Discontents* (Cambridge: Harvard University Press, 1998), 232. One of the exceptions to the general rule of downplaying ideas in the history of the New Left is James Miller's superb *"Democracy Is in the Streets": From Port Huron to the Siege of Chicago* (New York: Simon and Schuster, 1987), especially his chapter on C. Wright Mills. See also, for a book that examines the intellectual roots of the 1960s (although relatively diffusely, from my standpoint), Andrew Jamison and Ron Eyerman, *Seeds of the Sixties* (Berkeley and Los Angeles: University of California Press, 1994).

argued that the New Left created a mishmash of ideas, but it is nevertheless important for the historian to reconstruct the coherence that *did* exist. In understanding New Left ideas better, we get a stronger sense of what the New Left meant in the context of American political and intellectual history—and, potentially, for the present.[6]

In emphasizing ideas, I am not suggesting that the thinkers studied here were the most significant influence on the activists and social movements that we normally take as crucial to the New Left. Certainly, members of Students for a Democratic Society (SDS) and the Student Non-Violent Coordinating Committee (SNCC) read C. Wright Mills and Paul Goodman, as well as European thinkers like Albert Camus. Tom Hayden, whose writings helped define SDS, relied on C. Wright Mills; the ideas of Arnold Kaufman, as we will see, can be found in the Port Huron Statement of SDS. But New Left activists could be terribly ignorant of their intellectual predecessors. Pete Seeger's and Bob Dylan's folk music, along with the sneering rebellion of movie stars like Marlon Brando and James Dean, probably had more influence on many New Left activists than the sometimes complex books and articles discussed here. The historian Doug Rossinow has shown, too, that the social teachings of Christianity had an influence on activists in the Mid- and Southwest. When activists sought out something more than Brando's tough looks or the lyrics of a Dylan song, however, they very often turned to the pages of these thinkers.

Even so, my interest here is less in the direct impact of ideas and more in the intellectual questions that ran alongside the development of the New Left—ideas that had a life of their own. By taking ideas seriously, I will also try to introduce "normative" questions into the study of history. For I am as interested in what the New Left could have been as in what it actually *was* historically. The study of ideas is the best place to get a sense of this.[7]

6. On the New Left's lack of intellectual coherence, see Peter Clecak, *Radical Paradoxes: Dilemmas of the American Left, 1945–1970* (New York: Harper and Row, 1973), 71.

7. Early historians of the New Left make clear the influence of Mills and Goodman. See Jack Newfield's "informal survey" of New Left activists' reading patterns in his *A Prophetic Minority* (New York: New American, 1970), 87–88; see also Wini Breines, *Community and Organization in the New Left: 1962–1968 (The Great Refusal)* (New York: Praeger, 1982), 11. On the New Left's ignorance of its history, see Maurice Isserman, *If I Had a Hammer: The Death of the Old Left and the Birth of the New* (New York: Basic, 1987), 120–21. Doug Rossinow stresses Christianity, but also admits that "knowing" C. Wright Mills was an important mark of the New Left. See Rossinow's *The Politics of Authenticity: Liberalism, Christianity, and the New Left in America* (New York: Columbia University Press, 1998), 160–61.

To understand New Left ideas, we must first get the story straight. This history begins by following those who argue that what is often called the *spirit* of the 1960s did not start in the 1960s, but earlier. It is commonplace to see the New Left's inspiration emanating from much of the social criticism of the 1950s (books written by David Riesman and William Whyte, for instance) or from early debates among radical pacifists during the 1940s. I agree, and I therefore start by providing a concise background on American intellectual life during the 1940s, paying brief attention to *politics,* the small magazine that Dwight Macdonald formed during World War II and edited until 1949 (a difficult year in the tortured history of the Cold War). In its pages, writers developed some core strains of thought that helped lay the basis for things to come. I then examine the ideas and careers of two writers—C. Wright Mills and Paul Goodman—who started to write in the 1940s, often for *politics,* but whose careers took off during the 1950s. (Goodman actually started writing during the 1930s, but his ideas, I will argue, reflected the spirit of 1940s anarcho-pacifism.) Two other figures who encountered the early struggles for African American civil rights during the 1940s, William Appleman Williams and Arnold Kaufman, come next in my history. Finally, I complete the circle by examining two small magazines (both similar to and different from *politics*) launched in 1959 and 1960. *Studies on the Left* and *New University Thought* rose and fell during the crash-and-burn years of the 1960s. The younger intellectuals who edited and published these journals grappled with ideas developed by previous thinkers while creating their own. These publications—along with the work of Goodman, Williams, and Kaufman—allow me to see how ideas that developed during the 1940s and 1950s came into conversation with actual movements as well as a new generation of thinkers. I will then conclude by examining what this intellectual history tells us about current issues of American political thought and progressive ideas.[8]

8. On the influence of radical pacifism on the New Left, see Allen Smith, "Present at the Creation and Other Myths: The Port Huron Statement and the Origins of the New Left," *Socialist Review* 27 (1999): 1–27. For more on the periodization of the 1960s, see Andrew Hunt, "When Did the Sixties Happen?" *Journal of Social History* (Fall 1999): 147–61, and Wini Breines, "Whose New Left?" *Journal of American History* 75 (1988): 528–45. In claiming that these intellectuals played a central role in the thinking of the New Left, I should explain what some critics will obviously call oversights on my part. Perhaps most obvious is the glaring absence of Herbert Marcuse. Many think that Marcuse was *the* intellectual father of the New Left. Though he is important, I am most interested in explaining how the New Left grew from indigenous roots in American intellectual and political history. Marcuse, like his

I am not arguing that the ideas explored here simply popped up in 1945 and then died around 1970. History does not provide us with such clear-cut chapters. After all, the spirit behind the New Left did not originate in the late 1950s but in the mid-1940s. On the other hand, of the four major figures I study here, only one lived beyond 1972; the small magazines (if not their editors) had collapsed by this time as well. Thus, to a large extent, I am setting out a distinct period or episode in American intellectual history— one with a beginning and something of an end. With this said, though, I also believe that the ideas here lived on, precisely because so many of them fit within an even larger tradition of American radical thought that could never die so easily.

In researching this chapter in intellectual history, I became convinced that a synthetic treatment of New Left thinkers was needed. We already have biographies of each thinker studied here—Irving Louis Horowitz's on Mills; Taylor Stoehr's marvelous, though not complete, biography of Goodman and his relation to Gestalt therapy; Paul Buhle and Edward Rice-Maximin's insightful work on Williams. At first, I was prompted to focus on the nuances of Mills's political thinking, Goodman's activism, and Kaufman's mar-

---

other Frankfurt School comrades, moved to America during the 1930s (though unlike the others, he stayed), but he was always a deeply *German* thinker, even after living in America for twenty years. His philosophy is thoroughly Hegelian—with its emphasis on what his colleague, Theodor Adorno, called "negative dialectics"—and thus, in my opinion, stands outside the American intellectual tradition. As Morris Dickstein points out, Paul Goodman understood America much more than Marcuse did (in fact, as we will see, Goodman argued that Marcuse's philosophy failed to explain American protest movements). George Mosse made the same point by contrasting William Appleman Williams with Marcuse. For these reasons, Marcuse will hover in the background but will not be central. For examples of Marcuse's Hegelian thinking, see his *One-Dimensional Man* (Boston: Beacon, 1964), 141, and *Reason and Revolution: Hegel and the Rise of Social Theory* (Boston: Beacon, 1960), 27. See also Morris Dickstein, *Gates of Eden: American Culture in the Sixties* (New York: Basic, 1977), 74. George Mosse makes his point in his contribution to *History and the New Left: Madison, Wisconsin, 1950– 1970,* ed. Paul Buhle (Philadelphia: Temple University Press, 1990), 235. Besides Marcuse, I will also pay little attention to Norman Mailer; I see him more as a novelist—and really as a narcissistic self-promoter whose politics veered all over the place—than an intellectual. He can best be contrasted with Paul Goodman, who also began as a novelist and then turned into a social critic (but was much better at it than Mailer). Other intellectuals and activist-intellectuals to be discussed here, but not treated thoroughly, include the editors of *Liberation* magazine, Bayard Rustin, Martin Luther King Jr., Saul Alinsky, David Riesman, Albert Camus, Hannah Arendt, Nat Hentoff, Michael Harrington, I. F. Stone, Betty Friedan, and Irving Howe. These thinkers *will* enter into the picture, but only in the margins. By examining some of the debates that the central characters in this work had with other thinkers, I will clarify the reasoning behind my inclusions and exclusions.

riage of ideas and activism in the teach-in movement. Eventually, though, I began to see that the whole was bigger than the parts. We understand Mills's legacy better, for instance, when we see how Arnold Kaufman tried to build upon it during the mid-to-late 1960s. We get to see how important certain ideas were because they showed up in both Goodman's and Williams's writings. We sense an "intellectual culture," so to speak, by studying the correspondence between Kaufman and Williams when the two discussed shared ideas about the future of the peace movement. To assess the intellectual legacy of the New Left requires concentrated attention to each individual as well as a capacity to draw out larger themes that encompassed all of their work. I will therefore organize this book around each individual's life and how it interacted with certain themes.[9]

The Intellectual's Role in Political Change

The easiest theme to start with focuses on these intellectuals themselves—and more specifically, on how they conceived of their own work. All of their efforts come back to a single question: What role should intellectuals play in effecting political change? These thinkers realized that intellectuals are a peculiar "social type," a group of people concerned with the often abstract world of ephemeral ideas. Hovering in the background was the warning that intellectuals are at their best when distant from politics and power. As historian and critic Christopher Lasch once argued, only when intellectuals step back from governing institutions will they be able to "speak truth to power." Though the intellectuals studied here believed that power could easily corrupt even the most honest of writers and thinkers, they did not allow this to negate the importance of political involvement. Indeed, they hoped to balance the capacity to speak truth to power with engagement in projects of political change. And yet they had no desire to become legislators or aides to those in power; rather, they wanted to help create deliberative and democratic publics of thoughtful citizens capable of confronting those in power.

They saw the intellectual engaged in the collective pursuit of truth with

9. Irving Louis Horowitz, *C. Wright Mills: An American Utopian* (New York: Free, 1983); Taylor Stoehr, *Here, Now, Next: Paul Goodman and the Origins of Gestalt Therapy* (San Francisco: Jossey-Bass, 1994); Paul Buhle and Edward Rice-Maximin, *William Appleman Williams: The Tragedy of Empire* (New York: Routledge, 1995).

fellow citizens—a process they conceived as political. The intellectual's peculiar role in change required asserting more control over the "cultural apparatus." These thinkers wanted to ensure that intellectuals appearing on television would not lose ownership of their ideas, for instance, and that writers
expressing their thoughts for reading publics would communicate in accessible and clear ways (which often meant writing more pamphlets than books).
They also believed in a responsibility to help nurture—directly, and through
their own initiative—the publics with which they spoke. This meant going
into the world and getting citizens to deliberate in face-to-face forums.
During the civil rights movement, some helped form "Freedom Schools,"
in which intellectuals spoke directly with the poor and disenfranchised.
Others organized "teach-ins," where academics and intellectuals criticized
American foreign policy and debated political leaders. Still others founded
small magazines to be read by activists who would make them into forums
for alternative politics. In all of these ways, these intellectuals hoped to speak
to and with movements, balancing a concern with truth and intellectual
integrity with a need to be effective in the complicated world of political
change.[10]

To make this line of thinking clear, I will combine a number of different
approaches to historical inquiry. First, I will explore biography, explaining
how each figure's life intersected with the wider context of intellectual history and how each thinker came to develop his central ideas about political
change. My focus here will be on political commentary (for instance, Paul
Goodman's idea of decentralization as it related to the Free Speech Movement). Of course, such a focus often requires an assessment of the social or
psychological theory each thinker used to justify his vision of political
change. But—as a cautionary note to readers—I admit to bracketing certain
areas of thinking within each intellectual biography. This said, I also believe
in understanding ideas and not simply putting them in historical context. I
will therefore spend considerable time analyzing each thinker's political philosophy—discussing the origins of ideas but also explaining their internal
logic (or lack thereof). In his biography of John Dewey, Robert Westbrook

10. For Christopher Lasch's thinking on intellectuals and social change, see *The New Radicalism in America, 1889–1963: The Intellectual as a Social Type* (New York: Norton, 1965), and
Robert Westbrook, "Christopher Lasch, *The New Radicalism,* and the Vocation of Intellectuals," *Reviews in American History* 23 (1995): 176–91. For more on the tension between
political commitment and intellectual integrity in New Left political thought, see Richard
Flacks, *Making History: The American Left and the American Mind* (New York: Columbia University Press, 1988), 174.

quoted the intellectual historian, Morton White: "If you are going to talk about the causes and consequences of philosophical beliefs, you had jolly well better know a lot about what these beliefs are." I, too, heed White's words. But I also believe that something matters aside from philosophical beliefs. What matters, and sometimes matters more, is how intellectuals try to communicate their ideas to other citizens—the practices and institutions through which intellectuals nurture democratic publics. Much of my history, then, will take into account where intellectuals worked, whether in academia (sometimes comfortably, more often not), progressive think tanks (for instance, the Institute for Policy Studies), activist and movement organizations, or democratic forums like teach-ins. I believe that such activities tell us a great deal about the merits of these thinkers' ideas as they relate to political change.[11]

Just as important is how these intellectuals spoke to their publics. In the field of cultural studies today, much ink has been spilled over the relation of the intellectual to the purported end of "modernity" and the dawn of "postmodernity." The age of speaking in "universal" terms is supposedly past. When intellectuals allude to Enlightenment ideals, such as truth, justice, and equality, we are told that they really cloak their own self-interest and desire for power in the name of values that have lost credibility. New Left intellectuals would have been puzzled by the current anxiety of English professors writing about postmodernity and intellectuals. Mills, Goodman, Williams, Kaufman, and the editors of small magazines were at ease with their social and political roles. They were usually comfortable "speaking American," that is, referring to values embedded in the nation's identity, such as democracy and equality. They were "connected critics," in Michael Walzer's evocative phrase, who used their nation's best ideals to criticize their nation's worst practices. This becomes clearest in their critique of American foreign policy, especially in Cuba and Vietnam. Some of them were also comfortable evoking "universal values"—e.g., truth and justice—that transcended national ideals. At the same time, these New Left intellectuals believed that universal and national principles needed to find their way into particular, institutional, and historical practices and transformations. At their best, New Left intellectuals argued both for ideals and for "strategies" and believed that

---

11. Robert Westbrook (quoting Morton White), *John Dewey and American Democracy* (Ithaca: Cornell University Press, 1991), xii. On the "social history of intellectuals," see Thomas Bender, *Intellect and Public Life: Essays on the Social History of Academic Intellectuals in the United States* (Baltimore: Johns Hopkins University Press, 1993).

the two were inseparable, that they fed off one another. The responsibility of intellectuals was to balance universalistic inspiration with a capacity to speak to particular (local and national) communities and events.[12]

What a Left Could—and Should—Be

In considering the role of intellectuals in political change, the thinkers studied here also examined the relation of culture to politics. They questioned a long tradition in American radicalism that associated intellectual leftism with countercultural radicalism. From the time of *The Masses* magazine and the artistic experiments of Greenwich Village in the early twentieth century, intellectual radicalism and cultural rebellion seemed wedded. But New Left thinkers scrutinized this connection, and those historians who see the major contribution to intellectual life at this time as a "new sensibility"—alternative lifestyles and expressiveness—miss this somehow. New Left intellectuals were, I will show, deeply critical of the limits of cultural rebellion and self-expression as an ethic. After all, cultural rebellion could easily be taken over by a popular culture industry and turned into an empty commodity of stylized anger or hip withdrawal that failed to challenge the status quo. C. Wright Mills said as much about the "Angry Young Men" in England, Paul Goodman about the Beats, and Arnold Kaufman about the late-1960s hippie counterculture. Cultural radicalism, these thinkers noted, always threatened to displace the more challenging and serious work of political transformation.[13]

12. On the idea of "connected critics," see Michael Walzer, *The Company of Critics: Social Criticism and Political Commitment in the Twentieth Century* (New York: Basic, 1988), 23. The writings of those within cultural studies are too many to cite here. For a fairly representative example, see Andrew Ross, "Defenders of the Faith and the New Class," in *Intellectuals: Aesthetics, Politics, Academics,* ed. Bruce Robbins (Minneapolis: University of Minnesota Press, 1990). For the relation between postmodernity and intellectuals, see Zygmunt Bauman, *Legislators and Interpreters: On Modernity, Post-Modernity, and Intellectuals* (Ithaca: Cornell University Press, 1987). And for a good critical overview of these ideas, see John Michael, *Anxious Intellects: Academic Professionals, Public Intellectuals, and Enlightenment Values* (Durham: Duke University Press, 2000).

13. For interpretations that stress a connection between the intellectual history of the 1960s and a "new sensibility," see Ronald Berman, *America in the Sixties: An Intellectual History* (New York: Free, 1968), and Dickstein, *Gates of Eden.* More recently, Doug Rossinow has argued that cultural liberalism seems the only serious outcome from the activities of the New Left: see *Politics of Authenticity,* 294.

Instead of identifying a New Left transformation with cultural radicalism, the intellectuals studied here believed in a rational and reform-minded political transformation. They drew less upon Marxism (or a confidence in the working class as an agent of change) and more on the political concept of participatory democracy. The roots of this concept grew out of a "radical republican" tradition of politics, one that related to the writings of Thomas Jefferson. This tradition—with its faith in small virtuous farmers building an egalitarian commonwealth—was then updated in the modern intellectual explorations of John Dewey (especially his classic, *The Public and Its Problems*). The New Left intellectuals relied on this variety of political thought, which sometimes made their work seem nostalgic and unrealistic. Indeed, when they stood upon a republican foundation, they seemed more moralistic than political; their jeremiads sounded like pinings for a golden age (often the eighteenth or nineteenth century) now forgotten and difficult to recreate under present conditions. At the same time, their ideas about decentralized, participatory democracy suggested how ordinary citizens could participate in processes of deliberation and decision making within the confines of modernity.[14]

But even this more modern idea of participatory democracy could conflict with an Old Left belief in social and economic justice—something that seemed best protected by a strong, activist state. The civil rights movement, for instance, provided some of the intellectuals studied here with hope that citizens could organize for change in local communities. On the other hand, it also made clear the need at times for a strong federal government capable of correcting what Arnold Kaufman called "municipal tyranny." The conflict between decentralized, participatory democracy and the need for centralized institutions capable of ensuring equality and justice could either become a source of intellectual creativity or, at its worst, a source of intellectual confusion. What it makes very clear, though, is that there was a strong tradition of leftist thought that did not tend toward bureaucratic statism. Nonetheless, the legacy of republican political theory, which inspired thinkers such as Goodman and Mills with its emphasis on vigorous citizen participation, and the demands of progressive thinking (especially a concern for a strong government capable of overseeing redistribution of income and

14. On the radical republican strain as it relates to American intellectual history, see John Thomas, *Alternative America: Henry George, Edward Bellamy, Henry Demarest Lloyd, and the Adversary Tradition* (Cambridge: Belknap Press, 1983).

power) remained unresolved in New Left thinking. The demand to resolve this conflict challenges us still, and it should inspire much critical thinking today.

New Left intellectuals left behind another complex legacy in relation to political change. Often their social and political analysis—C. Wright Mills's malaise about a growing number of passive white-collar workers, or William Appleman Williams's despair that corporate liberalism could hamper radical alternatives—contradicted their hope that society could be transformed. Even someone as optimistic as Arnold Kaufman, who criticized other writers' obsession with "cooptation," started to write in more pessimistic, fateful tones during the late 1960s. Because these thinkers rejected Marxian ideas about the inherent, systemic collapse of capitalism and the objectively necessitated dawn of utopia, their concept of democracy relied upon ordinary citizens committing themselves to projects of political change. Nonetheless, it was never clear what political will stood behind their vision, or whether their hopes were simply dreams meant to counteract the pessimistic conclusions of their own analyses of contemporary American society. When social and political movements started to emerge, these intellectuals drew a certain amount of inspiration from them, but also expressed concern about their misdirection and limits at times. Central questions I will be asking here are: Were the expectations of these intellectuals about the potential for change in America legitimate? Was their vision of a New Left actually realizable, or not? The answers provided by a historical account are often ambivalent, which only makes their current ramifications more important.

Between Radicalism and Liberalism

In addition to the role intellectuals played in political change and these thinkers' understanding of what a New Left should look like, I am concerned with the relationship between radicalism and liberalism. As with the other questions explored here, this one is charged with both historical and contemporary concerns. Liberalism in today's political culture seems eviscerated. Crudely stated, being a liberal today makes a political candidate likely to lose an election. Few Democratic Party politicians will defend the need for an activist state capable of sustaining public welfare in the strong terms that LBJ once did during the 1960s. At the same time, to be a liberal intellectual means facing attack from the left for being too universalistic—ignoring the constitutive power of gender and race—or from the right for trouncing the practices of local customs and religions. Critics have portrayed liberalism as lacking any sense of wider public purpose aside from protecting the "entitlements" of a litany of "special interest" groups. At the same time, crucial tenets of modern liberalism—the belief that citizens must be assured of a certain minimal amount of social justice, balanced against a fear of a too-powerful state bureaucracy—seem central to any rebirth of a progressive vision of American politics. Bereft of liberalism, American politics has careened far to the right. In the context of this book, it is important to take into account how historians explain the current state of affairs. After all, one of the historical reasons for the death of liberalism is the attack mounted by the New Left of the 1960s. The New Left—though not completely of its own will—helped kill liberalism, the worrisome story goes.[15]

This interpretation goes along with a story about the fate of liberalism in the post–World War II era. By the time of the New Deal, liberals had shed all attachment to laissez-faire economic positions and embraced the regulatory state (albeit a weak one, in comparison to those growing in Europe). They wanted to counteract the inequalities inherent in an unregulated market. But liberals also became strongly associated with another phenomenon—Franklin Delano Roosevelt, whose personality became synonymous with modern liberalism during the 1930s. When FDR died in 1945, liberalism faced an identity crisis. Truman's personality could never replace FDR's; instead, the times demanded principles capable of sustaining themselves beyond certain leaders. Truman also had to battle one of FDR's more popular protégés over the future identity of liberalism. For in 1948, just after Truman's inherited presidency came to an end, Henry Wallace—once FDR's vice president—tried to rebuild the Popular Front of the 1930s (including communist influence within its ranks) and oppose Truman via a newly formed third party, one of the last of its kind. For Wallace, the New Deal's legacy needed to be social equality, tinged with populism and embodied in a strong state, public planning, and the nationalization of industry. As one historian (more sympathetic than most) admitted, Wallace's 1948 campaign was "a complete disaster." Quite simply, Wallace was routed. Truman, then, in the minds of many, discarded Wallace's more radical form of liberalism

---

15. The best statement of this interpretation can be found in Allen Matusow, *The Unraveling of America: A History of Liberalism in the 1960s* (New York: Harper and Row, 1984). On the contemporary state of liberalism, see my "Remember Liberalism?" *Social Theory and Practice* (forthcoming).

with the support of liberals in Americans for Democratic Action (ADA). As Mary Sperling McAuliffe points out, by 1948, "with the Wallace supporters on the left routed and the Republicans on the right at least temporarily subdued," it seemed that the future belonged to a set of leaders that many historians label "Cold War liberals."[16]

Starting with Truman, liberalism became wedded to a weak welfare and strong warfare state. FDR's more moralistic language—his call, at the beginning of the New Deal, to drive the "unscrupulous money changers" from the temple of democracy and to embrace "a sacred obligation of duty" to fellow citizens—was replaced with a more technical language. Indeed, the arguments during the 1950s for an "end of ideology" among certain New York Intellectuals influenced liberal politicians who spoke less of combating greed and more of political tinkering in order to facilitate economic growth. The state would now regulate the economy (along with labor unions, where viable), enhancing production through what Alan Brinkley has called "commercial Keynesianism," that is, mild adjustments meant to grow the economy and mitigate deep busts and booms. As Allen Matusow explains, liberals now "had no disposition to revive the old crusade against concentrated economic power, redistribute wealth, or restructure existing institutions." This new disposition was best symbolized in John F. Kennedy's pledge as president to pass a tax cut before any other policy initiative, a tax cut "that sought no redistribution of wealth and power" but rather "helped to stabilize and rationalize the corporate economy [and] underwrite its risk taking and guarantee its market." This "prudent Keynesianism" symbolized JFK's conceptualization of politics as technocratic problem solving. As the president himself put it, "The fact of the matter is that most of the problems . . . that we now face are technical problems, are administrative problems . . . that do not lend themselves to the great sort of passionate movements which have stirred this country so often in the past. They deal with questions which are now beyond the comprehension of most men." Kennedy combined this technocratic domestic policy with an aggressive foreign policy fueled by anticommunism (best captured in his personal resolve to do battle

16. Norman Markowitz, *The Rise and Fall of the People's Century: Henry A. Wallace and American Liberalism, 1941–1948* (New York: Free, 1973), 295 (see 73 on FDR's personality cult as the key thing that held the New Deal together, and see 125 and 137 on Truman's betrayal of radical liberalism); Mary Sperling McAuliffe, *Crisis on the Left: Cold War Politics and American Liberals, 1947–1954* (Amherst: University of Massachusetts Press, 1978), 47. See also Alonzo Hamby, *Beyond the New Deal: Harry S. Truman and American Liberalism* (New York: Columbia University Press, 1973).

with Castro). The end result of this foreign policy would, of course, be the Vietnam War, the bitter opposition of the New Left, and the eventual "unraveling" of liberalism.[17]

There is more to this story, I would argue. First, there is the tradition of a more independent and "radical" liberalism that grew up alongside the presidencies of Truman and Kennedy. This tradition is best associated with John Dewey, who, during the New Deal, developed a vision of "Jeffersonian socialism." Dewey's political thinking was far to the left of the New Deal and found expression in the League for Independent Political Action (LIPA), an organization led by Alfred Bingham and based on a vision of "middle class radicalism" and the idea of a "cooperative commonwealth." Bingham's and Dewey's political vision differed from Marxism, as the historian Donald Miller points out, in that it imagined "a new cooperative social ethic" achieved through "peaceful change" and "the existing organs of democracy." Radical liberalism posed an alternative to the real threat of fascism and authoritarian collectivism so prevalent in the 1930s. Dewey himself believed that his vision of social equality could also be squared with the idea of participatory democracy found in *The Public and Its Problems*. Radical liberals believed that politics needed to balance the educative role of public participation in a democracy with institutions strong enough to protect the general welfare.[18]

Elements of this tradition lived on during the 1960s. All one has to do is follow the debates within ADA to recognize that liberals had not accepted Kennedy's vision of politics. In fact, a pungent critique of JFK as a technocrat came from within ADA's ranks—and ADA contacted thinkers like Paul

17. Franklin Delano Roosevelt, "First Inaugural Address," in *Great Issues in American History: From Reconstruction to the Present Day*, ed. Richard Hofstadter (New York: Vintage, 1969), 353, 356; Alan Brinkley, "The New Deal and the Idea of the State," in *The Rise and Fall of the New Deal Order, 1930–1980*, ed. Steve Fraser and Gary Gerstle (Princeton: Princeton University Press, 1989); Matusow, *Unraveling of America*, 11, 59; Bruce Miroff, *Pragmatic Illusions: The Presidential Politics of John F. Kennedy* (New York: McKay, 1976), 168; John F. Kennedy quoted in Christopher Lasch, *The Culture of Narcissism* (New York: Warner, 1979), 145. For more on "growth liberalism," see also David Farber, *The Age of Great Dreams: America in the 1960s* (New York: Hill and Wang, 1994), 104–5.

18. Westbrook, *John Dewey and American Democracy*, 455–58; Alfred Bingham, *Insurgent America: Revolt of the Middle Classes* (New York: Harper and Brothers, 1935), 29, 99; Donald Miller, *The New American Radicalism: Alfred M. Bingham and Non-Marxian Insurgency in the New Deal Era* (Port Washington, N.Y.: Kennikat, 1979), 31. For more on this tradition of radical liberalism, see Alan Lawson, *The Failure of Independent Liberalism, 1930–1941* (New York: G. P. Putnam's and Sons, 1971), and Eugene Tobin, *Organize or Perish: America's Independent Progressives, 1913–1933* (New York: Greenwood, 1986). It should be pointed out that Bingham later supported the New Left: see Donald Miller, *The New American Radicalism*, 205.

Goodman to discuss how to develop a richer and more culturally grounded liberal vision. Additionally, if we include the United Auto Workers (UAW) and the UAW's leader, Walter Reuther, in the circle of postwar liberals, as most historians and liberal intellectuals such as Arthur Schlesinger suggest we should, then we see how liberalism retained a sometimes muted connection to social activism and social democracy, the sort that John Dewey had developed earlier (and SDS later). And we must take note of the rise of "qualitative liberalism" during the 1950s, a vision articulated by intellectuals such as Schlesinger and John Galbraith. Galbraith argued that an increasingly affluent society might cater to certain material needs, but that it would never satisfy the more qualitative needs for civilized and public-minded goods. This qualitative liberalism, with its emphasis on spiritual and sometimes communitarian values, even found its way into LBJ's "Great Society" program. Not only did LBJ's Community Action Programs hope to reinvite citizens into public life and active decision making, but the president himself also articulated a moral vision for national politics. As he explained, the Great Society's goal was to combat "soulless wealth" and "advance the quality of our American civilization." Essentially, "radical liberalism"—an idea that Arnold Kaufman rediscovered and explored most fully during the 1960s—remained a vital force in American politics even as liberalism became technocratic, obsessed with anticommunism, and plagued by disarray. What radical liberalism—as a set of ideas and of practices—showed, I will argue, is that liberalism and radicalism need not have been in absolute or deadlocked conflict. In fact, by illustrating how liberalism responded to its intellectual critics, we get a better sense of what its potential really was.[19]

If liberalism was not one-dimensional, neither was the critique of it made by New Left thinkers. In the first place, many of the thinkers studied here seemed more intent on attacking liberals in positions of power rather than

19. Lyndon Baines Johnson, quoted in Taylor Branch, *Pillar of Fire* (New York: Simon and Schuster, 1998), 311. For conflicts within the ADA, see Steven Gillon, *Politics and Vision: The ADA and American Liberalism, 1947–1985* (New York: Oxford University Press, 1987), 19 and 150–51, for instance; for the ADA critique of Kennedy's technocracy, see Richard Reeves, *President Kennedy: Profile of Power* (New York: Simon and Schuster, 1993), 655. On the UAW, Reuther, social activism, and social democracy, see Peter Levy, *The New Left and Labor in the 1960s* (Urbana: University of Illinois Press, 1994), 6; Nelson Lichtenstein, *The Most Dangerous Man in Detroit: Walter Reuther and the Fate of American Labor* (New York: Basic, 1995), 155. On Schlesinger's inclusion of Reuther within his "vital center" liberal grouping, see *The Vital Center: The Politics of Freedom* (1949; reprint, New York: Da Capo, 1988), 148, 169. For Galbraith's vision, see his *Affluent Society* (New York: Mentor, 1958). On Schlesinger's "qualitative liberalism," see also Lasch, *The New Radicalism,* 310.

liberalism per se. Even when someone like C. Wright Mills did criticize liberalism as a political philosophy, he chided it for being outdated, not necessarily wrong. To a large extent, Mills performed what can be called an immanent critique. He took from liberal political philosophy what he still thought was radical and left behind what he thought was unsalvageable. For instance, Mills's political theory of democracy, as we will see, could not have been developed without drawing on the nineteenth-century liberal conception of a democratic public—of deliberating citizens capable of holding political representatives in check. Mills (and William Appleman Williams) fully accepted the premise of representative democracy, and hence American constitutionalism, two key doctrines of the liberal faith. Mills's idea of a public also relied upon the tradition of classical liberalism explored in the thinking of John Stuart Mill and others. Arnold Kaufman was quick to point this out during the late 1960s. As I will show, Mills wanted to find ways to make key liberal ideas speak to changing historical circumstances—not simply discard all of them.

When necessary, New Left intellectuals also wound up defending liberalism against certain attacks from more aggressive portions of the left. Take, for instance, Paul Goodman, a staunch critic of liberalism's over-reliance on technocratic planning. When activists within Students for a Democratic Society started to adopt Leninist political philosophy and criticized "bourgeois civil rights," Goodman was the first to defend these rights, and hence the liberal political philosophy from which they sprang. I take Goodman's defense seriously: when thinkers have their backs to the wall, they often spell out their political philosophy most clearly. What it suggests is that there was the potential for a *symbiotic* relation, not simply a combative one, between radical thinking and liberalism. The fact that this healthier relationship between radicalism and liberalism (and the political possibilities that stemmed from that relationship) eventually disintegrated is tragic—precisely because it was neither predestined nor inevitable.

Perhaps the most important exploration of this potentially symbiotic relation is Arnold Kaufman's idea of "radical liberalism," his political strategy of coalition politics, and his activism within the New Democratic Coalition and the Poor People's Campaign. I want to explore Kaufman's thinking and career precisely because it offers an alternative to the interpretation that liberalism and radicalism inherently conflicted during the heyday of the New Left. Radical liberalism may also represent an important alternative to the malaise and disarray that has resulted from the aftermath of the 1960s.

This becomes especially clear when we set it in the wider context of the late 1960s—a time when the civil rights movement had "come north" and had started trying to create a coalition politics based on a "poor people's movement" that could successfully transform American politics. This was an important—though bungled—opportunity in American history, one that I want to recover today. Though I will not lay out specific plans by which to recuperate this tradition under changed historical circumstances, I do think it is worth exploring radical liberalism not simply as a dead idea from the past but as a suggestive way to think critically about America's political future. That is what makes this final theme so important. I intend this book, after all, as both a work of history and contemporary political criticism.[20]

These themes and questions—the relation of intellectuals to political change, the tensions within New Left political thinking about political possibilities, and the creative tension between radicalism and liberalism—tied together the thinking of the intellectuals studied here. But these commonalities should not distract us from the very real differences among their ideas. The most obvious differences derived from the academic disciplines within which they worked. While these intellectuals sometimes identified with the strengths of their respective disciplines, they also criticized the main drift within those disciplines. For instance, Mills embraced the "sociological imagination" while criticizing sociologists' tendency to rely on statistics and the "grand theory" and evasive thinking of Talcott Parsons. Paul Goodman, the least academic of these intellectuals, became a practicing psychotherapist and grounded his political and social vision in psychological theory. At the same time, he embraced radical Freudianism and Gestalt therapy—theories completely antithetical to the neo-Freudianism on the rise within mainstream psychology. William Appleman Williams never ceased believing that history was the "queen" of all the disciplines, but he also criticized the growing power of the "consensus school" in American history and tried to recover the radical legacy of Progressive-Era historians like Charles Beard. Arnold Kaufman was certainly an academic philosopher, but like his British colleague, Ernest Gellner, he argued that the recent trends in linguistic and analytical philosophy made the profession increasingly aloof in the face of political questions. All of these thinkers, no matter their academic specialization, were humanists. They did not think of themselves as specialists or

20. For a not entirely satisfactory attempt to rethink the possibility of coalition politics, see William Julius Wilson, *The Bridge Over the Racial Divide: Rising Inequality and Coalition Politics* (Berkeley and Los Angeles: University of California Press, 1999).

experts (certainly not technocrats), but as intellectuals concerned with questions of public importance.[21]

In addition to their disciplinary divisions, these thinkers differed substantively in their political thinking. Though I find their commonalities stronger and more interesting, I will do my best not to downplay the differences. Paul Goodman, for instance, identified with the tradition of anarchism, while Mills pledged himself to democratic socialism and, to a lesser degree, anarchism. The two men also disagreed on the relevance of psychology to radical politics. Within publications like *New University Thought* and *Studies on the Left,* we will find a whole range of political thinking—precisely what makes going back to those magazines so interesting. My aim here will be to point out differences, but also to make a claim that there was more coherence and connection than might be immediately apparent. Even so, the work of these thinkers was marked by tension. It was not always clear, for instance, if they were dismissing liberalism or performing what I often call an "in-house" critique. By revisiting these tensions, I hope to rethink what these ideas mean today. I want to continue a conversation with this legacy—to uncover insights and mistakes in addition to conflicts and potential resolutions.

It goes without saying that all of the figures studied here were white men writing before the rise of the modern women's movement. Their political thought reflected certain limitations. Goodman, for instance, simply swept the problems of young women (those about which Betty Friedan was writing) under the rug. These thinkers believed in an integrationist model of emancipation, in which differences—cultural or otherwise—would not trump a wider social good. Some will obviously argue that this reflects purely a weakness on the part of these intellectuals. I would argue that it illustrates a form of New Left political thought that was not wracked by many of the problems critics—on the left and right—associate with "identity politics" and the prioritizing of race and gender above all else. Whatever the case may be, the mode of thinking charted here was quite different from the fragmentation of the New Left that many historians associate with the rise of the black power and women's movements of the late 1960s and early 1970s.[22]

21. For a discussion of intellectuals related to issues of expertise, see Carl Boggs, *Intellectuals and the Crisis of Modernity* (Albany: State University of New York Press, 1993).

22. One of the classic works that examined the women's movement in relation to the New Left is Sara Evans, *Personal Politics: The Roots of Women's Liberation in the Civil Rights*

By focusing on the intellectuals chosen here and their historical context, I hope to show what they have to teach us about the possibilities of democratic radicalism. Some will be surprised that a Gen X-er wants to go back to all of this. To many, it may seem dated, inherently restricted by its own time frame. But I think that the debates surrounding community organizing, a democratic public, coalition politics, and other ideas found here still have much to offer. So do the conceptions of intellectual work that these thinkers developed. Perhaps just as important, Mills, Goodman, Williams, and Kaufman first started writing during a very conservative age, the 1950s, and then saw this age melt—and sometimes explode—into an era marked by a rise in political engagement. I myself write during a very conservative and apathetic time in American history. There are certainly movements working to change things today, but they seem to be struggling against a conservative tide. I have no delusions that our future will recapitulate the course of history that these intellectuals witnessed. To a large extent, I hope that it does not. I fully recognize just how out of the mainstream many of the ideas I write about here really are. But I write about them in the hope that some of them might begin to speak more meaningfully to us. That—as the epigraph to this introduction makes clear—is precisely the purpose of historical inquiry. It is always for the future that we look to the past.

Movement and the New Left (New York: Knopf, 1979). Evans seems to veer between seeing the early New Left's "intellectualism" as inherently male and problematic and seeing it as limited but not necessarily oppressive. She argues that "the intellectual mode [of the early New Left] meant that women in the new left occupied a position much like women in society as a whole" (111). But at other times, she speaks of the "oppressive *use* of intellectual and verbal skills" in the early New Left (166, my emphasis). It is not clear from her writing whether intellectualism *necessarily* entailed or only *potentially* became a form of white male aggression. Here, I believe, we see some of the early formulations that worried critics on the left— especially Russell Jacoby, Todd Gitlin, and Richard Rorty—who believed that identity politics had devastated any hope for a rational left in America.

A Preface to the *politics* of Intellectual Life in Postwar America: The Possibility of New Left Beginnings

The end of ideology closes the book, intellectually speaking, on an era, the one of easy "left" formulae for social change. But to close the book is not to turn one's back upon it.
—Daniel Bell, *The End of Ideology*, 1960

We seem to be in the early stages of a new concept of revolutionary and socialist politics, where we can hope for the present only to clear the ground, to criticize the old methods that have landed us in a blind alley, and to grope in a new direction.
—Dwight Macdonald, "The Root Is Man (II)," 1946

The 1940s are often taken as a decade of American triumph. In 1941, the famous and wealthy publisher of *Life* magazine, Henry Luce, wrote that the twentieth century "is ours not only in the sense that we happen to live in it but ours also because it is America's first century as a dominant power in the world." This sort of bold enthusiasm seemed appropriate. America, after all, was victorious in World War II and now stood as a leading world power. Even if communism challenged the "American way of life," as increasing numbers of writers referred to it at the time, there at least was a well-defined enemy that only helped highlight America's own excellence. After all, World War II unleashed economic prosperity, represented in the cornucopia of commodities made available to large numbers of Americans. In the 1950s, when debating Nikita Khrushchev, Vice President Richard Nixon simply unveiled a model of a modern American kitchen to his Soviet sparring partner. It seemed that the abundance of commodities was enough to prove America's superiority over Russian totalitarianism.[1]

Intellectual life in America reflected this rising prosperity and confidence. As Richard Pells explains it (without endorsing the view), there has been a fairly standard and sweeping interpretation of the shifts in intellectual life

1. Henry Luce, *The American Century* (New York: Farrar and Rinehart, 1941), 27. My interpretation of the "kitchen debate" is indebted to Stephen Whitfield, *The Culture of the Cold War* (Baltimore: Johns Hopkins University Press, 1991), 73–74.

from the early twentieth century up to the 1950s: "Starting out as exuberant reformers in the Progressive Era, writers are supposed to have gained wisdom as rebels during the 1920s and as radicals in the 1930s, before reconciling themselves to society in the 1950s. . . . By the 1950s, they had finally grown up and settled down." Prosperity induced intellectual comfort, so the story goes. The intellectual historian Stephen Longstaff argues that American "culture" during the Cold War "not only had careers, comfort, and fame to offer. It also wanted distinguished intellectuals to provide some tone to public sanctions at home and abroad, and it expected them to take their place among the representatives of the various interests and constituencies that make up the country's official and unofficial elite." As with the rest of the country, intellectuals grew fat and comfortable during the Cold War.[2]

This is typically seen in the path taken by a group of writers now known as the New York Intellectuals—the most important grouping of intellectuals in the post–World War II period. These modernist thinkers gathered around magazines like *Partisan Review* and *Commentary* and included Sidney Hook, the philosopher; Lionel Trilling, the literary critic; Norman Podhoretz, the social critic and editor; and many others. Bound together by similar experiences, many historians refer to these writers as the "New York Family." Most members had grown up in Jewish enclaves within New York City, coming of age during the Great Depression and eventually attending the City University. As young thinkers, they debated their new secular faith of Marxism. Defining themselves predominantly as anti-Stalinists, many of them found consolation in the arguments of Trotsky, who preserved the revolutionary and vanguardist teachings of V. I. Lenin against Stalin's practice of "socialism in one country." These New York thinkers despised the Popular Front and its primary agent, the American Communist Party. They especially eschewed the populist sentiments they saw, rightfully or not, operating in the Popular Front culture of the 1930s, a culture that limped on into the 1940s. The New York Intellectuals embraced instead the intellectualism of high modernism in literature and art. They tried to marry—and it was an odd marriage indeed—the modernism of a T. S. Eliot with the revolutionary politics of a Trotsky.

World War II, though, challenged their Trotskyist assumption that America acted solely as an imperialist power, rather than as a committed opponent

2. Richard Pells, *The Liberal Mind in a Conservative Age: American Intellectuals in the 1940s and 1950s* (Middletown: Wesleyan University Press, 1989), 117; Stephen A. Longstaff, "The New York Family," *Queen's Quarterly* 83 (1976): 567.

of fascism. After the war, the New York Intellectuals gave up on Marxism entirely and started to drift to more centrist and liberal views. As Irving Howe, once a Trotskyist himself, explained, "No version of orthodox Marxism could retain a hold on intellectuals who had gone through the trauma of abandoning the Leninist *Weltanschauung* and had experienced the depth to which the politics of this century, most notably the rise of totalitarianism, called into question the once sacred Marxist categories." With the advent of the Cold War, these thinkers grew increasingly comfortable, since "there was money to be had from publishers [and] jobs in the universities," he pointed out. Or, as the historian Alexander Bloom has quipped, "New York Intellectuals began, in a phrase which became infamous in time, to 'make it' in the postwar world."[3]

Indeed, the New York Intellectuals became increasingly willing to celebrate the "American way of life" and debunk any communist alternative. In 1952, the editors of *Partisan Review* held a symposium strikingly entitled "Our Country, Our Culture." Here, they declared that "more and more writers have ceased to think of themselves as rebels and exiles. They now realize that their values, if they are to be realized at all, are to be realized in America and in relation to the actuality of American life." Many historians believe that the conservatism of these intellectuals is best symbolized in the founding of organizations like Americans for Intellectual Freedom (AIF) in 1949. AIF began as a protest group against the Waldorf Conference—a gathering of American writers and artists who argued for a friendlier foreign policy toward the Soviets, based upon the incorrect assumption that both countries shared the concept of cultural freedom (something of a reassertion of the earlier Popular Front and the unity found during World War II). AIF protested Soviet totalitarianism and showed its willingness to lend intellectual weight to America's battle abroad, which was becoming consolidated through Kennan's containment policy and the Truman Doctrine, both fueling more aggressive military actions on the part of the United States against Soviet expansion abroad. The group worked with the Congress for Cultural

3. Irving Howe, "The New York Intellectuals," in *The Decline of the New* (New York: Harcourt, Brace, and World, 1970), 219; Alexander Bloom, *Prodigal Sons: The New York Intellectuals and Their World* (New York: Oxford University Press, 1986), 310. For more on the New York Intellectuals, see Terry Cooney, *The Rise of the New York Intellectuals:* Partisan Review *and Its Circle* (Madison: University of Wisconsin Press, 1986); Hugh Wilford, *The New York Intellectuals: From Vanguard to Institution* (Manchester: Manchester University Press, 1995); Neil Jumonville, "The New York Intellectuals: Defense of the Intellect," *Queen's Quarterly* 97 (1990): 290–304.

Freedom (CCF), an international organization, becoming in the process the American Committee for Cultural Freedom (ACCF). The CCF espoused anticommunist ideas in a variety of forums, including conferences, festivals, and magazines (most notably *Encounter* in England), and provided intellectual justification for fighting a cultural version of the Cold War. Perhaps the organization's ultimate purpose only became clear in 1966, when it was officially confirmed that the group had received funding from the Central Intelligence Agency (something Paul Goodman and others suspected long before). For a critic like Irving Howe, this simply made obvious what he knew all along—that "the impulses of the New York intellectuals" were "increasingly conformist and conservative."[4]

Prosperity Yes, But Also Anxiety

Howe's interpretation and those of others seem largely accurate. In fact, C. Wright Mills and Paul Goodman would do much to pioneer this sort of interpretation during the 1950s. But something is missing from this story. First, the generalizations drawn about American culture during the Cold War fail to capture the spirit of the time. Certainly many Americans felt enchanted by prosperity, but many also expressed anxiety during the 1940s and 1950s. After all, there was the power of the atomic bomb hovering in the background; there was also the sinister force of communism that some (including, eventually, the famous senator from Wisconsin, Joe McCarthy) saw seeping into every crevice of life. No wonder the historian William Graebner termed the 1940s an "age of doubt." The *zeitgeist* crystallized in

4. "Our Country, Our Culture," quoted in Jackson Lears, "A Matter of Taste: Corporate Cultural Hegemony in a Mass-Consumption Society," in *Recasting America: Culture and Politics in the Age of the Cold War,* ed. Lary May (Chicago: University of Chicago Press, 1989), 40; Howe, "The New York Intellectuals," 233. On the Waldorf Peace Conference protests and the formation of AIF, see Job Dittberner, *The End of Ideology and American Social Thought, 1930–1960* (Ann Arbor: UMI Press, 1979), 106; on the ACCF, see Bloom, *Prodigal Sons,* 262–63. For the CIA support, see Frances Stonor Saunders, *The Cultural Cold War: The CIA and the World of Arts and Letters* (New York: Free, 1999), especially 54–56. For more on the CCF and ACCF, from quite different perspectives, see Christopher Lasch, *The Agony of the American Left* (New York: Vintage, 1969), chapter 3, and Peter Coleman, *The Liberal Conspiracy: The Congress for Cultural Freedom and the Struggle for the Mind of Postwar Europe* (New York: Free, 1989). The political differences between Lasch and Coleman explain their contrasting interpretations, but so does Lasch's more keen focus on the damage done to American intellectual life (versus Coleman's interest in Europe).

the opening pages of Arthur Schlesinger's *The Vital Center* (1949): "Western man in the middle of the twentieth century is tense, uncertain, adrift. We look upon our epoch as a time of troubles, an age of anxiety." The purported stability of the 1950s did not necessarily change this. As John Patrick Diggins described the decade, it was "an age of stable nuclear families and marital tension, of student conformity on campus and youth rebellion on the screen and phonograph, . . . of suburban contentment with lawns and station wagons and middle-class worry about money and status, of high expectations of upward mobility and later some doubts about the meaning and value of the age's own achievements." Clearly, prosperity and the assumption of world power could not do away with Americans' anxieties and fears.[5]

So it was with intellectuals. Consider especially their awareness of totalitarianism—represented in the rise of the Nazi regime and then the consolidation of the Soviet Union. There was the increasing concern that America faced a power so completely absolutist that it deserved nothing less than abject fear. George Kennan, the architect of containment, declared that the United States faced "a political force committed fanatically to the belief that with the U.S. there can be no permanent *modus vivendi,* that it is desirable and necessary that the internal harmony of our society be broken." A few years later, Hannah Arendt, a German expatriate, warned that totalitarianism created "a system in which men are superfluous" at home and promised "the elimination of every competing nontotalitarian reality" abroad. This was scary enough, but there was even more to worry about: Arendt argued that totalitarianism grew out of a mass culture and society. Totalitarianism required people to think of themselves as "masses" and certainly "not citizens with opinions about, and interests in, the handling of public affairs." The problem was that America, too, was turning into a mass society and culture. Many popular social critics, including William Whyte, David Riesman, and Vance Packard, began arguing in the 1950s that American citizens were turning apathetic, becoming passive receptacles for the products of a consumer economy. Thus, democracy was threatened not only from outside—by the international forces of communism—but also from within. Intellectuals, if they cared about democracy, could not sit tight.[6]

5. William Graebner, *The Age of Doubt: American Thought and Culture in the 1940s* (Boston: Twayne, 1991); Schlesinger, *The Vital Center,* 1; John Patrick Diggins, *The Proud Decades: America in War and Peace, 1941–1960* (New York: Norton, 1989), 219.

6. George Kennan quoted in John Lewis Gaddis, *The United States and the Origins of the*

To get a sense of just how conflicted many intellectuals were during this period of time, examine the intellectual biography of Daniel Bell. Bell's life fit the standard narrative of the New York Intellectual. He began as a young socialist in 1932 (at the ripe age of thirteen), supported America's entry into World War II while remaining a social democrat, and then became increasingly centrist. By the late 1950s he wrote about a supposed "end of ideology." "For the radical intellectual who had articulated the revolutionary impulses of the past century and a half," Bell explained, there had been "an end to chiliastic hopes, to millenarianism, to apocalyptic thinking—and to ideology. For ideology, which once was a road to action, has come to be a dead end." Ideologies like communism needed to be tossed aside, because they were too rigid, too simplistic. It is no surprise that Bell's thinking helped frame the work of the anticommunist CCF. But none of this meant that he thought all was well in America. In fact, while pronouncing ideology dead, he worried, as Richard Pells points out, how "modern work" had an "inherent inability to offer satisfaction to the employee." This was no small fear, as many Americans spent most of their time during the day at work. The "discontents" of such work, especially within large bureaucratic corporations, meant that Americans had not overcome their anxieties about the future, as far as Bell was concerned.[7]

Though Bell had suggested that ideology could no longer be counted on to respond to social and political problems, not all intellectuals gave up on the search for some sort of radical alternative. The rejection of Stalinism and the Soviet Union certainly led many intellectuals to gravitate toward the right during the Cold War (becoming no less ideological, it should be noted). For instance, writer James Burnham changed from Trotskyist to one of America's Cold War faithful—endorsing John Foster Dulles's fervent call to not just "contain" but even "roll back" communism. Max Eastman, radical bohemian and Trotskyist throughout World War I, wound up an editor

---

Cold War, 1941–1947 (New York: Columbia University Press, 1972), 303; Hannah Arendt, *The Origins of Totalitarianism* (1950; reprint, Cleveland: World, 1958), 457, 392, 308. For the rise of social criticism during the 1950s, see Pells, *Liberal Mind,* chapter 4.

7. Daniel Bell, *The End of Ideology: On the Exhaustion of Political Ideas in the Fifties* (New York: Free, 1960), 393; Pells, *Liberal Mind,* 194. For the connections between the CCF and Bell's "end of ideology" thought, see Dittberner, *The End of Ideology and American Social Thought,* especially 132–33. See also Howard Brick, *Daniel Bell and the Decline of Intellectual Radicalism* (Madison: University of Wisconsin Press, 1986).

at William Buckley's conservative publication, *The National Review,* during the 1950s. Sidney Hook and Irving Kristol made similar odysseys. This was only one path taken, though. Other intellectuals, of course, moved to the center (like Daniel Bell himself). But there was also another possibility: to reject Marxism—with its inaccurate descriptions of capitalism's downfall—while looking for alternative forms of progressive thought. In other words, anti-Stalinism did not *necessitate* conservatism. The anxiety of the times could just as easily spur new thinking about the future of the left.[8]

In fact, as the editors of *Liberation* magazine made clear in the mid-1950s, there were numerous historical strains of thought that could inform a reconstruction of what they called "independent radicalism" (a term also used by the editors of *Dissent* around the same time). They cited the prophetic tradition in Judeo-Christian theology, the radical democratic thought of a Thomas Jefferson or Tom Paine, the decentralized and democratic socialist tradition that informed the work of a Eugene Debs, the radical nonviolence espoused earlier by Reinhold Niebuhr and eventually by Martin Luther King Jr., and a communitarian version of anarchism. They even admitted that there could be something learned from the "humaneness and tolerance" taught by the liberal tradition (something that will become more apparent later in this story). The editors at *Liberation* believed that these strains lived on, even into the Cold War. And they knew that they had found their strongest expression in *politics* magazine (1944–1949), even if only briefly. As Irving Howe described the magazine, it was "the one significant effort during the late forties to return to radicalism." Precisely because it became something of a seedbed for later New Left thinking, I want to examine it briefly here. This exploration is not intended to provide a comprehensive view of the publication or of its editor, Dwight Macdonald. Rather, I want to set out some of the intellectual tools that thinkers possessed during the 1940s, tools that could be used to develop radical thought into the future. As Daniel Bell himself put it, *politics* magazine was a "unique place in American intellectual history." This is especially true in the context of New Left intellectual history.[9]

8. John Patrick Diggins, *Up from Communism: Conservative Odysseys in American Intellectual History* (New York: Harper and Row, 1975).
9. "Tract for the Times," *Liberation,* March 1956, 3–6; Howe, "The New York Intellectuals," 235; Bell, *The End of Ideology,* 307. See also "A Word to Our Readers," *Dissent* 1 (1954): 3.

The Politics of *politics:* "New Roads" Ahead?

By 1944, when Macdonald founded *politics* magazine, he was beginning to jettison his previously held faith in Trotskyism. Here he was following the path of other New York Intellectuals at the time. But he wanted this new publication to allow a broad range of thinkers on the left to think through the future of radicalism. As he expressed it in the opening editorial, *politics* was to "create a center of consciousness on the Left, welcoming all varieties of radical thought." His former colleagues at *Partisan Review* (where he had once been an editor) were drifting much further to the right, thus placing Macdonald squarely on the left side of the spectrum of intellectual life. On the other hand, for those who clung to Trotskyism and orthodox Marxism, Macdonald's foray into new territory simply showed off his "flighty character" (James Farrell) and produced a "grab bag of modern confusionism" (Irving Howe, then still a Trotskyist). Though clearly aligned with the left— *contra* the opinions of dogmatic Marxists—Macdonald was better at opening up questions than answering them definitively. In his search for a new politics, Macdonald established a pattern for the journal. He would have what he called "younger, relatively unknown American intellectuals" write exploratory pieces on subjects like pacifism or ethical individualism, then debate these thinkers in the journal, and then often come around to restating these lesser-known authors' positions in his own words. Readers witnessed Macdonald's "conversion" processes to new political ideas in the pages of *politics.* The magazine became, through these encounters, a collaborative learning effort about the future course of radical thought. Indeed, one of its most important contributions was to introduce readers to key thinkers who helped formulate New Left thinking—especially C. Wright Mills and Paul Goodman.[10]

Macdonald's first and most important move in the magazine was to reject Trotskyism specifically and Marxism more broadly. Trotskyism became too authoritarian for Macdonald's liking at the time, due to its reliance on

10. Dwight Macdonald, "Why Politics?" *politics,* February 1944, 6; James Farrell, in a letter to *politics,* March 1946, 89; Irving Howe, "The 13th Disciple," *politics,* October 1946, 329. Howe was still a believer in Trotskyism—more precisely, its Schachtmanite version. The best book on *politics* is Gregory Sumner, *Dwight Macdonald and the* politics *Circle: The Challenge of Cosmopolitan Democracy* (Ithaca: Cornell University Press, 1996). For biographical details on Macdonald, see Michael Wreszin, *A Rebel in Defense of Tradition: The Life and Politics of Dwight Macdonald* (New York: Basic, 1994), and Stephen Whitfield, *A Critical American: The Politics of Dwight Macdonald* (Guilford, Conn.: Archon, 1984).

Lenin's belief in intellectuals leading a vanguard party. Macdonald's anti-Leninism drew from an increasing number of anarchists writing for the magazine. Marxism overall seemed dated and inaccurate in the face of the realities of post–World War II society. Marx's predictions about the imminent crisis of Western capitalism never came true: the working class had never become a revolutionary force in advanced Western societies in the way Marx had predicted. The prosperity of the postwar American economy and its dispersion of consumer goods to the working class would make this especially unlikely. Additionally, Marxism was a product of the scientific spirit of the Enlightenment—the same Enlightenment, for Macdonald, that had just created the atomic bomb recently dropped on Hiroshima. Marxism's faith in progress and its teleological read on history (all roads leading to a communist ending) did not speak to the tragedy Macdonald had witnessed during the 1940s, symbolized by events like the Holocaust and the use of the atomic bomb on civilian populations. Of course, the result of this line of thinking might have been to shift the grounding of Marxism away from scientific prediction toward ethical reasoning. For a time, Macdonald supported such a shift by publishing thinkers aligned with humanist socialism, critics of the scientistic and objectivistic forms of Marxism. Though Macdonald clearly saw socialist humanists as closer to his thinking than doctrinaire Marxists, he nonetheless seemed to suggest that one of his major goals was to "criticize the dominant ideology of the left today—which is roughly Marxian" and replace it with something else. When Macdonald saw faulty assumptions at the core of a philosophy, he was prone to reject it outright—which he did with Marxism.[11]

Understandably, Marxists became especially defensive while reading *politics,* and Macdonald had promised to make his magazine responsive to the views of its readers. Macdonald admitted to a certain amount of "negativism" (his own unironic term) found at *politics.* At the same time, though, while rejecting Marxism, Macdonald still embraced "utopian aspirations." But it was unclear just what the nature of this critical utopia would be. Increasing numbers of readers wanted to know what it would look like.

11. Dwight Macdonald, preface to "New Roads in Politics," *politics,* December 1945, 369. For Macdonald's critique of Leninism, see his "Revolution, Ltd.," *politics,* July 1945, 218–21; for a socialist-humanist viewpoint, see Helen Constas, "A Critique of Marxian Ideology," *politics,* January 1946, 12. Looking ahead, it should be noted that a large part of Macdonald's rejection of Marxism drew from Paul Goodman's thought in "Revolution, Sociolatry, and War," *politics,* December 1945, 376–80.

Listening to his readers, Macdonald felt compelled to respond to the charges of "negativism" by creating two series—the first entitled "New Roads in Politics," the other "Here and Now." Both were dedicated to exploring new approaches to radical politics. And both laid the ground for what would constitute New Left political ideas in America.[12]

The first place in which Macdonald saw new forms of leftism was in the activities of conscientious objectors (COs) during World War II. As was typical, Macdonald came to this idea by publishing a devotee of pacifism, Don Calhoun, and then debating him. Calhoun's most important argument was against those who believed that pacifists and COs were guilty of with-drawing from political activities in order to retain their moral purity. The accusation worked because draft resistance during the 1940s seemed marked by a strong tendency toward radical individualism (something Paul Good-man, as we will see, embraced at the time). Calhoun, though, made a strong argument against this characterization of pacifism, insisting that nonviolent resistance engendered an active commitment to changing a system bent on war—a thoroughly political and thus collective commitment. In his debate with Calhoun, Macdonald rebuked him, but admitted that he had made some convincing points. As Macdonald went on to worry about America's mass culture and society—pioneering the sort of social criticism made more famous during the 1950s—and to argue that impersonal structures destroyed the individual conscience, pacifist and conscientious objection started to take on a more radical dimension for him. One year after his encounter with Cal-houn, Macdonald dropped his remaining doubt about COs and praised "how much serious and original thinking is being done by CO's these days," going so far as to contrast it with the "routinized Socialist and Trotskyist press." As he explained later, the CO "is especially concerned with the problem of how the individual can act decently in a world whose indecency is coming to exceed all bounds." After all, he reasoned, with the rise of Hitler's Germany "it is not the law-breaker that we must fear today so much as he who obeys the law." A bit later, Macdonald practically mimicked Calhoun's arguments in his endorse-ment of burning draft cards as both an individual act of conscience and commitment to political change. With these ideas in mind, Macdonald de-cided to work with and write about pacifist organizations of the 1940s,

---

12. For Macdonald's defense and use of the term "negativism," see his response to George Elliot, *politics*, September 1944, 250; Dwight Macdonald, "The Root Is Man," *politics*, April 1946, 99.

including the Committee for Non-Violent Revolution and, later, the Peace-makers.[13]

In coming to see Calhoun's side, Macdonald also suggested that activist intellectuals might manage to resist a mass society and engender a new form of radicalism. Here again was a break from Marxism, which always placed its faith in the proletariat as an agent of change. Most pacifists were either religiously or intellectually motivated, and very few of them came from the ranks of the working class. As the historian Lawrence Wittner points out, "The conjecture that the World War II pacifist constituency contained an inordinate number of middle class intellectuals is buttressed by examination of the education level of C.O.'s." C. Wright Mills actually drew this line of reasoning out to its fullest extent, arguing in a 1944 article in *politics* that "the independent artist and intellectual are among the few remaining per-sonalities equipped to resist and to fight the stereotyping and consequent death of lively things." Macdonald never directly suggested that intellectuals should become a new agent of change (that is, they were never given the same sort of status the proletariat held in Marxist theory), but his support of the COs leaned in that direction.[14]

This embrace of conscientious objection to governmental actions also led Macdonald to take seriously the political philosophy of anarchism in all its variations. The radical individualism of draft resisters suggested a more broadly construed libertarianism. Here the legacy of Randolph Bourne, the famous renegade intellectual who had condemned John Dewey's support of World War I, resurfaced. With the advent of total war, Macdonald started to reason, the centralization of state and military power became just as per-

13. See Don Calhoun, "The Political Relevance of Conscientious Objection," *politics*, July 1944, 177 (Macdonald's response follows). See also Dwight Macdonald: "Conscription and Conscientious Objection," *politics*, June 1945, 165; "The Responsibility of Peoples," *politics*, March 1945, 90; comments on his compiling of CO writings, *politics*, November 1945, 342; "Why Destroy Draft Cards," *politics*, March–April 1947, 55. On the Committee for Non-Violent Revolution, see Don Calhoun's documentary article, "The Non-Violent Revo-lutionists," *politics*, April 1946, 118–19; Dwight Macdonald, "Peacemakers," *politics*, Spring 1948, 136–37. For fine histories of radical pacifism that discuss the Committee for Non-Violent Revolution and Peacemakers, see Lawrence Wittner, *Rebels Against War: The American Peace Movement, 1933–1983* (Philadelphia: Temple University Press, 1984), and Isserman, *If I Had a Hammer.*

14. Wittner, *Rebels Against War,* 48–49; Mills, "The Social Role of the Intellectual" (1944) in his *Power, Politics, and People: The Collected Essays of C. Wright Mills,* ed. Irving Louis Horowitz (New York: Oxford University Press, 1963), 299.

nicious as the abuse of economic power (something, again, Marxism could not account for with its prioritization of economic over political power). Those who elevated the conscience of the individual above the state's will, therefore, became exemplary. Macdonald celebrated the "Anarchists' uncompromising rejection of the State." Engagement in almost any kind of *mass* political action—changing institutions of power, such as the federal government, through electoral politics—now seemed suspect, as far as Macdonald was concerned. All power appeared corrupt. Decentralization seemed to take priority over any need for a centralized state looking out for the common good and social justice. This line of thinking pushed him to embrace the individualistic (or libertarian) strain of anarchism—that which made the individual the ultimate good, rising above all other obligations. And so in "The Root Is Man"—one of his most famous essays, the title of which said so much in itself—he argued that radicals must put at front and center the "full development of each individual, and removal of all social bars to his complete and immediate satisfaction in his work, his leisure, his sex life, and all other aspects of his nature." Radicalism now seemed to turn into unfettered individualism.[15]

Yet Macdonald was far too much of a communitarian to become a full-fledged libertarian. After all, things like work, leisure, and sex were inherently social acts, not the behavior of lone individuals. So Macdonald started to show interest in the rise of what came to be known as "intentional communities" in the United States. Indeed, as he pledged himself to radical individualism, he also called—in the same essay—for a new conception of "political action" cast on "a modest, unpretentious, personal level" that could only be found in "small groups of individuals . . . grouped around certain principles and feelings." Soon after making this statement, Macdonald ran a piece on the Macedonia Community, a small intentional community in the South. The author who wrote this piece argued that what drew the members together was not simply their shared "pacifism" but also their "disillusionment with modern industrial society." Other intentional-community advocates (such as George Woodcock, a British anarchist), argued that these sorts of communities might do nothing to transform political

15. Dwight Macdonald: "The Root Is Man," 115; on how mass politics is useless, "Truman Doctrine," *politics,* May–June 1947, 86–87; "The Root Is Man (II)," *politics,* July 1946, 208; see also "The Root Is Man," 99. Much of Macdonald's thinking stems from the tradition of "personalism" in radical thought. On this point, see James Farrell, *The Spirit of the Sixties: Making Postwar Radicalism* (New York: Routledge, 1997).

systems or society at large but were still worthy as ends in themselves. By supporting such arguments (even if only by publishing them), Macdonald signaled his debt to other thinkers, especially Paul Goodman. In the pages of *politics,* Goodman had argued much earlier on (while Macdonald himself was still something of a Marxist) that radicals "must—in small groups—draw the line and at once begin action directly satisfactory to our deep nature." Once again, Macdonald came around to other thinkers' viewpoints and suggested that intentional communities might be an important component of future radicalism. Though they were not individualistic in nature, it should be pointed out that almost all such communitarian experiments withdrew from mass political action.[16]

Macdonald's reasoning did not address whether he thought a purely decentralized society could ensure justice and equality. In fact, Macdonald's penchant for decentralization only prompted bigger questions. How could a decentralized society, even one bonded together partially through communities, be able to address issues of inequality—especially inequality between communities that possessed different levels of resources or that perhaps practiced racial exclusion? On these points, Macdonald had few answers, leaving behind instead numerous contradictions and paradoxes with which later New Left thinkers struggled. His withdrawal from mass political action implied that little could be done on a widespread scale to change sociopolitical structures.

There was also the tension between Macdonald's individualist anarchism and communitarian anarchism. In this context, it seems productive to discern what elements were shared by both philosophies. They both made political action into something premised on free will and choice. Marxists had traced out objective crises operating in capitalist societies that ensured the eventual victory of communism. Macdonald eschewed this sort of social scientific prediction about an imminent future. Instead of being about the transformation of large political structures or institutions or about participation in mass politics as it presently existed, Macdonald suggested that radical

16. Macdonald, "The Root Is Man (II)," 209; David Newton, "The Macedonia Community," *politics,* Winter 1948, 28; George Woodcock, "The English Community Movement," *politics,* August 1946, 233; Goodman, "Revolution, Sociolatry, and War," 378. It should be noted that Staughton Lynd (see Chap. 6 below) lived in the Macedonia Community for some time. For more on this experiment, see W. Edward Orser, *Searching for a Viable Alternative: The Macedonia Community Cooperative, 1937–1958* (New York: Burt Franklin, 1981). See also Wreszin, *A Rebel in Defense of Tradition,* 186, and Sumner, *Dwight Macdonald and the politics Circle,* 150.

politics came down to individuals acting upon their consciences and *freely choosing* certain ways of life—including whether to live communally. As historian Robert Westbrook explains, "Resistance to the process of rationalization and 'massification,' Macdonald concluded, must rest less in class struggle than in exemplary acts of moral courage." The big acts of history that previous revolutionaries committed themselves to—the Bolshevik Revolution or Gandhi's mass nonviolent movement—paled before the more authentic act of choosing to live one's life a certain way. When he explained what could be done to prevent war, for instance, Macdonald said that ordinary people—scientists who might be in the position to build bombs or citizens who paid taxes that enriched the military—could "simply" stop "playing the game." Politics, for Macdonald, was turned into individual choice about personal behavior. A new definition of a radical followed from this. A radical must be committed to moderation, personal change, and a refusal to go along with mass politics and society. He admitted that the term "radical would apply to the as yet few individuals" such as "anarchists, conscientious objectors, and renegade Marxists like myself" who committed themselves to thinking about "the ethical aspect of politics." Because Macdonald was one of the first to publish in America the writings of Albert Camus, and because his own thinking stressed the threat of a mass society, it is not surprising to find him attempting to ground political action in the act of willing a new self into existence.[17]

Dissolution and New Beginnings

At the same time that Macdonald became clearer on some radical alternatives to the new mass society of Cold War America, he also faced a crisis within *politics.* No matter that he wanted the magazine to be a collaborative project; the editorial and managerial tasks always fell to him. This created two major problems. First, money: in 1946, Macdonald wrote to Paul Goodman and complained that the magazine's funding was running dry. Lack of funds plagued *politics* until its death. But even if the magazine's finances had become secure, *politics* would still have suffered from its second

17. Robert Westbrook, "The Responsibility of Peoples: Dwight Macdonald and the Holocaust," in *America and the Holocaust,* ed. Sanford Pinsker and Jack Fischel (Greenwood, Fla.: Penkevill, 1983), 54. For Macdonald's characterization of radicals, see "The Root Is Man (II)," 210, and "The Root Is Man," 100.

and more significant problem: Macdonald's personal burnout. Simply put, being the only real editor at *politics* exhausted him. In 1948, Macdonald tried to recruit C. Wright Mills to help with editorial duties; Mills refused. In that same year, Macdonald explained that the magazine had been delayed because "*politics* has been a one-man magazine, and the man (myself) has of late been feeling stale, tired, disheartened, and—if you like—demoralized." Macdonald's personal life hit a rocky period, and the single-handed running of a magazine simply became too burdensome.[18]

But another, more significant reason for *politics*'s crash was that Macdonald faced an irresolvable intellectual conflict of his own making just at the moment that he began formulating his new theory of radicalism. In one prominent way, his intellectual life paralleled that of other New York Intellectuals. Macdonald's anti-Stalinism—like that of his fellow ex-Trotskyists—had hardened by the late 1940s. Increasingly, Macdonald portrayed Stalin in terms used by both liberal and conservative anticommunists. In the spring of 1948, Macdonald went so far as to equate Stalin with Hitler, moving toward a position remarkably close to Kennan's and Truman's emerging policy of containment. More and more, Macdonald made an issue of Stalin, arguing that he had underplayed the dictator's significance before. Just as important, though, Macdonald started taking aim at Henry Wallace's 1948 campaign, exposing communist influence. C. Wright Mills and Paul Goodman grew increasingly wary of Macdonald's attacks on Henry Wallace. They never denied that he had a point about communist infiltration (nor did they support Wallace as a candidate), but they did not think it merited the sort of attention Macdonald paid to it. Here we start seeing some of the fissures that would come to constitute major divisions within New Left thinking after the collapse of *politics*.

In 1949, Macdonald made his political leanings clearer by helping form AIF. Along with Sidney Hook, who was turning from Trotskyism to anticommunism at the same time, Macdonald protested the lack of cultural freedom in the Soviet Union. Mills's and Goodman's suspicions about his intensified obsession with communists seemed to be bearing out. Macdonald's commitments made it increasingly difficult to tell his political lean-

18. Dwight Macdonald to Paul Goodman, October 15, 1946, Dwight Macdonald Papers, Sterling Library, Yale University, Division of Manuscripts and Archives; on Macdonald's attempt to recruit Mills, see Wreszin, *A Rebel in Defense of Tradition,* 212 (and see also Mills's refusal, in his letter to Macdonald dated November 20, 1948, Dwight Macdonald Papers, C. Wright Mills folder); Dwight Macdonald, "A Report to Readers," *politics,* Winter 1948, 58.

ings apart from those within liberal anticommunist organizations like Americans for Democratic Action (ADA), or even within groupings of more centrist anticommunists.[19]

Except, of course, for his pacifism—the final strain of his thought still limping leftward. Macdonald admitted to a major intellectual conflict between a growing desire to overthrow Stalinism and his pacifist intention to resist World War III. A year after admitting this dilemma to his readers, Macdonald wrote to Mills that he was "in a state of transition to something quite different from any past viewpoint I have had, including the pacifist. (I recently resigned from the 2 pacifist groups I belonged to.)" Apparently, Macdonald was resolving the tension between pacifism and anticommunism in favor of anticommunism at this point. In fact, after the 1948 election, he accused Norman Thomas—an anticommunist (and largely pacifist) socialist for whom C. Wright Mills would vote throughout the 1940s—of being soft on communism. The next year, Macdonald shut *politics* down. The tension in his thought became overwhelming, especially when combined with his personal burnout and financial difficulties.[20]

Three years after shutting down shop, Macdonald gave a speech in which he declared his intention to "choose the West" in light of the Cold War. At the same time, he decided to say "goodbye to utopia" and any possibility of a "revolutionary alternative." As he explained, "Pacifism does not have a reasonable chance of being effective against a totalitarian enemy." This was not a statement made with glee, of course; Macdonald was clearly disturbed by his choice, feeling backed into an intellectual wall. Nevertheless, anti-totalitarianism—in this case, anticommunism—beat out radical pacifism, and it seemed to take with it intentional communities, anarchism, socialist humanism, ethical individualism, or any alternative whatsoever. In his newly polarized worldview, the West was *it*. To make clear his new orientation, he stopped writing political criticism and took up cultural commentary, landing a writing job with *The New Yorker*. Though Macdonald never became as

19. Dwight Macdonald: "USA vs. USSR," *politics*, Spring 1948, 75; letter to C. Wright Mills, May 28, 1949, Dwight Macdonald Papers, C. Wright Mills folder; "Henry Wallace," *politics*, March–April 1947, 34–42; and "Henry Wallace (Part Two)," *politics*, May–June 1947, 96–117. On AIF, see Dwight Macdonald, "The Waldorf Conference," *politics*, Winter 1949, 32A–32D. See also Wreszin, *A Rebel in Defense of Tradition*, 239.

20. Dwight Macdonald, opening editorial, *politics*, Summer 1948, 149, for his dilemma; Macdonald to Mills, May 28, 1949, Dwight Macdonald Papers, C. Wright Mills folder (the two groups were the Committee for Non-Violent Revolution and Peacemakers); Dwight Macdonald, "On the Elections," *politics*, Summer 1948, 204.

rabidly anticommunist as Sidney Hook, his colleague from AIF, he certainly put an end to any search for a radical alternative, even while writing social and cultural criticism. He jettisoned *politics*—and politics.[21]

Around the same time, he jeopardized his friendship with C. Wright Mills. The friendship finally crashed over a mean-spirited review that Macdonald wrote of Mills's *White Collar* in 1951. The tensions between them, however, were clear before this event, and they tell us a great deal about how the closing down of *politics* related to the future of New Left political thinking. These two intellectuals had "met" when Mills sent Macdonald a critical essay he had written about James Burnham's theory of the "managerial revolution." (For more on this, see Chap. 2.) They also corresponded about their common concern over the fate of pragmatism as a philosophical tradition. Indeed, Mills and Macdonald got into a debate over whether radicals should defend universalistic values (Macdonald's view) or be content with the historical relativism implicit in pragmatism (Mills's argument). Mills started contributing to *politics* and never shied away from banging out a letter to Macdonald about what he thought of the latest issue. Indeed, Mills became increasingly critical of his colleague. When Macdonald's essay, "The Root Is Man," came out, Mills told him that it was "a splendid piece." This exuberance must have referred solely to the cultural and ethical analysis that Macdonald had pulled off in the essay—his warnings about the dangers of a mass society and its concomitant decrease in personal and civic responsibility. In a later letter, Mills explained that politically, the two of them "differ like hell," and that this difference emerged in his reading of "The Root Is Man." Mills elaborated: "There is a terrific let down, for me at least, . . . when you come to political action. . . . This political action outcome . . . is so weak that it would have been much better not to have included anything on the topic at all." Mills argued that Macdonald's cultural analysis was insightful, but that his political prescriptions paled in comparison. He clearly thought little of personalism or individualism as a solution to the problems Macdonald had outlined. (This would parallel another debate Mills had with Goodman: see Chap. 3.) Mills harangued Macdonald at one point to get

21. Dwight Macdonald, "I Choose the West," reprinted in *Politics Past: Essays in Political Criticism* (New York: Viking, 1957), 198. On this speech and its aftermath, see Whitfield, *A Critical American,* 89; Wreszin, *A Rebel in Defense of Tradition,* 236; Sumner, *Dwight Macdonald and the politics Circle,* 223; and Pells, *Liberal Mind,* 180. Christopher Lasch argues that this speech signaled the end of Dwight Macdonald's "first career" and the beginning of his second: see his *New Radicalism,* 323. On how *Partisan Review* moved closer to the ACCF, see Longstaff, "The New York Family," 563.

back to "hard hitting political analysis." He still believed in a political alternative to Macdonald's increasing gravitation toward ethical individualism and
saw no reason why anarcho-pacifism or humanitarian socialism could not
fuel a formidable type of radicalism—one that still had something to say
even about *mass politics.*[22]

Mills did not form his own magazine, though he considered it. Indeed,
when he turned down a shared editorship with Macdonald in 1948, he
probably clinched the end of their tension-filled intellectual friendship. Macdonald explained to Mills in 1949 that he had "underestimated the depth of
differences between us—on such questions as the labor movement, the possibility of socialist action today, the application of scientific thinking to politics, etc." This difference would be set in stone once Macdonald reviewed
White Collar in 1951. Though their split took on very personal tones, it is
important here to see that it was mostly about political and intellectual disagreements. For in these disagreements we begin to see how Mills started to
carve out the basis of future New Left thought—a basis that was deeply
indebted to Macdonald's prior intellectual explorations. One year after the
review of *White Collar* appeared, Norman Thomas invited Mills and Macdonald to debate one another. Mills refused and explained why in a letter to
Thomas: "I hold quite firmly to certain old-fashioned beliefs, including socialist and humanist and certainly secular ideals; I do not think Dwight is
capable of fixing his beliefs in any warrantable way." Instead, Mills argued,
Dwight made a "fetish of confusion and drift." Mills—fairly or not, since
Macdonald would eventually change course once again—placed Macdonald
in the general "drift" of the New York Intellectuals toward the status quo.
Against this impulse, Mills had developed his own view of the intellectual as
an agent of change. As Mills saw it, there was still the possibility of thinking
seriously about radicalism in the changed context of the Cold War. Macdonald, for Mills, had simply forgotten that.[23]

Mills had grown disgruntled with Macdonald's penchant for anticommunism, which had prevented Macdonald from pursuing a democratic radical-

22. All of the letters quoted here are found in the Dwight Macdonald Papers, C. Wright
Mills folder: Mills to Macdonald, May 8, 1946; Mills to Macdonald, July 22, 1946; Mills to
Macdonald, undated. For the review of *White Collar,* see Dwight Macdonald, "The Mills
Method," in *Discriminations: Essays and Afterthoughts, 1938–1974* (New York: Grossman,
1974).

23. From the Dwight Macdonald Papers, C. Wright Mills folder: Macdonald to Mills,
May 18, 1949; Mills to Norman Thomas, March 18, 1952, copied to Macdonald with the
words "Dwight, So to hell with guys like you!" scrawled across the top.

ism rooted in American thought and traditions. Of course, *politics* had always relied on European thinkers more than American ones. (It should be noted that Mills himself, though, had mined European social thought for his own thinking.) But Macdonald *had* opened up the possibility of envisioning a democratic radicalism by providing a platform for new ideas; he had helped chart a course independent of the irrelevant Trotskyism of his past. It was up to others to continue going down this route to discover its fullest possibilities, while making older traditions speak to the anxieties of Americans living in a new postwar world.[24]

There were some more concrete lessons as well. In its pages, *politics* showed that radicalism could ground political action on a new basis, emphasizing decentralized communities, humanitarian and libertarian socialism, individual conscience, and personal free will. Macdonald saw how pacifism and nonviolent direct action could serve as important political alternatives. He believed that the concept of mass culture was deeply political, not simply cultural, and that mass politics was increasingly corrupt and superficial. He also left behind a critical tension between a gloomy depiction of a social reality that closed out alternatives—"bureaucratic collectivism," as he often called it, or what others labeled a conformist "mass society"—and hope for political change. All of these themes and their inherent tensions played themselves out in the later thinking of New Left intellectuals. This is most clearly and immediately evident in the developing thought of C. Wright Mills and Paul Goodman. Mills, in some ways, picked up on the humanist and democratic socialism that Macdonald had explored briefly (later in life, Mills also considered nonviolent theories), while Goodman continued to develop the anarcho-pacifism to which Macdonald had been briefly attracted. It is to these thinkers' work—and the inheritance that came their way through *politics* and the general context of American intellectual life at the time—that we now turn.[25]

24. Gregory Sumner shows how Macdonald stayed away from the American predecessors to his own radical thought. See his *Dwight Macdonald and the* politics *Circle,* 126. See also Alan Wald, *The New York Intellectuals: The Rise and Decline of the Anti-Stalinist Left from the 1930s to the 1980s* (Chapel Hill: University of North Carolina Press, 1987). The odd thing about Wald's work is his complete comfort with sectarianism—what I take to be one of the silliest and most destructive elements in left-wing intellectual thought.

25. Sumner, *Dwight Macdonald and the* politics *Circle,* 18. On the tension between Macdonald's analysis and his hope for change, see Westbrook, "The Responsibility of Peoples," 59–60.

2

The Godfather, C. Wright Mills: The Intellectual as Agent

> The image which unites the Hemingway man and the wobbley . . . and both of them with my "real" occupational role as a professor of social science . . . is the image of the political writer. This is the idea of the man who stands up to nonsense and injustice and says no. Says no, not out of mere defiance or for the sake of the impudent no, but out of love of truth and joy in exercising intellectual skills.
> —C. Wright Mills, "For Ought?"

> The Age of Complacency is ending. Let the old women complain wisely about "the end of ideology." We are beginning to move again.
> —C. Wright Mills, "The New Left," 1960

When C. Wright Mills met Dwight Macdonald in 1942, the two men hit it off well, both enjoying the art of argument. In fact, as Macdonald's biographer put it, "Dwight claimed that [Mills] could argue longer and louder about any subject than even he could." While Mills lived outside of New York City (in Wisconsin and then in Maryland), he sent Macdonald numerous pieces published in *politics* and other articles published elsewhere— purely for the sake of discussion. Mills was Macdonald's junior and learned quite a bit from his elder; he also confronted their differences in a fairly substantive correspondence. In setting out what drew the two of them together and then explaining why they drew apart, we get a better sense of not only their intellectual friendship but also the origins of New Left thinking. For when Macdonald reviewed Mills's *White Collar* harshly and Mills followed suit by "breaking ranks" from Macdonald, the origins of the New Left could be glimpsed, even if just in embryonic form. C. Wright Mills would essentially take a great deal from Macdonald's explorations at *politics,* but would resist his final choice of the West.[1]

A generation gap always informed their relationship. Although Mills

---

1. Wreszin, *A Rebel in Defense of Tradition,* 134.

graduated from high school in 1934 and began attending college the same year, he did not come of political age during the 1930s. Texas, after all, was not exactly a hotbed of radical sectarianism like New York City. Mills explained, "I did not personally experience 'the thirties.' At the time, I just didn't get its mood." Nor did he get Marxism. He was too busy rebelling against the military regiment of Texas A&M (where he spent, in his own words, "one unhappy year"), reading Nietzsche, and writing fiction and poetry. Marxism was foreign to this "native American radical who could speak with indigenous accents," as Irving Howe described him. For this reason, Mills could write confidently later in his life, "I've never been emotionally involved with Marxism or communism, never belonged in any sense to it." This absence of Marxism and radical sectarianism explained a core difference between Mills and Macdonald (and other New York Intellectuals). Mills started with something of a blank slate when he began his search for a New Left.[2]

Mills's first experience of anything at all "radical" was his discovery—via his professor at the University of Texas at Austin, Clarence Ayres—of the liberal philosophy of pragmatism (which made him more willing than Macdonald to entertain "liberal" ideas in general). Mills explained in 1938, "My intellectual godfathers were pragmatists. When I first awoke I discovered myself among them." This debt became clearer when Mills attended graduate school at the University of Wisconsin in 1939. Here he decided to write his dissertation on pragmatism, the indigenous American philosophy that argued for no absolute fixed principles other than experimentation. One of the things that drew him nearer to Macdonald was that he was increasingly wary about pragmatism's political consequences. He wrote to Macdonald in 1942, in a clumsy style not yet overcome, "I am growing a little fearful that the only positive value, with the aid of which you sustain radical society

2. Mills quoted in Richard Gillam, "Richard Hofstadter, C. Wright Mills, and 'the Critical Ideal,'" *American Scholar* (Winter 1977–78): 72; Mills, autobiographical fragment in the C. Wright Mills Papers, 1934–1965, Center for American History, University of Texas at Austin, box 4B389; Irving Howe, "On the Career and Example of C. Wright Mills," in *Steady Work: Essays in the Politics of Democratic Radicalism, 1953–1966* (New York: Harcourt, Brace, and World, 1966), 247; C. Wright Mills to Hallock Hoffman (of the Center for the Study of Democratic Institutions), October 7, 1959, C. Wright Mills Papers, box 4B398. For biographical details on Mills, I rely on Richard Gillam's published essays as well as his marvelous and unpublished dissertation, "C. Wright Mills, 1916–1948: An Intellectual Biography" (Ph.D. diss., Stanford University, 1972). In addition, I have drawn upon the very helpful time line printed in *C. Wright Mills: Letters and Autobiographical Writings,* ed. Kate Mills (Berkeley and Los Angeles: University of California Press, 2000).

hopes, is the 20th century formality of 'scientific method.' I hope to show in a sociological history of the pragmatic movement, which should be finished in six or eight months, that this is not too firm an anchor for political shipping." Though Mills never questioned pragmatism's conception of knowledge (indeed, a little later, he would defend Dewey against Max Horkheimer's more dismissive read in *The Eclipse of Reason*), he concerned himself with the political consequences of its seeming relativism. Recognizing Randolph Bourne's influence, Mills argued that John Dewey's support of World War I showed off his "technologism" and lack of substantive values. Mills believed that Dewey's acceptance of the war, among other things, suggested he was "too technological and not deeply enough political." The emphasis here was on the *political* consequences of pragmatism surrounding war, not the philosophy's primary teachings. Mills disagreed with Macdonald when the latter once decided to defend objective idealism—a belief in absolute values like justice and truth that stood outside of history and that could inform a critique of horrors like the Holocaust. Nonetheless, he *did* believe that pragmatism required substantive values to guide its instrumentalist framework. Though these values might be historically contingent, thinkers needed them in order to transcend the more short-term, instrumentalist patterns in pragmatist thinking (an idea that Arnold Kaufman would later explore in fuller detail). Like Macdonald, he showed a heavy debt to Bourne, who had retained a faith in pragmatism even while criticizing the political mistakes made by its key exponent.[3]

At the University of Wisconsin, Mills not only pursued his interest in pragmatism but also imbibed the institution's legacy of Progressivism. The university was known for its liberal ideal of public service and committed

3. C. Wright Mills: quoted in Gillam, "C. Wright Mills, 1916–1948," 69; letter to Macdonald, February 6, 1942, C. Wright Mills Papers, box 4B369; *Sociology and Pragmatism: The Higher Learning in America* (New York: Oxford University Press, 1969), 422–23 (this work is Mills's doctoral dissertation); "Pragmatism, Politics, and Religion" (originally published in *The New Leader*, 1942), in *Power, Politics, and People*, 166. Mills would later write, "I have never found either a transcendent or an immanent ground for moral judgment. The only moral values I hold I've gotten right inside history." See his "'The Power Elite': Comment and Criticism," *Dissent* 4 (1957): 32. For Mills's rejection of Max Horkheimer's dismissal of pragmatism, see his report to Margaret Nicolson, October 15, 1945: "I don't see any evidence that Horkheimer has really gotten hold of pragmatism except . . . in a rather vulgar form" (C. Wright Mills Papers, box 4B389). For an important work that examines the indigenous roots of Mills's thought, including his indebtedness to pragmatism, see Rick Tilman, *C. Wright Mills: A Native Radical and His American Intellectual Roots* (University Park: The Pennsylvania State University Press, 1984).

intellectual work. Wisconsin professors—such as historian Frederick Jackson Turner and sociologist Edward Ross—had played an enormous role in Progressive-Era intellectual inquiry. When Mills came to Wisconsin, he began to show interest in Charles Beard, the most important political historian to live during the Progressive Era, and he delved into the social thought of Thorstein Veblen, whose socioeconomic analysis influenced activists and politicians at the turn of the century. While reading these great Americans, Mills also encountered (largely through his mentor, Hans Gerth) the thinking of key European social theorists like Max Weber and the Frankfurt School. This increasing interest in European intellectual sources also drew Mills closer to Macdonald, who eventually published Mills's and Gerth's translation of Max Weber's essay on "Class, Status, and Party" in the pages of *politics*.[4]

But aside from these interests, what really drew Mills to Macdonald was World War II. Though he had missed the Great Depression and the political decade of "the thirties," Mills confronted the war with a growing sense of personal anxiety and intellectual interest in leftist politics. The clearest way in which the war broke into Mills's consciousness—as it had for the conscientious objectors Macdonald had applauded—was through the military draft. Though he was no pacifist, Mills did not want to take part in battle or submit himself to the military regimentation he so hated at Texas A&M. He tried to figure out ways to dodge the draft. The military, however, eventually turned him down due to hypertension. (Unconfirmed stories go that he drank a massive amount of coffee right before his military examination.) Mills came to feel sympathy for Macdonald's later criticisms of the depersonalization of World War II, even if he never embraced Macdonald's temporary pacifist orientation. Mills's opposition to the war also led him to pursue a "sociology of the left," as he called it in a letter to Macdonald in

4. On the University of Wisconsin, see Paul Buhle's introduction to his edited collection, *History and the New Left,* and Allan Bogue and Robert Taylor, eds., *The University of Wisconsin: One Hundred and Twenty-Five Years* (Madison: University of Wisconsin Press, 1975). On Beard, see the chapters on him in Richard Hofstadter, *The Progressive Historians: Turner, Beard, Parrington* (New York: Vintage, 1970). On Beard's influence on Mills, see Gillam, "C. Wright Mills, 1916–1948," 167, and the C. Wright Mills Papers, box 4B368, U.S. History folder. Mills once stated that Weber and Veblen were the most relevant social theorists of modernity: see his and Hans Gerth's "A Marx For Managers" (1942), in *Power, Politics, and People,* 53; on the influence of Weber and the Frankfurt School, see John Eldridge, *C. Wright Mills* (London: Tavistock, 1983), 19; for more on Mills's influence, see the list of thinkers he compiled in his "Readings for Sociologists," C. Wright Mills Papers, box 4B374.

1945. Though this might have sounded like a social scientist's interest, it was becoming deeply personal for Mills. One of the key sectors of the left that drew Mills's attention was Macdonald's own strain of radicalism. Here was the foundation of their intellectual and political friendship.[5]

Breaking Ranks: Joining the Family Only to Escape It

In corresponding with Dwight Macdonald and writing for *politics,* Mills moved closer to the orbit of the New York Intellectuals. In 1945, he literally moved closer: he relocated from the University of Maryland (situated in the planned community of Greenbelt) to New York City. Here Mills first worked for Paul Lazarsfeld's Bureau of Applied Social Research and then taught full-time at Columbia University. New to the city, Mills moved to a building in which Daniel Bell—another young sociologist writing for *politics*—lived. In addition to learning from Macdonald, Mills took a great deal from his friendship with Bell, who knew New York City quite well. But eventually Mills would also split from him. By briefly contrasting Mills with both Macdonald and Bell, we learn where his thinking was heading within the general context of American intellectual life, and more specifically within the context of the New York Intellectuals.[6]

When Mills met Bell, the latter's prime occupation was editing the *New Leader,* an anticommunist, socialist newspaper. Here Bell helped develop critical concepts like the "permanent war economy" and the "monopoly state"—ideas that Mills took up but that Bell eventually dropped after World War II in order to embrace his "end of ideology" centrism. Though Mills

5. For Mills's statement on "sociology of the left," see Mills to Macdonald, February 5, 1945, Dwight Macdonald Papers, C. Wright Mills folder. On Mills's draft experience, see Gillam, "C. Wright Mills, 1916–1948," 185–86; see also Guy Oakes and Arthur Vidich, *Collaboration, Reputation, and Ethics in American Academic Life: Hans H. Gerth and C. Wright Mills* (Urbana: University of Illinois Press, 1999), 95. Mills explained that he was still fearful, even after this rejection, that he might face the draft: again, see his letter to Macdonald from February 5, 1945. For Mills's general radicalization during World War II, see James Miller, "Democracy and the Intellectual: C. Wright Mills Reconsidered," *Salmagundi* 70–71 (1986): 86–87.

6. For Mills's relocation to New York City, see Gillam, "C. Wright Mills, 1916–1948," 270–71. A reflection of Mills's attitude toward the University of Maryland is captured in his December 7, 1943, letter to Macdonald: "Everything here is as dull and unrewarding as usual" (Dwight Macdonald Papers, C. Wright Mills folder). For his move, see the letter dated "Fall, 1944" in the same collection. For Mills becoming a part of the New York Intellectual group, see Irving Louis Horowitz, *C. Wright Mills,* 77.

waited until 1945 to relocate to New York City, Bell had published some of Mills's early pieces in the *New Leader* from 1942 to 1943. It is clear that one of Mills's most important debts to Bell, besides his conceptual framework, was the public forum that Bell provided for his ideas, a forum that encouraged him to write more lucidly. Indeed, until 1942, most of Mills's prose was clunky and often impenetrable, laced with sociological jargon and passive, almost Germanic language. In his articles for the *New Leader,* the clarity of Mills's later prose began to develop.[7]

In addition to clarity and political concepts, Mills and Bell shared an increasing interest in the work of Max Weber and of Franz Neumann, another German political sociologist connected to the Frankfurt School. Moreover, Bell would join Mills in criticizing the alienation created within modern work systems. But he refused to criticize mass culture, and he would certainly have been displeased by Mills's later political twist on the mass culture thesis. For Bell, those who focused on "the debaucheries of mass culture" forgot that "these problems are essentially cultural and not political." Instead of characterizing mass society as apathetic, Bell portrayed Americans as "joiners" engaged in voluntary associations. Though Mills agreed that Americans were neither dupes nor completely passive, he certainly believed that mass culture did irreparable damage to the civic virtues that Bell trumpeted. The most significant difference between them, though, was signaled when Bell dropped his former Marxism for a more conservative form of anticommunism, a shift made explicit when, in 1952, he joined the Congress for Cultural Freedom (the organization that sprang from Americans for Intellectual Freedom). Bell argued that his own transformation from radicalism applied to the New York Intellectuals in general. In his famous book, *The End of Ideology* (a compilation of essays he had written during the 1950s), Bell would use terms remarkably similar to those of Mills: he argued that "the excitement of the 1930s had evaporated" in the postwar world, that "[t]he political intellectuals became absorbed into the New Deal." Unlike Mills, though, Bell was completely comfortable with this transformation. By 1952, Mills had broken with Bell, lumping him in with the general

---

7. Dittberner, *The End of Ideology and American Social Thought,* 165. On Bell's intellectual development, I rely upon Brick, *Daniel Bell.* On Mills's academic jargon, one can simply read anything that he published in the early 1940s; see also Gillam, "C. Wright Mills, 1916–1948," 75–76, 175. In a letter dated February 13, 1941, to R. H. Williams, a professor at the University of Buffalo, Mills admitted that he was trying to write more clearly (C. Wright Mills Papers, box 4B377).

"drift" taken by the New York Intellectuals as a whole (including, of course, Dwight Macdonald).[8]

Mills's break from Bell was similar to his break from Macdonald. Again, Mills would take certain things from both thinkers and then criticize their drift toward anticommunism as the primary basis of their political views. Here we see the origins of New Left thinking. As the previous chapter demonstrated, Mills embraced Macdonald's cultural criticism while abhorring his political stances. Throughout his career, Mills remained devoted to cultural criticism. Moreover, Mills adopted from Macdonald a critique of the concept of progress, with its inevitable faith that the world tended toward improvement. When Mills wrote in the late 1950s that "the moral insensibility of our times was made dramatic by the Nazis" as well as "by the atomic bombing of the peoples of Hiroshima and Nagasaki" and "the brisk generals and gentle scientists who are now rationally—and absurdly—planning . . . the strategy of World War III," he tipped his hat to Macdonald, while updating his insights for the late 1950s. When Mills condemned "depersonalized inhumanity," he clinched his debt. Mills also openly cited Macdonald's essay, "The Responsibility of Peoples," in his later work and retained the sort of ethical commitment that Macdonald, while editing *politics,* placed at the center of his own radicalism.[9]

But while recognizing his debt, Mills had always eschewed what he perceived as Macdonald's "snobbishness." Writing to Robert Lynd, a sociologist at Columbia University, Mills argued that *politics* would be a success as long as Macdonald "doesn't get too 'self-indulgent' about it." Macdonald's self-indulgence was far more politically significant for Mills than it might at first appear. Citing *politics* in an article that he wrote for *Labor and Nation,* Mills argued that Macdonald's vision of the left was "frequently overwhelmed by vision without will." Here his split with Macdonald was largely codified, at least intellectually. Mills would never be content with a politics

8. Bell, *The End of Ideology,* 313, 303. For Daniel Bell on Americans as "joiners," see Pells, *Liberal Mind,* 142. For Bell's joining of CCF, see Dittberner, *The End of Ideology and American Social Thought,* 176. For Mills's break, see his "Commentary on Our Country, Our Culture," *Partisan Review* 19 (1952): 446–50. Their disagreements would become even more ferocious once Mills published *The Power Elite,* a book that Bell spent a great deal of time trying to refute.

9. C. Wright Mills, "The Intellectuals' Last Chance," *Esquire,* October 1959, 101, and "The History Makers," *Social Progress* (October 1959): 7. For Mills's critique of progress, see also Richard Gillam, "C. Wright Mills and the Politics of Truth: *The Power Elite* Revisited," *American Quarterly* 26 (1975): 476. For Mills's citation of Macdonald's "The Responsibility of Peoples," see his *Causes of World War III* (New York: Simon and Schuster, 1958), 76–78.

without will—in fact, the search for an effective form of leftism defined much of his later intellectual work. He believed that politics needed to be about widespread social and political change and that a writer needed to show what concrete sources there were for this sort of change. Just as important, it made clear what Mills hated the most in Macdonald: his tendency to write about political alternatives as if they were just things to be played around with by a detached intellectual. At one point, Mills labeled Macdonald the "Peter Pan of the Left." From 1947 onward, Macdonald served as something of a counterexample for Mills, even as Mills relied upon a great deal of Macdonald's earlier thinking.[10]

Two of Mills's accusations about Macdonald—his snobbishness and tendency toward "drift"—became the backbone of Mills's general attack on the overall deradicalization of the New York Intellectuals. Some of this was personal. Mills always felt alienated from the New York Intellectuals, even as he became closer to them. As an Irish Catholic Texan, he did not fit in well with the cosmopolitan and Jewish backgrounds of most New York Intellectuals (Macdonald himself being a peculiar exception to the rule). Mills appeared to be a crude populist—and even spoke with a southern twang at times—in comparison with a Lionel Trilling or a Daniel Bell. But to personalize this difference is to ignore the fact that Mills largely played up his alienation, even going so far as to *affect* an accent in the presence of certain New York Intellectuals. Mills wore many masks, and in certain ways, he was just as cosmopolitan (if not more so) than most members of that group. Though there was a personal disaffection, certainly, Mills's major complaints about his fellow thinkers were more substantive, focusing on their drift away from what he took to be the central tasks of intellectuals—to be social critics and seekers of political alternatives.[11]

10. C. Wright Mills: quoted in Richard Gillam, "*White Collar* from Start to Finish," *Theory and Society* 10 (1981): 23; letter to Robert Lynd, undated, C. Wright Mills Papers, box 4B343; "Five 'Publics' the Polls Don't Catch," *Labor and Nation,* May–June 1947, 24; quoted in Wreszin, *A Rebel in Defense of Tradition,* 237. It should be noted that Robert Lynd's book, *Knowledge for What? The Place of Social Science in American Culture* (1948; reprint, Princeton: Princeton University Press, 1970), formulated a vision of social theory and criticism that influenced Mills's later thinking on sociological inquiry.

11. It is interesting to note that Mills's background was much more cosmopolitan and broad than that of the often parochial New York Intellectuals, some of whom seemed almost frightened to leave the confines of New York City. Indeed, Mills would go on to travel quite extensively throughout America and abroad, including visits to Europe, Eastern Europe,

Mills complained about the New York Intellectuals' tendency to *personalize* politics. As he would point out in his later writings on the New Left (where his criticisms of the "Old Futilitarians" came to the fore), thinkers like Daniel Bell universalized their deeply personal, autobiographical rejection of socialism. They used their own experiences with communism in order to reject radicalism completely. As Mills explained, these thinkers' "disillusionment with any real commitment to socialism" led them to reject "*all* ideology." Their own "guilt" about having once been communists also limited their ideas. These thinkers became "trapped by the politics of anti-Stalinism," as he put it. Ensnared, they played into the hands of the great "American celebration," an imperative created by the Cold War. In countering this tendency among the New York Intellectuals, Mills began to develop the model of committed intellectualism that became so central to his concept of radical politics and the New Left. Though Mills had personal confrontations with Bell and Macdonald, in another way, he needed them: they served as negative examples, counters to his own alternative. Additionally, their backgrounds clarified how his own personal experience—precisely, the absence of communism in his early life—gave him an advantage in reflecting on democratic radicalism. While breaking from Macdonald, Bell, and the rest of the "New York Family," Mills was charting his own course for democratic radicalism.[12]

Russia, and Latin America. At one point, he considered moving permanently to England. For interesting reflections on Mills's many masks and his tendency toward personal posturing, see Gillam, "C. Wright Mills, 1916–1948." For more on Mills's "posing," see his notes in *C. Wright Mills: Letters and Autobiographical Writings*, ed. Kate Mills, 27.

12. C. Wright Mills, "The New Left" (1960) and "The Decline of the Left" (1959), in *Power, Politics, and People*, 248 (italics in original), 223, and *Causes of World War III*, 126. The clearest statement of Mills's rejection both of the New York Intellectuals and of the "American celebration" is his "Commentary on Our Country, Our Culture." (See also Mills's footnote in "On Knowledge and Power" [1955] in *Power, Politics, and People*, 603.) One of the other authors critical of the New York Intellectuals in the "Our Country, Our Culture" *Partisan Review* symposium was Irving Howe. In fact, we should note that in many ways, Mills's attempt to stick to the idea of democratic radicalism was enormously influential in the formation of *Dissent* magazine in 1954. Mills was an important figure here, even though he would eventually break from Howe over their later debates regarding the peace movement and Cuba. Howe himself pointed out that when *Dissent* was originally attacked after its first issue appeared, "Among prominent intellectuals only C. Wright Mills came to our defense." See Edward Alexander, *Irving Howe: Socialist, Critic, Jew* (Bloomington: Indiana University Press, 1998), 97. For more on the background of *Dissent* as it relates to the future New Left, see Isserman, *If I Had a Hammer*, chapter 3.

The Role of the Intellectual and the Old Left

I am one of those who have decided to throw in with the little groups that cannot win.
—C. Wright Mills, "The Politics of Skill," 1946

While rejecting Macdonald and searching for a vision that had some real possibility of transforming social and political institutions, Mills flirted with Trotskyism briefly during the 1940s. But Trotskyism seemed like a foreign language to Mills and was a ghettoized vision for a small band of intellectuals anyway. He quickly rejected it and then landed squarely within the camp of organized labor that also included liberals and social democrats. (Mills, it should be noted, voted for Norman Thomas throughout the 1940s.) From America's entry into World War II to about 1949, Mills believed that labor unions might provide the source for an effective left in America. Here he resisted Macdonald's tendency to speak poorly of "lib-labs." Mills had his reasons for optimism. After all, 1946 was a major year for organized labor. As historian John Patrick Diggins explains, in that year "America witnessed one of the most severe periods of unrest in American labor history. Strikes broke out in almost every industry: steel, coal, electrical, lumber shipping, railroads." Walter Reuther, heading the United Auto Workers (UAW), made an unprecedented move by not only leading a walkout from General Motors but also demanding that the corporation open its books to public scrutiny—arguing, along social democratic lines, that this economic monopoly had public obligations. Mills took note of this labor upsurge.[13]

Not surprisingly, Mills was especially drawn to the UAW. After covering one of its conventions for *Commentary,* Mills came back with a glowing report. In what was clearly a reflection of his own autobiographical tendencies, Mills reported that UAW members exemplified "the old populist mood of the frontiersmen from the Southern and Western border states." These were truly "home grown radicals" who formulated a distinct "non–middle class culture." But, as Mills pointed out (again with autobiographical overtones), they combined this populist exuberance with "political sophistication" and a propensity for deliberation and discussion. Though Mills was not overly impressed with Reuther, the president of the UAW who was drifting

---

13. For Mills's flirtation with Trotskyism, see Gillam, "C. Wright Mills, 1916–1948," 330–31; Diggins, *The Proud Decades,* 101; on Walter Reuther, see Lichtenstein, *The Most Dangerous Man in Detroit,* and Kevin Boyle, *The UAW and the Heyday of American Liberalism, 1945–1968* (Ithaca: Cornell University Press, 1995).

toward anticommunist liberalism at the time, he admitted that Reuther was a democratic leader committed to working with the rank and file and formulating the closest thing to a truly social democratic vision for America. Broadening his thinking in *The New Men of Power: America's Labor Leaders* (1948), Mills argued that labor leaders were "the only men who . . . could organize the people and come out with the beginnings of a society more in line with the image of freedom and security common to left traditions." Here was a political vision that had strength and institutions behind it.[14]

But if labor unions like the UAW were to become truly radical and resist incorporation into the status quo, Mills believed that they needed to think politically. As he put it in 1943, "Unless trade unions unify into an independent political movement and take intelligent political action on all important political issues, there is danger that they will be incorporated within a government over which they have little control." Mills repeated this sentiment in his more overt call for the "formation of an independent labor party." There is reason to believe that Reuther himself tended in this direction in the wake of World War II. In a letter to Hans Gerth in 1948, Mills wrote hopefully about how "Reuther is coming out this fall for a new party." But soon after this statement, Mills's hopes were dashed. Having witnessed the communist influence within the Wallace campaign in 1948, Reuther sided with Truman—positioning the UAW within Americans for Democratic Action (ADA), a liberal organization that was avidly anticommunist and that rarely broke from the Democratic Party (though it was often critical of it). A third party now seemed out of the question. There was already the Taft-Hartley Act (1947), which, in the words of labor historian Nelson Lichtenstein, created a "collective bargaining straitjacket that restricted the social visions and political strategies advocated by the laborite left." By 1948, then, it was clear that Mills's hopes were just that—hopes. Unions would now focus solely on securing contracts for their workers and eschewing radical politics. Mills's political vision—like Macdonald's—lacked will.[15]

14. C. Wright Mills, "'Grass-Roots' Union with Ideas: The Auto Workers—Something New in American Labor," *Commentary*, March 1948, 241, 242, 247, and *The New Men of Power: America's Labor Leaders* (New York: Harcourt, Brace, 1948), 30. It should be noted that Mills's enthusiasm for the UAW was shared by Irving Howe, who was breaking with Trotskyism at the time. See his and B. J. Widwick's *The UAW and Walter Reuther* (New York: Random House, 1949). It is also important to note that the UAW would help fund SDS later on: see, in general, Levy, *The New Left and Labor*.

15. C. Wright Mills, "The Political Gargoyles: Business as Power" (1943), in *Power, Politics, and People*, 75–76; "The Case for the Coal Miners," *The New Republic*, May 24, 1943,

Nonetheless, what Mills really found in the labor movement was an opportunity to think critically about the intellectual's relation to political
change—the central basis of his future idea of a New Left. During the years
immediately following World War II, he mostly concerned himself with
what he called a "tragic split between the radical intellectual and the rank
and file of organized labor." In trying to merge the two, he pushed his
thinking about intellectuals forward and, in the process, discovered other
intellectuals who promised a better model than Macdonald's and Bell's, intellectuals who suggested how ideas could inform progressive politics in a
significant way.[16]

Research and writing served as the two major paths by which Mills could
best engage the labor movement. At the Bureau of Applied Research, he
performed a great deal of research directly helpful to unions. This brought
him into the editorial circles of Labor and Nation, an important publication
that tried to bridge the "tragic split" that Mills lamented. Most important,
Mills met the editor of Labor and Nation, J. B. S. Hardman, with whom
he worked and had many conversations. Hardman was an immigrant Jew
from Tsarist Russia. When he came to the United States, he flirted with the
Communist Party and Trotskyism, but then eventually joined the Socialist
Party and worked with numerous trade unions. During the 1940s, he
formed the Inter-Union Institute, an institution that coordinated labor's research activities. For Mills, Hardman served as a political intellectual committed to effective change—a counterexample to Dwight Macdonald's lack
of experience in any serious type of political organizing. Mills described
Hardman as "a wonderful old man" and someone "in revolt against bore-
dom in the labor movement."[17]

697; and letter to Gerth, September 26, 1948, reprinted in C. Wright Mills: Letters and Autobiographical Writings, ed. Kate Mills, 121; see also Lichtenstein, The Most Dangerous Man in
Detroit, 261. On Reuther siding with Truman and deciding against a third party, see Boyle,
The UAW, 51. For two historical views on labor tending to move away from radical politics,
see Steven Fraser's and Nelson Lichtenstein's essays in The Rise and Fall of the New Deal Order,
ed. Fraser and Gerstle. Mills's vision of a third party representing labor lived on in the pages of
the American Socialist, a publication that ran from 1954 to 1959. This magazine was much
more loyal to a Marxist alternative than Mills ever was; it faithfully argued for labor to break
with the Democratic Party. See, for instance, "The Labor Party Debate at the CIO Convention," American Socialist (January 1955): 5. Clearly, Mills's vision did not disappear when he left
it behind. Nonetheless, it became much less feasible, as the folding of the American Socialist
showed. I am indebted to Paul Buhle for making me aware of this publication.

16. Mills, "'Grass-Roots' Union," 248.
17. Mills to Hans Gerth, January or February 1946, in C. Wright Mills: Letters and Auto-

In the pages of *Labor and Nation,* Mills explained how he thought intellectuals should relate to the labor movement. In the first place, he believed that intellectuals were increasingly recognizing their own alienation from the places in which they worked—in academia, for book publishers, for political institutions (what Mills would later call "the cultural apparatus"). He wrote, "Many of the new research people are disaffected and morally unhappy: they sell their minds to people they don't like for purposes they don't feel at one with." Labor held out an appealing opportunity for purposeful commitment. But in linking up with labor, Mills argued, intellectuals should not think of themselves as leaders. Indeed, he was quite critical of the "illusions" of "Fabianism," where intellectuals turned themselves into reformist advisers who assumed positions of political power. Nor should intellectuals think that their ideas would be immediately useful to labor. They needed instead to *make* them useful by listening to what labor leaders wanted (e.g., public opinion research that might discern how much support there was for a strike). Additionally, since intellectuals were themselves white-collar workers, they should try to help out in organizing efforts among other white-collar employees. In a speech to the Inter-Union Institute in 1946, Mills argued, "Instead of talking in general about all that the intellectuals could contribute to unions if 'they would only accept us,' the intellectual ought to help organize" workers, especially those in the white-collar ranks. In all of these ways, politically engaged intellectuals had to make themselves useful while reminding labor of its larger aims and political vision.[18]

---

biographical Writings, ed. Kate Mills, 96–97. Mills's involvement in Hardman's work can be gleaned from a memo that states: "Mills has been made an advisory editor of [*Labor and Nation*] and has spent a great deal of time helping to get this magazine out and advising on policy of the Institute" (memo to Paul Lazarsfeld, January 28, 1947, C. Wright Mills Papers, box 4B368). Mills was also going to edit a book with Hardman entitled *Politics and Labor: An Inquiry into American Social Dynamics.* This book never came about: see box 4B395. For more background on Hardman, see Gillam, "C. Wright Mills, 1916–1948," 334–35. I also thank Jeffrey Boxer for finding out more about Hardman.

18. C. Wright Mills, "The Politics of Skill," *Labor and Nation,* June–July 1946, 35; "The Intellectual and Labor Leader," speech at the Inter-Union Institute, January 18, 1946, C. Wright Mills Papers, box 4B343; and "No Mean Sized Opportunity," in *The House of Labor: Internal Operations of American Unions,* ed. J. B. S. Hardman and Maurice Neufeld (New York: Prentice-Hall, 1951), 519. Mills put his own philosophy of useful research into practice in a number of articles that he wrote for *Labor and Nation:* "What the People Think: Review of Selected Opinion Polls," *Labor and Nation,* November–December 1946, 11–13; "What the People Think," *Labor and Nation,* March–April 1947, 258; "Notes on White Collar Unionism," *Labor and Nation,* March–April 1949, 17–21, 42; "White Collar Unionism," *Labor and Nation,* May–June 1949, 17–23. It is not surprising to find renewed interest in Mills's work

Ironically, when Mills paid attention to the bigger questions of politics and social reform, he grew increasingly disaffected from labor. In certain ways, Mills showed another key debt to Daniel Bell, who had begun writing off the radical potential of labor within the pages of *politics*. By 1948, Mills had started to depict organized labor as "opportunistic," and in 1949 he described it as a "vested interest." Mills saw labor as a bureaucratic institution that was now a part of the status quo of managerial capitalism. By 1950, Mills could not envision organized labor as an institution that would push for progressive change. This sometimes verged on a flat-out rejection of labor (he wrote his friend Harvey Swados in 1955 that the same UAW members he had once praised in *Commentary* were now "serene idiots"). Mills generally seemed to characterize labor as flotsam and jetsam, though, capable of floating in a radical or conservative direction. In *White Collar* (1951), Mills speculated that in "being watchdogs over the economy, as against being merely an interest group within it, the unions will be *forced* to take on a larger cultural and political struggle." The word *forced* was crucial here, for Mills could no longer see organized labor as a proactive leader in an effective left; labor was merely *potentially* reactive if history were to change. His previous hope in labor closed out as the last gasp of the old liberal left. It was now time to search for a *new* left while seeing which way labor would go and while building on the idea of a committed intellectual.[19]

The "Retreat" to Social Criticism: A Moralist Figuring Out the World

I know most of the younger men in American sociology, men like myself who got degrees within the past 5 or 6 years and have published since then, and I am bound to say that not more than two of them can be trusted to do anything other than what the older men have done. They are all so craven and so anxious for career chances that they would sell out their own ideas if they had any for the right kind of job. The fact is that they don't even know where to stand politically, they are so repressed and full of fear of every possible move.

—C. Wright Mills to Dwight Macdonald, January 3, 1944

---

among contemporary thinkers who are trying to rebuild the links between intellectuals and labor. See, for instance, Nelson Lichtenstein, "Falling in Love Again? Intellectuals and the Labor Movement in Post War America," *Labor Forum* (Spring–Summer 1999): 18–31.

19. C. Wright Mills: *New Men of Power,* 164; "White Collar Unionism," 19; letter to Harvey Swados, May 1955, C. Wright Mills Papers, box 4B411; *White Collar: The American Middle Classes* (New York: Oxford University Press, 1951), 321.

During the 1950s, Mills drew back from political engagement with the labor movement in order to get a better sense of what was happening in American society. He remained a moralist, but also became a social critic who tried to tease out insights developed in the world of academic research. H. Stuart Hughes described Mills best in calling him a "moralist who has chosen to put on the ill-fitting garment of the systematic theoretician of society." Though I will not delve into his writing during this time in great detail, it is evident that Mills was formulating his political vision through what might appear to be his less politically charged work of the 1950s. In becoming a social critic, he was also making clear what role intellectuals should assume in public life—a crucial step toward his formulation of the New Left. He also assessed the traditions upon which a future left could and could not rely.[20]

Mills was perhaps best known as a critic of professional social science. To put it simply, he believed that the act of describing social life was an inherently moral one. In *The Sociological Imagination* (1959), a book that drew out the principles behind the sociological inquiry he did throughout the 1950s, Mills explained: "Whether he wants it or not, or whether he is aware of it or not, anyone who spends his life studying society and publishing the results is acting morally and usually politically as well." Precisely for this reason, the sociologist faced an imperative—the demand to communicate findings to the people being studied (and therefore to write in a clear and concise way for a wide reading public of fellow citizens). One of his major criticisms of professional social science was that "the sociologist of applied social research does not usually address 'the public'; he has specific clients with particular interests." Mills eschewed this sort of specialized writing for small, selective audiences. In all of his own work, he wanted to "take it big," to make his findings speak to a wider readership committed to political self-understanding. For this reason, he was not accepted as a professional sociologist, but was seen instead as a "popularizer"—a term that took on increasingly pejorative tones at this time.[21]

20. H. Stuart Hughes, "A Politics of Peace," *Commentary*, February 1959, 118.

21. C. Wright Mills, *The Sociological Imagination* (New York: Oxford University Press, 1959), 79, 102. For the accusations of his being a popularizer, see Jamison and Eyerman, *Seeds of the Sixties*, 40. On "taking it big," see Dan Wakefield, "Taking It Big: A Memoir of C. Wright Mills," *Atlantic Monthly*, September 1971, and Wakefield's introduction to *C. Wright Mills: Letters and Autobiographical Writings*, ed. Kate Mills. C. Wright Mills also argued against any analogy between social and natural science (*Sociological Imagination*, 114) and instead suggested an analogy between his sociological work and the work of a "modern novelist" (a term he used in typewritten notes: see the C. Wright Mills Papers, box 4B373). In all of these

It also meant that Mills had to seek out an alternative way of approaching social theory, one that evaded the statistical, abstract, or theoretical approaches of his fellow social scientists (especially Talcott Parsons). To do so, he reached back into intellectual history. From Hans Gerth, he got Max Weber, who focused on broad issues like centralization and bureaucratization. (Weber's works were, in fact, being translated by Gerth at the time.) But as Gerth himself explained, Veblen was probably the biggest influence on Mills, if only because—from an American standpoint—he was more approachable. As Mills put it, "Thorstein Veblen is the best critic of America that America has produced." Veblen's legacy offered Mills a glimpse of what it meant to be a social critic and a model intellectual. Mills called Veblen one of America's "masterless men," an intellectual kindred spirit to "the Wobblies." Notably, after labor failed to provide him with a home base, Mills refused to place himself squarely within *any* institution. Mills loved Veblen, in large part, for his ability to stand outside of institutions and serve as a critic who could still speak in tones that would attract a wider public. But there was one problem: Mills deplored Veblen's well-known tendency toward irony. For Mills, social criticism was not to be ironic, but *moral*. In an introduction to Veblen's seminal book, *Theory of the Leisure Class,* Mills wrote, "Veblen laughed so hard and so consistently at the servants and the dogs and the women and the sports of the elite that he failed to see that their military, economic, and political activity is not at all funny." The sort of social criticism Mills would pursue would draw from Veblen's independent spirit but be much more moral and political in tone.[22]

---

ways, he seemed to articulate what Anthony Giddens later called a "post-positivist" social science. See Giddens, *Social Theory and Modern Sociology* (Stanford: Stanford University Press, 1987).

22. C. Wright Mills, introduction to *The Theory of the Leisure Class,* by Thorstein Veblen (New York: Mentor, 1953), vi, xvi–xvii. Weber's influence on Mills can be seen throughout his work, but it is especially clear in his and Gerth's *From Max Weber: Essays in Sociology* (New York: Oxford University Press, 1946). For Gerth's comment about Veblen's influence, see Hans Gerth, "C. Wright Mills, 1916–1962," *Studies on the Left* 2 (1962): 9. Another influence on Mills was forced upon him by Dwight Macdonald. Macdonald got Mills to review James Agee and Walker Evans's *Let Us Now Praise Famous Men* (Boston: Houghton-Mifflin, 1939). Mills argued that Agee left behind a challenge to future writers—to balance objective social science against the "personal meanings" of the observer. For Mills, Agee was too "self-indulgent" and had not discovered the need for "self-discipline" and "craftsmanship," a term he would increasingly use to describe his later work. See Mills, "Sociological Poetry," *politics,* Spring 1948, 125. It should also be noted that in and around 1959–60, Mills planned to write *The Very Bottom: Down and Out,* a book on America's poor. See the C. Wright Mills Papers, box 4B412. Of course, Michael Harrington wound up publishing something similar to that idea later in *The Other America.*

White Collar served as a transitional work for Mills, moving away from the model of the committed labor intellectual toward that of the detached social critic. Nonetheless, read in this context, the book was deeply political. In the first place, the research that went into it originated with Mills's concern over whether white-collar employees might join unions—a pressing interest of organized labor during the post–World War II period, when white-collar ranks skyrocketed throughout American society. But Mills's work must also be put into the context of previous thinking on the middle classes in America. Key here were two sociological and political thinkers that Mills had read: Lewis Corey and Alfred Bingham. Corey, a Marxist, argued that since white-collar classes were being proletarianized—that is, they worked increasingly for salaries rather than owning property—they could be relied upon to build a popular front with the working classes. Bingham, a radical liberal, differed from Corey. Though he believed that white-collar members faced proletarianization, his vision for them was to build a "cooperative commonwealth" through electoral politics. What both men shared, though, was an optimism about the potential radical visions of white-collar workers.[23]

Mills wanted radicals to put many of these hopes to rest. He disliked Corey's Marxist and Bingham's liberal and progressive assumptions. Mills was more of a classical republican political theorist when it came to thinking about white-collar employees. That is, he believed that the loss of property signaled a serious loss of independence. Mills described the white-collar classes as "more often pitiful than tragic." Bereft of property, white-collar people faced work conditions that lacked any serious meaning and took on "a generally unpleasant quality." No social thinker should assume, Mills argued, that white-collar employees would become a progressive force in American society, especially because the working class had already failed on that count. White-collar employees might join unions, but even that was uncertain, due to their status anxiety. Mills's pronouncement on this class's political future was gloomy: "They are no vanguard of historic change; they are at best a rear-guard of the welfare state." Summing up his critique of Bingham's "middle class radicalism" and making his own republican political jeremiad even clearer, Mills argued, " 'Middle class radicalism' in the United States has been in truth reactionary, for it could be realized and maintained

23. Mills's original concern with white-collar unionization can be seen in his articles for *Labor and Nation:* see note 18 above. On Bingham's ideas, see his *Insurgent America.* For Corey's position, see his *Decline of American Capitalism* (New York: Covici, Friede, 1934). See also Richard Pells, *Radical Visions and American Dreams* (New York: Harper Torchbooks, 1973), 91–95.

only if production were kept small-scale." Mills concluded that just because they were growing in number and their work was being proletarianized did not mean that white-collar employees would serve as a force for radical or liberal change in America—and he refused to declare the white-collar classes a replacement for the Marxist proletariat.[24]

Many of Mills's fellow New York Intellectuals thought his critique of white-collar life too severe. But even if his overall assessment of their political future was negative, he did not dismiss white-collar workers outright. Mills believed that they might unionize. And when asked by a disgruntled white-collar worker about what political actions he could take, Mills was quick to offer advice, making clear that the situation was not hopeless. In a rare correspondence (one demonstrating that he still thought of himself as a political intellectual while writing sociological tracts during the 1950s), Mills doled out his thoughts to a "Mrs. Harold Gossman," who had pressed him on what could be done about the situation among members of the white-collar class. He suggested that this white-collar citizen form "a discussion group among friends" and put together "a White Collar Center" that could address issues around wages and prices, maybe even going so far as to form co-ops (advice that would have made Bingham smile). At one point, Mills berated his listener: "Don't moan about your loss of status: think politically." In a follow-up interview to this advice, Mills argued that white-collar workers promised little in terms of progressive politics. But it was clear from his advice to Mrs. Gossman that he would not rule out the potential for the very sort of "middle class radicalism" that Bingham had espoused. It was just not on anything more than purely wishful grounds—as his own jeremiad made clear. Indeed, during the 1950s, Mills's social analysis typically portended doom for radical visions even though his own moral and political hopes never vanished.[25]

While the political messages of *White Collar* were mixed, *The Power Elite*

24. C. Wright Mills, *White Collar,* xii, 219, and "The Structure of Power in American Society" (1958), in *Power, Politics, and People,* 34. For more on Mills's apparently republican leanings, see his commentary on Noah Webster's belief in "a general and tolerably equal distribution of landed property" as the basis of "national freedom" (*White Collar,* 8). See also his seemingly romantic belief that the older petite bourgeoisie had more "civic spirit" (ibid., 45). It should be noted that Mills himself practiced petit bourgeois practices such as (briefly) growing his own food. See his comments on running a "subsistence farm, producing about half of our foodstuffs": autobiographical fragment, C. Wright Mills Papers, box 4B389.

25. The advice given to "Mrs. Gossman" was in "Hope for White Collar Workers," *American Magazine,* May 1951, and in the C. Wright Mills Papers, box 4B376. For the New York Intellectuals' critique of Mills's read of white-collar employees, see Irving Louis Horowitz, *C. Wright Mills,* 248–53.

(1956) made Mills's political vision clearer. This book drew from another 1940s concern that a "permanent war economy" was consolidating. (The permanent war economy was a concept explored by Daniel Bell while he was at the *New Leader* and by Macdonald in the first few issues of *politics*. Mills expanded on it in an early piece for *Common Sense,* Alfred Bingham's publication—and one that Bell also edited for a brief period.) For Mills, the "permanent war economy" was an empirically grounded concept taken from observations in 1945 that elites such as the Secretary of the Navy and the president of General Electric were collaborating, jointly envisioning "an image of a militarized capitalism in the defense of which they would conscript America." With the advent of modern war—and its concomitant centralization of military institutions and economic corporations—powerful elites assumed the mantle of leadership in America. With further empirical research, carried out after 1945, Mills's thesis of a "power elite" can be taken essentially as an updated account of a permanent war economy in the immediate wake of World War II.[26]

Mills's increasing indebtedness to Weber showed through in his power elite thesis. Weber, as Mills knew well, moved beyond Karl Marx's account of power in modern society. As Marx saw it, economic class rule was the sole source of domination. For Weber, this was far too simplistic. He focused on the dynamic of centralization and domination not just within the economy, but also within the state and cultural life. Mills followed Weber's lead, arguing, "The history of modern society may readily be understood as the story of the enlargement and centralization of the means of power—in economic, in political, and in military institutions." He traced out this centralization in the change from small standing armies during the Revolutionary period to large centralized military forces, starting with America's entry into World War I. He documented the massive centralization of corporate power and the death of small entrepreneurs during the Gilded Age, and he then showed how modern war provided greater demand for concentrated industrial production. The stock market only furthered these tendencies. Though Mills portrayed America's political state as weak, arguing that the wealthy could always break laws and evade regulation, he also saw its power growing as it tried to correct for some of the brutal injustices incurred by capitalism

26. C. Wright Mills, "The Conscription of America," *Common Sense,* April 1945, 16. For examples of Mills's later use of the permanent war economy concept, see his "Balance of Blame," *The Nation,* June 18, 1960, 528–29; *Causes of World War III,* chapter 10; "The Intellectuals' Last Chance," 112; and *The Power Elite* (New York: Oxford University Press, 1956), 19, 167, 215.

and to manage conflicts created by the Cold War. The power elite was thus composed of leaders of the corporate sector (the most powerful of all), the military (growing in power with the Cold War's decreasing reliance on classical ambassadorship and nonmilitaristic diplomacy), and the political apparatus (the least strong, due especially to a weak civil service).[27]

Critics—including Daniel Bell—attacked Mills's conception of the power elite, seeing it as too simplistic. But what must have worried social scientists the most was not Mills's thesis but the fact that *The Power Elite* was much less a sociological study than a moral and cultural jeremiad. Mills fashioned himself in the tradition of the muckrakers who had unveiled corporate abuse and political corruption at the turn of the century, the most famous and articulate of whom was Henry Demarest Lloyd, himself a republican-inspired social critic. Mills never shied away from moral judgment about those who wielded power in America. He called them, quite simply, "mindless." He waxed nostalgic about the founding fathers—America's first elite—arguing that "once upon a time, at the beginning of the United States, men of affairs were also men of culture." The contrast with his own time was easy to make. While George Washington read Voltaire, Mills pointed out, Eisenhower "reads cowboy tales and detective stories." In an unpublished piece entitled "The Politics of Truth," Mills made even clearer his moralism and tendency toward cultural jeremiad, complaining about the "advertising ethos and package mentality displayed through Eisenhower's million dollar campaign." He argued, "We are against certain rather deep lying trends in American society itself, which are now taken for granted, and some of which cannot be dealt with by legislation . . . or . . . administrative action only. It is a realization of this immoral tone that sets the depth of our pessimism, and that lends an anarchist touch to our mood, and it is this realization that makes us appear, often correctly, as impractical and utopian." But this signaled a major tension in Mills's thought, for while hinting at utopian anarchism, it also seemed that Mills would have been quite content with an elite that was more intelligent than unsophisticated leaders like Eisenhower.[28]

27. Mills, "Structure of Power," 25. See also *The Power Elite,* from which I draw the rest of this analysis of Mills's "power elite" theory. To a certain extent, Mills's concern about the growing centralization of military power also betrayed his republican concerns; it even suggests a near romanticism about citizen armies of the Revolutionary period in American history. At a recent symposium on Mills's work, Norman Birnbaum called Mills a "left Weberian" (symposium for the release of *C. Wright Mills: Letters and Autobiographical Writings,* ed. Kate Mills, New York Public Library, September 20, 2000).

28. Mills, *The Power Elite,* 356; "On Knowledge and Power," 604, 605; and "Politics of

Just what Mills wanted in the face of a centralized power elite was never entirely clear. As a social critic, the real question was what political or social theory he would use to describe how power worked (and could thus be reworked). First, he rejected a group of sociological thinkers known as elite theorists—Vilfredo Pareto, Gaetano Mosca, and Robert Michels. These European theorists believed that societies inevitably developed strong elites. (An "iron law of oligarchy" was Michels's term.) By way of rejecting these thinkers, Mills rejected James Burnham, the writer who had popularized them for an American audience in his book, *The Machiavellians*. For Mills, these thinkers simplified things. "It is not my thesis," Mills wrote, "that in all epochs of human history and in all nations, a creative minority, a ruling class, an omnipotent elite, shape all historical events. Such statements, upon careful examination, usually turn out to be tautologies, and even when they are not, they are so entirely general as to be useless in the attempt to understand the history of the present." Mills would admit that business elites were, to a certain extent, "self-circulating," a term used by elite theorists. They came from the same Protestant and wealthy backgrounds and went to the same prep schools and Ivy League colleges. Nonetheless, Mills saw an "iron law of oligarchy" as too fatalistic even for what often became his own fatalistic mind-set and his own hope for self-willed resistance.[29]

Mills also rejected Marxism as an explanation of how power worked. He especially lambasted the Marxist assertion that the state was "the committee of the ruling class," his quick and easy retort being: "I don't believe it is quite that simple." That is why he used the term "power elite" rather than "ruling class." He explained that "the political apparatus" is not "merely an extension of the corporate world." It is rather "a network of 'committees,' and other men from other hierarchies besides the corporate rich sit upon these committees." Since its members were diverse, "this instituted elite is frequently in some tension." This might have suggested that the elite could be changed by splitting it, so to speak (something that William Appleman Williams would later suggest). Though Mills never suggested this exact point,

Truth," C. Wright Mills Papers, box 4B414. Mills called himself a "god-damned anarchist" in a letter to Harvey Swados, November 3, 1956, reprinted in *C. Wright Mills: Letters and Autobiographical Writings,* ed. Kate Mills, 218.

29. Mills, *The Power Elite,* 20; on the business elite, see 127. For more on elite theorists, see Vilfredo Pareto, *Sociological Writings* (London: Pall Mall, 1966), especially 128–35; Gaetano Mosca, *The Ruling Class* (New York: McGraw-Hill, 1939); Robert Michels, *Political Parties* (New York: Free, 1962); James Burnham, *The Machiavellians* (New York: John Day, 1943).

he would later see citizen movements capable of challenging the elite's domination of political life. Nonetheless, Mills never went so far as to argue that the elite lacked power. Any conception of the "elite as impotent" was as absurd as Marxist conspiracies. Power, influence, and centralization existed as very real social and political forces for Mills. From this perspective, he eschewed political scientists who argued that diverse interest groups had influence on government, making it impossible to say that any one set of actors had more influence than others. Those who refused to recognize the influence of the power elite—those whom Mills increasingly called "liberals"—were merely "obfuscators." In fact, his critique of pluralist political scientists, a group of thinkers that often overlapped with the New York Intellectuals, became the clearest connection between Mills's sociological analysis and his search for a radical political theory and a New Left.[30]

Liberalism as Salvageable: Scrapping the Tradition, or Discovering the Possibilities of Radical Liberalism?

In starting to push beyond liberal political theory, Mills started a tension-ridden pattern within New Left thinking. He was clearly trying to search out some alternative to liberalism, while at the same time suggesting that liberalism held certain necessary features for any future left. Mills was not always clear, though, about whether he wanted to scrap liberalism or salvage critical elements from it. Some younger New Leftists could see him as junking liberalism; others, such as Arnold Kaufman (see Chap. 5), believed that he was carving out a form of "radical liberalism." At the least, Mills believed that those within the liberal tradition needed to think more critically about their past and present accomplishments. He seemed neither celebratory nor completely dismissive, but he also made some mistakes in interpreting the strengths and weaknesses of the liberal tradition.

30. See Mills, "'The Power Elite': Comment on Criticism," 31, and his *Power Elite,* 170, 276, 16. Mills's critique of the Marxist theory of the state needs to be understood alongside his critique of the Marxian notion of class consciousness, an analysis that Mills developed in his studies of white-collar workers. Mills argued that white-collar workers might face proletarianization (as Lewis Corey argued), but that this did not lead to an inevitable development of proletarian class consciousness on their part. For Mills, such a position derived from "a metaphysical belief" in shifting consciousness—an astute criticism of Marx's mechanical theories of society. See Mills, "The Sociology of Stratification" (1951), in *Power, Politics, and People,* 319–20. On the general influence of "pluralism" in American political science, see Diggins, *The Proud Decades,* 253.

Interestingly enough, Mills's arguments about liberalism shared a great deal with some New York Intellectuals who were drifting toward the sort of liberal anticommunism he criticized. Lionel Trilling and Richard Hofstadter (the latter a personal friend of Mills who criticized many of his ideas) were both New York Intellectuals who believed that liberalism was the dominant ideology of American political thought. As Trilling put it in the opening to *The Liberal Imagination,* "In the United States at this time liberalism is not only the dominant but even the sole intellectual tradition." Daniel Boorstin, an avid ex- and anticommunist, believed that the "genius of American politics" was that it tended toward one set of ideas, both pragmatic and liberal. Louis Hartz, though not a New York Intellectual, wrote an entire book on how America lacked any aristocratic or feudal background, making liberalism the only game in town—and a hollow one, precisely because it lacked contenders. Mills was certainly privy to these ideas, and even helped develop some of them. What made him different, again, was that he refused to accept liberalism's shortcomings or the idea that it was the *only* political vision available.[31]

Of course, the key question here is what Mills meant by "liberalism," a term that is as loose as "democracy." Mills recognized the most obvious and major shift within liberal political thought—one that correlated with a change from the eighteenth to the twentieth century (perhaps best captured in the career of John Stuart Mill, who himself formulated this shift). During the eighteenth century, "classical" liberalism meant the political thinking of entrepreneurs and property owners, concerned with defending small free markets and open trade against the encroachment of mercantile economic policies and governments. Classical liberalism—as Tocqueville pointed out in his treatise on America—also prized local voluntary activities and associa-

31. Lionel Trilling, *The Liberal Imagination: Essays on Literature and Society* (Garden City, N.J.: Anchor, 1950), vii; Richard Hofstadter, *The American Political Tradition* (New York: Vintage, 1948), especially viii; Daniel Boorstin, *The Genius of American Politics* (Chicago: University of Chicago Press, 1953); Louis Hartz, *The Liberal Tradition in America* (New York: Harcourt, Brace, 1955). For a good synopsis of these thinkers' views on liberalism, see Pells, *Liberal Mind,* 135–62. It is interesting to note that the argument about the lack of a feudal background missed the aristocratic nature of slavery and the importance of the South in relation to a conservative intellectual tradition in America. On Hofstadter's and Mills's friendship, see Gillam, "Richard Hofstadter, C. Wright Mills, and 'the Critical Ideal.'" Charles Frankel (who served as Arnold Kaufman's adviser in graduate school) was another friend—and liberal opponent—of Mills. Frankel once remarked that Mills was "an extraordinary human being" in "Legend of the Left," *Newsweek,* May 11, 1964, 92. For more on Frankel, see Chapter 5 below.

tions. But by the twentieth century, liberals had shifted their thinking away from laissez-faire principles. "Modern" liberals started to recognize the inequities created by industrial society and called for stronger governments that could create systems of welfare capable of protecting older ideals like freedom and individuality. In American intellectual history, this shift was best captured in Herbert Croly's belief that "Hamiltonian means"—strong government and regulatory policies—were needed in the modern world to ensure "Jeffersonian ends"—freedom and equality. By the 1930s, liberals were known as advocates for strong welfare states.[32]

Mills took note of this shift, but he argued that the "classical" conception of liberalism still had great influence in American life. Here he followed Hartz and Hofstadter, who premised their arguments on America's lack of any feudal remnants. Due to this historical circumstance, Mills explained, "the middle classes have been predominant—in class and in status and in power." "Liberalism" was therefore "paramount" in American political thought. And yet, small markets and petit bourgeois entrepreneurs had disappeared. Mills explained, "Over the last hundred years, the United States has been transformed from a nation of small capitalists into a nation of hired employees; but the ideology suitable for the nation of small capitalists persists, as if that small propertied world were still a going concern." Liberal ideology—or what he sometimes called "liberal rhetoric"—thus wound up "masking social reality." Mills's critique paralleled the idea of "cultural lag," the notion that ideas often take some time to catch up with the social realities they purportedly justify. Mills disliked cultural lag theory because it lacked any normative framework. Why, he asked, should ideas simply capture social reality rather than push us to think *beyond* social realities? Nonetheless, his criticism of classical liberalism suggested not that it was substantively *wrong,* but that it failed to capture social reality in any meaningful way. Classical liberalism's tendency to become mere "rhetoric" did not mean that its core values were baseless, but that they were often outmoded.[33]

32. The story of this transition within liberal political thought has been told in many different venues. Those interested in a thorough explanation of it can consult James Kloppenberg, *Uncertain Victory: Social Democracy and Progressivism in European and American Thought, 1870–1920* (New York: Oxford University Press, 1986). See also Herbert Croly, *The Promise of American Life* (New York: Macmillan, 1909).

33. C. Wright Mills: "The Conservative Mood," in *Power, Politics, and People,* 211 (the essay was originally published in 1954, in the first issue of *Dissent*); *White Collar,* 34; "Conservative Mood," 30; "The Intellectuals' Last Chance," 101. For Mills's critique of the "cultural lag" theory, see his "Professional Ideology of Social Pathologists" (1943), in *Power, Politics, and*

Indeed, Mills himself seemed partial to numerous classical liberal assumptions. He never questioned the Enlightenment's legacy of rational inquiry into social and political problems or its central place within the liberal tradition. He seemed comfortable with the epistemology of pragmatism—if not with all of John Dewey's political positions. Nor did he ever argue, the way some radical Marxists did, that "bourgeois civil rights" merely covered up injustices. Rather, his criticism during the Cold War was that liberals often championed the principle of civil rights—especially those rights that protected critical and free speech—but rarely put the principle into practice. As Bourne did with Dewey around World War I, Mills performed an "in-house" or friendly critique of liberals, one that pushed them on their self-professed ideals. "Post-war liberals," Mills wrote, "have been so busy celebrating civil liberties that they have had . . . neither the time nor inclination to *use* them." Mills here picked up on an old way of thinking about freedom, stressing "positive" freedoms—the right to speech that was *effective* in determining political decision making—over "negative" freedoms—the mere protection of any speech, be it effective or not. The British political theorist T. H. Green had, by the late nineteenth century, defined a positive freedom as "a positive power or capacity of doing or enjoying something worth doing or enjoying, and that, too, something that we do or enjoy in common with others." This sort of thinking lay at the basis of Mills's position here. Nor did Mills ever question the importance of democratic, voluntary associations—those institutions, in his own words, that linked "individuals, smaller communities, and publics . . . with the state." While Daniel Bell, criticizing mass culture theorists, thought that these voluntary associations operated unimpeded in the modern age, Mills argued that modern society tended to marginalize them. Finally, in assessing classical liberalism, Mills never questioned its ethic of reform. Within the American context, Mills always believed in the gradualism counseled by the liberal tradition of political reform. In all of these ways, Mills remained a classical liberal of sorts, albeit one who radicalized liberalism's core assumptions. Liberalism seemed to have something critical to offer.[34]

People, 544–45. For more on the cultural lag theory, see Pells, *Radical Visions*, 24–25. Mills's arguments on liberalism and small entrepreneurs were also developed by the Frankfurt School, especially Max Horkheimer in his *Eclipse of Reason*, 141. (Mills reviewed *Eclipse of Reason* for Oxford University Press.)

34. T. H. Green, "Lecture on 'Liberal Legislation of Freedom of Contract'" (1881), in *Lectures on the Principles of Political Obligation and Other Writings*, ed. Paul Harris and John

If Mills seemed partial to classical liberalism, what did he think of its modern variant? Here he was less enthusiastic. For Mills, modern liberalism congealed around the New Deal—with its welfare (1930s) and warfare (1940s) states. Since it relied on centralized government and administration, liberalism's grassroots moral fervor had declined. He explained, "Liberalism, now almost a common denominator of U.S. politics, becomes administrative liberalism, a powerful and more absorptive state framework, within which open political struggles are being translated into administrative procedures and pressures." As it became reliant on "law or administration," it lost its connection to "grass roots" movements and thus failed to cultivate "new leaders" or ideas; by turning itself into "a set of administrative routines," liberalism had no "program to fight for." Indeed, since liberal policies relied upon a hierarchical conception of administrative "expertise," any further "public discussion" about moral direction had become moot. Mills updated his earlier critique of pragmatism (itself a modern liberal doctrine) when he argued, "Liberal practicality tends to be apolitical or aspire to a kind of democratic opportunism." When they position themselves solely for state power, liberals became craven, amoral, and inherently conservative. This suggested that modern liberalism was not such a good inheritance for radical thinkers, that it would resist more radical possibilities.[35]

Morrow (Cambridge: Cambridge University Press, 1986), 199. For the tight association Mills made between liberalism and the Enlightenment, see his and Hans Gerth's *Character and Social Structure* (New York: Harcourt, Brace, and World, 1953), 464; Mills, *The Power Elite,* 334; Mills, "Culture and Politics" (1959), in *Power, Politics, and People,* 242. Mills's embrace of reform can be seen in his positive review of *Yankee Reformers in the Urban Age,* by Arthur Mann, in the *New York Times Book Review,* October 17, 1954; his sympathetic treatment of how sociology was once connected to reform movements (see *Sociological Imagination,* 84); and his citation of L. T. Hobhouse, an important figure in liberal political thought, as one "whose creed I share" (see Mills, *Listen, Yankee: The Revolution in Cuba* [New York: Ballantine, 1960], 179). Richard Gillam recognizes that Mills was a reformer, not a revolutionary: see his "C. Wright Mills and the Politics of Truth," 478. See also Weber's classic defense of liberalism, portrayed in Steven Seidman, *Liberalism and the Origins of European Social Theory* (Berkeley and Los Angeles: University of California Press, 1983). As we will see in the later chapter on Arnold Kaufman, Mills's thinking here formed the basis of what Kaufman called "radical liberalism."

35. C. Wright Mills: *White Collar,* 321–22; "On Knowledge and Power," 601; *Sociological Imagination,* 88; and "Characteristics of Our Times," a speech to the Division of Home Missions, National Council of the Churches of Christ, Atlantic City, New Jersey, December 10–13, 1958, C. Wright Mills Papers, box 4B389, 6. Dwight Macdonald had set out this interpretation of modern liberalism in "The Death of F. D. R." (1945), in *Politics Past.*

Mills seemed to err in some important ways here. By calling liberalism the "official political philosophy" of America, he underplayed how a variety of conservatism—one that actually parodied the classical liberal arguments for smaller markets and a weaker state—persisted (and was about to gain steam in the late 1950s and early 1960s within the Goldwater wing of the Republican Party). Ironically, Mills had recognized this grouping in his *New Men of Power,* calling them "the practical right," an odd turn of phrase. But as the 1950s dawned and as Eisenhower pledged Republican Party loyalty to the welfare state, Mills directed most of his animosity toward liberalism. Unfortunately, liberalism was not the only game in town. Of course, some might argue that Mills could not have been expected to notice this, since the conservative tendency did not really make a dent until later (although it was evident in the early southern protest against federal intervention for the civil rights of African Americans as well as in more avid forms of anticommunism during the 1950s). But Mills's argument can certainly be blamed for its own reductionism, that is, for ignoring how modern liberals still spoke a morally charged language—one with a vigorous faith in democratic equality and hatred for communist authoritarianism. Perhaps Mills did not agree with what he found here, but Schlesinger's *The Vital Center* and Reinhold Niebuhr's *The Children of Light and the Children of Darkness*—perhaps the ultimate statements of liberal anticommunism—were certainly charged with moral language. It was neither fair nor accurate of Mills to suggest that liberals could never muster moral tones. Finally, Mills left behind a tension for the New Left. Was his an "in-house" critique of liberalism—one that placed its faith within the tradition while pushing it to embrace its more radical claims—or a dismissal? Later, in his assessment of Third World radicalism, Mills's critique of liberalism became increasingly strident, associating liberalism solely with First World prosperity. (As we will see, other New Left intellectuals faced this question and tried to answer it in different ways.) Mills, then, helped fuel tensions between radicalism and liberalism that were never entirely resolved by thinkers and activists of the New Left.[36]

36. Mills, *New Men of Power,* 23–27. For Mills's more crude association of liberalism with First World privilege, see *The Marxists* (New York: Dell, 1962), 29. A number of political theorists have explored the moral underpinnings of modern liberalism: see, for instance, William Galston, *Liberal Purposes: Goods, Virtues, and Diversity in the Liberal State* (Cambridge: Cambridge University Press, 1991). See also my "Remember Liberalism?"

Radical Democracy as Political Vision

Democracy implies that those who bear the consequences of decisions have enough knowledge—not to speak of power—to hold the decision-makers accountable.
—C. Wright Mills, *The Power Elite,* 1956

By reflection and debate and by organized action, a community of publics comes to feel itself and comes in fact to be active at points of structural relevance.
—C. Wright Mills, *The Power Elite,* 1956

If liberalism failed on key accounts to provide answers for those intent on political change, what other alternatives existed? In many ways, Mills was painting a fairly grim picture of American society during the 1950s. After all, from the descriptions found in *White Collar* and *The Power Elite,* America was a land of alienated, passive white-collar employees, a mass culture, and an elite accountable only to itself. So what political theory could serve as an alternative to this gloomy scenario and still suit Mills's reformist (and sometimes liberal) tendencies and his search for a vision that did not lack political effectiveness? It would seem that Mills's only response to this question was the idea of radical democracy.

This theme was already evident in *The New Men of Power,* Mills's book on the labor movement. In a chapter entitled "Alternatives," Mills criticized the "formal democracy" of American politics and liberal managerialism. With American democracy, participation was essentially saved for voting, not an everyday activity. For Mills, "the left" should try to "democratize modern society" and "establish a society in which everyone vitally affected by a social decision, regardless of its sphere, would have a voice in that decision and a hand in its administration." In support of his vision, Mills cited G. D. H. Cole, the main proponent of "guild socialism," a radical vision for worker-managed firms and decentralized decision making about industrial matters. Mills would stick to this vision of robust and everyday democracy when he later defined his vision as one of "collective self-control" and "effective decision-making" being shared by as many citizens as possible. Yet as Mark Starr pointed out in an important critique of Mills's celebration of guild socialism, Cole had already jettisoned a great deal of his own belief in democratic participation by the time Mills cited him. Starr's critique came just at the time that Mills questioned labor's role in radical change. Mills might still have been able to defend the argument, but at least should have stopped to think about the implications of Starr's point. While questioning labor's role in democratic political change, though, Mills would never question democracy's pivotal role in his radical vision.[37]

For his idea of radical democracy, Mills went back in history once more, returning to his own image of what American society was like during the eighteenth and nineteenth centuries and to the thinking of John Dewey. At the heart of his democratic theory was the idea of a public. Again, this was a core component of classical liberal thought. A democratic public, for Mills, was a collection of citizens who deliberated on political decisions. Within it, Mills explained, "virtually as many people express opinions as receive them" through "discussion" that is free from "authoritative institutions." The public was defined by the natural give-and-take of conversation, or what Mills called the "chance immediately and effectively to answer back to any opinion expressed." Since this necessitated a certain amount of face-to-face interaction, it was not surprising that for Mills, the democratic public's high point had occurred in the eighteenth century, when small town meetings served as a principal form of self-governance in America. According to Mills, "The public, so conceived, is the loom of classic eighteenth-century democracy." Indeed, the small public mirrored the local free market. Mills described eighteenth-century America in this way: "Here is the market composed for freely competing entrepreneurs; there is the public composed of circles of people in discussion." Mills radicalized classical liberalism here, showing how its core teachings could make for key criticisms of the present state of politics.[38]

37. Mills, *New Men of Power*, 252–53, and *Sociological Imagination*, 116, 188. Mark Starr's criticism can be found in his review of *New Men of Power* in *Labor Zionist*, March 18, 1949; see also Mills's response, "Dogmatic Indecision," in *Labor Zionist*, April 15, 1949. It is interesting to note that Mark Starr also worked closely with *Labor and Nation*. Mills would continue to assert that the act of voting was a paltry definition of what made a democratic citizen. He once wrote, "Voting is the specialized activity of the public in the age of specialization" (remarks in typed MS, C. Wright Mills Papers, box 4B413). Mills's vision of radical democracy has been picked up by numerous thinkers, including John Alt, "Reclaiming C. Wright Mills," *Telos* 18 (1985): 15. It should be noted that as much as Mills was a radical democrat, he *was* willing to sacrifice his democratic principles for other principles, such as social justice. About Cuba, Mills wrote: "Without social justice, democracy is not possible. For without it men would be slaves of property" (*Listen, Yankee*, 99).

38. C. Wright Mills: *The Power Elite*, 303–4; "Mass Society and Liberal Education" (1954), in *Power, Politics, and People*, 355; *The Power Elite*, 299; "Structure of Power," 36. For how Mills went back in history for his political vision, see Pells, *Liberal Mind*, 259. Mills's conception of a democratic public anticipated Jürgen Habermas's thought, during the 1960s, on the "bourgeois public sphere": see *The Structural Transformation of the Public Sphere* (Cambridge: MIT Press, 1989).

As much as Mills got this idea from his own understanding of American history, he also got it from one of his "pragmatic godfathers," John Dewey. In his dissertation, Mills pointed out that Dewey was raised in a small Vermont town. Many interpreters would agree with Mills when he argued that Dewey's background colored his political philosophy. Dewey had, of course, placed the conception of the public squarely at the heart of his democratic theory, best expressed in his *The Public and Its Problems* (1927). He had also located its source within "local community life." Dewey's political theory was largely a retort to Walter Lippmann's argument that, with the discovery of psychological irrationality, the power of the unconscious, and the effectiveness of manipulative propaganda during World War I, public opinion could no longer be trusted with democratic governance. Dewey argued that "the primary problem of the public" was to "achieve . . . recognition of itself," since he admitted that the social and political forces discussed by Lippmann had done a great deal of damage. Dewey believed that the public—which, for him (and later for Mills), relied upon face-to-face deliberation—needed to be reconstructed under modern conditions. He wrote, "Democracy must begin at home, and its home is the neighborly community." The public needed to rediscover itself through "improvement of the methods and conditions of debate, discussion, and persuasion." Thereby, it would gain "weight in the selection of official representatives and in the definition of . . . responsibilities and rights." Mills picked up on these ideas and updated them for his own era and set of intellectual concerns.[39]

Since the idea of a democratic public came from eighteenth-century American history and John Dewey's political philosophy, Mills believed that it fit squarely within the American grain. And yet with the current low ebb of American democracy, Mills argued, the idea of a public had become quite radical. Mills explained, "When many policies—debated and undebated—are based on inadequate and misleading definitions of reality, then those who are out to define reality more adequately are bound to be upsetting influences. That is why publics of the sort I have described . . . are, by their very existence in such a society, radical." Here was, once again, the radical

39. John Dewey, *The Public and Its Problems* (Denver: Swallow, 1927), 216, 77, 213, 208; Mills, *Sociology and Pragmatism,* chapter 15. For more on Dewey's political theory, see Westbrook, *John Dewey and American Democracy,* 300–318. On the historical experiments that informed Dewey's democratic theory, see Kevin Mattson, *Creating a Democratic Public: The Struggle for Urban Participatory Democracy During the Progressive Era* (University Park: The Pennsylvania State University Press, 1998).

liberalism so central to Mills's political thought. The liberal nature of this radicalism was clearly seen in Mills's willingness to accept representative systems of government (another debt to *classical* liberalism). In fact, Mills was no direct democrat; he saw a democratic public acting in concert with political officials delegated to make decisions. "Public opinion," in Mills's formulation, "judges specific policies and actions of those in authority." A democratic public was both radical and politically reformist. Mills contended that the "two things needed in a democracy are articulate and knowledgeable publics and political leaders who if not men of reason are at least reasonably responsible to such knowledgeable publics as exist." Mills's political vision here did not wipe the slate clean to start anew. Rather, it hoped to rebuild institutions that once existed and that once worked within the confines of America's constitutional republic.[40]

The problem, of course, was *how* to rebuild the democratic public. This had been a problem for Dewey, and it remained one for Mills. After all, if the democratic public was akin to the free market, then was it not threatened by massification and centralization? Indeed, Mills spoke mostly of the public's *absence* from contemporary politics. He wrote, "The most decisive comment that can be made about the state of U.S. politics concerns the fact of widespread public indifference." The reason, for Mills, was clear: "What were called 'publics' in the eighteenth and nineteenth centuries are being transformed into a society of masses." Masses did not deliberate like publics; rather, they remained passive in the face of propaganda. In explaining this social and political transformation, Mills spread the blame around. First and foremost, Mills focused on two primary suspects: bureaucratization and centralization of the means of political power. Mills argued that these forces had an impact on the voluntary associations in which discussions once took place. "Voluntary associations," he asserted, "have become larger to the extent that they have become effective; and to the extent that they have become effective, they have become inaccessible to the individual who would participate by discussion in their policies." This tendency was only made worse by a rise in "expertise" and "public relations," which pushed the

40. C. Wright Mills, *Sociological Imagination,* 191; "Mass Media and Public Opinion" (1950), in *Power, Politics, and People,* 580; and "On Knowledge and Power," 613. That Mills was no direct democrat might stem from his unwillingness to experience any sense of solidarity or "fraternity" in his own life—not exactly a distrust of masses of people, but certainly not a trusting attitude. See Mills's remarks on fraternity in *C. Wright Mills: Letters and Autobiographical Writings,* ed. Kate Mills, 250.

voices of regular citizens out of political discussion. The educational system was also responsible. Mills cited Jefferson's original wish that education could "make citizens more knowledgeable." With the advent of modernity, education moved from forming "the good citizen in a democratic republic" to molding the "successful man in a society of specialists." Most important of all was that "media markets" were fast overrunning "primary publics." The mass media, with its increasing range of communication, marginalized small discussions and their role in determining public debate. Mills was blunt: "The mass media, especially television, often encroach upon the small-scale discussion, and destroy the chance for the reasonable and leisurely and human interchange of opinion."[41]

With these forces allied against it, why would Mills have any hope in a democratic public resuscitating itself? He had his reasons. First, Mills refused to depict America as a "one-dimensional" society (to use Herbert Marcuse's evocative phrase) in which citizens had been so manipulated that they could think of no alternatives. He explained, "No view of American public life can be realistic that assumes public opinion to be wholly controlled and entirely manipulated by the mass media." Here he tipped his hat to thinkers like Daniel Bell, who argued that the mass culture thesis, when taken to its logical conclusion, turned citizens into dupes with no control over their lives, thus failing to describe social realities. Mills had done studies of opinion change within small towns, and his findings became a source of optimism about the possibility of citizens resisting the impact of the mass media. He also cited the fact that the mass media had reported incorrectly on the way citizens were going to vote during the 1948 presidential election—a fact captured in the famous pictures of President Truman grinning while holding up a newspaper that read "Dewey Defeats Truman." The mass media, for Mills, was not all-powerful. Discussion, with its give-and-take and its embodied (versus mediated) experience, still seemed strongest in affecting people's ideas. He argued, "It is people talking with people, more than people listening to, or reading, or looking at, the mass media that really causes opinions to change." The conclusion from all of this was obvious: "The American public is neither a sandheap of individuals each making up his own mind, nor a regimented mass manipulated by monopolized media of

41. Mills: *White Collar,* 328; *Sociological Imagination,* 52; "Mass Society and Liberal Education," 360; "The History Makers," 11; "Mass Society and Liberal Education," 368; *White Collar,* 266; "Mass Media and Public Opinion," 581; *The Power Elite,* 314.

communication." Mills added to this empirical argument the idea that critics needed to assume a public if they wanted to effect change that would be democratic in nature. Here he adopted the sort of politics he got from Macdonald—calling on his fellow citizens to resist what seemed insurmountable obstacles. As he saw it, "the formal means of democratic public life are still enough available" for intellectuals to engage in political discussion with the hopes of changing political decision making.[42]

What was required was concerted effort to resuscitate a democratic public. This was no small challenge. As Mills put it, "The United States today I should say is democratic mainly in form and in the rhetoric of expectation. In substance and in practice it is very often non-democratic, and in many institutional areas it is quite clearly so." According to James Miller, Mills came up short in his response to this weighty demand, since he never specified how democracy could work under modern conditions. There is much truth to this claim. Mills could sound awfully abstract when he called for a return to "the ancient sense of clarifying one's knowledge of one's self" as the first step in the reconstitution of a democratic public. And yet Mills did provide some answers that demand our attention. Following his friends in the British New Left, he thought, at one point, that adult education could help rebuild a democratic public. By creating a "hospitable framework for . . . debate," the adult college could "fight all those forces which are destroying genuine publics and creating an urban mass." Mills went on to say that the adult school could "help build and strengthen the self-cultivating liberal public." But even the adult school seemed a meager hope. What Mills really believed in was the creation of "movements" that could reenergize public debate in America by engaging citizens in political causes. For Mills, the only things that could help re-create publics was "to make, in the union drive, all the workers militants; in the electoral campaign, all the electorate precinct workers"—that is, to engage citizens in the sort of political work that only vigorous social movements could provide. From here, democratic deliberation would spill over into other realms of society. Mills thus connected his sociological research with his political hopes. He explained (in an unpublished piece), "Out of the little circles of people talking with one another, the big forces of social movements and political parties

42. Mills, "Mass Media and Public Opinion," 577, 590, 586, and *Causes of World War III,* 136.

develop." Since "discussions of the primary public" could never be elimi-
nated, Mills still had some reason for optimism.[43]

A New Politics with Will: The Transformative Possibilities of New Protest Movements and the Rise of a New Left

When Mills is studied in the context of the New Left, he is typically seen as
a thinker who directly and indirectly influenced later movements, as someone who formulated ideas before they were acted upon. During much of
the 1950s, Mills thought of himself in these terms—as someone in a holding
pattern, waiting for things to change. In 1952, after *White Collar* was published but before *The Power Elite* was completed, Mills explained that "without a movement to which they might address political ideas, intellectuals . . .
become indifferent." In the face of such despair, and to counteract the withdrawal of his fellow New York Intellectuals, Mills counseled patience: "In my
own thinking and writing I have deliberately allowed certain implicit values
which I hold to remain, because even though they are quite unrealizable in the
immediate future, they still seem to me worth displaying. . . . One just has to
wait, as others before one have, while remembering that what in one decade is
utopian may in the next be implementable." Mills's gloomy depiction of
America as a mass society ruled by irresponsible elites did not make him any
more hopeful a few years after making these comments. But by the later 1950s,
and until his death in 1962, Mills started seeing some cracks in the edifice of
Cold War America—namely, political movements that offered hope and demanded his attention. After 1957, with one exception (*The Sociological Imagination*), Mills stopped writing longer academic works on sociology. Instead,
he became more of a "political intellectual," writing pamphlets and articles
that explored just what could make his democratic vision a reality and what
movements should do in order to be radical. Here Mills started doing more

---

43. C. Wright Mills: *Sociological Imagination,* 188; *The Power Elite,* 318; "Mass Society and
Liberal Education," 370, 368; typewritten notes, C. Wright Mills Papers, box 4B413; "Public
Opinion" (unpublished MS for Russian-language journal, *Amerika*), C. Wright Mills Papers,
box 4B375; James Miller, "Democracy and the Intellectual," 98. On adult education, Mills
was clearly indebted to his colleagues in the British New Left: see below. At the same time,
the idea of radical adult education was a deeply American tradition. See, for example, Leon
Fink, *Progressive Intellectuals and the Dilemmas of Democratic Commitment* (Cambridge: Harvard
University Press, 1997), chapter 8, and Aldon Morris on the Highlander Folk School in his
Origins of the Civil Rights Movement (New York: Free, 1984), 141–57.

than simply waiting for movements—he laid the ground for them. He started to define the contours of a New Left.[44]

The central challenge for a future left was to ensure that American democracy would become more than mere rhetoric. For Mills, the biggest impediment to meeting this challenge was the Cold War, which flattened every political view out to being "either capitalist *or* communist." He believed that the fear of communism stifled domestic political thinking and debate. Of course, watching Dwight Macdonald shift from radical exploration to "choosing the West" served as a case in point. Mills explained, "We [in the West] celebrate civil liberties much more than we use them." The challenge was, then, to make the rights to free speech real, that is, to engender public deliberation with political consequences. For this reason, Mills showed a great deal of interest in one of the first movements that constituted the New Left—a movement coalescing around protests against the House Un-American Activities Committee (HUAC). This government agency had taken the lead in probing for communists in America, especially in Hollywood and academia. When protests erupted against HUAC at San Francisco's city hall in 1960, Mills joyfully lent his name in support. Clearly, his enthusiasm stemmed from his belief that the reconstruction of a democratic public relied upon an open atmosphere in which different ideas would, at the least, be tolerated—and perhaps even be taken seriously.[45]

More important than anti-HUAC sentiment was the emerging peace movement of the late 1950s. Once again, Mills watched with hope as organizations like the National Committee for a Sane Nuclear Policy (SANE) formed and as *Liberation* magazine (a magazine that Paul Goodman worked on and Mills voraciously clipped) started discussing mounting protests against

44. Mills, "Commentary on Our Country, Our Culture," 448, 450.
45. "Interview with C. Wright Mills, 'On Latin America, the Left, and the U.S.,'" *Evergreen Review* 5 (1961): 113; speech to the American Studies Conference on Civil Rights, October 16, 1959, C. Wright Mills Papers, box 4B400 (Martin Luther King Jr. was also at this conference); Richard Fried, *Nightmare in Red: The McCarthy Era in Perspective* (New York: Oxford University Press, 1990), 69. Mills's support for the anti-HUAC protests can be seen in his correspondence with Bowman and Wanda Collins in the C. Wright Mills Papers, box 4B389, and in his support of a letter of protest against HUAC led by the Fellowship of Reconciliation: see the C. Wright Mills Papers, box 4B415. For more on the anti-HUAC protests, see Todd Gitlin, *The Sixties: Years of Hope, Days of Rage* (New York: Bantam, 1987), 82–83, and Jerold Simmons, "The Origins of the Campaign to Abolish HUAC, 1956–1961, the California Connection," *Southern California Quarterly* 64 (1982): 141–57. It should be noted that Mills also supported the sit-in movement led by southern students in 1960. See the C. Wright Mills Papers, box 4B415.

nuclear weapons. This was the most important movement he had seen yet. He explained, "We *can* begin to create a Left by confronting issues as intellectuals in our work, and is it not obvious that *the* issue is now World War III?" These movements for disarmament were important not only because they protested the militarization of society under the Cold War. They were also experimenting with "new forms of action" that included "direct, non-violent" forms of protest. (Interestingly enough, Mills had never shown an interest in pacifist or nonviolent theory until this point.) For instance, though Mills did not refer to it, in 1958 the captain of the ship known as the *Golden Rule* protested a testing zone for nuclear weapons by sailing into it—thus breaking the law. Mills understood that with actions like these, it was not just the aims that mattered, but also the methods used. In the same vein, he believed that peace protests could open up democratic debate because they addressed an inchoate public about political matters and asserted direct pressure on the power elite to stop relying on military power (what Arnold Kaufman later called "radical pressure"). Notably, Mills believed that civil disobedience and protest needed to be coupled with the re-creation of a democratic public—that without deliberation, protest offered very little. Citizens in the peace movement refused to be locked out of public discussion by a power elite. In one of his first pamphlets in support of the peace movement, *The Causes of World War III,* Mills explained that "it is now sociologically realistic, morally fair, and politically imperative to make demands upon men of power and to hold them responsible for specific courses of events." Seemingly, then, the power elite thesis did not necessarily lead to political pessimism—just to a limit on the *possibilities* of political transformation. The new challenge made by peace protesters coalesced nicely with Mills's hope for movements re-creating democratic publics with coercive but not revolutionary power.[46]

To be effective, Mills argued that the peace movement needed to become international. Here again, there were reasons for hope. In the year *The*

46. Mills, "The Decline of the Left," 234–35, and *Causes of World War III,* 95. For Mills's support of SANE, see box 4B414 in the C. Wright Mills Papers; for his reading of *Liberation,* see 4B395. Mills also collected the writings of one major peace movement figure, A. J. Muste (see box 4B416). Muste wound up defending C. Wright Mills's thinking against Irving Howe. See his position in "C. Wright Mills' Program: Two Views," *Dissent* 6 (1959): 189. On the formation of SANE and *Liberation* magazine, see Wittner, *Rebels Against War,* 237–47. It should be noted that *The Causes of World War III,* if read critically, is little more than *The Power Elite* simplified, combined with calls to political action and the formation of a peace movement. On the *Golden Rule,* see Isserman, *If I Had a Hammer,* 151–66.

Causes of World War III was published, for instance, Bayard Rustin had led an independent group of citizens to visit the USSR and plead for disarmament. Mills himself praised Cyrus Easton, a wealthy industrialist in Nova Scotia who invited intellectuals, politicians, and scientists from both the East and West to discuss peace issues. Easton himself went on to call for nuclear disarmament. Tongue in cheek, Mills chided his government: "The House Un-American Activities Committee has shrewdly seen through one multimillionaire's attempt to bring Russian agents—disguised as scientists—to a meeting at Pugwash, dangerously close to many of our Vital Centers." What Easton did, Mills believed, was to have citizens directly break their own country's laws, travel to meet the "enemy," and then try to solve pressing problems outside the influence of governments. Here was a radical and direct democratic program for the peace movement. And yet, the movement probably *still* had to change the elite's mind—even if it was an international elite.[47]

Mills's most basic aim was less ambitious than this, but no less radical within the context of the Cold War. He simply wanted to have the peace movement begin a democratic debate about American foreign policy and the centralization of military power. As Mills saw it, "There is no possible . . . combination of interests . . . that has anywhere near the time, the money, the manpower, to present a point of view on the issues . . . that can effectively compete with the views presented day in and day out by the warlords." The result was the reign of "military metaphysics—the cast of mind that defines international reality as basically military." Mills sometimes labeled planning for World War III "crackpot realism." What he meant by this term was "an outlook and a style of mind that is unfitted to apprehend reality, but which justifies its false and feeble views as reality itself." Since no nuclear war could really be seen as "winnable," the reasoning went, most military planning during the Cold War was absurd. Mills believed that the peace movement had to break the hold of "crackpot realism" on America's leaders. To do his part, Mills tried to construct an alternative vision for American foreign policy, one that he hoped the peace movement would adopt. Again, demonstrations without intellectual activity and the re-creation of a democratic public were not enough.[48]

47. C. Wright Mills and Saul Landau, "Modest Proposals for Patriotic Americans," *Tribune* (London), May 19, 1961, 5. On Rustin's activities, see Bayard Rustin, "To the Finland Station," *Liberation,* June 1958.

48. Mills, *The Power Elite,* 221, 222, and notes in "Crackpot Realism" folder, C. Wright Mills Papers, box 4B417.

For the most part, Mills followed William Appleman Williams's thinking on the Cold War. For that reason, I will not plumb Mills's thought here (for Williams, see Chap. 4). Mills agreed with his fellow New York Intellectuals that the Soviet Union was totalitarian. But in a debate with Irving Howe, Mills asserted, "I do not believe the Soviet system is absolutely evil." As he made clear, anticommunism had become a suffocating impediment to U.S. foreign policy and the capacity of leaders to assess whether to intervene in the world. Soviet communism—due to the totalitarian thesis—was conceived of as unchangeable, and Mills believed that this showed up containment's futility. Mills argued against a reliance upon NATO (and the Warsaw Pact) and called for America to support the United Nations. Though he believed that the USSR should not be trusted, he also argued that America's leaders were mostly to blame for the heated nature of the Cold War. Soviet communism needed to be accepted as "fact," and the only foreign policy option he outlined was coexistence.[49]

Changing foreign policy was only the beginning, as far as Mills was concerned. He believed that the critique made by the peace movement should lead to a thorough restructuring of domestic policy and decision making in the United States. To challenge the "Permanent War Economy"—a term he continued to use throughout his later writings on the Cold War—Mills proposed a "Permanent Peace Economy." He laid out his plans for such an economy in a crude set of notes: "(1) Take the boom out of war (2) our basic means of production—open *all* the books (3) approximate equality of incomes (4) approximate equality of the sexes (5) make war decisions democratic." Since the war machine relied upon private corporate production for weaponry, Mills argued for democratic socialism: "The privately incorporated economy must be made over into a publicly responsible economy. I am aware of the magnitude of the task, but either we take democracy seriously or we do not." He also called for the military to lessen its demands on scientific research and education. Since the military was "now the largest single supporter and director of scientific research," this would be no small feat. Indeed, Mills called for a "public Science machine, subject to public control." Unlike Dwight Macdonald during the heyday of *politics* magazine, Mills did not question

49. C. Wright Mills, "Intellectuals and Russia," *Dissent* 6 (1959): 297; "The Balance of Blame," 527; and *Causes of World War III*, 5. For evidence that Mills read Williams, see boxes 4B417 and 4B418 in the C. Wright Mills Papers. For Mills's comment that the USSR was totalitarian, see his "Mass Society and Liberal Education," 358. On Mills's call for the U.S. to support the UN and not NATO, see his "A Program for Peace," *The Nation*, December 7, 1957, 423.

science as a whole: rather, he critiqued its misapplications within a permanent war economy. Mills believed, essentially, that the peace movement's conclusions should introduce democratic socialism—with a real emphasis, of course, on a democratic public having sway in political judgment and being capable of "checking" the books and decisions of its leaders.[50]

The peace movement should also lead, Mills believed, to a reassessment of American foreign policy in the Third World (what he called the "hungry nation bloc"). For many Americans, this need was made explicit by the Cuban Revolution of 1959, in which Fidel Castro led a band of scroungy rebels and seized power away from the United States-supported Batista regime. In facing up to Cuba (which entailed a short visit there), Mills became a vociferous critic of U.S. foreign policy. In *Listen, Yankee,* he published his criticisms in a paperback pamphlet that sold four hundred thousand copies— more than any of his other books. For Mills, hysterical anticommunism— which had both economic and noneconomic motives—fueled the negative reaction on the part of the United States to the Cuban Revolution. In fact, Mills questioned the idea that imperialism sustained America's economic prosperity (after all, he pointed out, America was quite well-off *before* it expanded at the turn of the century). He argued that America's earlier support of the Batista regime gave rise to a moral responsibility to listen to what the revolutionaries were demanding. At one point, Mills, in an exceptional bit of nostalgia for the 1930s, compared the Cuban Revolution to the Spanish Civil War, the *cause célèbre* of radicals at that time. Unfortunately, his analogy did not work. The Cuban Revolution of 1959 was really akin to the Spanish-American War of 1898, especially as it related to Mills's own thinking.[51]

In writing on Cuba, Mills made clear his debt to another "pragmatic godfather," William James. During the Spanish-American War, James was a vocal critic of American imperial expansion in Cuba (and later in the Philippines). As a public intellectual who was inspired by older republican ideals, James argued that America's expansion and annexation of Cuba and the Philippines forced America to "puke up its ancient soul," that imperial con-

50. "Permanent Peace Economy" comments in typed MS entitled "What, Then, Ought We Do To [sic]?" in C. Wright Mills Papers, box 4B395. (Most likely, this was a speech Mills gave—something he did more and more during this time.) See also Mills, *Causes of World War III,* 120; *The Power Elite,* 216; and "A Program for Peace," 422.

51. Mills, *Listen, Yankee,* 7. For his critique of an economic interpretation of imperialism, see "On Latin America," 116–17. On four hundred thousand copies sold, see James Miller, "Democracy and the Intellectual," 95. For Mills's reference to the Spanish Civil War, see his comments in box 4B394, C. Wright Mills Papers: "Whether or not they know it, for the generation just coming to maturity, the revolution in Cuba is their 'Spanish Civil War.'"

quest was inimical to America's democratic values. As a philosopher and radical pluralist, he condemned the "blindness" of conquerors who went to foreign lands only to impose their will. James kept his discussion of the Cubans and Filipinos to a minimum. Instead, he aimed his criticisms at Americans who, he claimed, had forgotten their republican and democratic values in trying to build an empire.[52]

Though *Listen, Yankee* was written from the perspective of an invented Cuban persona, Mills, like James before him, reserved most of his invective for America. In doing so, he hoped to recuperate what James had called America's "ancient soul." Mills wrote, "Cuba—listen, Yankee—Cuba is your big chance. It's your chance to establish once again what the United States perhaps once did mean to the world." Complicit with the Batista regime, America now had to transcend its collective blindness and listen to the voices of the revolutionaries. That this was not happening made Mills fume. At one point, Mills called JFK's attempt to reseize power in Cuba—culminating in the infamous Bay of Pigs invasion—the behavior of a "spoiled child." One of his demands was for American corporations to pull out of Cuba (due to their earlier complicity in turning it into a sugar-producing colony) and for the U.S. government to give humanitarian aid with no strings attached. If it did not, Mills argued, America would simply "force" Cuba into the arms of the Soviet Union, and a great opportunity would be missed. In *Listen, Yankee,* Mills wrote a jeremiad—a wake-up call for America to be great again simply by *listening* to those who at first appeared to be its enemies. (The title of the book itself carried its major political suggestion.) He thus became what Saul Landau, a young graduate student who traveled with Mills in Cuba, called "a pamphleteer, the Tom Paine of the New Left." In Mills's work, Paine's legacy joined that of William James.[53]

Mills went one step further than James, though, and actually embraced—and tried to speak in the voice of—the revolutionaries. He literally merged his voice with that of the Cuban rebel. As he explained in the introduction to *Listen, Yankee,* "My major aim in this book is to present the voice of the Cuban

52. See, for instance, William James, "On a Certain Blindness in Human Beings," in *The Writings of William James,* ed. John McDermott (Chicago: University of Chicago Press, 1977). See also George Cotkin, *William James, Public Philosopher* (Baltimore: Johns Hopkins University Press, 1990). That Mills was aware of James's example is clear from his *Sociology and Pragmatism.* See the interesting remarks by Irving Louis Horowitz on the parallels between Mills and James in his introduction to *Sociology and Pragmatism,* 11–12.

53. Mills, *Listen, Yankee,* 149; Mills's comment on Kennedy in the C. Wright Mills Papers, box 4B421; Saul Landau in *History and the New Left,* ed. Buhle, 112.

revolutionary, as clearly and emphatically as I can." The desire to understand the revolutionary was noble, but Mills did something more here. He lost sight of his own conception of a critical intellectual, distant from any direct institutional loyalty with those in power (revolutionary or otherwise). The desire to merge his voice with that of the Cuban revolutionaries trapped Mills, leading him to project his own political thinking on a set of actors who were quite different from him. Mills lost the critical distance central to his own self-conception and his belief in the role of the intellectual.[54]

To say that Mills romanticized the Cuban revolution is an understatement. At times, he stopped being a critical intellectual and became a sycophant. In *Listen, Yankee,* he wrote, for instance, "Now we feel so strong, we feel so free, we feel so new." The exaltation of feelings was exactly what went wrong in *Listen, Yankee.* Mills replaced Enlightenment rationality with revolutionary fervor. In doing so, he lost critical distance; exuberance displaced reason. Sounding like a Jacobin during the French Revolution, Mills wrote, "Revolution is a way of defining realities." In the next breath, he justified "the dictatorship of workers and peasants." Though his claim that social justice might have to trump democracy under certain conditions seemed defensible, here Mills crossed a line and supported not just dictatorship but also the idea that revolutionaries constituted their own reality and hence could not be contested on rational grounds. His criticism of America's democratic values was replaced by a romantic vision of dictatorship.[55]

At the same time, Mills projected his autobiographical details onto the Cuban revolutionaries, forcing his own ideas upon them. He did this by placing them within his developing conception of a "new left." For Mills, "young intellectuals" made the Cuban Revolution happen. The fact that

54. Mills, *Listen, Yankee,* 8. It is interesting to note that other left-leaning thinkers *were* critical of the Cuban Revolution's authoritarian tendencies from an earlier point. This became evident in the pages of *Liberation* magazine. One editor, Roy Finch, blamed both Cuban authoritarianism and America's aggressive policy in his "Interview with Cuban Libertarians," *Liberation,* March 1961, 9. This brought Finch into debate with Dave Dellinger, an editor much more partial to Castro. In fact, it eventually led to Finch's resignation: see Roy Finch, "Cuba and Liberation: An Editor Resigns," *Liberation,* May 1961, 3–5. This point is especially important, since, as is clear from clippings in his archives, Mills definitely read *Liberation.* It also makes clear that there was dissent on the left about the Cuban Revolution. See, on this general point, Van Gosse, *Where the Boys Are: Cuba, Cold War America, and the Making of a New Left* (New York: Verso, 1993).

55. Mills, *Listen, Yankee,* 118, 18, 119. At other points in the book, Mills recognizes the possibility of "dictatorial tyranny" in Cuba, but downplays it: see 179, for instance.

someone like Fidel was a young, educated intellectual who happened to have read *The Power Elite* was an empirical fact. But Mills quickly started to revise the Cuban revolutionaries' story. He argued that these Cubans had not lived through Stalinism. True as this was, Mills suddenly made Fidel Castro and others sound as if they were a part of his own orbit—the disgruntled sons of the "New York Family." Mills contrasted the Cuban revolutionaries with "those ex-radicals who at least verbally cling to socialist kind of ideals, but when you get down to it, do not dare get their hands dirty and refuse to confront the real issues and the terrible problems that every revolution in the hungry world" faces. Cuban revolutionaries suddenly sounded less like guerrilla warriors and more like students booted out of a seminar run by Daniel Bell, where they happened to read Max Weber's ruminations on the ethic of responsibility. Mills also assumed that his own projections would make his visions come true. Describing the Cuban revolutionary as "neither capitalist nor communist" and as a "socialist . . . , both practical and humane," Mills made them seem a bit more than they were. No wonder he would argue that Cubans could get resources from the Soviet Union without strings attached—a superhuman feat indeed. When his friends pressed that Cuba was becoming something of a pawn of the Soviet Union, Mills wrote, "Please know that I too see a lot of 'unpleasantness' in the Cuban possibilities—but most of them, I think are being brought on by US action and inaction." Needless to say, Mills's projections about an independent form of socialism dawning in Cuba faltered; the pressures of the Cold War were simply too strong. History did not serve Mills well on this count.[56]

Why did Mills err? To a large extent, the answer was a combination of ignorance and wishful projection. In turning to Cuba for answers to his own political concerns, Mills spent only two weeks there, traveling maniacally and then cramming the notes he took quickly into *Listen, Yankee*. He faced a culture very different from his own, in which he hoped to find foot soldiers for his own version of the new left. Unlike William James, he felt comfortable speaking for those he did not really know all that well. This was partly due to Mills's sense that he had to move quickly: by 1960, he faced worsening heart problems, ones that would kill him two years later; moreover, Cuba was being forced into the orbit of the USSR. As he described his life in 1960, it seemed marked by "too much fast writing, too many decisions of moral and intellectual types made too fast, on too little evidence." E. P.

---

56. *Listen, Yankee,* 43, 149, 181–82, 90–92; Mills to Frank Freidel, October 31, 1960, in *C. Wright Mills: Letters and Autobiographical Writings,* ed. Kate Mills, 319.

Thompson correctly described Mills as a "moody, deeply-committed, and in his last years, impatient man." Saul Landau, who traveled with Mills at the end of his life, called him "desperate." In searching for a vision of political change, Mills was simply too quick to see what he hoped to see. *Listen, Yankee* therefore became something of a detour before arriving at a more sound judgment about the New Left in First World countries.[57]

Mills was, of course, better at speaking about things he actually knew. And what he knew best was America and other First World countries. As has been made clear, some of Mills's best thinking about a New Left came from the early protest movements in America. But it also came from his encounter with the New Left in Britain. In England, Mills met people who spoke his language, literally and figuratively. In many ways, the intellectual leaders of the New Left in England—E. P. Thompson, Ralph Miliband, and Stuart Hall—made Mills aware of how far the American New Left would have to travel in terms of developing radical programs and ideas. These thinkers elaborated both their differences from and similarities to Mills, which helped him consider more carefully the context in which the New Left would have to operate. For instance, Stuart Hall wrote Mills, "I am, like you, without a 'past' in the CP." In the same letter, though, Hall argued that England had escaped the suffocating atmosphere of McCarthyism and anti-communist hysteria. Mills admitted that the European New Left, especially England's, was far ahead of the United States, in large part due to the reasons Hall had stated. With its freedom from the Cold War stalemate, England had developed a much stronger peace movement and public debate surrounding nuclear weapons than America had. It also had a stronger tradition of human-ist socialism—one that paid a heavy debt to the liberalism of thinkers like Hobhouse. And during the 1950s, younger intellectuals were trying to com-bine this tradition with participatory democracy, connecting it with guild socialism and radical adult education. Mills realized that he had something to learn from England (indeed, he thought at one point of moving there perma-nently). And unlike his experience with Cuba, he would not have to jettison his own intellectual traditions to do this. When he decided to return to the United States after staying in Europe for some time, he explained that "my argument lies in America and has to be worked out there." Mills was com-

57. Mills to E. P. Thompson, Fall 1960, in *C. Wright Mills: Letters and Autobiographical Writings,* ed. Kate Mills, 320; E. P. Thompson, "C. Wright Mills: The Responsible Crafts-man," *Radical America* (July–August 1979): 63 (originally published in 1963); Saul Landau, "C. Wright Mills—The Last Six Months," *Root and Branch,* no. 2 (1963–64): 15.

mitted to being what Michael Walzer calls a "connected critic," one who spoke to his nation's fellow citizens in meaningful ways.[58]

While in England from 1956–57 and 1960–61, Mills started formulating his idea of the New Left more thoroughly than he had ever done before. Unfortunately, he died before he was able to develop his vision to the fullest extent. In dialogue with E. P. Thompson, he started making connections between his 1940s thinking about the intellectual's role in political change with his contemporary hopes for a New Left. Here we find the culmination of Mills's political thought as it related both to his social theory and to his understanding of how things were developing in First World countries.

The Role of the Intellectual in the New Left

We cannot fail to smash our own little routines and become political in the larger manner that integrates political consciousness with everyday life and into the very style with which we live ourselves out. But we do not seem able to take the initiative. The very way in which we live has whittled away our capacity for exasperation. We have become tired before we have done anything and before anything was done to us by an enemy we could make explicit. We've never really declared war as a truly American left. There is no American left.

—C. Wright Mills, quoted in Irving Louis Horowitz, "The Unfinished Writings of C. Wright Mills: The Last Phase," 1963

Mills never believed that a New Left would be entirely new. There would be carryover from previous traditions, including liberal and socialist ideals. Mills took up what Dwight Macdonald had once developed in the pages of *politics,* as well as what some Eastern European intellectuals and his British colleagues argued for—namely, the sort of humanitarian socialism that resisted mechanical Marxism and, of course, Stalinism. Here is how he defined his own political vision, when asked what "the causes" of the present should be:

58. Stuart Hall to C. Wright Mills, June 3, 1960, C. Wright Mills Papers, box 4B388; C. Wright Mills to his parents, October 17, 1961, in *C. Wright Mills: Letters and Autobiographical Writings,* ed. Kate Mills, 338. Mills's admission that Europe was ahead of America in terms of developing a New Left can be already found in his "La Gauche Americaine: Savoir Attendre," *Esprit,* November 1952, 693. On the Cold War's lesser impact on Britain, see Mills, "The Balance of Blame," 526. On the British New Left, I rely upon Michael Kenny, *The First New Left: British Intellectuals After Stalin* (London: Lawrence and Wishart, 1995); Paul Jacobs and Saul Landau, *The New Radicals* (New York: Random House, 1966), 9; Lin Chun, *The British New Left* (Edinburgh: Edinburgh University Press, 1993); and Kate Soper, "Socialist Humanism," in *E. P. Thompson: Critical Perspectives,* ed. Harvey Kaye and Keith McClelland (Philadelphia: Temple University Press, 1990).

"'The causes' are what they've been since the 18th century: to make men free, to master history, to abolish war, to improve the quality of everyday life, to abolish the poverty of 2/3rds of mankind, to make the everyday life of ordinary men and women everywhere a work of art, to heighten the level of moral sensibility." There was very little new about this pronouncement. Nor was there much new about his calls to strengthen government—particularly the "legislative bodies"—in order to "investigate the corporate, the military, the political bureaucracies." What Mills meant by a "left" was also not that different from what Eugene Debs or Norman Thomas might have envisioned. For Mills, the left grew out of "structural criticism and reportage and theories of society" capable of making political "demands." Mills's New Left sounded, at times, quite old.[59]

Where Mills added something new to the picture was not in radical democracy (in certain ways, Eugene Debs had articulated this belief earlier), but in his conception of the intellectual's role in political change. Mills modified his political thinking over the years, especially on labor, but his interest in the intellectual remained a constant. As we have seen, Mills wrote a piece for *politics* in 1944, in which he asserted, "The independent artist and intellectual are among the few remaining personalities equipped to resist and to fight the stereotyping and consequent death of genuinely lively things." Though the artist would drop out of this sentiment by the late 1950s, the intellectual would only continue to grow in significance. As Mills explained in a piece written close to his death: "It has been said in criticism that I am too much fascinated by power. This is not really true. It is intellect I have been most fascinated by, and power primarily in connection with that." While Mills dismissed the idea that labor would be an effective agent for historical change, he still showed interest in the concept of agency itself. Indeed, he called "the problem of the historical agency of change . . . the most important issue of political reflection." At times, Mills simply put intellectuals in the place where, for Marxists, labor was, in a hurried gesture of providing agency to his own political theory.[60]

Of course, when placed within the context of radicalism, this could sound like Bolshevism's theory of intellectuals serving as the vanguard. Even

59. C. Wright Mills, typed MS, C. Wright Mills Papers, box 4B395; *Causes of World War III*, 143; and "The New Left," 253.

60. Mills, "The Social Role of the Intellectual" (originally published as "The Powerless People"), 299; quoted in Irving Louis Horowitz, "The Unfinished Writings of C. Wright Mills: The Last Phase," *Studies on the Left* 3 (1963): 17; and "The New Left," 254–55. On Debs's belief in radical democracy, see Nick Salvatore, *Eugene Debs: Citizen and Socialist* (Urbana: University of Illinois Press, 1982), 259.

an ally like Saul Landau suggested this to Mills. If we place Mills within the liberal and pragmatic tradition, his thinking paralleled that of William James, who believed in the "college bred" as the leaders of reform (an idea that Mills discussed in his dissertation). Fortunately, Mills corrected for these elitist or vanguardist tendencies in his thought. He balanced his call for intellectual engagement with a serious understanding of the limits of intellectuals. Here I will quote Mills at length (in part because this quotation was later picked up by Arnold Kaufman):

> If he is to think politically in a realistic way, the intellectual must constantly know his social position. This is necessary in order that he may be aware of the sphere of strategy that is really open to his influence. If he forgets this, his thinking may exceed his sphere of strategy so far as to make impossible any translation of his thought into action, his own or that of others. His thought may thus become fantastic. If he remembers his powerlessness too well, assumes that his sphere of strategy is restricted to the point of impotence, then his thought may easily become politically trivial.

Picking up on Weber's thinking about the "ethic of responsibility" versus the "ethic of ultimate ends," Mills also argued that intellectuals always had to balance "detachment" (the pursuit of "truth") with political engagement (the pursuit of effective impact). While these statements were made for his article in *politics* (1944), he still echoed them in 1955 when he called for the intellectual to practice "the politics of truth" and to serve as the "moral conscience of his society." As he put it in 1959, "To transcend by their understanding a variety of everyday milieux, but not be able to modify, to change the structural forces that are at work within and upon these milieux; to sit in judgment, but not to have power to enforce judgment; to demand but not be able to back up their demands—that is the general position of most political intellectuals, at least of the Western societies today." This sentiment, with its peculiar balance of detachment and engagement, remained with Mills until his death.[61]

Perhaps the way Mills made his balancing act clearest was in his apprecia-

61. Saul Landau in a conversation with Mills reported in his "C. Wright Mills—The Last Six Months," 10. C. Wright Mills: *Sociology and Pragmatism,* 264; "The Social Role of the Intellectual," 300–301; "On Knowledge and Power," 611; and "To Tovarich" (1959), in *C. Wright Mills: Letters and Autobiographical Writings,* ed. Kate Mills, 276.

tion of Veblen's "Wobbly" and "masterless" qualities. Mills never suggested that intellectuals should actually assume positions of power or even give advice to those who held power. For Mills, the idea of a "philosopher-king" was "rather foolish." Critical independence—the "politics of truth"—was necessary for intellectuals to practice their craft and retain critical insights on the way in which power was abused. When intellectuals forgot this and groveled at the feet of power, they ignored what their real role was: "The man of knowledge has not become a philosopher king; but he has often become a consultant, and moreover a consultant to a man who is neither king-like nor philosophical." On the other hand—and here was the balancing act playing itself out—intellectuals should *not* pull back from political engagement due to the corruption of power. There was an alternative to this either-or scenario of assuming power or withdrawing, as Mills saw it, and that was "to remain independent, to do one's own work, to select one's own problems, but to direct this work *at* kings as well as *to* 'publics.'" Again, the power elite could be persuaded, but only through the active deliberation of a critical public.[62]

It was precisely Mills's central idea of the democratic public that decentered the intellectual from any vanguard role. Mills explained the major task of the intellectual: "What he ought to do for the society is to combat all those forces which are destroying genuine publics and creating a mass society—or put as a positive goal, his aim is to help build and to strengthen self-cultivating publics." In order to accomplish this enormous task, intellectuals should educate their fellow citizens—in adult schools and elsewhere—and expose the powerful through muckraking (the sort that Mills did in *The Power Elite*). They should also write pamphlets on the topics of the day. In doing this, they would, of course, work with other citizens and share their ideas through democratic means of deliberation. By helping build "self-cultivating publics"—and the term self-cultivating is crucial here—intellectuals saw their role within a democratic process of education. This was no vanguardism or Jamesian elitism.[63]

---

62. See Mills's introduction to the Mentor edition of Thorstein Veblen's *Theory of the Leisure Class,* ix, and *Sociological Imagination,* 180, 181. It is interesting to note that against Mills's own wishes, a friend actually suggested his name to the Kennedy administration as an adviser. See the letter from Nicholas Holt to Mills, July 20, 1960, C. Wright Mills Papers, box 4B389. Clearly nothing came of this—as if Mills would join Schlesinger!—but unfortunately, I could not find out whether Mills had responded to Holt's query.

63. Mills, *Sociological Imagination,* 186. Some of these themes are explored in Christopher Lasch, "A Typology of Intellectuals," *Salmagundi* 70–71 (1986): 105.

For Mills, though, the question remained: why were intellectuals not acting in the way he thought they should? The first reason was historical. After the "fashionable Marxism" of the 1930s disappeared off the radar screen of intellectual life in America, writers and thinkers—including Mills's colleagues—had become increasingly conservative. After being incorporated into government during World War II, thinkers during the 1940s embraced a "tragic" view of life that simply justified their "political failure of nerve." Then, by the 1950s, they had become ensconced in organizations like the Congress for Cultural Freedom—as Dwight Macdonald's own career testified. They became cowed by McCarthyism. They also articulated their own arguments for ending debate, hiding behind slogans like "the end of ideology" that bolstered what Mills called their "complacency." All of this was self-willed passivity. He wrote about his fellow New York Intellectuals: "Nobody locks them up. Nobody has to. They are locking themselves up—the shrill and angry ones in the totality of their own parochial anger."[64]

Self-willed marginality, though, could not account for the entire picture. After all, the New York Intellectuals were a mere subset within American intellectual life, and they were typically older. What about the younger generation? Though Mills had hope for younger intellectuals, he noticed, in England, that certain countercultural tendencies became diversionary for many young thinkers. Following the lead of his New Left colleagues, Mills focused his critical sights on a group of writers known as the "Angry Young Men." Leading this group was John Osborne, author of *Look Back in Anger*, whose main character, Jimmy Porter, expresses rage at a lack of "causes" in his life and then proceeds to take his alienation out on his timid wife. The audience for this famous play was expected to take Porter as a rebel (a more literary rebel than James Dean in *Rebel Without a Cause*). But cultural rebellion and its sneering sort of anger, for Mills, was not radical at all. Here we begin to see the difference between the New Left and cultural rebellion, a difference that would be better developed in Paul Goodman's critique of the Beats and Arnold Kaufman's and William Appleman Williams's critique of youthful countercultures of the late 1960s. Mills argued, "Personal radicalism

64. Mills: *White Collar*, 146; "The Social Role of the Intellectual," 294; "The New Left," 247; *Causes of World War III*, 127. Mills's understanding of the "tragic sense of life" was quite limited. He failed to comprehend the ancient and Christian underpinnings of this idea, simply dismissing it as a form of apolitical cynicism. This might have partially explained the concept, but it tended toward reductionism. For more on the intellectuals' relation to McCarthyism, see Pells, *Liberal Mind*, chapter 5. On page 345, Pells himself uses the expression "self-censorship," showing the impact and legacy of Mills's own thinking on historians.

ought to be imputed to political frustration." There was very little that was radical about this sort of personal anger, because it never truly challenged political or social institutions. The resulting "complacency of the literary young" mirrored the withdrawal of "old Futilitarians" such as Daniel Bell.[65]

Mills added to these cultural problems a very serious institutional one. The central culprit here was the "cultural apparatus." This was composed of "the organizations and milieux in which artistic, intellectual, and scientific work goes on, and of the means by which such work is made available to circles, publics, and masses." Thus, the cultural apparatus could be described as the means by which information is "produced and distributed . . . and consumed." Mills explained, "It contains an elaborate set of institutions: of schools and theaters, newspapers and census bureaus, studios, laboratories, museums, little magazines, radio networks." Mills's thinking on the cultural apparatus was central to his idea of the New Left. As he explained in a 1961 interview, just one year before his death, "My own idea of a New Left (which I am now trying to develop, but which I have not gotten straight) to replace the old Left, which has collapsed or become ambiguous, is going to center, first of all, upon the cultural apparatus and the intellectuals within it." By understanding his idea of the cultural apparatus, we better understand Mills's final arguments about a New Left.[66]

Mills situated intellectuals within the broader rubric of white-collar workers and, therefore, described their social experience as one of proletarianization. In *White Collar*, Mills explained that "the means of effective communication are being expropriated from the intellectual worker." Or as he put it in a later essay on "The Cultural Apparatus": "The cultural workman has little control over the means of distribution of which he becomes a part." Mills's portrayal of American intellectual life in this case paralleled his other arguments about the transition from eighteenth- to twentieth-century America. As small shops became large corporations, as citizen armies became military monoliths, as town meetings turned into political bureaucracies, so intellectual life shifted from "the world of pamphleteering open

---

65. C. Wright Mills, "The Complacent Young Men" (1958), in *Power, Politics, and People,* 388, and "The Decline of the Left," 225. For an overview of the "Angry Young Men" phenomenon, see Kenneth Allsop, *The Angry Decade: A Survey of the Cultural Revolt of the 1950s* (New York: British Book Centre, 1958), and the collection of writings found in *The Beat Generation and the Angry Young Men,* edited by Gene Feldman and Max Gartenberg (New York: Citadel, 1958).

66. Mills, "The Cultural Apparatus" (1958), in *Power, Politics, and People,* 406, and "On Latin America," 122.

to a Tom Paine" to "the world of radio and motion pictures." Modernity proletarianized its cultural workers. Hollywood encouraged "ghost writing," and the same book system that produced "best sellers" also produced an army of "hacks and failures." Even the supposedly pristine world of academia threatened to constrict intellectual life. As early as 1942, Mills recognized that the academic was "a salaried employee in a semi-bureaucratic organization." Being members of a bureaucracy limited the independence of intellectual workers, especially as it encouraged small-minded specialization. As Mills explained, "Others who own and operate the mass media stand between us [intellectuals] and our potential publics." Essentially, the cultural apparatus prevented intellectuals from helping create "self-cultivating publics"—and, hence, it challenged Mills's hope for a New Left.[67]

Mills had personal experience with intellectual proletarianization. He always felt that Columbia University never gave him the support he deserved. His private papers include numerous exchanges between him and the deans at Columbia, letters in which he complained about feeling alienated from the institution. Mills's experience with publishers produced the same sort of animosity. At one point, he wrote Dwight Macdonald that he felt like "a slave to Prentice Hall." And in the same piece where he described himself as a "modern novelist," Mills admitted that because he was unwilling to bend on many issues related to the cultural apparatus, his work was meant for "intimate publics, especially today when the mass public is exploited and ruined by the competition of debasing products of the mind." Or, as he put it when he was in even a darker mood, working on *The Power Elite,* "And nobody but friends will read [the book] anyway. They'll just ignore it." For Mills personally, the cultural apparatus produced despair by reducing and cutting him off from his public of fellow readers and citizens.[68]

67. C. Wright Mills: *White Collar,* 152; "The Cultural Apparatus," 418; "Mass Media and Public Opinion," 578; *White Collar,* 150–51; review of *The Academic Man,* by Logan Wilson, *American Sociological Review* 7 (1942): 445; *White Collar,* 130–31; "The Cultural Apparatus," 419.

68. Mills to Dwight Macdonald, October 1944, Dwight Macdonald Papers, C. Wright Mills folder; Mills in C. Wright Mills Papers, box 4B373; C. Wright Mills to Ken Stampp, undated, C. Wright Mills Papers, box 4B411. One of the few places that at least entertained providing Mills with support was the Center for the Study of Democratic Institutions, hosted by Robert Hutchins's liberal Fund for the Republic. Much of this is captured in Mills's favorable correspondence with Hallock Hoffman in the C. Wright Mills Papers. For more on this institution's important role during the Cold War, see Frank Kelly, *Court of Reason: Robert Hutchins and the Fund for the Republic* (New York: Free, 1981). On Columbia's lack of support, see, for instance, Mills's letter to Jacques Barzun (then a dean at Columbia), September 28, 1959, in which he complains about insufficient help.

The only response that Mills could formulate to this gloomy scenario was for intellectuals to reappropriate the cultural apparatus. Intellectuals, Mills argued, should "use" the means of the cultural apparatus "as we think they ought to be used." Mills spoke like a true republican workman, unwilling to accept any terms but his own. He counseled, "We should write and speak for these media on our own terms or not at all." Mills doled out the same advice to professors in academia: "I grow weary of complaining professors in America who allow themselves to be exploited—turned into tired and routine people, or into effective entertainers—rather than demand that staffs be enlarged sufficiently to enable men and women to be properly educated, and educators to control the serious work they have to do." To explain the reasoning behind his call to cultural independence, Mills used the principle of "craftsmanship" as it applied to intellectual production (the term itself was most fully developed and used earlier by Thorstein Veblen). The independent craftsperson—a fixture in republican political thinking—produced things independently, finding pride in that sort of working environment. Mills described "craftsmanship" as "the central experience of the unalienated human being and the very root of free human development." Essentially, by writing and speaking on their own terms and as craftspeople, intellectuals could, through their own actions, show what sort of society they wanted in the future.[69]

In considering this political vision, E. P. Thompson posed some very tough questions for Mills. He asked him just how intellectuals were supposed to reappropriate the cultural apparatus. Thompson queried, "In what sense have they ever possessed it?" Mills's response would have been Tom Paine and pamphleteering, even though Mills's own pamphleteering had been done through a mass media company. But Thompson's toughest question went to the heart of Mills's vision. He wrote, "You advise intellectuals to 'write and speak for these media on their own terms or not at all.' O.K. Supposing the answer of those who control the media is 'not at all'? What then? Are there not enough of John Adams' 'bad men' to fill the gaps?" Admitting the weakness of his own position, Mills wrote in the margins of this letter from Thompson: "Yes, we can only embarrass them," meaning

69. Mills, *Causes of World War III*, 141; MS (probably a speech), C. Wright Mills Papers, box 4B395; and "Man in the Middle: The Designer" (1958), in *Power, Politics, and People*, 386. Mills's comments about academia lead naturally, or so it seems, to the views of many in the contemporary academic labor movement. For more on this movement, see my "New Year, New Organizing Efforts on Campuses," *The Nation*, October 5, 1998, and "The Academic Labor Movement: Understanding Its Origins and Current Challenges," *Social Policy* (Summer 2000): 4–10, as well as the essays that follow.

those "bad men" Thompson mentioned. This was not exactly a position that suggested strength; rather, reaction to the mass media might very well not reach any significant audience. Finally, Thompson asked Mills, "How are we to fight our ideas out of the universities? How are we to prevent our books and journals from becoming means of communication within a closed circuit, isolated minority speaking to isolated minority?" On this point, Mills drew a blank. After all, he admitted that his own work only reached "intimate publics." How would New Left intellectuals ensure that their ideas were not simply marginalized? Or to pose the question differently, why would Mills have any hope in New Left intellectuals accomplishing anything of major impact?[70]

Perhaps Mills had hope in intellectuals for the same reason that he thought primary publics had not been entirely destroyed in America. Intellectuals might be able to participate in the discussions already occurring within primary publics. But most of Mills's arguments on these counts actually wound up being less sociological and empirical in nature, more idealistic and wishful. He coaxed his fellow intellectuals into understanding that they were "free to decide what they will or will not do in their working life." At times he almost seemed to berate his younger cohorts: "There's no public, no movement to address your ideas to? How do you know? What ideas? First off, be your own public, let others listen who will listen in." The only thing that Mills could counsel those who argued that the institutions were stacked against them was that they needed to act *as if* there was a receptive public available. Here again was the lasting debt Mills paid to Macdonald—delivering an almost absurdist call to political action in the face of a hostile social system. As he saw it, there was nothing to do but hope.[71]

Conclusion

A man should follow a plow or lay a woman or ride a motorcycle at speed or live in a darkroom or lay in the sun or even talk a little. But he ought not to write. It is too hard. It is too revealing. It takes too much will. The reason you do it, of course, is that you want reasons for your anger and because you have no other means of power at your disposal.

—C. Wright Mills to "John," June 10, 1955

70. E. P. Thompson to Mills, April 21 (probably 1959), C. Wright Mills Papers, box 4B395. I would like to thank John Summers for bringing this letter to my attention again.

71. Mills, "The Decline of the Left," 231; typed MS on "angry young men," C. Wright Mills Papers, box 4B395; and *Causes of World War III*, 93.

One of the major inheritances Mills received from Macdonald was an intellectual schizophrenia. Both thinkers tended to draw up a gloomy social and political scenario and then counsel radical political action. Robert Westbrook described Macdonald's social thought as marked by a "tension between his hopes for a revival of responsibility and his dark view of the way the world was tending." The same could be said for Mills's political vision for the New Left. Mills's social criticism was indeed quite depressing. In America, he saw passive white-collar employees and a power elite with little accountability. He described America as a society of "cheerful robots"; its politics was "bureaucratized" and marked by "mass indifference." Worse yet, citizens in the "overdeveloped society" were "idiots." Though he never painted American society as completely "one-dimensional," Mills certainly saw that even critics could be incorporated into its institutions. As he explained in a letter to a friend, "What can we do in a society that loves criticism as well as applause? What can we do in a society that is so big and soft everything is just absorbed and melted into its folds?" And yet this same pessimist believed that younger intellectuals might be able to reappropriate the cultural apparatus, create "self-cultivating" publics, and thereby confront issues of war and inequality.[72]

Mills really had no grounds for calling on young intellectuals to act as if a public was available. His own sociological analysis told him otherwise. The only thing he really had—as an example of what he wanted all intellectuals to do—was his own life. He resisted the mindless careerism of academia (though was even guilty of some of this himself). He wrote pamphlets for a wide audience. He spoke and wrote on his own terms about political issues that mattered to him. He even considered leaving Columbia University altogether to do this. And ultimately, Mills's commitment killed him. In 1960, he accepted a televised debate with Adolf Berle, a famous liberal who served the Kennedy administration and its efforts in Cuba. In a letter to Irving Louis Horowitz, Mills expressed his own sense of responsibility to speak out, his deep pessimism about the potential of reappropriating the cultural apparatus, and how all of this wore him down: "I work now, nervously I suppose, for the Dec. 10th NBC dbate [sic] with AA Berle on Cuba. I hate such things; they can only be circuses, not enlightenment. . . . But I've got to do this if only because there is nobody else to do it." Mills's preparation for this

---

72. Westbrook, "The Responsibility of Peoples," 60. See also C. Wright Mills: *Causes of World War III*, 148; *White Collar*, 350; *Sociological Imagination*, 41; letter to "John," June 10, 1955, C. Wright Mills Papers, box 4B367.

debate led to a heart attack that would impair him for the rest of his life; he died in March 1962.[73]

As can be seen, Mills left behind a tough model of an engaged intellectual committed to repairing a fractured democratic public. He knew that his model did not encourage a great deal of hope: "If this—the politics of truth—is merely a holding action, so be it. It if is also a politics of desperation, so be it. To me it is the act of a free man who rejects 'fate'; it is an affirmation of one's self as a moral and intellectual center of responsible decision." But in addition to this difficulty, Mills also left behind other legacies for future New Left intellectuals. He showed how intellectuals could resist a pervasive conservative "drift." Against the Old Left, he showed that class exploitation in and of itself would not be sufficient to galvanize a new left within a changing historical context. Though he adopted European social theory, Mills also made clear that there were indigenous sources of radical thought in America—republican political theory, Thorstein Veblen, and even, at times, John Dewey and liberalism. He was not always certain whether liberalism needed to be transcended or could be built upon, and he suggested both things at once. At the least, liberalism bequeathed to the New Left the central idea of the American nation itself—democracy. Mills made democracy into something more than rhetoric. He showed the need for public deliberation and for intellectuals—in dialogue with regular citizens and social movements—to play a role in this process. This was the heart of his idea of a New Left.[74]

Mills left all these themes and arguments to later thinkers. As the pragmatists were for him, Mills became a "godfather" to the intellectuals who followed. No wonder younger thinkers, such as Arnold Kaufman and Tom Hayden, drew inspiration from him. But as should be clear, they inherited tensions from him as well. Mills certainly left a living legacy. We will see this legacy act itself out in the following pages—demonstrating its strengths and its weaknesses. New Left intellectuals seemed destined to build upon both.

73. Wright Mills to Irving Louis Horowitz, October 30, 1960, C. Wright Mills Papers, 4B390. Guy Oakes and Arthur Vidich discuss (rather mean-spiritedly) Mills's supposed lack of academic ethics and his egotistical careerism in their *Collaboration, Reputation, and Ethics.*

74. Mills, "To Tovarich," 295.

3

Paul Goodman, Anarchist Reformer: The Politics of Decentralization

Writers' words commit them, marshal their feelings, put them on the spot.
—Paul Goodman, "An Apology for Literature," 1971

The authentic democrat does not persuade people to his proposition but helps them formulate and realize their own propositions.
—Paul Goodman, *Five Years: Thoughts During a Useless Time,* 1966

In the last year of World War II, readers of *politics* witnessed C. Wright Mills exchange tough words with Paul Goodman. The matter at hand was the relationship between psychological theory and radical politics. In the context of a history of New Left intellectuals, the debate made clear the range of approaches and styles of thinking available to progressives. Before examining it, though, we should note just how many ideas Mills and Goodman shared. Their commonly held beliefs mattered far more than their differences. Setting these two thinkers side by side, we get a better sense of how there was something of a shared inheritance and emerging *Weltanschauung*—a common worldview—developing during the 1940s and 1950s among certain thinkers on the left.[1]

Goodman and Mills drew upon many of the same intellectual traditions. In the first place, both thinkers were Western rationalists and children of the Enlightenment. One of Paul Goodman's favorite essays, in fact, was Immanuel Kant's "What Is Enlightenment?" Here, Kant defined his central moral and political concept—autonomy—as the ability of humans to arise out of "self-imposed tutelage" and impose their own laws. As Kant explained in his writing on moral philosophy (which Goodman certainly read as an undergraduate or graduate student), "Autonomy . . . is the basis of dignity of human and of every rational nature." In defining his own variety of anarchist political theory, Goodman borrowed from Kant's moral and po-

1. I am not arguing here that Goodman directly influenced Mills or vice versa. I am simply pointing out commonalities in their thought.

litical thinking: "The chief principle of anarchism is not freedom but autonomy, the ability to initiate a task and do it one's own way." Goodman had
already articulated his debt to Enlightenment thinkers when he set out his
own core beliefs against certain libertarian, avant-garde writers. Sounding
like Mills, he claimed that he had "not given up on . . . vocation [i.e.,
purposeful work], rational politics, . . . the culture of the Western world," as
others had. These beliefs oriented Goodman's thinking from the 1940s until
his death. As he explained in an editorial letter at the end of his life, "I
regard myself as a loyal son of the Enlightenment."[2]

Goodman was as loyal as Mills was to a more specific intellectual tradition: pragmatism. Both thinkers shared a faith in core American values—the
sort expressed in Walt Whitman's poetry and John Dewey's philosophy.
Goodman praised "good humor" and the "classless and democratic" values
that had arisen out of the "frontier" culture of the eighteenth and nineteenth centuries, values that many Americans (Mills certainly included) still
shared in his own time. In everyday life, Goodman was a democrat: "I
address everybody with the same familiarity, disregarding their assumptions
and presumptions." This sort of experimental life, which did not necessarily
win Goodman friends, led him to sympathize with Dewey's philosophy. He
wrote (in prose that almost mimicked Dewey's), "It was the genius of American pragmatism, our great contribution to world philosophy, to show that
the means define and color the ends, . . . to make consummation less isolated, more in-process formed, to be growth as well as good." In the same
breath, though, Goodman—just like Bourne, Macdonald, and Mills—expressed how "melancholy" it was "to consider the fate of John Dewey's
instrumentalism." Goodman would never question the central philosophical
teachings of pragmatism—for instance, in his own words, that "truth is not
the description of a state of things but the orientation of an ongoing activity." Rather, he would point out pragmatism's misappropriation in American society. He went beyond Bourne, Macdonald, and Mills, who posi-
tioned themselves against Dewey's support of World War I. In sweeping and
largely unfair terms, Goodman further complained that "Dewey's pragmatic

2. Immanuel Kant, "What Is Enlightenment?" in *The Philosophy of Immanuel Kant,* ed.
Carl Friedrich (New York: Modern Library, 1949), 132, and Kant, *Fundamental Principles of the
Metaphysics of Morals* (Indianapolis: Bobbs-Merrill, 1949), 53. Paul Goodman, *Little Prayers and
Finite Experience* (New York: Harper and Row, 1972), 47; "Art of the Theater" (1965), in
Creator Spirit Come! The Literary Essays of Paul Goodman, ed. Taylor Stoehr (New York: Dut-
ton, 1977), 141; and letter to the *Honolulu Advertiser,* Paul Goodman Papers, Houghton Li-
brary, Harvard University, item 174.

and social-minded conceptions have ended up as the service university, technocracy, labor bureaucracy, suburban togetherness." Mills might not have agreed with all the details or with the dismissive tone, but he certainly would have agreed with the warning that stood behind this statement.[3]

Being a heartfelt American and pragmatist, Goodman stayed away from European theories of radicalism, especially Marxism. Though his brother claims that he briefly flirted with Trotskyism (though this is not entirely clear), Goodman never joined the Communist Party. Goodman explained, "I have always . . . been 'anti-Communist.'" He was more interested in indigenous sources of radicalism—in populism, for instance, and in the thinking of the "Young Americans." He cited Randolph Bourne's "anarcho-pacifist" arguments approvingly and drew upon Patrick Geddes, an intellectual who inspired Lewis Mumford's critique of suburban sprawl. He also shared Mills's praise for A. J. Muste, the Trotskyist turned pacifist activist. Goodman cooed, "A. J. Muste is the keenest political analyst in America." Indigenous radicals who clung to American beliefs in democracy always served as Goodman's heroes.[4]

Moving further back in history, Goodman also showed a penchant for classical republican political thinking—something that he, once again, shared with Mills. Eighteenth-century America (or at least his own read of it, which seemed remarkably similar to Tocqueville's read of nineteenth-century America) served as a backdrop for many of Goodman's criticisms of modernity. During this supposed golden age, Goodman argued, political decision making was "improvised" locally. Like Mills, Goodman also praised the idea of "craftsmanship" and used republican terms like "honor" in his jeremiads against America's moral and political deficit. But unlike Mills, Goodman's republican thinking grew from his reading of another favorite

3. Paul Goodman: *People or Personnel and Like a Conquered Province* (New York: Vintage, 1968), 353; "The Attempt to Invent an American Style," *politics,* February 1944, 17; *Five Years: Thoughts During a Useless Time* (1966; reprint, New York: Vintage, 1969), 29; *New Reformation: Notes of a Neolithic Conservative* (New York: Vintage, 1969), 199; *Little Prayers,* 55; *Five Years,* 186; *New Reformation,* 84. For more on pragmatism's influence on Goodman, see Taylor Stoehr's wonderful (though partial) biography, *Here, Now, Next,* 121–25.

4. Paul Goodman, "On Liberal Anti-Communism," *Commentary,* September 1967, 41, and *People or Personnel,* 224. For Goodman's citation of Bourne, see *New Reformation,* 143–49; for Mumford's influence, see *People or Personnel,* 56, as well as Neil Heims, "The Formulation of Freedom," in *Artist of the Actual: Essays on Paul Goodman,* ed. Peter Parisi (Metuchen, N.J.: Scarecrow, 1986), 58. Percival Goodman's claim that Paul Goodman was briefly a Trotskyist is in "Interview with Percival Goodman," *Artist of the Actual,* 139. This might be similar to C. Wright Mills's brief flirtation with Trotskyism.

philosopher—Aristotle. Goodman, in his own words, embraced "the Aristotelian notion that happiness consists in activity" and that "man is a political animal" whose fully realized self could only be discovered in the *polis*. For Goodman, the New Left would resuscitate a conception of politics that went beyond simply allocating resources or choosing political representatives, one that truly encouraged "self-actualization" and communal discourse via political participation. In so doing, it could renew older conceptions of the good life that Aristotle and eighteenth-century Americans seemed to understand better than modern citizens.[5]

Republican political theory, populism, and the decentralized politics of eighteenth-century America informed Goodman's concern with modern political centralization and its concomitant "psychology of powerlessness." This is probably the most important similarity in Goodman's and Mills's political thinking in relation to their conceptions of a New Left. Goodman agreed with Mills that America had a power elite (a term he used himself) and a mass society. Indeed, he depicted the power elite as even more unified than Mills thought it was. Goodman wrote, "The genius of our centralized corporations and bureaucracies is that they interlock, to form a mutually accrediting establishment of decision makers, with common interests and a common style that nullify the diversity of pluralism" and the beliefs of the "Marty Lipset School of Sociology" (i.e., the "end of ideology" thesis). What Goodman shared with Mills was made even clearer in his condemnation of President Eisenhower as "an unusually uncultivated man." Like Mills, Goodman's complaint about those in power was not always their power per se, but their crude mindlessness. Once again, Goodman shared

5. Paul Goodman: "A Conjecture in American History, 1783–1815," *politics,* Winter 1949, 11; *People or Personnel,* 132; *Growing Up Absurd* (New York: Vintage, 1960), 149; *People or Personnel,* 166; "What Is Man?" (1954) in *Nature Heals: The Psychological Essays of Paul Goodman,* ed. Taylor Stoehr (New York: Dutton, 1977), 251. Interestingly enough, Richard Hofstadter and Ken Stampp—two of Mills's friends at the University of Maryland (and Hofstadter later at Columbia)—commented on Goodman's piece about nineteenth-century America in *politics.* It should also be noted that Goodman sounded remarkably similar not only to Mills but also to Hannah Arendt. Listen to Goodman describe political speech: "Speaking is a special way of being in the world. It defines and actualizes the self rather than merely expressing it" (Goodman, "Society and the Writer," *Washington Post Book Week,* June 12, 1966, 1). Such a passage parallels Arendt's thinking in *The Human Condition* (Chicago: University of Chicago Press, 1958). For the ancients' influence, see also Percival Goodman and Paul Goodman, *Communitas: Means of Livelihood and Ways of Life* (New York: Vintage, 1960), 50.

Mills's analysis of what was wrong in contemporary American political culture—and his hope that something could be done about it.[6]

Finally, Goodman, like Mills, grew increasingly uncomfortable with the conservative political thinking of fellow New York Intellectuals. Mills would have nodded his head when Goodman complained to the *New York Times Magazine* about "the failure of the intellectuals during the late forties and fifties." As Goodman saw it, "Most of my intellectual generation sold out first to the Communists, and then to the organized system, so that there are very few independents around that a young man can accept as a hero." Goodman and Mills both cherished the idea of an "independent" intellectual. Goodman did not stop here in his harangue about the New York Intellectuals. As I will demonstrate later, Goodman saw the problem of the intellectual more broadly—as a problem related to the peculiar position of intellectuals within America's political culture and to what Mills called the "cultural apparatus." Goodman would take up Mills's call for intellectuals to become politically engaged, and he would formulate concrete policies that suggested how this could be done in the face of a cultural apparatus that stifled critical voices.[7]

6. Paul Goodman, "Last Public Speech" (1972), in *Drawing the Line: The Political Essays of Paul Goodman,* ed. Taylor Stoehr (New York: Dutton, 1977), 266. (The term "powerlessness" occurs throughout all of Goodman's writings.) See also Paul Goodman, "Comment," in *The Law School of Tomorrow,* ed. David Haber and Julius Cohen (New Brunswick: Rutgers University Press, 1968), 32, and *Growing Up Absurd,* 109. Goodman wrote, "There is a System and a Power Elite" in his "Anarchism and Revolution" (1970), in *Drawing the Line,* 227. In the "Comment" essay, Goodman also explains that he does not agree with C. Wright Mills. This is perplexing, because his language, ideas, and criticism of Seymour Martin Lipset's pluralism express a clear affinity for Mills's thinking in *The Power Elite.* It is not clear exactly how Goodman disagreed with Mills over the power elite thesis, because their ideas seem remarkably parallel. Goodman's critique probably related to his overall disagreement with Mills about human nature and social structure (a conflict that will be discussed later).

7. Paul Goodman, letter to the *New York Times Magazine,* February 11, 1968, Paul Goodman Papers, folder 206; Goodman quoted in Richard Kostelanetz, "The Prevalence of Paul Goodman," *New York Times Magazine,* April 3, 1966, 71. Beyond these similarities, I should mention just a few others. When Goodman argued that sociology should be "political and moral" and less obsessed with methodology, he sounded like Mills: see *Nature Heals,* 226. Goodman's critique of America's Cold War policies would also sound strikingly similar to Mills's condemnation of "crackpot realism." For an example, see Paul Goodman, *The Society I Live in Is Mine* (New York: Horizon, 1962), 151–52. Finally, Goodman shared Mills's distrust of organized labor as a force for political change.

The Debate: Should a Radical Check In with a Psychoanalyst?

With all these similarities in mind, it might seem strange that many readers of *politics* would think of Goodman and Mills as intellectual enemies. Needless to say, on one count, these two thinkers certainly differed, and this difference would continue to shape Goodman's political thinking. In 1945 and even up to his death, Paul Goodman would ground his radical visions in psychological theory. *What* psychological theory he favored would change over the years, as would Goodman's political vision. He began as a radical Freudian who embraced a psychology grounded in human instincts, and he followed Wilhelm Reich's later appropriation of Freudian theory for radical political causes as well. Goodman argued that without a belief in some sort of instinctual basis within human nature—what Freud termed the "id"—there would be no reason to hope that humans could resist the onslaught of conformist pressures. He celebrated the "rebellion of the instincts against the superficial distractions of the ego." The instincts were, as he put it, "beyond the influence of advertising slogans and political propaganda." For Goodman, a belief that human nature was "not so completely malleable" was necessary to garner faith that people could combat the demands of their society. This contrasted sharply with Mills's understanding of "social character" as connected to historical changes in social structure.[8]

Goodman's belief in Freud's and Reich's drive theories led him to criticize a school of thinkers known as neo-Freudians or ego psychologists (Karen Horney and Erich Fromm, most prominently). These thinkers argued that Freud had overemphasized instinctual drives and misunderstood the inherently social tendencies within human nature. For neo-Freudians, the ego developed naturally—not in violent conflict with the id. Goodman hated this idea because it led these thinkers to "diminish the role of instinctual drives." Goodman drew this argument out to its furthest extent (a strategy he pursued in almost all debates). Neo-Freudians like Fromm and Horney, Goodman argued, developed a "psychology" that "has as its aim to produce a unanimity of spirit in the perfected form of the present social system, with its monster factories, streamlined satisfactions, and distant representative government." Anyone who had read Fromm would probably have been con-

---

8. Paul Goodman, "Revolution, Sociolatry, and War" (first published in *politics*, December 1945), in *Drawing the Line,* 34; "Sex and Revolution" (1945) in *Nature Heals,* 74; "Human Nature and the Anthropology of Neurosis," in *Recognitions in Gestalt Therapy,* ed. Paul David Pursglove (New York: Funk and Wagnalls, 1968), 66.

fused by Goodman's line of reasoning; Fromm was, after all, a humanist and a socialist—someone who abhorred "monster factories." But Goodman believed that the *logic* of Fromm's psychology led directly to a form of thinking with no grounds for believing in the possibility of social change. Even if Fromm's politics were socialist, Goodman would argue, his psychology was conformist.[9]

Mills rushed to the defense of the neo-Freudians. Sounding like an angry, polemical New York Intellectual, Mills ridiculed Goodman's "metaphysics of biology" and his "gonad theory of revolution." Just as he had argued against Macdonald's resort to universalistic ethics in his battle against the atrocities of the twentieth century, Mills would argue against Goodman's universalizing of the instincts. Mills reminded his readers that "a socialist view of human nature will recognize fully that man is a historical creature." Goodman's view not only dehistoricized the psyche, but it also conceived of liberation in narcissistic terms: "If we accept Goodman's concept of freedom, the cultivation of biological 'release,' freedom becomes identified with the fixed irrationalities of the leisured and private life." Essentially, sexual liberation could never replace the older socialist demands for equality and democracy.[10]

Interestingly enough, Goodman conceded (partially) to Mills's last point. As he argued in a rejoinder to their debate, sexual liberation was not enough *in itself,* but it was an important feature of a radical program. He could foresee advertisers exploiting sexual liberation for their own greedy purposes; nonetheless, Goodman believed that radicals had to accept some sort of instinctual mechanism capable of counteracting alienation and conformist pressure. The only other alternative was a sociological and historical relativism that resulted in the idea of complete human malleability. Mills, on the other hand, believed particular values might be historically relative, but that fact did not prevent them from being useful in formulating criticisms of the

9. Paul Goodman, "The Political Meaning of Some Recent Revisions of Freud," *politics,* July 1945, 198; "A Touchstone for the Libertarian Program" (1945), in *Drawing the Line,* 20. For another example of Goodman's critique of neo-Freudians, see his review of *Infants Without Families,* by Anna Freud, *politics,* March 1945, 80. For more on debates among Freudian theorists, see Russell Jacoby, *Social Amnesia: A Critique of Conformist Psychology from Adler to Laing* (Boston: Beacon, 1975), and *The Repression of Psychoanalysis: Otto Fenichel and the Political Freudians* (New York: Basic, 1983). On Reich, see Paul Robinson, *The Freudian Left: Wilhelm Reich, Geza Roheim, Herbert Marcuse* (New York: Harper and Row, 1969).

10. C. Wright Mills and Patricia Salter, "The Barricade and the Bedroom," *politics,* October 1945, 314, 315.

present. Later, in *Growing Up Absurd* (1960), Goodman would insinuate that Mills was a sociological functionalist of sorts, since he situated ideas within their historical context and denied any "constant" within human nature. Though Goodman would change his psychological thinking quite a bit in the years between his debate with Mills and his writing of *Growing Up Absurd* (a book, it should be pointed out, that Mills read quite thoroughly), he never gave up on the idea that human nature inherently clashed with social pressures. This was the crucial and most significant difference between Goodman and Mills. Goodman could not imagine any radical program for change unless there was some fixed element in human nature that could provide its foundation.[11]

Growing Up in the New York Family

This was not the only difference between Goodman and Mills. Another difference was biographical. As noted earlier, Goodman was older than Mills. Born in 1911, he was raised in New York City. Facts of age and location meant that Goodman was a member of the "New York Family" in a way that Mills could never be. Indeed, Goodman was, first of all, a Jew. Second, he attended the college that all New York Intellectuals drifted toward (largely out of financial necessity): City College of New York. In addition, Goodman loved New York City, and saw it as his home. He argued that places like Manhattan "made people smart because of their mixed peoples, mixed manners, and mixed learning." Finally, Goodman wrote for the central institution of the New York Intellectuals—*Partisan Review.* He even asked to be made "an editor of PR." Of course, Goodman did not share the editors' Trotskyism, and his conception of a radical avant-garde in literature (which included himself) was much more experimental and critical than theirs. Nonetheless, he saw *Partisan Review* as an important magazine and as a space in which to develop ideas. He enjoyed dialogue with fellow New York Intellectuals. To make clear that he belonged to this larger group, Goodman referred to many of them, even in his public writings, by their nicknames (for instance, Daniel Bell became Danny Bell, and Seymour Mar-

11. Goodman's reply is in *politics,* October 1945, 315–16; Goodman, *Growing Up Absurd,* 226. Mills closely read "Growing Up Absurd" when it originally appeared in *Commentary,* as is evident from the Mills Papers.

tin Lipset became Marty Lipset). No wonder, then, that Irving Howe would place Goodman squarely within the New York Intellectual family.[12]

While Goodman had been born into the New York Family, he was also alienated from it for several reasons. First, he was always critical of Marxism. This immediately put him on the outs with most New York Intellectuals, at least during the 1930s and early 1940s. He explained, "What I myself noticed in the 30s and 40s was that I was excluded from the profitable literary circles dominated by Marxists in the 30s and ex-Marxists in the 40s because I was an anarchist." Goodman hung around not just New York Intellectuals but also a small, bohemian community in New York City that produced obscure anarchist publications like *Why?* (later called *Resistance*) and *Retort*. Here he developed his own version of anarcho-pacifism. Moreover, Goodman worked with the Living Theatre, a small experimental theater in New York City that performed some of his plays. In certain ways, the editors of *Partisan Review* embraced avant-garde literary innovation on an intellectual level, but Goodman *lived* and *practiced* it. Both his anarcho-pacifism and his literary experimentalism made the editors at *Partisan Review* squeamish. Add to this Goodman's bisexuality, and the origin of his alienation from other New York Intellectuals becomes clearer.[13]

12. Goodman, *Growing Up Absurd,* 74; Goodman to Dwight Macdonald, undated letter (with 1942–43 written in on top), Dwight Macdonald Papers, Yale University, Paul Goodman folder; Howe, *The Decline of the New,* 239. Goodman would have argued that Harold Rosenberg was another New York Intellectual who remained independent of the New York Family's general conservative drift: see Paul Goodman, "Essays by Rosenberg," *Dissent* 6 (1959): 305. In contrast with the "fellow traveling Liberals" and "pomposity of Danny Bell" (305), Goodman wrote, Rosenberg was able to "remain within fighting and dialogue range of the other writers without belonging to this 'intellectual' swim or that 'position-taking' magazine" (307). On Goodman's Judaism, see his "Judaism of a Man of Letters," *Commentary,* September 1948, 242–43. On Goodman's life, I rely upon Taylor Stoehr's biography as well as on folder 463 in the Paul Goodman Papers; the folder includes numerous résumés. On Goodman's love of New York City, see his "City Crowds," *politics,* December 1946, 390–91; his love of avant-garde literature, "Stale Marxism," *Kenyon Review* 9 (1947): 608–12. On his relation to the New York Intellectuals, see Kingsley Widmer, *Paul Goodman* (Boston: Twayne, 1980), 23–24, and on his studies at City College of New York, see David Hollinger, *Morris R. Cohen and the Scientific Ideal* (Cambridge: MIT Press, 1975), 70.

13. "The Politics of Being Queer" (1969), in *Nature Heals,* 218. For more on Goodman's anarchist community of the 1940s, see Taylor Stoehr's introduction to *Drawing the Line,* xvi, and his *Here, Now, Next,* 32; see also Tom Nicely, *Adam and His Work: A Bibliography of Sources About Paul Goodman* (Metuchen, N.J.: Scarecrow, 1979), 29. I also consulted copies of *Resistance*—formerly known as *Why?*—housed in the Tamiment Labor Archives at New York University. The politics here were not simply anarchist but also libertarian and individualistic. On the Living Theatre, see Richard Kostelanetz, "Paul Goodman: Persistence and Preva-

This also explains what drew Dwight Macdonald to Goodman. As discussed in Chapter 1, Macdonald took many of his ideas from Goodman (and from his brethren within the anarchist movement). And—as it had for Mills and Macdonald—World War II fully politicized Goodman, transforming him from an avant-garde author with anarchist inclinations to a politically minded pacifist and advocate for decentralized democracy, one with a very strong tendency toward libertarianism and personalism. At *politics,* Macdonald continued to rely upon Goodman's thinking to formulate his first steps toward an independent form of radicalism. Goodman not only put his pacifism into practice during World War II (which, as his brother Percival explained, almost landed him in jail), but he also continued to develop these ideas throughout the late 1940s, even while Macdonald was rejecting pacifism for "the West." Macdonald simply gave Goodman a forum in which to write social and political criticism.[14]

All these ideas—anarchism, pacifism, literary avant-gardism—fueled Goodman's thought during the 1950s and his criticism of his fellow New York Intellectuals. Like Mills, Goodman gravitated toward the pages of *Dissent,* but later fell out with the editors over their rigid anticommunism (as witnessed in Irving Howe's dismissal of Mills's *The Causes of World War III*). During the 1960s, Goodman wrote Irving Howe that *Dissent* should have done more to expose the CIA funding of the Congress for Cultural Freedom. Goodman prodded Howe, "Why has *Dissent* not put out a full-dress inquiry on this subject of paid intellectuals? . . . My guess is that the reasons are squeamishness, friends, timidity." The result of such timidity, Goodman argued, was the alienation of younger readers from the magazine. Similar concerns also led to Goodman's debate with Dwight Macdonald. In the late 1940s, Goodman claimed that he was angry with *politics* for focusing too much wrath on liberals like Henry Wallace. (He saw bigger targets in the earlier enemies of the magazine, such as the "permanent war economy.")

---

lence," in his *Masterminds* (New York: Macmillan, 1969), 284. For a good statement of Goodman's political philosophy during this time, see his "Reflections on Drawing the Line," "On Treason Against Natural Societies," and "A Touchstone for the Libertarian Program," all in *Drawing the Line.*

14. "Interview with Percival Goodman," 150. See also Colin Ward, "The Anarchist as Citizen," *New Letters* 42 (1976): 237–45, and Joseph Epstein, "Paul Goodman in Retrospect," *Commentary,* February 1978, 70. For Goodman's vision of what *politics* should be, see "The Unalienated Intellectual," *politics,* November 1944, 319. Goodman always felt that he was *expelled* from *Partisan Review* for his views. See his comment in *Five Years* (146): "I have never left anybody who has access to a printing press!"

Another complaint came later in 1958 when Goodman, in reviewing *Memoirs of a Revolutionist* (a collection of essays originally printed in *politics*), criticized Macdonald for taking the historical change of New York Intellectuals—their conversion from Marxists to ex-Marxist conservatives or liberals—as the only legitimate intellectual transformation. Goodman felt that there was no reason to start with Marxism or to end with conservatism. Clearly, a great deal of Goodman's vision of a New Left drew from a frustration he shared with Mills about the complacency of fellow New York Intellectuals. The biographical differences between Goodman and Mills, though—along with their philosophical disagreements over human nature and psychology—led them to express their frustration in dissimilar ways.[15]

Changing Intellectual (Pre)Conditions: Becoming a Connected Critic During the 1950s

Naturally, for men of letters, our new status is personally unfortunate. We were trained in a tradition where letters had a quite different ambition and scope; our adolescent fantasies of becoming major artists are doomed to be fantasies.
—Paul Goodman, "Reflections on Literature as a Minor Art," 1958

By the late 1940s many of the elements of Paul Goodman's radicalism—decentralism and pacifism, for instance—were in place. Nonetheless, he had to find ways to make this political theory speak to a larger audience. His ideas had grown out of a dialogue within marginal subcommunities, like small cooperatives, not-so-widely read anarchist publications, avant-garde theaters, and bohemian clusters in New York City. Before making the teachings of these groups speak to a wider public, Goodman went through two major transformations in his intellectual development. The first was a change in his psychological theory. The second was in his view of social criticism—a move away from simply "drawing the line" and resisting conformity toward "connected criticism" and writing patriotic jeremiads. To a large extent, Goodman would reject the "negativism" that Dwight Macdonald formulated at *politics*. He started to see that concrete proposals for

15. Goodman to Howe, December 8, 1966, Paul Goodman Papers, folder 177; Paul Goodman, "Our Best Journalist," *Dissent* 5 (1958): 84. In his retort, Macdonald made a significant point about the "hasty and formless" quality of Goodman's writing: see Dwight Macdonald, "The Question of Kitsch," *Dissent* 5 (1958): 399. The Goodman-Macdonald debate was not as nasty as that between Mills and Macdonald.

reform needed to be made in a language accessible to a wide public. This served as the basis of his developing conception of a New Left that could be effective in political transformation.

Goodman began to change his thinking about psychology when he reconsidered the work of Wilhelm Reich. Reich had personally berated Goodman for writing anarchist interpretations of his ideas in *politics*. Quite simply, Reich was no anarchist; he was a Marxist, and this forced Goodman away from his psychological hero. Needless to say, there were not just negative reactions at work here but also other intellectual sources that inspired Goodman's rethinking of psychology. His Aristotelian philosophy, for instance, provided a view of human nature quite distinct from the conflict model—and the bombardment theory of socialization—favored by Freud and Reich. Aristotle's belief in a "soul" moving toward an inherent *telos* suggested a more benign understanding of socialization. So too did Goodman's Kantianism, which saw the self as an "integrator" of experience. As Goodman pointed out, Kant had posited the self as "the *synthetic* unity." Essentially, the self was a healthy combination of internal (universalistic) mechanisms—those things that constituted "human nature"—and the external (pluralistic) world. In retrospect, Goodman explained his late 1940s reassessment of Reich's individualistic and id psychology this way: "It is more profitable to think of the self as a process of structuring the organism-environment field." In other words, self and society could be integrated without succumbing to conformity.[16]

At the time Reich rejected him, another psychological thinker, Fritz Perls, contacted Goodman. Perls was also questioning Reich, which made their new intellectual friendship that much more important. Together they formulated a new psychological theory—Gestalt therapy—which was capable of replacing Reich's theory as a grounding for Goodman's radicalism. Though Gestalt therapy shared certain traits with radical Freudianism, the differences between the two theories were more significant. Like Reichian theory (and unlike classical Freudian theory), Gestalt therapy stressed the *present* in people's lives, not their childhood or their past. An emphasis was

16. Frederick S. Perls, Ralph Hefferline, and Paul Goodman, *Gestalt Therapy: Excitement and Growth in the Human Personality* (New York: Julian, 1951), 235. (The words are undoubtedly Goodman's. For more on the writing of this book, see Stoehr, *Here, Now, Next.*) See also Paul Goodman, "Great Pioneer, but No Libertarian," *Liberation,* January 1958, 9. On Goodman's understanding of Aristotle's self-actualizing "soul," see his "Essay," in *Freedom and Order in the University,* ed. Samuel Gorovitz (Cleveland: Press of Western Reserve University, 1967), 31. On Reich's Marxism, see Paul Robinson, *The Freudian Left,* 41.

also placed on conscious activity, not the unconscious realm of dreams. Gestalt therapists demanded that their patients interrogate their present-day behavior and habits for unresolved tensions, thus finding their true selves: "When you relinquish your determination to make your behavior fit the arbitrary, more or less fixed pattern that you have taken over from 'the authorities,' aware need and spontaneous interest come to the surface and reveal to you what you are and what is appropriate for you to do." Self-awareness then led directly to individuals confronting their social environment.[17]

The result of such a confrontation was not a pleasureless conformity, however (as Freud had seemed to suggest in his classic work, *Civilization and Its Discontents*). Psychology need not settle for reconciling a patient with the general unhappiness of everyday life, to paraphrase Freud. Rather, Gestalt therapy held out, in Taylor Stoehr's words, an ideal of health that involved "lively engagement with the unpredictable world of the next moment." At times, such therapeutic technique verged on feel-good release. In celebrating "spontaneity," Perls and Goodman blurted out at one point, "Whatever you do, try to get it off your chest!"—as if simply talking about things made them better. They corrected for this tendency, though, by stressing the need for "creative adjustment" between the individual and his or her social environment. Perls and Goodman believed that the patient's desires were strong enough to justify engagement in social change: "Reality is not something inflexible and unchanging but is ready to be remade." In a set of personal and cryptic notes on Gestalt therapy, Goodman wrote, "Change in social role of Psychotherapy. . . . Progressively dim view of social norms: morals, regimentation and bureaucracy, emptiness of standardization and loss of unique careers in the social roles: need to remake society." From therapy, the move to social criticism and political engagement seemed natural.[18]

On this point, the role of the therapist in Gestalt therapy became increasingly important and the difference with classical psychoanalysis that much more significant. Freudian practice demanded near silence on the part of the analyst, because the patient would reveal truth through free association during the sessions (the patient was not even able to see the analyst, who sat

17. Perls et al., *Gestalt Therapy*, 112, viii, 3, 40, 464, 120. For more on the relationship between Perls and Goodman, see Stoehr, *Here, Now, Next*.

18. Stoehr, *Here, Now, Next*, xiii; Perls et al., *Gestalt Therapy*, 305, 144, 230, 246; Goodman, notes in Paul Goodman Papers, folder 1143 (Notes for lectures on various subjects, 1994–95).

behind the patient). Goodman, who was a practicing therapist during the 1950s, believed in a more active role. The psychotherapist should "confront the patient with the reality," he once suggested. Instead of being distant, the therapist was to be a friend to the patient, a "fellow citizen and comrade," as Taylor Stoehr puts it. Indeed, Goodman ran collective therapy sessions with his patients that turned into "mutual criticism" meetings similar to those held at the nineteenth-century Oneida Community, in which citizens discussed collective means of improving their lives. As Richard King put it, "[t]he goal of the therapist" for Paul Goodman "was not to cure a sick person, but to aid the creative adjustment of the patient to reality on his own terms." But there was a higher responsibility as well. Based on observations of the shared difficulties of patients, the therapist had a special responsibility to become a social critic—to show just why fellow citizens suffered from "blocked potentialities." Conversely, social criticism had to justify itself in well-grounded views of human health. Here was the basis of Goodman's future New Left political vision. As Taylor Stoehr explained, "Gestalt Therapy was not superseded in Goodman's thought by New Left politics, but rather served as that politics' grounding in a theory of human nature and face-to-face community." With Gestalt therapy in his intellectual toolkit, Goodman could more easily turn to social criticism and engage in debates as a politically minded intellectual.[19]

There were still other impediments to Goodman's becoming an effective social critic. Most important was how he understood his role as a writer. Up to and through the 1950s, Goodman had spent much of his time writing avant-garde fiction, poetry, and drama. Though I will not explore this writing here (as a full intellectual biography would have to), I want to discuss, briefly, Goodman's experience as an artist. His growing dissatisfaction in this role during the 1950s became a major source of his later social criticism and engaged political work. As much as he moved from radical Reichianism to a more complex psychological theory, he moved from avant-garde artist to connected, even patriotic, social critic.

Writing and publishing fiction and poetry during the 1950s frustrated

19. Goodman, *Five Years*, 12; Stoehr, *Here, Now, Next*, 18, 266; Richard King, *The Party of Eros: Radical Social Thought and the Realm of Freedom* (Chapel Hill: University of North Carolina Press, 1972), 98. For Goodman's explanation of his move from Gestalt therapy to social criticism, see his *Little Prayers*, 39–41. It is not surprising to find that Goodman's own therapeutic specialty was "career block": see his undated letter (late 1959) to Robert Davis, Paul Goodman Papers, folder 33.

Goodman. During the later 1950s, he wrote his friend, George Dennison, a letter that reflected his general mood: "I need to embark on a big work of some kind (whether literary or otherwise), and I simply don't have a big vision—it doesn't break on me. I actually go to sleep wishing I'll have a telling dream." This frustration—and important inclination that he might stop writing "literary" works for something else—grew out of Goodman's pieces being rejected from numerous publications and his own books of fiction and poetry not selling very well. In the journals that he kept during the 1950s, Goodman opined, "I guess I am the most widely unknown writer who is so highly esteemed by a few." Though he worried about the quality of his writing, he concerned himself mostly with the state of his audience. In an unpublished piece called "On Being a Writer" (1951), he declared, "My works have no social audience." Instead, they were destined for a small circle of fellow citizens. Not surprisingly, Goodman felt frustrated, as did Mills, about writing unread works.[20]

Of course, this sort of feeling could lead in different directions. Most obviously, it could engender alienation and bitterness. This was always a possibility for Goodman, since he saw the artist suffering from a tension between being "unconventional, . . . marginal, and unsafe" and being, at the same time, "the chief bearer of the common culture." But instead of expressing alienation or turning his back on his audience, Goodman decided to make good on the promise of being the bearer of culture. Even by 1949, he had called on artists to "fight back for our audience." He believed that the artist had a responsibility to *constitute and create* an audience; this sense only continued to grow throughout the 1950s. To re-create a community that was "deep enough for creativity" and not so passive in the face of culture became Goodman's task. This required the artist to face the "difficulty of the proprietary control of the media by the tribe of intermediary bureaucrats," or what Mills labeled the "cultural apparatus." The artist essentially had to build back a critical public and audience against the forces of commercialization and cheap and easy entertainment. To do this, the artist would have to criticize what was wrong with society, thereby improving its

---

20. Paul Goodman, letter to George Dennison (undated, but many of the other letters to Dennison clearly were written during the 1959–60 period), Paul Goodman Papers, folder 34; *Five Years,* 10; and "On Being a Writer," Paul Goodman Papers, folder 455. Goodman's difficulty in getting his fiction published is seen in letters to the Bobbs-Merrill Company from 1958 onward: see Paul Goodman Papers, folder 6. On the poor sales of Goodman's fiction, see Stoehr, *Here, Now, Next,* 36.

capacity to appreciate a wider array of art and culture. The public for art would have to be reconstructed—precisely through the reappropriation of the cultural apparatus, as Mills had argued. Goodman's personal frustration as an artist led him to this challenge.[21]

This artistic demand coalesced with a general life crisis for Goodman. Starting in the mid-1950s, Goodman's personal life seemed to fall apart. He faced difficulty in getting the last installment of his novel, *The Empire City*, published; there was a new licensing law for lay therapists to which he failed to respond; and, at the same time, his daughter contracted polio. After caring for his daughter, Goodman decided to relieve the pressures in his life by getting away to Europe in 1958 (a year after Mills was there). What happened there can probably be best described as a conversion experience. In Europe, he felt a stirring sense of patriotism. In a letter to George Dennison written during the summer of 1958, Goodman explained, "My most consistent and 'adding up' attitudes have been (1) a deep and worsening gripe about the physical ugliness of America; shame for it; (2) a general feeling that it's a lousy world, hard for decent folk; (3) a yearning for a simple manly patriotism that makes an effort and that I heard in the voice of a farmer deep in the Alps: '*Hier ist Canton Uri!*'—I'll tell you about this, it haunts me as the best thing I have experienced." This mix of increasing pain at social conditions in America and respect for Swiss patriotism drove Goodman into writing social criticism. Becoming lonely during his travels (which only furthered his love of America), he came back to the States, feeling "agitated by the need to do something for my country." Just as Mills had felt that his arguments needed to take place in America, so too did Goodman. Any idea of expatriation—the sort popular among intellectuals in the 1920s—was ruled out. Swept up by patriotism, Goodman started to read some of the founding fathers' writings at this time, especially those of George Washington and Thomas Jefferson. He also set to work on writing *Growing Up Absurd*—the work of social criticism that would provide him with a much wider reading audience and that would define his career from that point onward. He was now to be a "connected critic," to use Michael Walzer's phrase, and would speak a patriotic language that a wider circle of citizens could understand, rather than hector from the margins. In taking on the

---

21. Paul Goodman, "The American Writer and His Americanism," *Kenyon Review* 21 (1959): 478, and "The Chance for Popular Culture" (1949), in *Creator Spirit Come!* 79, 86, 87.

roles of patriot and critic, Goodman would formulate his vision of a New Left.[22]

Why Cultural Rebellion Failed in Building a New Left

My own tone in this book sounds like an Angry-Middle-Aged Man, disappointed but not resigned.
—Paul Goodman, *Growing Up Absurd*, 1960

Like C. Wright Mills, Paul Goodman politicized the cultural critique that dominated so much of American intellectual life during the 1950s. David Riesman had shown how transformations in the culture of work and personality types turned previously self-directed individuals into other-directed conformists. But when it came to politics, Riesman tended toward liberal and pluralist ideas (the sort Mills criticized and Goodman would later condemn). William Whyte (who, Mills felt, had stolen his ideas) showed how large bureaucratic workplaces created alienated white-collar workers whom he called "organization men." Solutions, though, were not forthcoming. Whyte explained, "The conflict between the individual and society has always involved dilemma; it always will, and it is intellectual arrogance to think a program would solve it." The only counsel he offered was for individuals to "fight the Organization" *as* individuals. Finally, Vance Packard made many of the same criticisms as Riesman and Whyte. Writing popular social criticism, Packard exposed the manipulative nature of advertising, but he suggested only that people examine the moral impact of this activity—nothing more. Goodman developed ideas that were similar to those of Riesman, Whyte, and Packard when he wrote *Growing Up Absurd;* to a large extent, the book synthesized a decade's worth of social criticism. But unlike these critics (and more like Mills), he made clear that what often appeared as cultural problems—conformity and alienation—had political roots and demanded serious social reform. In fact, Goodman wanted *Growing Up Absurd*

22. Paul Goodman, letter in Paul Goodman Papers, folder 34, and *Five Years,* 197–98. Goodman's crisis is documented in Stoehr, *Here, Now, Next,* 223–27. On Michael Walzer's idea of "connected criticism," see his *Company of Critics.* It should come as no surprise that Goodman's patriotic experience occurred in Switzerland—known for its decentralized political system.

to "appear before the 1960 campaign," believing that it had a political message.[23]

Goodman's central thesis in *Growing Up Absurd* was that "organized society" had destroyed the older conception of a vocation, while creating "synthetic demands" through manipulative advertising. Advanced capitalism, for Goodman, relied upon an "artificially induced demand for useless goods" that resulted in "jobs for all and good profits for some." Since work consisted mainly of routine jobs and manipulating one's image within a bureaucratic corporation—positioning oneself closer to those in power—young people felt increasingly disaffected. Goodman believed that the "organized society" (discussed by Whyte) and manipulative advertising (analyzed by Packard) had very serious social consequences. One of Goodman's major goals in *Growing Up Absurd* was to explain the growing amount—or the *perception* of a growing amount—of juvenile delinquency during the 1950s. For Goodman, young people's disaffection was quite understandable. The "organized society" of faceless bureaucracies "dampens animal ardor. It has no Honor." Young people therefore rebelled and sought alternatives to the organized society. *How* they did this, though, was not entirely satisfactory for Goodman. While he saw the potential for healthy rebellion that could take a political direction, he also saw a great deal of diversion for disaffected youth—the sort that Mills saw in the Angry Young Men of England.[24]

The leading diversion was the major countercultural formation of the 1950s—the Beat rebellion led by Jack Kerouac and Allen Ginsberg. Goodman applauded these writers' interest in pacifism and communitarianism. But he objected to other tendencies in Beat writing. In the first place, much of it was simply *bad* writing. At a poetry reading, Goodman complained publicly that Kerouac "will probably never learn to write" and that Gregory Corso was "an infant" when it came to penning poetry. Goodman was

23. William Whyte, *Organization Man* (Garden City, N.J.: Anchor, 1956), 443, 448; Goodman, *Five Years*, 222. See also David Riesman et al., *The Lonely Crowd* (New York: Doubleday, 1955); Vance Packard, *The Hidden Persuaders* (New York: McKay, 1957); Daniel Horowitz, *Vance Packard and American Social Criticism* (Chapel Hill: University of North Carolina Press, 1994); Pells, *Liberal Mind*. Of all the major social critics, Riesman did support "utopian" ideals and was sympathetic toward Goodman's work. See David Riesman, "The Search for Challenge," *New University Thought* 1 (1960): 11.

24. *Growing Up Absurd*, ix, 30, 12. For the historical context of juvenile delinquency, see James Gilbert, *A Cycle of Outrage: America's Reaction to the Juvenile Delinquent in the 1950s* (New York: Oxford University Press, 1986). It should be pointed out that Goodman thought the Angry Young Men held much more promise than the Beats did.

especially critical of Kerouac's famous novel and memoir, *On the Road*. An avant-garde writer familiar with experimental techniques, Goodman disliked Kerouac's penchant for automatic writing, his tendency to let words spill out onto the page (often under the influence of Benzedrine). Sounding like Truman Capote, who famously quipped that *On the Road* was "not writing but typing," Goodman argued, "Nothing is told, nothing is presented, everything is just 'written about.'" This writing style illuminated a more significant problem in the way the Beats approached problems. The passivity of recording each and every event reflected their general lack of engagement with the world. Goodman explained that the Beat writers "have the theory that to be affectless, to not care, is the ultimate rebellion." On this point, Goodman asserted, the Beats reflected back the pathologies of powerlessness created by the society against which they were supposedly rebelling.[25]

This was an important critique of how countercultural rebellion could fail to push beyond the limits of mainstream culture. Goodman went so far as to analogize hipsters (young people who were still in the system, but rebelled against it) and the organization men that William Whyte had depicted: "Playing roles and being hip . . . is very nearly the same as being an Organization Man, for *he* doesn't mean it either." Goodman showed how countercultural rebels turned their alienation into passivity and settled for simplistic moral relativism. For instance, he analyzed the use of the word "like" in hipster and Beat conversation. When a young person said, "'Like if I go to like New York, I'll look you up,'" this indicated that "in this definite and friendly promise, there is no felt purpose in that trip or any trip." This might seem to make too much of Beat lingo, but Goodman believed that more serious consequences of this language showed up again in how young people discussed important political issues. He wrote, "In a Beat group it is bad form to assert or deny a proposition as true or false, probable or improbable, or to want to explore its meaning." The result was that Beats gave up on any normative framework, just like the organization men who passively accepted bureaucratic regimentation. Personalized rebellion substituted for social and political change.[26]

25. Goodman's comments on Kerouac and Corso, Paul Goodman Papers, folder 1218; *Growing Up Absurd,* 279, 281. For an interesting confirmation of Paul Goodman's points, see Gerald Nicosia on the relation between nihilism and the Beat philosophy of "kicks" in his *Memory Babe: A Critical Biography of Jack Kerouac* (New York: Penguin, 1983), 149–50. Even by 1957, though, Kerouac might have recognized much of what Goodman worried about: see the incident recounted by Nicosia on 546.

26. *Growing Up Absurd,* 67, 172–73, 175.

Goodman believed that the Beats embraced willful ignorance. Here his criticism bordered on the hysterical reaction of Norman Podhoretz, who had written a scathing critique of Kerouac and Ginsberg as "know-nothing bohemians." Podhoretz argued that the Beats represented "a revolt of all the forces hostile to civilization itself" and a "movement of brute stupidity." Goodman's position was different, though, because he was more sympathetic toward the Beats' dissatisfaction with the conformity of American life. More importantly, he did not see in the Beat movement such a threat to Western civilization; Podhoretz, from Goodman's standpoint, had made a mountain out of a molehill. Nonetheless, Goodman did complain that the Beats knew very little either about Western culture or politics and that this damaged the legitimate aspects of their rebellion. He described the Beats and the characters of their novels as "touchingly inarticulate because they don't know anything." The Beat rebellion was no threat to civilization; if anything, it propped up the very system that the Beats complained about—precisely because their condemnation was so limited by ignorance.[27]

Goodman worried that the Beats had neglected an opportunity to face squarely the "missed and compromised revolutions" that were constricting the present and that fell "most heavily on the young." He outlined these missed revolutions at the end of *Growing Up Absurd,* and they became the basis of his future political vision. There was the compromise of the labor movement when it "gave up on the ideal of workers' management" and settled for negotiating higher wages. (This argument seemed to echo Mills's critique of labor during the late 1940s.) There was the failure of the "New Deal," which could not find the appropriate "social balance between public and private works. The result is an expanding production increasingly consisting of corporation boondoggling." Another result was that consumption—facilitated by higher wages—became the imperative and sole form of leisure available to citizens. There was the failure of "the democratic revolution," which succeeded in "extending formal self-government" but at the same time "gave up the ideal of the town meeting, with the initiative and

27. Podhoretz quoted in Gitlin, *The Sixties,* 49; Goodman, *Growing Up Absurd,* 280. To a certain extent, Goodman's attitude paralleled that of liberal thinker James Wechsler. Wechsler actually debated Kerouac and then wrote his criticisms up in *Reflections of an Angry Middle-Aged Editor* (New York: Random House, 1960). Goodman reviewed Wechsler's book and argued that he had not taken the Beat critique of liberalism seriously enough. See Paul Goodman, "'Challenge to the Beat Generation,'" *The New Leader,* June 20, 1960, 25–26. Nonetheless, Goodman agreed with Wechsler that the Beats' rebellion was far too apolitical for his liking.

personal involvement that alone could train people in self-government." There was the failure of "progressive education" to "introduce learning-by-doing" into education such that "real problems" were solved by students. These core issues (as well as others raised by Goodman) supported his vision for a New Left, which was to face the failed revolutions of the past. The New Left would have to make clear that cultural problems, such as alienated work environments, a schlocky consumer culture, passivity, and bureaucratic education, had political roots and could therefore be changed.[28]

Like Mills, Goodman refused to remain quiet after spelling out his political vision. He continued to write social criticism, but for wider and wider audiences, and he counseled radical political action. If anything, he was much more committed to helping activists than Mills, who was content with the simple act of writing. For instance, during the late 1950s, he was already embracing "actions like the Golden Rule" and the "recent beautiful resistance to spurious Civil Defense" drills. When *Liberation* magazine formed amid these events, Goodman was quick to lend a hand. He praised the editors of *Liberation* for getting "personally engaged in the events" about which they wrote. He celebrated the early civil rights movement, believing that it provided young people with new political avenues. As early as 1962, Goodman gave a speech to Students for a Democratic Society (SDS), a group he would later call the "best of the youth groups." (He was accompanied at this convention by Arnold Kaufman and James Weinstein, a major editor at *Studies on the Left*.) Clearly Goodman was looking for movements that could capture his political vision. He knew that the 1950s had been marked by social criticism—including his own later version—and was hoping that the 1960s might become an era in which young people took up his teachings and gave them political meaning.[29]

This point brings us to what might be the biggest difference of all between Goodman and C. Wright Mills—one that drew, once again, from the fact of biography. Goodman lived until 1971. He actually watched movements come to fruition during the 1960s and was given an opportunity to

28. Goodman, *Growing Up Absurd,* 217, 219, 220, 231.

29. Goodman, *The Society I Live in Is Mine,* 49; *Nature Heals,* 133; and undated letter to A. J. Muste, Paul Goodman Papers, folder 195. For Goodman's speech to SDS, see Kirkpatrick Sale, *SDS* (New York: Vintage, 1974), 86. For Goodman's assessment that the 1950s were marked by social criticism that was acted upon during the 1960s, see *People or Personnel,* 255 (*People or Personnel,* it should be pointed out, was originally published in 1963). Goodman also edited a selection of articles that appeared in *Liberation:* see Paul Goodman, ed., *Seeds of Liberation* (New York: George Braziller, 1964).

have a dialogue with activists whom Mills never met as a result of his early death. In a certain way, Goodman became a "movement intellectual," in all the different senses of this term. He pressed activists to think harder about the issues they confronted and come up with concrete policy suggestions for reform. He criticized the limits of movements as they came into being. Most of all, he tried to bring his ideas into conversation with a new set of political actors. In so doing, this "Angry-Middle-Aged Man," Goodman's own term for himself, suddenly found himself in dialogue with the young. As it should for any democratic intellectual, the conversation that took place was two-sided. It defined Goodman's intellectual biography from that point onward.

Searching for a New Left Agent of Change: The Free Speech Movement and Young America

The chief hope is in the young.
—Paul Goodman, "Two Little Essays on Democracy," 1966

The young come to us—it is not the other way; they have made up their minds but are sorely in need of support.
—Paul Goodman to Max Lerner, January 18, 1968

Paul Goodman had clearly rejected the idea that cultural rebellion would be enough to bring together a New Left capable of political transformation. But he now had to explain what set of actors could create true social change. Here, rather than theorizing abstractly, he took his lead from actually emerging political movements. While C. Wright Mills had placed his early hope in anti-HUAC protests held in San Francisco, Goodman had high hopes for the Free Speech Movement (FSM) that erupted at the University of California at Berkeley in 1964. These movements shared more than just geographical proximity. Both confronted the obstruction of democratic speech in Cold War America. They made clear that the re-creation of a democratic public was central to the New Left, that without open and public dialogue, a left would be closed out of existence. They also provided a way in which intellectuals could draw out bigger visions based upon their local activities. Goodman developed theories of politics and education from what he saw happening within the FSM; at the same time, he applied his already developed ideas to explain the significance of the movement. This movement, he argued, illustrated that young people had moved beyond the "voluntary ignorance" of the "young Beats" to "return to involvement" in politics. (This would be William Appleman Williams's take on the New Left's basis as well: see Chap. 4.) Here was the dawn of the New Left.[30]

The FSM took off when administrative leaders at the University of California at Berkeley prevented students from setting up literature tables in Sproul Plaza (a central gathering place for students). Students engaged in recruiting civil rights workers were especially annoyed and decided to stage a sit-in. Protests mounted as students confronted university police. Amid their protests, they formed "free universities" that nurtured open and decidedly political discussions. Mario Savio, a student of philosophy at Berkeley, stood on top of a police car to give rousing speeches to student gatherings. One of his speeches, entitled "An End to History," eventually became a defining document in New Left thinking. Savio began by equating his work with the civil rights movement in the South with his protest against the University of California. He made issue of the "depersonalized, unresponsive bureaucracy" that he and other students faced at the University of California, especially as they tried to change its policy. He justified the movement by citing "the right to participate as citizens in a democratic society." Savio argued that the university should not simply be an institution for corporate or defense research but rather a "place where people begin seriously to question the conditions of their existence." For good reason, then, *Dissent* asked Paul Goodman to go to California and cover the events while thinking about what they meant for the dawn of a New Left.[31]

Goodman saw in these events much more than a desire on the part of the students to discuss politics openly. The revolt reflected a new form of politics. Goodman listened to student leaders, and he then brought to bear on their actions the political vision that Dwight Macdonald had articulated earlier at *politics*. Berkeley student Michael Rossman told Goodman that the FSM was "the first human Event in 40,000 years." Goodman dismissed such

30. Goodman, "Berkeley in February" (1965), reprinted in *Drawing the Line,* 140.

31. Mario Savio, "An End to History," in *The New Student Left,* ed. Mitchell Cohen and Dennis Hale (Boston: Beacon, 1967), 249, 251. For more on the FSM, see Gitlin, *The Sixties,* 164; Sheldon Wolin and John Schaar, *The Berkeley Rebellion and Beyond* (New York: Random House, 1970), essay 1; the essays collected together in *Revolution at Berkeley,* ed. Michael Miller and Susan Gilmore (New York: Dial, 1965); and Seymour Martin Lipset and Sheldon Wolin, eds., *The Berkeley Student Revolt* (Garden City, N.J.: Anchor, 1965).

hyperbole, but nonetheless believed the students had rediscovered that *all* political action required self-willing action in the face of insurmountable odds. Goodman wrote, "The existential theory seems to be that by acting in freedom they made history, and conversely, the historical event made them free." Just as important was the form their protests took. When students created a Free University, Goodman argued, they resisted hierarchical leadership. The student rebellion against bureaucracy took on antibureaucratic forms. Essentially, young people rediscovered not only existential politics and the power of democratic speech but also decentralized activism. Goodman therefore felt legitimate in describing the FSM events as "a kind of hyper-organized anarchy."[32]

In paying such attention to this new student-led movement, Goodman made a bit too much of it at times. Mills had elevated young intellectuals to a high position in his radical theory, and Goodman followed suit, arguing that "only the young seem to recognize" that society's central struggle was "between a world-wide dehumanized system . . . and human decency." The FSM might have made this a defensible point (though, as Goodman admitted, the civil rights movement of African Americans had preceded and framed the FSM, and this was made up of people of all ages). But the next step in Goodman's line of reasoning was off. He argued, "At present in the United States, students—middle class youth—are the major exploited class." He explained that "Negroes, small farmers, the aged" were so "out-caste" that "their labor is not needed and they are not wanted." Of course, this qualification failed to explain why students were more *exploited* than "Negroes" and "small farmers." Middle-class youth might have felt pressure to play a role in economic production (through their future careers as organization men), but this did not make them an exploited class. After all, some students were destined to become leaders of their society and assume power. In writing about the FSM, Goodman magnified the importance of young intellectuals and seemed to suggest that they had enough agency to transform society due to their standing within it. There was a Marxist and Hegelian aspect about the reasoning, placing mythical powers of transformation in a portion of the population. Oddly enough for a purported anarchist, voluntarist, and experimentalist, Goodman seemed ensnared, at this moment, in the grip of agency theory, of believing that one social group deserved a leadership role or a privileged position in social and political

32. Goodman, "Berkeley in February," 133, 137.

change. Students appeared to serve as Goodman's proletariat within an otherwise open-ended and pragmatic theory.[33]

Goodman was much better at analyzing what the FSM said about the state of American education. He understood that students asked serious questions about the purposes of education in a democratic society. Drawing together his earlier interest in progressive education with what he saw of the FSM and the Free Universities movement, Goodman developed his own radical theory of education. At its core was a belief in education as "a natural community function" that "occurs inevitably." Education was best when "incidental," flexible, and grounded in community life. By centralizing and institutionalizing educational processes, schools (at all levels) routinized and devitalized them. In so doing, educational institutions became obsessed with policing their students rather than nurturing free discussion and political debate. As Goodman saw it, the FSM allowed students "a chance to learn something" through their own self-willed activities and confrontation with power. This was more powerful than classroom lectures. In another context, Goodman elaborated on the point: students could "learn more social and political science" from "extramural development like community development, organizing migrant farm labor, or getting shot at in Selma" than they could in most political science courses. He saw this nonformal education taking place when civil rights workers organized "Freedom Schools," which educated southern citizens and organizers, and when SDS students took up community organizing in the North. Though he would defend the classical conception of the liberal arts college (free from the pressures of the Cold War research industry), Goodman believed that the student movement could renew a conception of education grounded in learning by doing, in the activities of non-school-based institutions, and in the natural processes of public deliberation and political engagement. Through their critical education into politics, these students were also discovering the basis of the good life. Taking this idea of education seriously, the New Left could confront substantive issues—racial inequality in the South and the bureaucratization of universities in the North—while improving the means of debate and political education at the same time.[34]

33. Paul Goodman, *People or Personnel,* 253, and "Thoughts on Berkeley," in *The Berkeley Student Revolt,* ed. Lipset and Wolin, 316. It should be noted that SDS leaders would eventually embrace the idea that students were a new working class capable of displacing the proletariat: see, for instance, the selections reprinted in section 16 of *The New Left: A Documentary History,* ed. Massimo Teodori (Indianapolis: Bobbs-Merrill, 1969).

34. Paul Goodman: *Compulsory Mis-Education and The Community of Scholars* (New York:

In writing and commenting on the FSM, Goodman had opened up dialogue with a new movement. He was ready to do more of this—willing both to listen and to debate. By becoming a best-seller, *Growing Up Absurd* had made Goodman a better-known writer; still, he lacked an institutional affiliation. After all, he had never felt comfortable in academia. He explained, "I realize that I am not a scholastic nor a university man . . . I am a humanist, that kind of Renaissance free-lance." This too paralleled Mills's earlier consideration of leaving Columbia in order to write full time. Goodman was too much of a "public intellectual" to find fulfillment in the confines of the modern university. At the same time, he wanted a space to develop his ideas with others, an institution where intellectuals talked to movements and vice versa. He found such a place at the Institute for Policy Studies. From 1964 to 1965, Goodman worked at the IPS, developing "practical proposals" that grew out of his own thinking and dialogue with new social movements. No longer just "drawing the line" or counseling individual resistance, as he had in the 1940s, Goodman tried to make his ideas matter in ways he had never done before.[35]

The Role of the Engaged Intellectual in Political Change: Paul Goodman's Years at IPS and the Idea of Decentralization

Naturally, my own hope is that, having gotten a bellyful of centralized managerial capitalism and mass-media democracy, people will rally to decentralized economy and politics and communitarian ideals. But although the peace movement cuts across class-lines, color-lines, and national-lines, and is non-conformist and raggedly organized, I do not as yet see that it presages any particular political shape.
—Paul Goodman, "Declaring Peace Against the Government," 1962

In most histories of the sixties, the Institute for Policy Studies (IPS) gets short shrift. It deserves much more attention, especially in the case of an intellectual history of the New Left. Founded in 1963, IPS served as a major progressive think tank in America. The fact that there were (and are) no other places like it betrays its significance. Ironically, the right, during its rise

---

Vintage, 1964), 16; "The Present Moment in Education" (1969), in *Drawing the Line,* 76; "Berkeley in February," 140; "Comment," in *The Law School of Tomorrow,* ed. Haber and Cohen, 29; *Compulsory Mis-Education,* 47.

35. Goodman, *Five Years,* 41. On public intellectuals, see Russell Jacoby, *The Last Intellectuals: American Culture in an Age of Academe* (New York: Basic, 1987).

to power in the 1980s, took IPS as a model. As Marcus Raskin, a founder of
IPS, points out, "The right-wing Heritage Foundation published a fifty-
page report at its inception on how it intended to copy the Institute for
Policy Studies and its organizing methods." Even by the late 1960s, IPS had
become an institution known for hosting left-leaning intellectuals who formulated practical alternatives for American politics and who engaged in political action.[36]

Though it was founded in October 1963, the history of IPS went back to
the late 1950s. Two of its founders, Marcus Raskin and Arthur Waskow, met
in Washington, D.C., in 1959 when they worked for Congressman Robert
Kastenmeier of Wisconsin. Both recognized a need for dialogue between
progressive intellectuals and elected officials. They formed the "Liberal Project," which took as its model the British Fabian Society and tried to recruit
progressive thinkers (including, unsuccessfully, C. Wright Mills) to talk with
politicians like Kastenmeier. Many of the politicians involved in the project
failed to win reelection in 1960, and the project fell apart. Around the same
time, Raskin and Waskow were just completing *The Limits of Defense,* a
book that developed out of thinking done in the burgeoning peace movement and that critiqued nuclear containment theory. As the book neared
publication, though, Raskin struck his name from the title page. Through
the help of his teacher, David Riesman, he had been offered a position with
McGeorge Bundy, senior adviser to President John Kennedy (and potential
participant in the National Teach-In discussed in Chap. 5). *The Limits of
Defense* would not look good on the c.v. of someone who was to work with
the National Security Council. This move of authorial abnegation seemed
worth it, though, since the reward was to see how ideas could actually speak
directly to power.[37]

Unfortunately, power was not always willing to listen. Raskin found him-

36. Marcus Raskin, *Visions and Revisions* (n.p.: Olive Branch, 1998), 322.

37. For this history of IPS, I rely upon the report by the Institute for Policy Studies, *The
First Three Years: 1963–1966* (Washington, D.C.: IPS, 1966); John Friedman, introduction to
First Harvest: The Institute for Policy Studies, 1963–1983, ed. John Friedman (New York: Grove,
1983); and the highly critical essay by Rael Isaac, "The Institute for Policy Studies: Empire on
the Left," *Midstream* (June–July 1980): 7–18. More important were the telephone interviews I
did with Marcus Raskin (December 8, 1999) and Arthur Waskow (November 8, 1999), as
well as the helpful advice of Gar Alperovitz, another founder of IPS. See also Kai Bird, *The
Color of Truth: McGeorge Bundy and William Bundy, Brothers in Arms* (New York: Simon and
Schuster, 1998); Arthur Waskow, *The Limits of Defense* (Garden City, N.J.: Doubleday, 1962),
and "Marc Raskin," *Social Policy* (Winter 1999): 59–63; and James Roosevelt's introduction to
The Liberal Papers (Garden City, N.J.: Anchor, 1962).

self marginalized and on the defensive within the administration. When his views on nuclear disarmament were discovered, Bundy became uncomfortable. Eventually, Raskin was transferred to the Office on Budget in order to prevent his dismissal. This sort of marginalization was bad enough; then came the Cuban Missile Crisis. At this point, Raskin—along with his colleague Richard Barnet of the National Arms Council—decided to leave altogether. On the heels of their departure, Raskin and Barnet formed IPS, taking as their core principle a refusal to accept federal funds for their programs. Goodman himself described them as "bright youngsters who went to Washington with Kennedy" and then "set up as independent consultants across the street." It made sense for Goodman to be attracted to their efforts. He had grown increasingly glum about intellectuals who joined the Kennedy administration. As he saw it, intellectuals like Arthur Schlesinger Jr. "have given up citizenly independence and freedom of criticism in order to be servants of the public and friends of the cops." Writing to David Riesman (who had gotten Raskin his position in the Kennedy administration), Paul Goodman complained: "You keep giving 'critical support' to Kennedy exactly as the Trotskyists give 'critical support' to Khrushchev. This is miserable pedagogy. People are thirsting for a real alternative that is not admittedly evil. To explore this and develop it is the proper use of intellect. You people muddy up the water and are, it seems to me, a typical *trahison des clercs.*"

For Goodman, the young intellectuals at IPS had made the right move by going independent. The challenge would be to balance their effectiveness as social and political critics with the responsibility of speaking truth—precisely the challenge that C. Wright Mills had earlier outlined for radical intellectuals. Though Goodman believed that truth telling came first, he also understood that intellectuals needed to find effective ways of communicating ideas to a wider public—to ensure that their ideas had an impact.[38]

There were other things that made Goodman appreciate being invited to join IPS. In the first place, the Institute teased out the more radical side of liberalism, especially the democratic features of John Dewey's pragmatic phi-

---

38. Paul Goodman, *People or Personnel*, 87; "The Devolution of Democracy," *Dissent* 9 (1962): 10; and letter to David Riesman, printed in *The Society I Live in Is Mine*, 160. In my interview with him, Arthur Waskow explained that during the Cuban Missile Crisis, Raskin had even been offered a special position in an air-raid shelter if he were to stay on with the administration. Needless to say, this was not enough to keep him, especially since they had only room for him and no other members of his family!

losophy. John Friedman argues that IPS grounded its work in "existential pragmatism." Practical engagement in public affairs always informed the work of IPS scholars. As Arthur Waskow described it, "The Institute is not just an ordinary research center because it's committed to the idea that to develop social theory one must be involved in social action and in social experiment." This principle obviously attracted Goodman, as did the Institute's insistence on making "practical proposals" to democratize society, its close ties with SDS, and its focus on decentralization as a political principle. Not surprisingly, Goodman felt entirely comfortable here; he relished the conversations held between scholars, activists, and political officials and worked diligently on political writing. To a large extent, Goodman found a home in IPS.[39]

Goodman tried to philosophize *from* the dialogue he had with social movements while at IPS. A few years after departing from IPS, he would explain that protests against the Vietnam War prefigured a better society. They reflected "the kind of America I want, one with much more direct democracy, decentralized decision-making, a system of checks and balances that works, less streamlined elections." Goodman saw things in the FSM and the civil rights movement that confirmed his own political philosophy of decentralization. He took note of the "spontaneity, localism, and decentralist federation of the Negro civil rights movement" in 1963. The empirical grounding of this statement is contestable; historians who have studied the civil rights movement have shown a great deal of structure and leadership provided by black churches, the Southern Christian Leadership Conference, and Martin Luther King Jr. And many civil rights leaders, King included, believed that they needed the federal government to step in, that their own local activities were not enough on their own. Nonetheless, Goodman was right to think that others *believed* the movement to be decentralized (call it an organizing "myth"), especially as students in SDS and SNCC engaged in local neighborhood organizing drives during the mid-1960s. Goodman argued that these movements needed to be taken seriously—that their principles deserved attention from political theorists.[40]

39. John Friedman, introduction to *First Harvest,* xi; Arthur Waskow, "Looking Forward: 1999," *New University Thought* 6 (1968): 36; Raskin, interview.

40. Paul Goodman, "Reflections on Civil Disobedience," *Liberation,* July–August 1968, 14; *People or Personnel,* 21; and "Urbanization and Rural Reconstruction," *Liberation,* November 1966, 9. On the civil rights movement and organizational structure, see Morris, *Origins of the Civil Rights Movement.* On the community organizing attempts of SDS and SNCC, see Chapter 6 below and James Miller, *"Democracy Is in the Streets,"* chapter 10.

Decentralization moved to the center of Goodman's political thought while he was at IPS. Echoing C. Wright Mills, Goodman wrote, "Over-centralization is an international disease of modern times." The result of the disease was "powerlessness," a sense of being "trapped" by "so little say or initiative." The role of the intellectual engaged in movement discussions was to show how powerlessness could be overcome by extending the principle of decentralization beyond protest into other realms of policy. Here Goodman moved beyond the libertarian anarchism he had developed during World War II. Then he was counseling resistance to and refusal of a war machine— resistance based on his Freudian belief in the immutable nature of the individual. Now, Gestalt therapy suggested that cooperation and purposeful collective work were more necessary to a healthy life. Goodman accepted the need for centralization in certain areas of life (perhaps as a consequence of his planning background, captured in his earlier work with his brother, *Communitas*). Instead of fundamentalist anarchism or individualism, the philosophy he favored during World War II, Goodman embraced a pragmatic and reformist kind. He explained, "We ought to adopt a political maxim: to decentralize where, how, and how much is expedient. But where, how, and how much are empirical questions; they require research and experiment." Or as he put it elsewhere, showing his debt to John Dewey's pragmatism, "We must prove by experiment that direct solutions are feasible." Goodman took it upon himself to pursue this line of reasoning while at IPS.[41]

Goodman made numerous proposals based on the principle of decentralization. Sometimes these seemed almost tossed out at his readers, with little sense of just how realistic they were (few had serious empirical experimentation behind them). But some made a great deal of sense, especially those that had historical precedents. It is important to note that many of Goodman's proposals drew not from the eighteenth century (his seeming golden age) but from one of the greatest eras of state building in American his-

41. Paul Goodman, *People or Personnel,* 72, 5; "Some Prima Facie Objections to Decentralism" (1964), in *Decentralizing Power: Paul Goodman's Social Criticism,* ed. Taylor Stoehr (Montreal: Black Rose, 1994), 163; and *Utopian Essays and Practical Proposals* (New York: Vintage, 1964), 16. In a 1945 essay, Goodman had counseled "libertarians" to "work not to express our 'selves' but the nature in us. Refuse to participate in coercive or merely conventional groups" (*Drawing the Line,* 20). But this sort of spirit conflicted with *Communitas,* in which Paul and Percival Goodman argued for decentralized planning—the sort that could take care of centralized functions (such as transportation) while preserving the participation of citizens in local town life. The authors also saw the importance of coordinating certain functions so as to meet the basic needs of all citizens. See *Communitas,* 200–201 and throughout.

tory—the New Deal. Goodman envisioned partnerships between federal power and local initiatives. He called for "Youth Work Camps," like those pioneered by the Civilian Conservation Corps (CCC) during the Great Depression and by other federal programs dedicated to providing more opportunities in community service. He supported the arts projects under the Works Progress Administration (WPA) of the New Deal. Here funding went directly to community-based projects dedicated to creating local culture. This was distinct from the creation of the National Endowment for the Arts (NEA) under Lyndon Johnson; in Goodman's opinion, the NEA was over-centralized and created only "obnoxious official art of Arts Councils, glamorous culture centers, and suppers for the famous" rather than local and indigenous art experiments. In addition to local service and cultural programs, Goodman endorsed workers' self-management, something Mills had earlier supported. He believed that this required "wresting management from the businessmen." Goodman also called for community planners to take up "overall community planning" based on the ideal of an integrated neighborhood—with opportunities for work, play, and shopping all in one locale. All of these policies promised a certain amount of decentralization, even if they relied upon a strong government at the same time (i.e., planning). They also envisioned social change from a pragmatic standpoint, or what Goodman called "the pragmatist ideal of society as a laboratory for freedom and self-correcting humanity."[42]

Perhaps most important of all, Goodman applied the principle of decentralization to what Mills called the "cultural apparatus." Here Goodman unwittingly offered some answers to the questions posed by E. P. Thompson in his critique of Mills's theory of the cultural apparatus and its relation to the New Left. Goodman, like Mills before him, felt frustrated by the lack of control that an intellectual had once his or her work was appropriated by the cultural apparatus. For instance, a representative from CBS had approached

42. Paul Goodman: *Utopian Essays,* 266–73; "The Great Society," *New York Review of Books,* October 14, 1965, 8; *People or Personnel,* 59–60; *Growing Up Absurd,* 218, 220. Another tendency in the New Deal that Goodman clearly would have had sympathy for was the "grass roots democracy" of the Tennessee Valley Authority. For more on this tradition, see David Lilienthal's optimistic vision, *TVA: Democracy on the March* (New York: Harper and Brothers, 1944), and Philip Selznick's more pessimistic corrective, *TVA and the Grass Roots* (New York: Harper and Row, 1966). Though known for state building, many New Deal initiatives tried to build upon local activities. For more on this, see Harry Boyte and Nancy Kari, *Building America: The Democratic Promise of Public Work* (Philadelphia: Temple University Press, 1996), chapter 5.

Goodman about doing a show on him to be entitled "A Radical in Our Midst." Goodman knew of the dilemma that Thompson had raised in his letter to Mills and that Mills himself personally felt about his never-held televised debate on Cuba. If intellectuals went on television, their ideas were devalued or treated superficially; if they refused to go on the air, they did not reach people. With this dilemma in mind, Goodman wrote a scathing letter to the CBS representative, stating, "As an artist and intellectual I object immensely to having my brains picked and my personality exploited if I cannot really get across to the audience what I stand for and what I have to give." Essentially, Goodman was playing the hard line that Mills had counseled—work for the cultural apparatus on your own terms or not at all. But Goodman did more than this: he turned the principle into a policy. With James Baldwin, Norman Mailer, and the American Association of University Professors (a professional association started with the help of John Dewey in 1915 that protected academic faculty rights to free speech), he tried to place demands on the cultural apparatus when it turned to intellectuals for commentary. This was one of many ways in which something could be done, Goodman believed, to reform the cultural apparatus so that it facilitated intelligent and serious discussion.[43]

For Goodman, this reform was imperative for the New Left. As he saw it, "mass communications" made it almost "impossible to preserve substantive democracy." The centralization that worried him so much was clearly evident in the world of mass media. Goodman explained, "It is characteristic of our mass media that they interlock and reinforce one another." He therefore called on the federal government to "break up the networks." He also suggested a tax on mass media that could be used to fund independent and smaller media. All of this was in the hope of creating "thousands of small independent television stations, community radio stations, local newspapers that are more than gossip notes and ads, community theaters, high-brow or dissenting magazines." As he saw it, decentralized media would be *better* media—allowing more critical voices to enter public debate and exposing

43. Goodman to Herb Appleman (of CBS), October 10, 1963, Paul Goodman Papers, folder 6. For Goodman's statement on the question of whether to go on television, see his "Susskind and Sevareid," *The New Republic*, February 23, 1963, 26. It should be noted that Goodman's alliance with Norman Mailer here was a rare exception to his generally critical attitude toward this increasingly famous writer. At one point in an interview, Goodman described Mailer as an egotist and nihilist: see "An Interview on *Empire City*" (1965), in *Creator Spirit Come!* 261.

citizens to a diverse number of viewpoints. And going beyond Mills's vague call to reappropriate the cultural apparatus, Goodman showed how government could actually do something toward that end.[44]

In making these suggestions, Goodman became a movement intellectual. He took the principle of decentralization that he saw operating in the civil rights and peace movements—and that he had already developed himself— and extended it to public policy more broadly. At IPS, he found a way to speak *with and to* movements. Goodman never joined forces with those in power; rather, he lived up to Mills's ideal of an engaged intellectual who would "remain independent, do one's own work, select one's own problems, but direct this work *at* kings as well as *to* 'publics.'" Unlike Mills, though, Goodman lived long enough to find movements that would listen to his ideas. He had a chance to develop a theory of the New Left when movements were actually on the ground.

What a New Left Needed: Populism, Liberalism, or Both?

People don't want power as such. What they want is activity. They want to actualize potentialities, and insofar as they want power they want it in order to make decisions.
—Paul Goodman in "Power Struggles," 1962

Goodman's passion for the protest movements that were starting to make up the New Left drew him in long after his time at IPS. If anything, his interest in the movement only grew after 1965. At times, he became an activist intellectual with a propensity for overcommitment. When an organizer needed a speech made for a protest, Goodman made it. When a group needed a pamphlet, Goodman often promised to write it. Toward the end of his life, Goodman complained, "I have written more leaflets and sat at more press conferences than I like to remember." At the same time, though, he developed a political theory he hoped could help define the wider aims of

44. Paul Goodman: "Comment," *Liberation,* November 1965, 25; "Don't Disturb the Children," *The New Republic,* March 16, 1963, 28; "Television: The Continuing Disaster" (1963), in *Drawing the Line,* 103; *People or Personnel,* 212. Goodman wrote a series of articles for *The New Republic* on television (of which "Don't Disturb the Children" is one). Interestingly enough, he quit the series because of disagreements with the editors and because he found that he wrote too much about the behind-the-scenes centralization of the media rather than about what readers wanted—details on shows and programming. See "Goodman and T.V.," *The New Republic,* June 29, 1963, 31.

the movement. Here, Goodman spelled out some of the problems of modern liberalism. He admitted to "trying to sell" his own ideology to those in the New Left. The relation between the activist intellectual and the movement, then, went both ways. Goodman served the movement while trying to convince it of certain principles. His openness captured the democratic spirit that informed the work of New Left intellectuals.[45]

For Goodman, the New Left consisted of young people who were neither total conformists nor purely cultural rebels like the Beats (an idea simultaneously developed by William Appleman Williams). These young people took their education seriously and connected it with political engagement. He explained, "To my surprise, it is upon these kids that the social criticism by Riesman, Mills, Whyte, myself and others, has been having an effect." When Goodman wrote this in 1963, its sentiment clearly applied to the budding young intellectuals and activists who had founded Students for a Democratic Society (SDS), as well as to students engaged in the civil rights and peace movements (what many historians call the "first" New Left, which lasted until around 1965). By 1968, Goodman believed that "the Movement" consisted of those engaged in "anti-militarism, draft resistance, Negro rights, Student Power, Black Power." Essentially, the New Left had widened its membership and aims by 1968, largely due to the pressures placed upon it by the Vietnam War. Whether in its early incarnations or later ones, this was the movement that Goodman believed constituted "The New Left," a term that he used with a certain amount of critical distance.[46]

For Goodman, the New Left was unified by a critique of liberalism. Goodman's version of this critique was complex and deserves thorough attention. First, he followed C. Wright Mills in arguing that classical liberalism conflicted with an "economy dominated by monopolies." Free markets and decentralized politics were things of the past. Here Goodman suggested that he was not necessarily an enemy of liberalism but a critic who might be able to embrace certain strains within it. As he wrote in *Growing Up Absurd,* "Throughout the nineteenth and twentieth centuries, the radical-liberal program was continually compromised, curtailed, sometimes realized in form without content, sometimes swept under the rug and heard no more." The

45. Paul Goodman, *New Reformation,* 118, and "Transcript of Interview on the Subject of the New Left" (1968), Paul Goodman Papers, folder 529.

46. Paul Goodman, *Utopian Essays,* 280, and "In Praise of Populism," *Commentary,* June 1968, 30. On the periodization of the New Left, I follow James Miller's and Kirkpatrick Sale's accounts of SDS.

goal of the politically engaged critic here was to rediscover the radical hopes of liberalism and turn them into programs that a New Left could make real. This explains why a group like Americans for Democratic Action (ADA), one of the more important organizations for liberals at the time, would invite Goodman to speak at a gathering where members were trying to define a "qualitative liberalism." As John McDermott, the executive director of ADA, explained to Goodman, his organization wanted to examine the following: "What is involved in making work itself more satisfying? What is needed to make leisure time humanizing rather than debilitating?" The ADA took on these questions for reasons that warmed Goodman's heart: "We feel that not enough has been done to bring ideas and criticisms such as these within broad political and social conceptions which serve to re-ani-mate and re-direct progressive forces in this country." At times, this fit be-tween ADA's goals and his own social criticism suggested that Goodman might just be a radical liberal.[47]

But Goodman was like Mills in that his thinking about liberalism was dualistic. At times, he seemed to reject modern liberalism for being too *complicit* with centralization and state building. Goodman saw in modern liberalism a tendency toward technocratic policy and "social engineering." He aimed some of his animosity toward the "Great Society" programs, es-pecially the "War on Poverty." Goodman admitted that liberals had their hearts in the right place; after all, they *wanted* to empower the poor. But the bureaucratic nature of the welfare state "multiplied professional-client and patron-client relationships." Poor people were no longer citizens but passive consumers of state-provided services. Liberalism was then complicit with the "proliferation of social engineers" and the creation of "permanent clients." This critique could have conservative ramifications (in fact, during the late 1960s, neoconservatives appropriated this sort of language). Goodman never made it entirely clear whether these tendencies were *inherent* in the welfare state or whether they could be corrected for by more intelligent policy design. His own vision of renewing the New Deal and its partnership be-tween government and local communities might have suggested a certain

---

47. Goodman, *Growing Up Absurd*, 221, 15; John McDermott to Goodman, May 18, 1962 (this letter invites Goodman to an ADA gathering and includes a flyer from which I have quoted here). McDermott points out that "Mike Harrington" will be present. Paul Goodman seems to have participated in the event, since he outlined his speech in a set of notes available in the same folder. See "Notes for a talk to a meeting for Americans for Democratic Action (1962)," Paul Goodman Papers, folder 1149.

amount of optimism. But in the case of the Great Society, Goodman's critique seemed to reject the possibility of modern liberalism being democratic. After all, much of the Great Society's War on Poverty *had* tried to ensure "maximum feasible participation" through programs like the Community Action Program (CAP), under which local organizations played a role in welfare delivery. If Goodman saw passivity and bureaucracy *here,* where would he not? Indeed, Goodman seemed to suggest that modern liberals would always wind up generating bureaucracy and passivity. In 1966, he wrote, "If . . . money is spent for the usual liberal social engineering . . . it will not only fail to solve the problems but will aggravate them." When Goodman wrote like this, he suggested that modern liberalism was incapable of being democratic.[48]

Worse yet, Goodman's take on liberalism could tend toward hyperbole. Like other intellectuals during the 1950s, he at times depicted liberalism as the one and only political ideology in America. For instance, though he recognized a potential backlash against liberalism among conservative groups in America (including "businessmen and small-property owners . . . ; victims of inflation; displaced farmers"), he underestimated that possibility: "I do not think there is an important Radical Right in the United States." (Goodman was off in his political analysis here. Only three years after these words were written, Richard Nixon would band together precisely these groups of people—the "silent majority" who hated protesters and rioters— to combat the supposed excesses of the Great Society. Ronald Reagan had done the same thing two years earlier in the state of California, and George Wallace was starting to draw Democratic Party voters as well.) Suspecting that liberalism was the only game in town, Goodman made too much of it at times: "The rhetoric of Liberalism has become paternalistic and moderate and promises to lead us right to 1984." Worse yet, he suggested, "The liberal center is a corporate establishment tending to fascism." Goodman too quickly made generalizations about liberalism. Indeed, he admitted to liking the "apocalyptic rhetoric" developed by populists. Unfortunately, his tendency to use such rhetoric raised the object of his criticism—technocratic liberalism—to a stature it did not necessarily deserve.[49]

48. Paul Goodman: *People or Personnel,* 326; "The Great Society," 8; "The Liberal Victory," *New York Review of Books,* December 3, 1964, 7; "Urbanization and Rural Reconstruction," 8. For Goodman's equation of liberalism and centralization, see *People or Personnel,* 44–45. E. J. Dionne has recognized a certain similarity between the New Left's and New Right's critiques of the welfare state. See his *Why Americans Hate Politics* (New York: Simon and Schuster, 1992), chapter 1.

49. *People or Personnel,* 350, 32, 385, 348.

Goodman's alternatives to liberalism were better than his criticisms, and they could sometimes be seen as correctives, not rejections. Once again, he thought that certain tendencies within New Left movements offered the basis of his critique. Goodman situated the New Left student protests within a certain tradition in American history—one best described as Jeffersonian, populist, and democratic. Since the 1940s, Jefferson had been one of his heroes, and Goodman had always admired the populist revolt of the 1880s. When the New Left emerged, Goodman referred to the populist tradition (operating in the protest movements of the 1960s) as a corrective to the technocratic tendencies within liberalism. He wrote, "The promising aspect of [the movement] is the revival of populism, sovereignty reverting to the people. One can sense it infallibly during the big rallies. . . . The mood is euphoric, the heady feeling of the sovereign people invincible." As Goodman saw it, the nonviolent direct action used by movements for civil rights and against the Vietnam War was "an extension of traditional American populism." This was a powerful analogy. For as historians have shown, the original populists not only protested the demise of small farmers at the turn of the century but also called for government to support a decentralized cooperative system that could defend the farmers' way of life. The New Left could then be seen in a similar way—as an attempt to reawaken radical liberalism to its possibilities (its "missed revolutions") by infusing and energizing it with grassroots activism. Local initiative and national power could be married.[50]

Goodman wanted the New Left to follow the populists—to work through local power channels in order to reform the entire society along democratic lines. If the federal government could help by playing a role, Goodman argued, it should. After all, the civil rights movement succeeded by using "local action that has embarrassed and put pressure on Washington." Statements like these showed that Goodman wanted both local activity and the background assurance of social and political order. For Goodman, politics was about participation first and social stability second. Using his Aristotelian political philosophy, he explained that "a good polity is primarily a means of education to produce better people; it is only secondarily, though essentially, a means of balancing social interests and preserving social

---

50. Paul Goodman, *New Reformation,* 142, and "Reflections on Racism, Spite, Guilt, and Non-Violence," *New York Review of Books,* May 23, 1968, 18–23. For an important historical interpretation of the populist movement (one undoubtedly informed by New Left sentiments), see Lawrence Goodwyn, *The Populist Moment* (New York: Oxford University Press, 1978).

order." Therefore, Goodman asserted that local direct action needed to be squared with more conventional politics—including electoral and coalition politics as well as political structures ensuring stability. He embraced SDS's original call to "participatory democracy" and suggested that it could work within a representative system. Representative democracy succeeded, though, when politicians remained in contact with those who elected them and engaged in "public arguments" in town meetings. Goodman believed that the challenge was to mix participatory democracy and electoral politics. To do so, Goodman even wrote up a political platform in 1968, one that he wistfully hoped the California Peace and Freedom Party (a short-lived third party organized by white middle-class activists who were inspired by the peace and civil rights movements) might take up. The platform called for international monetary aid for local and indigenous attempts at social improvement, the dismantling of America's nuclear arsenal, the demilitarization of the universities, the provision of a guaranteed national income, and—of course—the decentralization of American society.[51]

Goodman's political thinking on the New Left produced interesting results. These can be seen in two areas: economics and race relations. Not surprisingly, Goodman eschewed state socialism. In fact, he conceded that "competitive free enterprise" was *better* than "socialist collectivism." But he argued that unregulated capitalism knew no bounds and wound up "parceling out . . . the commons as if it were on the market." He tried to balance out freedom and a public interest. He therefore endorsed the Scandinavian system, which created a "mixed economy" based upon consumer cooperatives, independent farming (the Jeffersonian touch), and some state-run industries. Local initiative—indeed, competition—needed to run alongside a state that was capable of looking after the public interest (and, if necessary, could take up some productive capacities). This did not seem too far from the mixed economy that liberals like John Kenneth Galbraith supported.[52]

51. Paul Goodman, *People or Personnel,* 13, 382–83, and "A Letter to John Lindsay," *New York Review of Books,* December 23, 1965, 9. Goodman's political platform is in "A Platform for Radicals," *Liberation,* February 1968, 6–7. His argument for a balance between direct democracy and conventional politics can be found in Goodman's "Comment" on a piece written by Richard Flacks in *Dissent* 14 (1967): 252. For a sample of Goodman's love of Jefferson, I rely upon his essay, "The Working Truth of Jefferson" (probably written during the 1940s). On the California Peace and Freedom Party, see James Elden and David Schweitzer, "New Third Party Radicalism: The Case of the California Peace and Freedom Party," *Western Political Quarterly* 24 (1971): 761–74.

52. Goodman, *Little Prayers,* 65; "Anarchism and Revolution," 223–24.

Another area of political thinking that Goodman took up was race relations. This, too, came out of dialogue with the civil rights movement, some
elements of which turned toward "black power" in the late 1960s. Goodman wanted to combine integrationism—which stemmed from his belief in
universalism and disgust for racism—and local power. Neither principle
could trump the other. Of course, this was easier for the early civil rights
movement than for the later black power movement, which dropped the
integrationist dimension for local control of black communities. The key
exponent of "black power," Stokely Carmichael, argued that African Americans should stop worrying about integration and instead organize themselves within the localities in which they found themselves—i.e., the communities that were often products of southern segregation (like Lowndes
County, the original home of the black power movement). Goodman appreciated the sentiment behind black power. He supported, for instance, the
Mississippi Freedom Democratic Party (MFDP), a predecessor to black
power protests. He even thought that the Student Non-Violent Coordinating Committee's 1965 decision to expel white members was "justified in
its claim that Negroes must work out their own emancipation." And, of
course, he supported decentralized communities taking on more power. At
the same time, though, he argued, "The reconstruction of society must in
the end transcend separatism." Here he sided with Martin Luther King Jr.'s
theory of nonviolence as a means of creating a "beloved community."
Goodman argued that those African Americans who expelled whites from
SNCC and hunkered down in local communities would still have to negotiate with whites in order to change the power structure. When they did, he
argued, they would have to rely upon guilt to get the attention of the white
people they had once pushed away. The result could not be healthy, for "no
good has ever come from feeling guilty, neither intelligence, policy, nor
compassion. The guilty do not pay attention to the object but only to themselves and . . . their anxieties." Such a politics would become anathema to
democracy. Goodman tried to balance integrationism (universalism) and local power (particularistic democracy). He wanted, in his own words, a
"structure open to 'integration' and containing a lot of Black Power" or
localism without "parochialism."[53]

53. Paul Goodman, "Objective Values," in *To Free a Generation: The Dialectics of Liberation,*
ed. David Cooper (New York: Collier, 1968), 126; "Reflections on Racism" (1968), in *Nature Heals,* 129; and "In Praise of Populism," 29. Goodman commented on the famous Ocean
Hill conflict, in which unionized teachers faced off against black parents who wanted more

Goodman's writing on race and the New Left clarified two things. First, it showed how he tried to balance radical democracy and decentralization with universal principles and wider political structures capable of monitoring these values. This was an important vision that other New Left thinkers would take up as well. Secondly, it showed that Goodman was very willing to criticize the course that the New Left was taking. His critique of black power was made from a sympathetic standpoint, but it was a criticism nonetheless. As the New Left moved into the chaotic time of 1968—marked by violent protests, assassinations, and bizarre political fissures within SDS—Goodman started to voice more criticisms, while never sliding toward neo-conservatism. Here we see the last stages of his committed intellectual work.

Criticizing the Brethren: The Intellectual's Delicate Balance of Engagement and the Politics of Truth

I don't think the movement is moving towards an ideology . . . I've been trying to sell them one myself for a long time, but it just isn't taking.
—Paul Goodman, "Transcript of Interview on the Subject of the New Left," 1968

I feel that if we in the revolutionary movement had more modest aims, we would make more sense.
—Paul Goodman, "Objective Values," 1968

---

control over their school. He sided with the union, but in a letter to the *New York Times Magazine* (February 23, 1969), he demonstrated where his own decentralist sentiments led: "Being powerful, the union should have been magnanimous. Though much in the right, it did not have to insist on its rights against these opponents, who needed to win" (12). Goodman's support of the MFDP can be seen in his "Great Society," 12. His balancing of universalism and regionalism are seen in his early essay on Jefferson, "The Working Truth of Jefferson," 2, and "A Southern Conceit," *Dissent* 4 (1957), where he wrote: "In the present economy and culture, almost the only earmark of the South as a region is the segregation; and if that's the case, forget it and draw the line elsewhere" (207). It is interesting to note that Goodman's critique of "identity politics" seems much more complex than many heard today. Goodman's appreciation of King's theory of nonviolence and the beloved community came out when he wrote, "In the end, all will have to live in community again. For this, a confronting conflict, mainly nonviolent, is better than either false peace or violence": see "The Duty of Professionals," *Liberation,* November 1967, 37. In "Reflections on Racism" (cited above), he explained that nonviolence "is the only realistic strategy, for it leads to, rather than prevents, the achievement of a future community among the combatants" (131). On black power's political philosophy, I rely upon Stokely Carmichael and Charles Hamilton, *Black Power: The Politics of Liberation in America* (New York: Random House, 1967). Goodman might have agreed with certain things in this book, but he would certainly have objected to its tendency to work from Third World examples (see below).

C. Wright Mills had bequeathed a difficult balancing act to New Left intellectuals. As he saw it, they could never give *complete* loyalty to an institution or movement. At the same time, they were *better off* engaging in movements that could rebuild democratic publics. This was not always an easy balance to strike. Goodman himself found it difficult. The nuances of his political thought never allowed him to torture reality in order to give undying support to the New Left. At the same time, he resisted the drift he had noticed early on in other New York Intellectuals toward neoconservatism (as it became labeled during the early 1970s). Instead, he criticized where criticism was due, making clear all the time that his arguments developed out of sympathy, not rejection.[54]

Many of Goodman's criticisms focused on certain political values and characteristics that seemed to be creeping up within the New Left. (Here he articulated what Irving Howe would later complain about in his writing on certain "styles" apparent within the New Left. Howe outlined negative patterns within student protest movements, patterns already under scrutiny in Goodman's own critique.) First, Goodman disliked the tendency toward political purity. For instance, when Staughton Lynd (then an avid spokesperson for the New Left: see Chap. 6 below) wrote a combative letter to *Liberation* against Bayard Rustin's condemnation of an anti–Vietnam War protest march in 1965 (which, from Lynd's standpoint, should not *exclude* communists), Goodman defended Rustin while making a larger point. He argued that when Lynd accused Rustin of compromising with those in power, he overlooked the fact that Rustin was "a brilliant tactician" who will "get more from Bobby Kennedy and Co." than vice versa. In accusing Rustin of selling out to the "Marines," Lynd threatened to become a "totalitarian moralist," Goodman argued. Ironically, Goodman started to see the limits of the *youthfulness* of the New Left—something he otherwise embraced—when it came to confrontations like these. He began seeing the importance of experience and wisdom in political activism. For instance, he counterposed A. J. Muste, a pacifist and anticommunist colleague of Rustin's, to younger New Leftists: "A. J. is an 'activist' as they, and they know that he is not going to compromise. . . . Yet he does not come on as though it were necessary to by-pass the present corrupt society and make, afresh, a paraworld. . . . He exists in human history and American history, whereas they cut themselves off from human history and American history." Moralism

54. On neoconservatives and their relation to the late 1960s, see Peter Steinfels, *The Neoconservatives* (New York: Simon and Schuster, 1979), and the conclusion to this volume.

and purity worried Goodman immensely, and he believed that history provided counterexamples upon which young New Leftists could draw.[55]

A tendency toward militant confrontation also bothered Goodman. Writing to a student leader engaged in antiwar protests in Berkeley (most likely
during the late 1960s), Goodman scolded, "Isn't it like the chief aim was to
confront the cops and cause disturbance, rather than directly to try to get
out of Vietnam?" Goodman was not simply a pacifist here. His complaints
were more serious than simply objecting to *any* use of violence. Indeed, he
admitted that "creative disorder"—including violence and riots—might be
necessary to prompt serious social change. He once wrote, "It seems that in
nonviolent civil rights protests it did not hurt to have some Black Panthers
in the wings." Goodman argued against any knee-jerk defense of "social
order"—the sort that neoconservatives were starting to articulate. But, as
Mills had argued, protest and civil disobedience relied upon public deliberation. Without this, they became meaningless, or were treated as reckless
behavior. Worse yet, as Goodman saw during the late 1960s, the New Left
could embrace confrontation for the sake of confrontation, for the pleasures
of feeling militant, rather than for bettering society. Groups like the Weathermen—the faction of SDS that started engaging in violent tactics, such as
bombings—made Goodman's point for him (a point that Arnold Kaufman
would take up later).[56]

Goodman argued that a philosophy of confrontationism did not draw
from anarchism; rather, it drew from authoritarian and vanguardist Leninism. Goodman hated the "neo-Leninist wing of the New Left" that started
to become more visible when students took over Columbia University in
1968. The students' protests against Columbia were legitimate, Goodman
argued, especially when they focused on the militarization of scientific research and the tendency of the university to treat the surrounding community of Harlem as a development zone for its own real estate interests (what
became known as gentrification). Nonetheless, there was a portion of SDS's
leadership—especially a new leader, Mark Rudd—that wanted to push
these protests toward needless confrontation. Goodman contended that

55. For Lynd's point about the protest and communists, see the piece in *Liberation,* November 1965, 31, and the writing in the A. J. Muste folder, Paul Goodman Papers, folder
470. For Howe's essay, see "New Styles in Leftism" (1966), in *Beyond the New Left,* ed. Howe
(New York: McCall, 1970).

56. Paul Goodman, letter to Marvin Garson, no date, Paul Goodman Papers, folder 165;
"The Duty of Professionals," 37, 36; *New Reformation,* 134.

young people like Rudd, hopped up on vanguardist power, provoked the police and refused to negotiate in hopes of prompting a "revolution." He saw this as youthful stupidity. Confirming Goodman's point, Rudd—who condemned Goodman's interpretation of the Columbia uprising in a letter to the *New York Times Magazine*—wound up joining the Weathermen.[57]

As Goodman saw it, the neo-Leninist tendency toward confrontation essentially denied the essence of *democratic political action*—that is, deliberation, compromise, and reform. The "neo-Leninist wing of the New Left," he argued, ignored "the piecemeal social revolution that is brightly possible." Goodman asserted that such a "piecemeal approach" was the "only safe and relevant way to transform our vastly complicated societies." He started drawing on resources within the liberal tradition—namely, the idea of tempered reform. The penchant New Leftists showed for models of authoritarian political change during the late 1960s betrayed their hopelessness. Indeed, Goodman saw militant confrontation and Leninism reinforced by a turn, among young leftists, toward Herbert Marcuse's theories of "one-dimensional society." Marcuse had argued that advanced industrial societies tended to close out possibilities of citizens thinking up alternatives to the status quo; rebels, therefore, had to embark on a "great refusal." Such thinking was dangerous and preposterous, as Goodman explained when he recounted a confrontation with Marcuse: "I can remember talking to Marcuse a year ago and I put it to him that the student revolt was very serious and he said, 'Ah, no, no. It will all be coopted.' But now since the episodes in Paris, he has changed entirely . . . He just doesn't read it right, and he just doesn't know the American scene at all; . . . he doesn't realize that the Americans have a long history of this populism." To think of society as one-dimensional, to deny the possibility of reform, to think of politics as confrontation, to embrace vanguardism—all of these tendencies militated against serious political activism. What was being ruled out here, according to Goodman, was "the politics of rational persuasion." This was the only firm and sane basis for radical activism.[58]

---

57. "The Black Flag of Anarchism," *New York Times Magazine,* July 14, 1968, 20, 15. Rudd's criticism of Goodman showed off his own pathology. Rudd lumped Goodman in with "most liberals," which was, needless to say, a serious mistake. See the *New York Times Magazine,* August 4, 1968, 56. Another student said that Goodman might have read too much into the students' refusal to negotiate, but confirmed that Rudd was far too manipulative. See J. P. Jordan's letter in the *New York Times Magazine,* August 25, 1968, 21. (Jordan represented Students for a Restructured University, a group that Goodman supported.)

58. Goodman: *New Reformation,* 158; "In Praise of Populism," 25; "Transcript of Inter-

Goodman was also concerned with a growing dislike for American values within the New Left (reflected in part by the popularity of European social theorists like Marcuse within the movement). Goodman's own discovery of patriotism during the late 1950s had never left him. When he listened to FSM activists in 1965, Goodman fretted about a "lack of patriotism" voiced by some. Significantly, Goodman did not see this attitude throughout the New Left—either within or outside of the Free Speech Movement. Indeed, he argued that draft-card burners were "intensely patriotic," counter to what most conservative critics believed. He tried his best to distinguish between a critical love of country and mindless loyalty. But he admitted to witnessing a growing propensity for anti-patriotism among New Leftists, especially those involved in the anti–Vietnam War protest movements during the later 1960s.[59]

In contrast to Mills, Goodman never pledged his support to Third World revolutionaries. Instead, he followed William James's critique of U.S. intervention during the Spanish-American War (see Chap. 2). Goodman was angry that America had betrayed its own democratic values of self-determination when it prosecuted the Vietnam War. He argued that "we drove the Vietnamese to heavy reliance on Russia and new China." But he never took the next step—endorsing the Vietcong. He purposefully stayed away from this: "I also think . . . that the North Vietnamese and many of the NLF have an ideological fanaticism that drives them beyond humanism and compassion." It became all too easy for New Leftists to embrace Third World revolutionaries, Goodman argued: "I am afraid that an advantage of the 'Third World' is that it is exotic, as well as starving; one does not need to know the inner workings." Ignorance made it all the easier to fetishize Third World revolution. That is why intellectuals like himself had to resist that tendency. Goodman suggested that protesters demand that "the U.S." get "out of Vietnam" but at the same time, "NOT side with the N.L.F." This might not have made for a catchy slogan, but the statement made perfectly clear Goodman's difference from C. Wright Mills, who had earlier

view on the Subject of the New Left"; *New Reformation,* 52. Goodman endorsed teach-ins in this spirit (an important point in relation to Arnold Kaufman's political thinking). See *People or Personnel,* 407.

59. Paul Goodman, "Comment," *Liberation,* November 1965, 26; Goodman to Mr. White, June 3, 1967, Paul Goodman Papers, folder 231.

decided to endorse the Cuban revolutionaries. Essentially, it was not necessary to embrace revolutionaries whom the United States was assaulting. Nor did the critic need to speak in the voice of the revolutionaries. A traditional American language of democracy and tolerance would suffice.[60]

All of this—anti-patriotism, confrontationism, a tendency to embrace foreign revolutionaries—represented an overall decline in the intellectual rigor of the New Left. During the later 1960s, Goodman complained that "nobody . . . is doing the . . . intellectual revolutionary job: philosophical discussion leading to program." Even those from whom he expected it failed to deliver. For instance, Goodman protested that *Liberation* had become "a movement sheet little better than the underground papers" (he took his name off the editorial masthead). Goodman argued that intellectual discussion in SDS seemed to stop sometime during the late 1960s. That explained the propensity for indefensible arguments against liberalism, a political theory that Goodman suddenly found himself defending. For instance, he argued, "In *New Left Notes,* we have lately heard of 'bourgeois civil liberties'; I hope we are not now going to hear of bourgeois clean air and water, bourgeois adequate space, bourgeois childhood, bourgeois mental health, etc." Sloppy thinking could explain a lot of the New Left's mistakes during the late 1960s, as far as Goodman was concerned. He made clear that the New Left relied upon the general intellectual infrastructure of liberalism—a faith in rights, freedom, and equality—that should never be discarded. As Arnold Kaufman would put it later, the New Left relied on the "finks" its membership lambasted. Once again, for Goodman, the *youthfulness* of the movement mattered here. Goodman argued that "the American young are unusually ignorant of political history" and philosophy in general. Barren of ideas, New Leftists within SDS embraced Third World Marxism or, worse yet, stopped thinking entirely in order to pursue militant protest.[61]

60. Paul Goodman: letter to the *New York Times,* December 15, 1965, Paul Goodman Papers, folder 205; letter to *Liberation,* no date, Paul Goodman Papers, folder 186; "Anarchism and Revolution," 222; letter to Dave Dellinger, no date, Paul Goodman Papers, folder 148.

61. Paul Goodman, letter to the editors of the *New York Review of Books,* no date, Paul Goodman Papers, file 203; letter to the editors of *New Left Notes,* Paul Goodman Papers, folder 198; "Black Flag of Anarchism," 10. Goodman's pessimistic view of SDS can be gleaned from his "Transcript of Interview on the Subject of the New Left."

Conclusion: The Intellectual as Ambivalent—but Never Resigned

Compared with the tempered enthusiasm of my previous books, this one is rather sour on the American young. In 1958 I called them "my crazy young allies" and now I'm saying that, when the chips are down, they're just like their fathers.

—Paul Goodman, *New Reformation: Notes of a Neolithic Conservative,* 1969

Goodman wrote these words in 1969. They reflected his deep pessimism about the future of the New Left. Still, Goodman never drifted toward neoconservatism. He still blamed his own intellectual colleagues—such as Danny Bell, Norman Podhoretz, and even the radicals at *Dissent*—for failing to provide young people with a set of ideas they could use to understand their world and frame intelligent political reform. In certain ways, the withdrawal and sellout of the New York Intellectuals drove the young into embracing crazy ideas like vanguard Leninism. Goodman was willing to criticize the New Left—to play the role of intellectual "wobbly," in Mills's terminology—while remaining sympathetic to its major goals. (After all, his own social criticism was responsible for many of those goals.) In that way, he remained a committed intellectual who never gave up on speaking the truth.[62]

Toward the end of his life (he died in 1972), though, Goodman grew tired. Even by 1964, he had expressed his psychological exhaustion with being a political intellectual: "I began to do more of this frantic practical proposal type of thing. But it was a reaction formation against despair. And I got tired." Five years later, as the epigraph to this section suggests, Goodman was showing serious signs of doubt about the promise of the New Left. He had thrown a lot of energy its way—had tried to "sell" it "an ideology," to use his own words—and watched as groups like SDS embraced neo-Leninism or took up mindless violence. Quite simply, Goodman had legitimate reasons to be disillusioned.[63]

Ending this story here, though, would be to miss the intellectual legacy that Goodman bequeathed younger activists and thinkers. He offered new ways to ground radicalism—both in American traditions of populism and psychological theory; he argued that universal aspects of humanity and national values could serve as the basis of New Left criticism. He showed the limits of a rebellion that was purely cultural in nature—namely, the Beats.

62. "On Liberal Anti-Communism," 41–42.
63. "Disturber of the Peace: Paul Goodman," *Mademoiselle,* February 1964, 105.

When movements emerged, Goodman demonstrated how an intellectual could listen to activists' demands while extending their insights beyond their inherent limits. Like Mills, Goodman made the reconstitution of a democratic public central to the New Left. Goodman also made clear that the New Left had to take decentralization seriously enough to propose policies that gave power back to average citizens. This included concrete policies—rather than Mills's frequent jeremiads—that decentralized the cultural apparatus enough to allow the voices of intellectuals to be heard by a wide range of citizens. He tried to balance participatory democracy and decentralization with the need for political and social stability. He showed how a love for the American republic and its core values need not become conservative. Most important, he showed how an intellectual could be both committed to a movement and critical of it at the same time. Essentially, Goodman put into practice the challenges of the New Left intellectual.

At the same time, Goodman manifested some weaknesses. Often, the proposals that he made in the name of practicality seemed *impractical*. It was hard to detect why he thought there was any political will behind them. For instance, Goodman never explained why a tax on centralized media conglomerates that would fund alternative media actually had a chance of becoming law. Michael Harrington and Christopher Lasch both complained that Goodman's political thinking and his "frantically written proposals" could sound terribly apolitical, essentially incapable of grappling with issues of political power or change. Goodman might have been proficient at writing proposals and even wished-for platforms that he hoped short-lived independent political parties would adapt, but he was not good at showing how those proposals could be enacted or those parties elected to power.[64]

There were other problems. Goodman's depiction of youth as a class seemed even more questionable than Mills's elevation of young intellectuals to the status of historical agents of change. Goodman never really defended the idea. Nor did he explain his criticisms of liberalism clearly. Like Mills, he sometimes dismissed liberalism and sometimes saw the good in it. When he came to defend liberalism against the silly attacks made by certain members of SDS, he sounded slightly hypocritical. After all, here was a writer who had once accused liberalism of tending toward fascism now arguing in favor of the same "bourgeois civil rights" that liberals had always faithfully de-

---

64. Michael Harrington, "On Paul Goodman," *Atlantic,* August 1965, 88–91; Christopher Lasch, "Getting Out of Power," *Commentary,* November 1965, 116–18.

fended. Finally, Goodman seemed to expect a bit too much from New Left protest movements. His political goal was to build upon the decentralized activism of the civil rights and peace movements, or as he put it, "to take similar democratic action toward other things that make life livable." However, taking principles that came out of protest movements and extending them to other areas of life was difficult. Protest movements had their own dynamics, and it was not clear that even the protesters believed that their decentralized methods should be applied elsewhere. For instance, many leaders of the civil rights movement *wanted* federal government intervention; they did not simply want to be held up as an example of decentralized power capable of handling everything at the grassroots level. On these counts, Goodman's political vision suffered from contradictions and a general lack of clarity.[65]

Nonetheless, Goodman's life and ideas made clear that Mills's hope for New Left intellectuals could be practiced without surrendering integrity (though not quite in the way Mills might have hoped). Goodman matched the principle of speaking truth with a fervid commitment to political causes in an almost unique way. What George Steiner said about him in 1963 applied at the end of his life as well: "Goodman has shown that a single person, backed by the pressure of vision . . . , can still initiate and sustain dialogue, amid the chaotic loudness of a mass society." That was precisely the role of the New Left intellectual, a role that Goodman practiced with courage.[66]

Of all Goodman's criticisms of the New Left, perhaps the most important was his argument that young people in the New Left needed to do a better job at setting out their intellectual vision. Movements, he believed, needed intellect, and vice versa. He was willing to provide some of that intellect, but he worried that young people did not have an appropriate insight into history, one necessary to make sense of his offerings. As he claimed, "The American young are unusually ignorant of political history." The challenge, of course, was to make the young understand what history could teach them. Goodman and other New Left intellectuals made their best efforts.

65. Paul Goodman, "The Children of Birmingham," *Commentary*, September 1963, 244.
66. George Steiner, "On Paul Goodman," *Commentary*, August 1963, 199.

4
William Appleman Williams, Republican Leftist: History as Political Lesson

The purpose of history is not to explain our situation so that we settle down as what C. Wright Mills has called Cheerful Robots in the Best of All Worlds. Neither is its function to propel us into orbit around some distant Utopia. . . . History's great tradition is to help us understand ourselves and our world so that each of us, individually and in conjunction with our fellow men, can formulate relevant and reasoned alternatives and become meaningful actors in making history.

—William Appleman Williams, *The Contours of American History,* 1961

History does not offer any answers. Men and women of the present must provide the answers. Hence the historian must return to his own society as a citizen and, with no quarter asked or given, engage other citizens in a dialogue to determine the best answers to these questions.

—William Appleman Williams, "The Crown on Clio's Head," 1970

William Appleman Williams tried to show the importance of studying history to the New Left and was once called "the dean of America's historical 'left.'" Of the intellectuals examined here, he most identified with his professional discipline. It follows that he was more comfortable with academia, though he, too, had serious doubts about the institution's capacity to nurture intellectual life. The fact that he was born in Iowa and never located for any extended period of time east of the Mississippi meant that he never made it into the orbit of the New York Intellectuals. He was too much of a midwestern populist and too enamored with the political leanings of Progressive-Era historians (e.g., Frederick Jackson Turner and Charles Beard) to travel comfortably in those circles. And unlike C. Wright Mills, a southwestern populist, he never tried.[1]

1. Flyer in the William Appleman Williams Papers, Ava Helen and Linus Pauling Papers, The Valley Library, Oregon State University, Corvallis, Oregon, folder of correspondence with Jeffrey Safford. For Williams's biography, I rely upon Buhle and Rice-Maximin, *William Appleman Williams,* as well as an extensive c.v. in the William Appleman Williams Papers, General Correspondence folder. Unfortunately, the papers from the period of Williams's life

Williams did share numerous traits with Mills and Paul Goodman, how-ever. First, he became politicized during World War II. But even here he was distinct. No pacifist or libertarian, he joined the Naval Academy in 1941 and served in the navy during the Good War. Even with this act of military patriotism, Williams would later recognize the "dehumanizing and undemocratic character" of the war machine that worried Goodman and Mills. At the time, he took note of a disturbing tendency documented thor-oughly in the pages of *politics*—the racist policies of the U.S. military and society at large. Still in the navy in 1945, Williams cut his teeth on political organizing by helping the National Association for the Advancement of Colored People (NAACP) with a local struggle for racial equality in Corpus Christi, Texas. African Americans in the town had demanded an end to discriminatory practices at local businesses and hoped to create what civil rights leaders would eventually call a more unified and "beloved commu-nity" in the process. Williams supported them and helped edit the NAACP newsletter, where he spelled out a democratic vision of racial equality. From this point onward, Williams clearly identified with the left. It is important that a desire to achieve racial equality—not economic equality—prompted his commitment.[2]

After serving in the military, Williams benefited from the G.I. Bill and attended the University of Wisconsin eight years after Mills had been there. While Mills took the pragmatists as his "intellectual godfathers," Progressive-Era historians served as Williams's intellectual inspiration. Like Mills, though, Williams pursued interdisciplinary studies and wound up being influenced by Hans Gerth, which made his historical work more attuned to current social issues and theories and hence more akin to Mills's pursuits. Like Goodman, Williams was also deeply influenced by the sort of teachings found among Gestalt therapists—especially the belief that self-actualization had to occur within face-to-face communities and through meaningful work. Indeed, like Goodman, Williams would become a vocal advocate of

---

that I focus on here—1945 to 1968—have largely been destroyed. Williams's interest in Pro-gressive-Era historians (among other things) placed him in opposition to the major historian among the New York Intellectuals, Richard Hofstadter.

2. Williams quoted in Buhle and Rice-Maximin, *William Appleman Williams,* 23; on Williams going left due to civil rights, see William Robbins, "William Appleman Williams: 'Doing History Is Best of All. No Regrets,'" in *Redefining the Past: Essays in Diplomatic History in Honor of William Appleman Williams,* ed. Lloyd Gardner (Corvallis: Oregon State University Press, 1986), 4–5.

decentralized communities serving as the basis of a future New Left and a healthy polity.[3]

This position emerged only after serious academic preparation in American history. At the University of Wisconsin, Williams decided to write a dissertation on a less-than-famous Progressive-Era activist and thinker, Raymond Robins. The focus on Robins framed the rest of Williams's intellectual life. Williams was impressed by Robins's Christian socialist beliefs and his work as an independent citizen-activist in the arena of foreign policy during and after the Bolshevik Revolution. Robins tried to carve out a more conciliatory foreign policy toward the Soviet Union in opposition to the adamant anti-Bolshevism of Woodrow Wilson. This focus on crafting an alternative vision for American foreign policy—through the pursuit of critical history—would always stay with Williams.[4]

The Young Academic

After completing his Ph.D. in 1950, Williams taught briefly at Washington and Jefferson College (outside Pittsburgh, Pennsylvania) and then drifted to Ohio State University, eventually landing a full-time position at the University of Oregon that lasted from 1952 until 1957. The same year he moved to the University of Oregon, he published his first book, *American-Russian Relations, 1781–1947*. Though a relatively dry monograph, the book established some major themes that Williams would pursue throughout his career. It also established him as a serious academic. An enormous collection of edited essays—*The Shaping of American Diplomacy: Readings and Documents*

3. On the influence of Gestalt therapy, see Buhle and Rice-Maximin, *William Appleman Williams*, 12. For Williams's view of meaningful work, see *The Great Evasion* (Chicago: Quadrangle, 1964), 171, and see 175 for an argument for decentralized economic production. On one count, Williams definitely differed from Mills and Goodman: he had absolutely no respect for pragmatism as a philosophy. He read it much as Lewis Mumford had read it in his classic book, *The Golden Day* (1926)—dismissively. William James became merely a bourgeois philosopher of laissez-faire, and Dewey's pragmatism was "an amoral if not actually unmoral philosophy" since it led to "an ameliorative adjustment to things-as-they-are." See *The Contours of American History*, originally published in 1961 (New York: New Viewpoints, 1973), 341, 405. But even on this point, I will show how Williams was actually closer to the pragmatists than he thought, especially when it came to his criticisms of America's foreign policy.

4. For more on Robins, see William Appleman Williams, *American-Russian Relations, 1781–1947* (New York: Rinehart, 1952), 128–35, and "The Outdoor Mind," *The Nation*, October 30, 1954, 384–85.

in American Foreign Relations 1750–1955—followed in 1956 and enhanced Williams's reputation. Indeed, by 1957, he was offered a teaching position at his alma mater, becoming a full-time professor at the University of Wisconsin until his departure in 1968—the period of time that I will focus on here.[5]

In *American-Russian Relations, 1781–1947,* Williams emphasized certain philosophies and events in the history of American foreign policy. Most importantly, he stressed the Open Door Notes issued by John Hay, Secretary of State, in 1898. In these notes, Hay turned his attention to the scramble for empire among European nations in what came to be known as the Third World. In relation to Asia, Hay declared that China should not be carved up by colonialists but rather made open to free trade. It was no accident, Williams never hesitated to point out, that the United States had an industrial surplus at this time, one desperately in need of a market. Here Williams followed Frederick Jackson Turner's emphasis on the closing of the frontier during the 1890s, situating the Open Door Notes within this historical juncture. Williams showed how America resolved the problem of a closing frontier by moving beyond its borders—making the world, quite literally, its market. He argued that this was as much a problem for intellectuals as it was for those who made foreign policy decisions. At the turn of the century, Brooks Adams, brother of the more famous Henry, asserted that America needed to prevent a slip toward "barbarism" by expanding into Asia. It would be necessary to do battle with Russia in order to pursue this course, Adams urged. In these arguments, Williams believed that he had glimpsed the future.[6]

He also perceived the future when the United States reacted to the Bolshevik Revolution during the aftermath of World War I. In *American-Russian Relations,* Williams documented how the United States installed troops in Russia and eastern Siberia in 1918, right after the Revolution, and aided the counterrevolutionary forces as much it could. Thus, for Williams, the Cold War did not begin in the aftermath of World War II or under President Truman's leadership; rather, it started in 1919. This historical fact served as a crucial part of Williams's overall argument. He would condemn those who lacked the historical acumen to understand the real origins of the Cold War.

5. This chapter will end its account in 1968, even though Williams lived until 1990. The reasons for leaving off here will become clearer as the narrative proceeds. I will briefly touch on his life after 1968 later in the book.

6. William Appleman Williams, *American-Russian Relations,* 30–33, and "Brooks Adams and American Expansion," *New England Quarterly* 25 (1952): 217–32.

By pushing those origins back to World War I, Williams stressed the hostility of the United States toward the USSR in the wake of its founding. He also pointed out that Americans like Senator William Borah and Raymond Robins protested their country's actions, even arguing for open trade and international aid for Russia. Williams believed, then, that the leadership of the United States had made a conscious and contested decision to pursue the Cold War as early as 1919.[7]

Of course, during the height of the Cold War, this sort of reasoning made one susceptible to charges of communism. Williams left himself open to such charges when he wrote, "The Soviets represented a desperate attempt on the part of the dispossessed to share the bounty of industrial civilization." To say this made Stalin seem as though he were just some misguided revolutionary with an understandable take on the state of poor people's bellies—not a dictator. This ran counter to the thinking about totalitarianism at the time (i.e., the political thought of Arthur Schlesinger or Hannah Arendt). In the context of Williams's relation to a budding New Left, it is important to note that while he blamed the United States for the origins of the Cold War, he never embraced Bolshevism or Stalinism. If anything, Williams argued, once radicals imported the model of the Bolshevik Revolution into America (which many members of the Socialist Party did in 1919, thus creating divisions and fissures within the Party), leftism became marginalized. Blinded by the supposed success of Lenin's triumph and ignoring the realities of American politics and society, radicals kowtowed to the Comintern and failed to discover their own indigenous traditions of communalism or socialism. Though he did not reject socialism completely, Williams saw no role for statist or Soviet communism in the thinking of a future New Left. Here, once again, was a legacy from the seedbed that Macdonald had laid down in *politics*.[8]

Williams ended *American-Russian Relations*, not surprisingly, with an anal-

7. *American-Russian Relations*, 105–6. On the resistance of Borah and Robins, see William Appleman Williams, "A Note on American Foreign Policy in Europe in the 1920s," *Science and Society* 22 (1958): 17, 19. For arguments that many Americans—especially liberals—ignored the deep-rooted history of the Cold War, see Williams, "The Cold War Revisionists," *The Nation*, November 13, 1967, 493.

8. William Appleman Williams, *American-Russian Relations*, 159; "A Proposal to Put the American Back into American Socialism," *New Politics* (Spring 1962): 41; Harvey Goldberg and William Appleman Williams, "Thoughts About American Radicalism," in *American Radicals: Some Problems and Personalities*, ed. Harvey Goldberg (New York: Monthly Review, 1957), 6. Williams's argument that the Bolshevik Revolution destroyed the possibility of an indigenous form of American socialism prefigured James Weinstein's book, *The Decline of Socialism in America, 1912–1925* (New York: Vintage, 1967). (For more on this work, see Chap. 6 below.)

ysis of George Kennan's doctrine of containment. As an ambassador to Moscow, Kennan had portrayed the Soviet Union as bent on foreign expansion. In 1947, Kennan called for the United States to take up "a long-term, patient but firm and vigilant containment of Russian expansive tendencies" and to pursue "adroit and vigilant application of counter-force at a series of constantly shifting geographical and political points." For Williams, Kennan's portrayal of the Soviet Union's "expansive tendencies" refused to recognize the *defensiveness* of the Soviet Union. Kennan conveniently ignored the fact that the United States "militantly opposed socialism long . . . before the existence of a Soviet State" and that it had stationed troops in Russia during the Revolution. Williams also believed that containment boded poorly for America, since it created a nervous posture among the foreign policy elite. He argued, "Freedom is not nurtured by states preparing for war. Rather does it find more opportunity to flower in the atmosphere of mutual accommodation achieved and sustained through negotiated settlements." Williams thus replayed the role of Raymond Robins during the Bolshevik Revolution and the 1920s. He argued for openness against what he perceived as his own age's form of Wilsonianism—containment.[9]

After completing *American-Russian Relations* and while editing *The Shaping of American Diplomacy,* Williams penned a number of more popular essays for *The Nation.* This famous leftist magazine was edited by Carey McWilliams, a historian himself and an activist who had worked for the civil rights of Mexican Americans. Largely with the guidance of McWilliams, Williams began to make a transition toward becoming a public intellectual. He already had some internal, intellectual nudging. After all, one of Williams's heroes was Charles Beard, who was acclaimed for his public writing skills. As Williams himself described Beard, "He considered the ivory tower as a refuge for the intellectual and moral coward—or scoundrel." Though more comfortable than Beard with academia, Williams tried, during the mid-to-late 1950s, to move beyond monographs like *American-Russian Relations* in order to write "sweeping and controversial works in the grand tradition," as one critic put it. By the early 1960s, just when Mills was considering a departure from Columbia University in order to write full time, Ronald Radosh, a graduate student, explained Williams's thinking on the

9. George Kennan, "The Sources of Soviet Conduct" (1947), reprinted in *Great Issues in American History,* ed. Hofstadter, 422, 423; Williams, *American-Russian Relations,* 281, 283. As Peter Novick points out, the idea that the USSR was predominantly defensive has largely been accepted by later historians: see Novick, *That Noble Dream: The 'Objectivity Question' and the American Historical Profession* (Cambridge: Cambridge University Press, 1988), 454.

matter in this way: "Williams . . . told me that he is thinking of stopping the writing of history and entering the debate on current questions, the role of the left, etc." In his *Nation* essays, Williams started to take some steps toward this point, turning away from being a purely academic historian to what Richard Hofstadter had labeled Charles Beard—a "public moralist."[10]

Williams's essays at *The Nation* are best situated within the cultural criticism of the 1950s—especially the more politicized sort that Mills and Goodman wrote. Like his two fellow New Left intellectuals, Williams put a distinct spin on cultural criticism. He did not condemn conformity as much as what he termed the "new Babbittry"—a small-minded conservatism that wallowed in economic prosperity. Sounding as if he had just read some Beat literature, he expressed concern about "apathy, unfocused discontent, and outright rebellion" and even cited Henry Miller's fear of an "air conditioned nightmare." Most important, Williams situated this general apathy alongside the blindness of containment thinking among America's foreign policy elite. Essentially, he merged his cultural criticism (which was admittedly much more impressionistic and thin in comparison with Mills's or Goodman's) with his criticism of America's foreign policy. After all, American prosperity could easily be connected to the Cold War and heightened military production, or what earlier New Left intellectuals had called the "permanent war economy." Among those studied here, though, Williams was the earliest thinker to connect cultural concerns about domestic America with its identity as a growing world power. Before the imbroglios in Cuba and Vietnam, Williams was clear that the cultural malaise condemned by the social critics of the 1950s had a direct relation to the realm of foreign policy.[11]

10. William Appleman Williams, "Charles Austin Beard: The Intellectual as Tory Radical," in *American Radicals,* ed. Goldberg, 299; Richard Melanson, "The Social and Political Thought of William Appleman Williams," *Western Political Quarterly* 31 (1978): 409; Ronald Radosh, undated letter to the editors of *Studies on the Left, Studies on the Left* Papers, Wisconsin State Historical Society, Madison, Wisconsin, box 8; Hofstadter, *The Progressive Historians,* 345. For more on Williams's love of Charles Beard's work, see David Noble, *The End of American History: Democracy, Capitalism, and the Metaphor of Two Worlds in Anglo-American Historical Writings, 1880–1980* (Minneapolis: University of Minnesota Press, 1985), 122. On McWilliams, see David Selvin, "Carey McWilliams: Reformer as Historian," *California Historical Quarterly* 53 (1974): 173–80. For McWilliams's views of Williams, see Carey McWilliams, *The Education of Carey McWilliams* (New York: Simon and Schuster, 1979), 244–45. For more on Beard as a public intellectual, see Thomas Bender's essay on him in *Intellect and Public Life.*
11. William Appleman Williams, "Babbitt's New Fables," *The Nation,* January 7, 1956, 3–6; "Needed: Production for Peace," *The Nation,* February 21, 1959, 152; and "American Century: 1941–1957," *The Nation,* November 2, 1957, 300.

Criticizing Empire: The Tensions of Republican Political Theory

America is neither the last best hope of the world nor the agent of civilization destined to destroy the barbarians. We have much to offer, but also much to learn.
—William Appleman Williams, "American Century: 1941–1957," 1957

Tragedy is defined by the confrontation and clash of two or more opposed truths.
—William Appleman Williams, "A Proposal to Put the American Back into American Socialism," 1962

When C. Wright Mills and Paul Goodman wrote their cultural criticism of the 1950s—*White Collar, The Power Elite,* and *Growing Up Absurd*—they rediscovered key values that stemmed from republican political theory. In writing on the white-collar classes, for instance, Mills reasserted the importance of property ownership in forging the independence of the older petite bourgeoisie. In criticizing the "organized society," Paul Goodman stressed honor and virtue as critical values of resistance. Williams renewed another republican theme—one that saw small polities constantly threatened by an inherent tendency toward corruption and empire. As historians like Bernard Bailyn and Gordon Wood have pointed out, this fear propelled the original American Revolution against what was perceived as a corrupt British empire. Trepidation about "the implications and consequences of empire" were passed down through the thinking of the anti-imperialists at the turn of the century, most famously William James. James had argued that America's "civic passions" should not be trumped by the sort of aggressive imperial expansion that he saw operating in the takeover of the Philippines. A deep-seated fear of empire was a strong intellectual tendency in American history.[12]

Williams belonged to this tradition, and his research into American foreign policy during the twentieth century confirmed the tradition's worst fears. The first book that came out of this research became his best-known work, *The Tragedy of American Diplomacy* (published in 1959, the same year as *Growing Up Absurd*). In many ways, this work followed the analysis already developed in *American-Russian Relations,* but organized itself around bigger themes, such as "tragedy" and "empire." The book highlighted Williams's shift toward becoming more of a public intellectual, albeit one who wrote

12. Robert Beisner, *Twelve Against Empire: The Anti-Imperialists, 1898–1900* (New York: McGraw-Hill, 1968), x. For James's critique of imperialism, I rely upon Cotkin's superb *William James, Public Philosopher.* See also chapter 1 of Thomas, *Alternative America.*

from within the academy. Looking back on the book in 1971, Williams argued that he took a "step back" from his monographic work and wrote "an analytical and interpretative essay directed to the *general public.*" The book mixed foreign policy analysis and political jeremiad. In it, Williams started to spell out a criticism of liberalism that would push him closer to the New Left constellation that was forming at the time, and the book's political messages will be our primary interest here.[13]

Once again, Williams followed the work of Frederick Jackson Turner (and Thomas Jefferson before him) in seeing the frontier as a defining factor in the American mind-set. He set the great "myth" of the frontier above another great myth: "This definition of the frontier as both a gate of escape from evil and an open door to prosperity and democracy is much more central to America's difficulties of perspective than the Gospel of Progress." The closing of America's frontier during the 1890s—the starting point of Frederick Jackson Turner's famous essay, "The Frontier in American History"—coincided with the death of laissez-faire capitalism and the rise of the modern bureaucratic corporation. The 1890s would remain the most important transitional decade in Williams's historical analysis, even as many other parts of his thinking changed. So too would the Open Door Notes, which he continued to situate alongside the growth of corporate power during the 1890s.[14]

In *The Tragedy of American Diplomacy,* Williams turned the Open Door Notes into what he called an American *Weltanschauung,* or worldview. The idea of the globe serving as an open door, essentially a market for America's goods and way of life, was developed in the thinking of key intellectuals during the 1890s (Brooks Adams and Frederick Jackson Turner, for instance) and gained staying power long past the turn of the century. It served, Williams argued, as "a classic strategy of non-colonial imperial expansion." America could stand up to imperialist countries that tried to colonize the Third World directly and brutally, thus appearing humanitarian, while also

13. William Appleman Williams, "America II Continued," *Partisan Review* 38 (1971): 67.
14. William Appleman Williams in "Foreign Policy and the American Mind," *Commentary,* February 1962, 157; *The Tragedy of American Diplomacy* (1959; reprint, New York: Delta, 1962), 21. In 1968, Williams still argued for the importance of the frontier: see his "Rise of an American World Power Complex," in *Struggle Against History: U.S. Foreign Policy in an Age of Revolution,* ed. Neal Houghton (New York: Washington Square, 1968). The centrality of the 1890s is still seen in his *Roots of the Modern American Empire* (New York: Random House, 1969), even though here he drove back America's expansionist philosophy to its earliest farmers.

defending its own self-interest—markets for its surplus production. Williams wrote, "The policy of the open door was designed to clear the way and establish the conditions under which America's preponderant economic power would extend the American system throughout the world without the embarrassment and inefficiency of traditional colonialism." Woodrow Wilson, for instance, epitomized the Open Door outlook, because he "integrated crusading idealism and hard-headed economics." It was not always clear if ideas (moralism) or material interests (corporate interests in foreign markets) drove the Open Door *Weltanschauung*. As Williams would explain later, the "demands of the corporation community and other economic groups were synthesized with theories of the intellectuals." Of course, this explanation did not necessarily clarify which—corporations or intellectuals, economic or idealistic interests—fueled America's ambition to expand. But for Williams, such clarification did not matter as much as the fact that this *Weltanschauung* prevented Americans from understanding their appropriate role in the world.[15]

While he believed that the Open Door *Weltanschauung* had a long history, Williams also found a contemporary leader who epitomized it. Here, he and C. Wright Mills shared an enemy. John Foster Dulles, Secretary of State under Eisenhower, symbolized all that Williams disliked in American foreign policy. When Dulles accepted his position in 1952, Williams argued, he "provided . . . the definitive statement of Open Door Policy." He explained this by alluding to Dulles's biography: "Synthesizing the moral imperialism of his missionary background with the necessity of economic expansion of his banking experience, Dulles announced that he would liberate the Russians and the Chinese from 'atheistic international communism' and usher in the American Century." Dulles provided a way for Williams to bring his analysis of the Open Door *Weltanschauung* up-to-date in order to face the changing terms of the post–World War II era. It was often difficult to see just what material interests drove America to "contain" or "roll back" Soviet expansion in Eastern Europe (and Williams never paid sufficient attention to this area). Nonetheless, Williams argued that the fear of a return to pre–World War II depression was much more pervasive than previously thought

15. William Appleman Williams, *Tragedy,* 43; "The Large Corporation and American Foreign Policy," in *Corporations and the Cold War,* ed. David Horowitz (New York: Monthly Review, 1969), 80; *Tragedy,* 67. For more on Williams's lack of clarity on material versus ideal interests driving foreign policy, see Bradford Perkins, "*The Tragedy of American Diplomacy,* Twenty-Five Years Later," *Reviews in American History* 12 (1984): 6.

and that this paranoia framed a great deal of American foreign policy thinking. For him, the Open Door philosophy undergirded the post–World War
II conflict with the Soviet Union: "The convergence of a sense of economic
necessity and a moral calling transformed the traditional concept of open
door expansion into a vision of an American Century."[16]

When forced, Williams usually placed most of the blame for the Cold
War on American shoulders. In 1953, Williams already saw some softening
in Stalin's foreign policy and worried that the United States did not react
appropriately. He argued, "The West's refusal to match Stalin's policy is risk-
ing the triumph within the Kremlin of those Soviet leaders who argue for
world revolution." Hence, America pushed Russia's back to the wall. It had
done this for quite some time, and nuclear weapons only made the situation
worse. Williams wrote, in *The Tragedy of American Diplomacy,* "Particularly
after the atom bomb was created and used, the attitudes of the United States
left the Soviets with but one real option: either acquiesce in American proposals or be confronted with American power and hostility." Though he
claimed that "to say this is not to say that the U.S. started or caused the
Cold War," it seemed that he clearly blamed the United States while depict-
ing the USSR as defensive. In doing this, Williams made the USSR a bit too
innocent, as if its conquest in Eastern Europe was *purely* motivated by fear.
Alternatively, he made the United States a bit too sinister and flattened out
tensions within its foreign policy. For instance, he labeled the Truman Doctrine and the Marshall Plan "two sides of the same coin of America's traditional program of open-door expansion." Though they might have had the
same ambition in mind—to prevent the spread of communism—the programs were also quite different; one called for military support of practically
any group opposed to Soviet communism, relying upon military force (and
the questionable act of giving aid to one's enemies' enemies), while the
other gave financial support to Western democracies, building back economies and polities. By collapsing the two approaches, Williams failed to
understand what made them significantly different. One led to overseas in-
vestment, the other to proxy wars. Williams thus overlooked a key distinc-
tion within liberal thinking on foreign policy.[17]

In certain ways, Williams's critique paralleled the development of a realist
position on American foreign policy, a view most clearly articulated by Wal-

16. *Tragedy,* 275–76, 232, 200.
17. "Moscow Peace Drive: Victory for Containment?" *The Nation,* July 11, 1953, 30;
Tragedy, 206, 270.

ter Lippmann. A Wilsonian in the direct wake of World War I, Lippmann had changed his mind in the aftermath of World War II on how much morality should play a role in framing foreign policy. Renewing an older conception of "spheres of influence," Lippmann believed that the United States must both accept Soviet expansion and develop a sense of its limited capacity to change the world in its own image. Williams implicitly agreed with many of Lippmann's arguments. To a large extent, Williams wanted America to realize its own hubris in thinking that it could turn the world into a new frontier for its own expansion or that it could force every other nation to emulate it. At the same time, though, Williams's arguments differed from Lippmann's. While Lippmann believed that there needed to be an American sphere of influence, Williams held to the principle of self-determination—even if it threatened America's backyard interests, such as Cuba. Here was Williams's own moralistic universalism. But even with this difference in mind, the similarities between Williams's budding New Left criticism of foreign policy and Lippmann's hardheaded realist approach are remarkable. It makes clear that original New Left thinking on foreign policy was not that far outside of the mainstream.[18]

The real question for Williams was whether America could change the course it had taken in foreign policy. Unlike Lippmann, he wanted the United States to rethink the idea that it had a right to its own sphere of influence. But it was unclear whether Americans could actually do this. The term "tragedy," especially, did not portend too well for galvanizing people to hit the streets in protest, conjuring up, as it did, feelings of passivity in the face of the uncontrollable. In fact, C. Wright Mills had criticized his fellow New York Intellectuals for using the term during the 1940s and 1950s, arguing that it betrayed these thinkers' passivity. Williams's use of the term, though, was complex.

There *was* an element of passivity. For instance, Williams wrote, "The tragedy is that none of" the bad things done in America's foreign policy were "done with evil intent." The frightening truth was that actions were carried out with little or no awareness of their consequences. Sounding like the pragmatists he criticized, Williams argued that Americans often acted on

18. For Lippmann's thought on foreign policy, I rely upon Ronald Steel, *Walter Lippmann and the American Century* (New York: Vintage, 1980), 408, and Diggins, *The Proud Decades,* 66. Perkins also notes that Williams's work shared certain things with the realists: see his "*Tragedy of American Diplomacy,*" 33. It should be pointed out that many historians believe the realist critique was most effective at ending the Vietnam War.

"abstractions" and reduced other countries and peoples "to things to be manipulated in the service of the verification of the abstraction." And yet there was still the possibility of enlightenment—of asking questions and overcoming what William James had earlier called the "blindness" of those who came to dominate others. Like Goodman and Mills, Williams was a rationalist. Though he believed in tragedy (an irrational and fatalistic belief stemming from antiquity and Christianity, many would argue), he also believed in rationally informed political change. While tragedy led to passivity or learning to live within certain limits, rationality led to deliberation and eventual change. Williams argued, "The truly essential need is to reexamine our conception of saving other people and societies." By calling into question their country's foreign policy aims, critics could feel confident that Americans might listen. After all, Williams argued, Americans were "neither hypocrites nor sophists, they simply accepted and believed the idea that American expansion naturally improved the world." The question still remained: how could the critic crack this naivete?[19]

This question was much like the one that Goodman faced as a critic during the 1950s, and Williams resolved it the way Goodman had. He became what Michael Walzer has called a "connected critic"; that is, he spoke the language of his fellow citizens and used their ideals critically to increase their self-understanding. He explained, "The tragedy of American diplomacy is not that it is evil, but that it denies and subverts American ideas and ideals." Williams believed that there were central concepts in the American political lexicon—especially democracy and self-determination—that could be used by critics waging a debate. Critics need not speak a foreign language to wake up their fellow citizens. Williams argued, for instance, that the "principle of self-determination" when "taken seriously . . . means a policy of standing aside for peoples to make their own choices, economic as well as political and cultural." Essentially, the American idea of self-determination—so influential in the nation's founding—conflicted with America's meddling in Third World affairs. Though he would come to criticize William James's philosophical pragmatism, he certainly sounded like the grand old pragmatist who had earlier

19. Williams: *Tragedy,* 173; "Rise of an American World Power Complex," 19; "Needed: Production for Peace," 153; *Tragedy,* 88. Robert Westbrook pointed out to me that Barton Bernstein used to distinguish between "hard" and "soft" anti-imperialism. The first view sees imperialism as inherent to American foreign policy (the sort of view espoused later by Gabriel Kolko); the latter sees imperialism more as something capable of being overcome. Williams would clearly fit into the latter tradition.

condemned the U.S. conquest of the Philippines. James had argued that imperialism—with its desire to impose a unitary vision on a pluralistic world—denied reality and the claims of the oppressed. Like James, Williams argued, "An acceptance of diversity is the key to a morally defensible and a pragmatically effective diplomacy." Here again there was a realist, pragmatist, and Lippmann-like component to Williams's arguments. At the same time, Williams balanced this with his own moralism. The critic, from his perspective, had to point out the contradiction between Americans' core values and their attempt to impose their way of life on the world. For Williams, America was not evil, just mistaken, as C. Wright Mills had argued about the Cuban Revolution and as Paul Goodman had asserted later about Vietnam.[20]

This argument seemed abstract at times. Was there really any existing alternative to the Open Door policy? Many would say that Williams had few answers to this question. In 1970, for instance, Michael Harrington argued that Williams's analysis tended toward gloomy conclusions; more recently, David Noble claimed that Williams "had no usable past, no significant American traditions" in which to ground his hope for change. These are compelling charges, and we will return to them later in more detail. For now, suffice it to say that Williams did see indigenous opposition to American foreign policy in the work of Raymond Robins and Senator Borah—both anti-imperialists who spoke an American language. Of course, some would argue (as many had when he was alive and active) that Borah was simply an isolationist. Williams conceded the point and tried to tease out the rational, radical, and morally compelling components in isolationist thought. He wrote: "The isolationists argued that the bedrock purpose and responsibility of a society involved transforming a social system into a true community, and that its humane and practical obligations to, and intercourse with, the rest of the world would be honored and fulfilled in direct proportion to its success in that eternal quest." Seemingly, isolationists renewed John Winthrop's famous conception of America as a "city on a hill"—a new country with a moral obligation to serve as an example to the rest of the world through its own *domestic* activities. Isolationists were not simply ducking out of responsibilities. Rather, they provided a rigorous alternative for Americans to practice, one that checked expansion and encouraged domestic democracy, an ideal that Williams embraced.[21]

20. William Appleman Williams, *Tragedy,* 292, and "The Irony of the Bomb," *The Centennial Review* 4 (1961): 380.

21. Noble, *The End of American History,* 132; Michael Harrington's contribution to "America II: A Symposium on the Work of William Appleman Williams," *Partisan Review* 37

Williams also rejoiced when Kennan turned away from containment policy during the 1950s by arguing that the policy made it difficult to discern what was a worthwhile battle and what was not. Williams explained that Kennan had recently called "for an end to the rigidity and single-track diplomacy that he had done so much to initiate." By recognizing his own faults, Kennan showed a great deal of humility, the sort that Williams desired from America's foreign policy elite. Indeed, Williams referred to the "eloquence" Kennan displayed when he recanted containment. Despite being a leftist and democrat, Williams always had a great deal of hope for changes within the elite ranks of American society (the sort of hope that Mills and Goodman had for a more cultivated and intelligent power elite). Of course, tension remained here, since so much else of his historical analysis cut against any expectation that the "tragedy" of American diplomacy could be surmounted by a change of mind-set among America's elites. Once again, the strains within New Left thinking emerged. Just how that tension played itself out in Williams's case will become clearer.[22]

Rejecting Invitations from Liberal Intellectuals

The Tragedy of American Empire received numerous reviews, some of them quite hostile. One of the relatively favorable reviews, though, was particularly notable. It was written by Adolf Berle, the man C. Wright Mills had been preparing to debate when Mills suffered his fatal heart attack. At the time he wrote the review, Berle was just about to accept President Kennedy's offer to become an adviser on Latin America. As a member of Kennedy's inner circle, Berle offered Williams the position of assistant. Williams refused. He shared the model of the intellectual developed by Mills and Goodman: for all three, the intellectual was to remain independent of institutions of power while remaining committed to political discussion and a democratic public. Williams's vision was made clearest in his comment on

---

(1970): 504; William Appleman Williams: "China and Japan: A Challenge and a Choice of the 1920s," *Pacific Historical Review* 26 (1957): 275; *Tragedy*, 122; "Taxing for Peace," *The Nation,* January 19, 1957, 53; "The Irony of the Bomb," 380. The idea that Williams renewed Winthrop's vision of a "city on a hill" is not far-fetched. Indeed, Williams cited Winthrop approvingly, arguing that he had developed a sort of Christian socialism and had a "sense of the general welfare." See *Contours of American History,* 94.

22. Williams, "American Century," 299; *Tragedy,* 7. For more of Williams's thoughts on Kennan's turnaround, see his "Second Look at Mr. X" (1952), in *A William Appleman Williams Reader,* ed. Henry Berger (Chicago: Ivan R. Dee, 1992).

the intellectual liberal who decided to work most closely with Kennedy, Arthur Schlesinger Jr. For Williams, as for Goodman, Schlesinger "valued his future influence more than his present morality." Or in words more suitable to Mills's framework, Schlesinger gambled away the politics of truth to embrace political efficacy.[23]

Williams disliked Schlesinger not only for his model of intellectual life but also for his liberalism, a political philosophy that received more and more of Williams's derision. The complaints about liberalism were many. First, as Williams saw it during the late 1950s and early 1960s, liberalism overlooked poverty and failed to acquire civil rights for African Americans. Of course, this would change under the presidency of LBJ, a leader Williams admired much more than JFK. But more important than these historical oversights was the general outdatedness of liberalism. As C. Wright Mills and Paul Goodman had argued, classical liberalism grew out of a nineteenth-century context of small businesses and government, and things had changed since then. Williams argued, similarly, that there was a "programmatic bankruptcy of traditional American liberalism. This failure stems not so much from having succeeded as from having survived without ideas for so long that the technique and the habit of thinking about basic problems are themselves threatening to become relics of another age." The idea seemed to be not that liberalism was rotten to the core, but rather dated and tired and in need of some rethinking and larger restructuring. Here again, Williams's political thought seemed akin to that of Mills.[24]

This restructuring might well have occurred—except that modern liberalism had made a Faustian pact with the bureaucratic corporation, as Williams contended in his next major work, *The Contours of American History.* He located this pact within the New Deal. In fairly abstract terms, he argued that "The New Deal saved the [capitalist] system. It did not change it." What he meant was that FDR—whom Williams labeled "one of the

23. William Appleman Williams, *The United States, Cuba, and Castro* (New York: Monthly Review, 1962), 152. The review and offer by Berle are documented in Buhle and Rice-Maximin, *William Appleman Williams,* 112–14, and Jordan Schwarz, *Liberal: Adolf A. Berle and the Vision of an American Era* (New York: Free, 1987), 320–22. For more on Berle and JFK, see Reeves, *President Kennedy,* 94. A good example of Williams's pride in being an independent intellectual can be seen in the way he described his own work. In the acknowledgments to *Contours of American History,* Williams embraced intellectual craftsmanship, writing, "This was not an organized project involving a vast farming out of various research assignments to students or colleagues." See also *Contours of American History,* 489.

24. William Appleman Williams, "Go Left or Go Under," *Liberation,* April 1957, 14.

most conservative representatives of the American feudal gentry to hold the Presidency"—simply accepted the large corporation and tried to ease its impact on American life. This was not exactly a Marxist pronouncement that the state was the "executive committee of the ruling class," but it came close. As the units of the economy grew in size, the government followed suit. Williams called the result "corporatist syndicalism"—larger and larger units in government and economic production. By regulating the corporate economy, modern liberals became complicit with it. Their pledge to the Open Door only highlighted their acceptance of corporate power. After the New Deal, these tendencies of liberalism grew worse. Yet at the same time, Williams waffled, asserting that the local relief efforts of the New Deal were "noble." He brushed aside this more nuanced and conflicted read of modern liberalism, though, when he pointed his finger at the Kennedy administration, staffed with liberal intellectuals. He minced no words in characterizing Schlesinger's pact with the JFK administration—a pact, he believed, that symbolized the poverty of American liberalism *tout court:* "In the United States, the so-called Vital Center—meaning a coalition of reformers and enlightened conservatives—has for some 75 years attempted to find or create a new frontier in overseas economic expansion, or in the Keynesian accumulation of capital from the taxpayer to sustain the corporation, or in a combination of both approaches." Liberalism seemed reduced to an insurance plan for corporate stability. This strain of reductionist thought wound up being popular with younger intellectuals and appeared in the pages of *Studies on the Left* (see Chap. 6).[25]

The result of corporate and governmental centralization was civic apathy. For as institutions grew in size and became bureaucratic, Williams argued, "the citizen" had no "effective, institutionalized leverage on the crucial and centralized decisions affecting every phase of his life." Williams complained that liberalism depleted the ideal of participatory democracy. He wrote, "In a syndicalist system composed of interest-conscious functional groups which exert extremely powerful and effective pressure on political leaders, how does the citizen–taxpayer either participate to any significant extent in the formula-

25. Williams, *Contours of American History,* 439, and "A Proposal," 41. On these points, see also "Go Left or Go Under," 15. Though Williams had no love for the New Deal, he seemed impressed by FDR's commitment to public works (see *Contours of American History,* 441), an admiration he shared with Goodman. This illustrated a tension in his assessment of liberalism, since the public-works principle was central to the New Deal philosophy of government.

tion of proposals or protect himself against decisions taken in his name which subject him to double jeopardy in matters of economics or civil rights?" Essentially, liberalism's pact with large corporations and with what would later be termed "big government" created a crisis for the American ideal of democracy. Sounding like Mills and Goodman, Williams explained, "The breakdown of dialogue and reciprocal influence between the tiny community of power and the society-at-large indicates a withering away of representative government and its replacement by administered choices, paralleling the contraction of the free marketplace and its replacement by administered products and prices." Liberalism failed to understand that its Faustian pact with large centralized corporations spilled over into a deadening impact on everyday politics and threatened the possibilities of a more participatory democracy.[26]

The point was made clearer in Williams's criticism of America's labor unions—central actors within America's liberal order. Williams extended Paul Goodman's and C. Wright Mills's views on labor unions into the areas of foreign policy and history. By the 1920s, Williams argued, labor unions had pledged themselves to "conservative syndicalism" and supported the foreign expansion orchestrated by American corporations. He stated, in the bluntest terms, "Labor foreign policy was (and is) corporation foreign policy." Labor unions—like liberals—failed to offer any alternative to corporate power, falling prey to lame pragmatism at home and abroad. Williams abhorred the "gimmie a bigger cut of the take" mentality he saw operating within unions. Like Mills, Williams was influenced by G. D. H. Cole and wanted labor unions to think beyond corporate forms of power and consolidation. He even suggested that unions take on the cultural apparatus, especially the mass media, at which Mills and Goodman aimed so much of their criticism. For instance, Williams argued that "communications workers" should call for a "passive resistance campaign against all merchandise advertised on TV until the quality of the programs ceased insulting their intellectual and emotional maturity." Though the point remained underdeveloped, Williams hoped that unions could make a qualitative criticism of the American way of life, rather than settle for higher wages negotiated through contracts. But aside from a few one-liners, he failed to explain how this might happen. Like Mills, Williams was deeply pessimistic about the possibility of unions (or liberalism more generally) to buck the status quo.[27]

In the end, Williams believed that liberals were far too acquiescent to-

26. Williams, *Contours of American History,* 448, 447, and *Great Evasion,* 18.
27. Williams: *Contours of American History,* 431; *Tragedy,* 129; "The Large Corporation," 73; "Go Left or Go Under," 15, 16.

ward the corporate economy. Their pact with institutional centralization—in the realms of government and of business—doomed any prospect of participatory democracy, an ideal that Williams increasingly embraced. Liberalism's pragmatism made it amoral in relation to questions of power. Unlike Mills and Goodman, Williams seemed to see little that was redeemable in liberalism, the classic or modern variant. His hostility would become clearer as American liberals faced one of their biggest challenges of the 1960s—the aftermath of the Cuban Revolution. Williams would become ever more relieved that he had refused Berle's offer. In so doing, he had personally rejected the tragic path taken in Cuba, a path that symbolized, from his perspective, the overall bankruptcy of American liberalism.

Cuba: The Endgame of Liberalism's Tragedy

The liberals are becoming mere role players in a Greek tragedy.
—William Appleman Williams, "The Cold War Revisionists," 1967

For C. Wright Mills, Cuba marked a crisis for America's foreign policy; for Paul Goodman, Vietnam expressed that crisis. Williams situated both events within an overall tragedy of American diplomacy. Like Mills, Williams started early in his anti-imperialist jeremiads by writing a pamphlet that protested U.S. intervention in Cuba. Williams's pamphlet failed to find the widespread audience that Mills's obtained, however. Nor did Williams write romantically in the voice of the rebels. Rather, Williams explored history to analyze current U.S.-Cuba relations and offer alternatives to military intervention (Mills did too, but not to such an extent). Williams's attitude toward Cuba ás an example of revolutionary practice, or what was referred to as "actually existing socialism," was not always clear. Nonetheless, as we will see, he was mostly concerned with American identity as it related to its attempted conquest and domination of Cuba.[28]

The case for history was not a difficult one to make. As Williams pointed out, President McKinley argued that America's original intervention in Cuba—during the Spanish-American War at the turn of the century—was forced upon him by the press and by those who had material interests there. JFK made a similar claim when he decided to intervene. Additionally, as

---

28. Williams's pamphlet was written to refute Theodore Draper's book on Cuba, *Castro's Revolution* (1962), which meant that it read, at times, like an extended book review. This inherently limited its reach and audience.

Williams showed, American intervention had its precedents, since after 1898, the United States had installed troops in Cuba in 1906, 1912, and 1917. The United States also had a long history of questionable diplomatic relations with Cuba, especially seen in FDR's befriending of Cuba's dictator, Batista. Accounting for this history, Williams argued, would lead to a reexamination of America's present role in Cuba.[29]

If it did reassess these events, America would recognize that its own policies—though originally framed by the Open Door—had become colonialist. The Open Door in Cuba became a closed door, so to speak. Originally an opponent of Spanish colonization, America became a colonizer itself. As Williams explained much later after the Cuban Revolution, "[t]he freedom that" America "wanted to extend Cuba so that it could develop its own potentialities as part of the American marketplace had within a generation been transformed into the liberty to define and practice freedom as approved by the United States." In the end, America was to blame for Cuba's dependency and poverty. When America beat Spain and gained control over the island, it "restored and consolidated the free-labor, one-crop sugar economy with its chronic underemployment and unemployment, reinforced the traditional pattern of land and crop control, and tied the trade and service sectors of the Cuban economy to the American market." Ironically, America replaced Spain's domination with its own. To a large extent, Williams pointed out, American foreign policy toward Cuba fit within the wider context of its developing Latin American policy. By the 1920s, the relation to Latin America had been "directed primarily toward obtaining raw materials for American factories and markets for the surpluses of that production." In the case of Cuba, raw materials mattered more than markets or any belief in self-determination.[30]

Williams documented how problems in U.S.-Cuba relations emerged early on. The first came when Batista, in 1940, supported a new constitution. Though a dictator, Batista was a "socially conscious conservative" whose constitution called for government-directed economic production and land distribution in order to help the poor. Befriending the peasants,

29. William Appleman Williams, "The President and His Critics," *The Nation,* March 16, 1963, 226, and *United States, Cuba, and Castro,* 8, 11.

30. William Appleman Williams, "Rise of an American World Power Complex," 14–15; "Cuba: Issues and Alternatives," *Annals of the American Academy of Political and Social Science,* no. 351 (January 1964): 75; and "Latin America: Laboratory of American Foreign Policy in the 1920s," *Inter-American Economic Affairs* 11 (1957): 19. For more on Castro's visit and the general context here, see Gosse, *Where the Boys Are.*

Batista angered the United States. But this was nothing compared to Castro's eventual revolution. Williams showed how Castro had originally been quite reasonable, coming to America and asking for help from the International Monetary Fund (IMF) and the United States government, all the while speaking the language of self-determination and democracy (not to mention reading Mills's *The Power Elite*). It was not so much the revolution that created animosity, but American unwillingness to listen to Castro's demands. Like Mills, Williams argued that "The rise of Russian influence in Cuba has been the result of the failure of American policy." America, after all, had refused to "make room for a nationalist, radical, implicitly socialist revolution in Cuba," and thus drove Cuba to embrace the Soviet Union. The overall "tragedy" of American foreign policy became explicit when the United States intervened in Cuba.[31]

The emphasis on tragedy allowed Williams to go a bit soft on Castro. Like Mills, Williams naively believed that Castro could let the Soviets in and still control the process. Of course, he had to take stock of Castro's growing tendency to act like a dictator. At one point, Williams admitted that "Castro's vigorous and assertive personal leadership in the writing of the Agrarian Reform Law was unquestionably an instance of quasi-dictatorial power." Nonetheless, Williams argued, Castro "was the premier." Pretending to sound like an objective political scientist who simply described different models of governance, Williams wrote, "The premier has great authority and responsibility in such a system of government." Williams went on:

> Winston Churchill remarked with his characteristic bluntness, during a crisis within the Allied coalition of World War II, that—whatever the ideal politics of compromise—"somebody has to play the hand." This is as true of a revolutionary movement as it is of a wartime partnership. Something is assigned second place in the hierarchy of values in every political situation. In the politics of the Agrarian Reform Law, as in other crucial episodes including many in the United States, decision by vote within the cabinet took second place. Castro used his power and accepted responsibility for what he did with it.

This was a far cry from Mills's neo-Jacobinism, in which revolutionaries redefined reality in the way they wanted. Nonetheless, Williams seemed to

31. Williams, *United States, Cuba, and Castro*, 59–60, 35–36, 96–97, 106–9, 176; "Cuba: Issues and Alternatives," 79.

allow justice to trump democracy a bit too quickly, as he would again in justifying Castro's agricultural cooperative plan without reservation. He never perceived that there might be a need to stop offering support. Here he betrayed the problems inherent in his own pluralistic approach toward foreign policy. It was never clear when pluralism turned a blind eye to forms of oppression within poorer and oppressed countries. When should a critic of American foreign policy also criticize Third World revolutionaries? When did a critic of American foreign policy become complicit with terror abroad? Williams never asked these crucial questions.[32]

Like his fellow New Left intellectuals, Williams was much better at criticizing his own country's policy and spelling out alternatives. While Mills called JFK a spoiled child, Williams lambasted his "urge to power and fear of failure." At the same time that he argued against JFK's belligerent intervention, Williams pleaded that protesters should not take an isolationist stand (a direction that his own work, as I have shown, could seem to suggest). In the case of Cuba, Williams argued that America had a moral responsibility— due to its historical relation to the island—to remain involved and to seek out some sort of accommodation precisely because it had done damage before. (This differentiated his views from those of realists.) He opined that America should accept "nationalization." Property owners in Cuba should be reimbursed by the federal government, and the government should try to get that money back once Cuba had successfully developed. This was not an outlandish or utopian position. It nicely meshed with a conception of reciprocity between the two countries; it also allowed Williams to maintain that America should take the first step in assisting Cuba's move toward nationalization. It also proved another point: Williams believed that America could overcome "tragedy" if it could accept a certain amount of pluralism in the world—a challenge that William James had set out at the turn of the century.[33]

Williams played the role of New Left critic quite well. He remained independent of the power structure—refusing Berle's offer—and spoke as an outraged, yet historically informed, citizen. Though he could drift toward an apology for dictatorship, he mostly spoke from the perspective of an American concerned with ideals of democracy, self-determination, and pluralism as they played themselves out abroad. At times, he even offered alternative and seemingly feasible policies. Nonetheless, the voice of the critic predominated. A

32. Williams, *United States, Cuba, and Castro,* 113–14, 137, 115.
33. William Appleman Williams, *United States, Cuba, and Castro,* 148, and "Protecting Overseas Investors," *The Nation,* August 26, 1961, 100.

key question remains: did Williams have any serious alternative to America's tragic tendency toward empire? As a historian, were there traditions upon which he could draw to sustain his hope for radical change?

Defining a New Left

I see . . . a pressing need to break free—a greater urgency, that is, to honor those of our traditional ideals, values, and practices that remain creative; and a more insistent necessity to create new visions, virtues, and procedures to replace those that have reached their potential and survive only as conventions and rationalizations that impede the building of an American community.
—William Appleman Williams, *The Contours of American History,* 1961

In his writing on Cuba, Williams offered a glimpse at his alternatives for American foreign policy and a New Left alternative to liberalism. First, there was a need to stop fighting the Cold War; here Williams urged the sort of existentialist refusal that C. Wright Mills had counseled: "Primarily, as C. Wright Mills has dramatized, it is simply time to assert our refusal as human beings to tolerate a policy which points so obviously toward disaster." And yet there was more offered here than an existential call to resistance. Williams argued for America to relax its rigid anticommunist stance, and provided, as concrete examples, Kennan's change of mind and Robins's earlier activism. Rather than containment, Williams believed in "radical internationalism" that supported "economic development while simultaneously accepting and furthering political and cultural independence." Here he followed the line of internationalist argument found in Mills's *The Causes of World War III.* Williams also sorted out the differences between his and the realists' position. Aid needed to be given to poorer countries; at the same time, Americans had to accept that these countries would experiment with nationalization and other forms of politics that made many in the United States uncomfortable. In the end (and perhaps most important), Williams believed that foreign policy could not change unless the terms of domestic life were modified by a New Left, one organized around a vision "based on self-containment and community instead of nationalistic expansion." Hence, New Left opposition would have to be both deeply internationalist and focused on domestic programs at the same time. The nature of this vision remained to be defined. In its definition, we glimpse Williams's idea of a New Left.[34]

Building on the strengths of the best isolationist arguments, Williams held

34. William Appleman Williams, "Needed: Production for Peace," 152; "The 'Logic' of Imperialism," *The Nation,* July 6, 1957, 15; and "Go Left or Go Under," 15.

that America needed to build "a true community" at home, or what he called "an exciting and creative commonwealth." In *The Tragedy of American Diplomacy,* Williams admitted that he was stumped when it came to this challenge. In certain ways, he faced the quandary Macdonald had already broached: how could his dark historical analysis ever result in a serious alternative to present social and political arrangements? With a great deal of honesty, Williams wrote, "This essay [*The Tragedy of American Diplomacy*] also points toward a radical but noncommunist reconstruction of American society in domestic affairs. And it is at this point that the irony appears: there is at present time no radicalism in the United States strong enough to win power, or even a very significant influence, through the processes of representative government—and this essay rests on the axiom of representative government." Here Williams accepted the limits set by liberalism—namely constitutional, representative democracy—but tried to supplement it with radical energy. Though Williams criticized liberalism, he did not suggest ignoring its strictures. He turned his attention to this demanding vision in his next two books, *The Contours of American History* (1961) and, even more important, *The Great Evasion* (1964). Here he set out an alternative vision for America—the sort that he hoped could galvanize a New Left.[35]

Of all the thinkers studied here, Williams was the most comfortable declaring himself an outright socialist. The devil, though, was in the details of his declaration. For though Williams expressed sympathy for the thinking of Karl Marx and wanted Americans to come to terms with his teachings (the long-winded subtitle of *The Great Evasion* was *An Essay on the Contemporary Relevance of Karl Marx and on the Wisdom of Admitting the Heretic into the Dialogue About America's Future*), he was predominantly a *Christian* socialist; his doctrine stemmed less from theories of capitalism's objective crisis (the arguments found in the three volumes of Marx's *Das Kapital*) and more from biblical teachings and moral angst about the inherent selfishness of bourgeois entrepreneurialism. Walter Rauschenbusch's "social gospel"—with its faith that all humans were created equal in the eyes of God and that humans must strive to realize the "Kingdom of God" on earth—mattered more than anything Marx had written in terms of Williams's political thought. Williams was also inspired by communitarian thinking, the sort of utopian thought Marx lambasted in *The Communist Manifesto* as inherently reactionary, as well

35. Williams, *Great Evasion,* 12; "A Proposal," 45; and *Tragedy,* 308.

as a critique of what came to be known as "possessive individualism"—the private egoism created by the pressures of a competitive capitalist market.[36]

Williams believed that the tradition he drew upon had a long legacy in American history. In fact, it originated in Puritan theology. Though some saw individualism within Puritanism (Max Weber, for instance), Williams saw a deeply communitarian element in believers who banded together through collective compacts with one another (the Mayflower Compact being the most famous). Williams embraced Jonathan Edwards's conception of a "corporate Christian commonwealth," and he thought that the early British "mercantilists" renewed this ideal by recognizing the need to subordinate individual business interests to a common good and "general welfare" protected by a paternalistic government. Though he never discussed them, it would seem that nineteenth-century communitarian experiments fit Williams's general hope here as well. The turn-of-the-century inheritors of Williams's radicalism included Edward Bellamy and Henry Demarest Lloyd. Williams believed that these thinkers "secularized and then reasserted with tremendous vigor the positive theme of early Christianity." They understood that "private property, since it emphasized and encouraged all the negative aspects of acquisition and competition, could not provide the basis for . . . a commonwealth." From Jonathan Edwards to Henry Demarest Lloyd, Williams saw a radical tradition with integrity and a great deal of continuity—one that drew upon Christian teachings in order to criticize the selfishness inherent in American capitalism.[37]

Williams mistakenly attributed the basis of this tradition to the thinking of Karl Marx. Though certainly legitimate in recognizing the importance of this great social theorist, Williams ignored how much *else* derived from Marx's work. Without delving too far into the details of academic debates about Marx's social thought, it needs to be pointed out that Marx's earlier writing was deeply influenced by Hegelian philosophy (indeed, he was first known as a "Young Hegelian"), but his later work tried to build upon the thinking of political economists who analyzed the macro-structures of modern capitalist economies. The younger Marx wrote a great deal about the human alienation inherent in the act of labor within a capitalist society, and

36. Williams, "A Proposal," 40.

37. Williams, *Contours of American History,* 483, 40–41, 387, 388. For more on the turn-of-the-century thinkers cited by Williams here, see Thomas, *Alternative America.* That radical Christianity had an influence on some members of the New Left (especially those outside eastern cities) is clear from Rossinow's *Politics of Authenticity.*

he focused on what is often referred to as the subjective damage done to individuals under capitalist relations. The later Marx wrote about the "falling rate of profit" inherent in the capitalist system and traced out objective crises that he saw operating within capitalist production. In *The Great Evasion,* Williams had nothing to say about the falling rate of profit or even about the objective conflict between the proletarian and bourgeois classes—a conflict that would eventually bury capitalism, Marx argued. For Williams, the crucial part of Marx's thought was "the nature of the relationships men had with each other in the course" of capitalist production. He argued that Marx believed that "capitalism is predicated upon an overemphasis and exaltation of the individualistic, egoistic half of men functioning in a marketplace system that overrides and crushes the social, humanitarian half of man." Though there *was* a humanitarian component to Marx's thought, there was much more that Williams simply ignored—precisely the objective analysis that seemed not to fit within Williams's own peculiar version of Marxism.[38]

Williams's belief in a humanitarian rather than a social-scientific approach to socialism seemed akin to the social thought of William Morris, even if he never discussed this British thinker. Morris had approached socialism as a result of his previous experience as an artisan. He believed that the capitalist division of labor destroyed the integral work patterns of earlier craftsmen and elevated egoism over a common good. As E. P. Thompson put it, Morris's "revolt against capitalism stemmed from moral revulsion rather than direct experience of poverty or oppression." So too for Williams. The relation to Morris is even clearer when we consider that he had stressed the need for a decentralized and participatory form of socialism as the right sort of corrective to capitalism. Through his reading of another British thinker, G. D. H. Cole (who was deeply and directly indebted to Morris), Williams picked up on these themes. At base, Williams was no Leninist; he did not believe in a vanguard party or a new class of intellectuals leading a revolution. Instead, socialism needed to be anchored in local communities, where

38. Williams, *Great Evasion,* 125, 19–20. Williams can be located in a tradition of Western Marxist thought—the sort that emphasized subjectivity and the qualitative critique Marx made of capitalism. Even so, I do not believe that Williams had a compelling understanding of the variations within Marx's thought, a point that Eugene Genovese made in his review of *The Great Evasion* in *Studies on the Left* 6 (1966): 73–76. It is confirmed by George Mosse, who was a colleague of Williams: see his "New Left Intellectuals/New Left Politics," in *History and the New Left,* ed. Buhle, 234. For more on Western Marxism, see Russell Jacoby, *Dialectic of Defeat: Contours of Western Marxism* (Cambridge: Cambridge University Press, 1981).

citizens could actualize themselves through democratic participation and meaningful work. Williams wanted to measure wealth less by money than by the level of participation and control citizens had over their lives. He explained, "The essential meaning of wealth has to do with an individual's effective, participating [sic] influence within his society." For him, the goal of any form of socialism was "active participation in the present and future affairs of one's own society" and the re-creation of an "American community." Decentralized and humanistic socialism became Williams's primary vision for a future left.[39]

To a large extent, this vision carried on a dissenting tradition in American intellectual history. A moral concern with what private property and egoistic pursuit of one's self-interest did to culture had always played a central role in American thought, from Melville to Whitman to Dewey. Williams was right to see his predecessors among figures like Henry Demarest Lloyd and "social gospel" theologians. There was a solid middle-class tradition of criticizing the central principles and degrading consequences of capitalism. This tradition did not question capitalism on the merits of performance, but on its moral and social impact—purposeless work, ugly and polluted cities, and a culture of selfishness. Waldo Frank captured the spirit of this tradition when he explained the work of a group of young social critics, the "Young Americans," at the turn of the century. Describing the efforts of Randolph Bourne and Lewis Mumford, Frank wrote, "We were all sworn foes of Capitalism, not because we knew it would not work, but because we judged it, even in success, to be lethal to the human spirit." Williams stood squarely within this tradition and spoke a distinctly American language—the language of a connected critic.[40]

Still, the problem of political transformation remained. A critique of capitalism's seamier consequences might have been intellectually persuasive, but not necessarily capable of galvanizing a social movement. The roots of republican political criticism—independent property ownership and armed citizens—disappeared during the modern industrialization of America. The

39. E. P. Thompson, *William Morris: Romantic to Revolutionary* (London: Lawrence and Wishart, 1955), 96; Williams, *Great Evasion,* 24, and *Contours of American History,* 487, 6.

40. Frank quoted in Casey Nelson Blake, *Beloved Community: The Cultural Criticism of Randolph Bourne, Van Wyck Brooks, Waldo Frank, and Lewis Mumford* (Chapel Hill: University of North Carolina Press, 1990), 4. The best source on the intellectual tradition that informed Williams's work is Thomas, *Alternative America;* for an account of how Lloyd actually met with William Morris, showing the intersection between an American and British critique of capitalism, see 149.

moralism that motivated middle-class activists and writers like Henry Demarest Lloyd and Jane Addams during the Progressive Era seemed to fade away into the prosperity and apathy of the 1950s—the world of "organization men" and suburban housewives about which social critics complained. Williams believed, though, that the spirit was recaptured in the civil rights movement that renewed "the ideal and the practice of a Christian community or commonwealth." He was right to pick up on the civil rights movement's language of re-creating a "beloved community"; nonetheless, it was not clear what *other* movements might actually invigorate his vision of decentralized socialism. Besides, the civil rights movement itself saw the necessity not only of local and community-based participation but also of the eventual attainment of individual rights. Some (especially recent critics, such as Shelby Steele) argue that the movement was strongly wedded to the American dream of individual success as much as to building community. With this in mind, it is hard to see any real source of political will for Williams's democratic and communitarian vision of socialism.[41]

Williams himself recognized numerous impediments to his own vision. First and most obvious, there was the frontier mentality that drove Americans to expand ever-outward and to suppress the need to create a real community at home. Secondly (and here Williams followed Paul Goodman), America had a tendency to produce rebels who actually mimicked the larger culture. Writing just before the hippie counterculture was to make inroads into the New Left—the first "Be-In" did not take place until 1967, two years after *The Great Evasion* appeared—Williams focused his attention on the counterculture's literary predecessors, the Beats. Like Goodman, he realized that there were good reasons for their alienation—precisely those sorts of things he thought were wrong with American capitalism and its meaningless work. But, as Williams argued, "their sub-culture is not based on values that are capable of creatively transforming society." They were too selfish and narcissistic to create a real community. Hence, the rebels (in whom critics might have otherwise placed their faith) wound up mirroring the pathologies of their own society, not transforming that society.[42]

Williams believed that this criticism applied to the budding feminist movement of his time as well. He had taken note of Marx's idea that capitalism had "torn asunder" older familial relations. He had also taken note of

---

41. Williams, *Contours of American History,* 486.

42. Williams, *Great Evasion,* 109. For more on the counterculture's emergence during the 1960s, see Allen Matusow's chapter on it in his *Unraveling of America.*

sociological reports on the damage done to poorer families as members had to move from job to job and women had to take on work outside the household. Williams discussed cases in which men had lost their self-respect because they could not support their families and openly fretted about the "disruption of family roles and relationships." Within this context, feminism appeared less than liberatory. Feminists—with their arguments for women to enter the workforce—became the rear guard of capitalism. Williams argued, "In defining emancipation in precisely the terms that describe the conditions of males in a capitalist political economy, the female alienates herself from the possibility of transforming the American family and society in a truly human and creative way."[43]

Williams's arguments came one year after the publication of the most famous feminist work of the 1960s—Betty Friedan's *The Feminine Mystique,* a book never mentioned in *The Great Evasion.* At first, it appears that Williams argued against Friedan's belief that women had to find creative work outside of what she called the "comfortable concentration camp" of the suburban family and its "housewife trap." And yet Friedan came out of a socialist background, and her arguments were far from a celebration of the capitalist job market. She held that women needed "creative work." At the same time, she warned: "But a job, any job, is not the answer—in fact, it can be part of the trap." From this, it would seem that Williams was taking a stand not necessarily against feminism, but against a certain strain within it that could fall prey to private, individualistic, and capitalistic values—values that Williams believed a New Left needed to transcend.[44]

Needless to say, his critique of feminism suggested that reformers could often take on their society's worst values. Not surprisingly, Williams approv-

43. Karl Marx and Friedrich Engels, "Manifesto of the Communist Party," in *Marx and Engels: Basic Writings on Politics and Philosophy,* ed. Lewis Feuer (New York: Anchor, 1989), 10; Williams, *Great Evasion,* 90, 112.

44. Betty Friedan, *The Feminine Mystique* (New York: Dell, 1963), 332. On Friedan's background, see Daniel Horowitz, *Betty Friedan and the Making of* The Feminine Mystique: *The American Left, the Cold War, and Modern Feminism* (Amherst: University of Massachusetts Press, 1998). I am indebted to a point made by Christopher Lasch, who argued that Betty Friedan's book complements Paul Goodman's oversight of women in his *Growing Up Absurd* (Goodman simply assumed that raising children was valuable work in itself). Lasch points out that both books are crucial in terms of what they say about modern work. He also points out that Friedan did not see work in a capitalist economy as necessarily liberating. See his "Sexual Division of Labor, the Decline of Civic Culture, and the Rise of the Suburbs," in *Women and the Common Life: Love, Marriage, and Feminism,* ed. Elisabeth Lasch-Quinn (New York: Norton, 1997), 105–16.

ingly cited Herbert Marcuse's *One-Dimensional Man* (1964). Williams believed that Marcuse exposed "the power of the system to define the choices
and impose them upon the individual." An air of "unfreedom"—a distinctly
Hegelian term used by Marcuse and his colleagues in the Frankfurt School—
defined late capitalism. This line of reasoning was not terribly encouraging
for those who wanted to change society. (Indeed, Marcuse put his faith in
the most marginalized groups in society—what Marx referred to as the
lumpenproletariat—to lead the "great refusal.") In his support of Marcuse's
social analysis and his critical read of the Beats and feminists, readers got a
sense that Williams was deeply pessimistic about the change that progressives
could create in America. The discouraging analysis found in Macdonald's
essays in *politics* and in Mills's depiction of the alienated white-collar class
seemed to reappear in Williams's *The Great Evasion.*[45]

There were other weaknesses in Williams's vision of a New Left based
upon decentralized, communitarian socialism. For instance, he never made
clear how the principles of equality and localism could be reconciled. What
if there were wealthier regions within a political system that wanted to use
localism to prevent a more equitable distribution of wealth? Which value
would win out? Or to use a more historical example, what about the issues
of slavery or segregation? What if certain communities created unjust institutions? Williams never explained how the values of social justice and democratic participation could work together. Though he praised the civil rights
movement, he failed to understand that the movement had identified a central problem for a democratic society—the need to ensure that local power
and participation (what Arnold Kaufman would call "municipal tyranny")
would not overrun equality. Though the civil rights movement leaders
spoke of creating a "beloved community," they also saw the need for a
centralized government to overturn the power of localities in order to ensure
individual liberties. This sort of paradox never seemed to catch Williams's
attention—and his political thought remained marred by these sorts of unresolved tensions.

More worrisome was the vagueness of so much of Williams's political
criticism. In defining his own form of democratic radicalism, Williams rejected numerous historical predecessors that he might well have appropri-

45. Williams, *Great Evasion,* 118–19. For more on Marcuse, see his *One-Dimensional Man;*
for more on the Frankfurt School, which deeply influenced both Williams and Mills, see
Martin Jay, *The Dialectical Imagination: A History of the Frankfurt School and the Institute of Social
Research, 1923–1950* (Boston: Little, Brown, 1973).

ated. He argued, for instance, that a new radicalism should not be based upon "palliatives snitched from the medicine cabinets of Populism, Progressivism, or New Dealism." This was quite a sweeping dismissal of actually existing reform traditions in American history, and hence the liberal tradition as well—an odd move for a historian. The extensiveness of this move can be seen in what Williams chose to embrace. He argued that a future left needed to be based upon "three essential propositions: decentralization, the quality of material and human production instead of its quantity, and the substance and tone of human relationships." On the first principle, Williams was no Goodman; he never set out any concrete means—any "practical proposals," to use Goodman's term—for creating a more decentralized society while protecting equality. The two remaining principles seemed rather murky. Williams was right to point out the moral damage done by capitalism. But to suggest that something needed to be done about "the substance and tone of human relationships" seemed utterly vague, especially in comparison to the concrete ideas proposed by the previous reformers he had rejected. It was not so much that Williams's ideas here were *wrong;* rather, they were empty. It might not come as a surprise, then, that when New Left social movements actually arrived on the scene and started filling in some of the gaps, much of Williams's vagueness turned to dismay. Like Goodman, Williams watched and participated in the New Left, but he also became a critic in the process. His vision for it and its reality did not always mesh.[46]

The Intellectual's Role in Political Change: Going Public, Then Ambivalent

A kind of sophisticated square is emerging from this new generation. This does not mean that [young new leftists] are merely sexually liberated Puritans or more efficient New Dealers. They are young men and women who are intelligent and perceptive enough to learn from their elders without making all the same mistakes. They have had enough of hipsterism as well as of the jet-set, and of the Old Left as well as of the Establishment. And they are aware that emancipation involves men as well as women, and that it concerns something beyond the freedom and opportunity to hustle their wares in the marketplace. They are morally committed to the proposition that the American system must treat people as people, and that the system must be changed . . . to achieve that objective.

—William Appleman Williams, "Pseudo-Debate in the Teach-In: Criticism Contained," 1965

46. "A Proposal," 45.

More at home in the university than either Mills or Goodman, Williams believed that his academic work could inspire future scholars committed to building the intellectual resources necessary for a New Left. At Madison, he supported graduate students who formed one of the first small magazines of the New Left—*Studies on the Left* (see Chap. 6). In a symposium on his work, a commentator called him "the spirit behind *Studies on the Left.*" And as the historian Jonathan Wiener has documented, Williams had a major influence on a second generation of historians who took his teachings seriously. As we will see in Chapter 6, many young scholars oriented toward activism and the New Left drew inspiration from Williams and the engaging classes he taught at the University of Wisconsin.[47]

At the same time, Williams became something of an activist oriented toward the world outside academia. As he explained in an autobiographical essay he wrote during the early 1970s, "There are moments when serious protest promises consequences and in those instants I have signed my name, written a private letter, walked the streets, or sent my money." Actually, Williams did much more. He wrote a pamphlet on Cuba that helped the small but burgeoning anti-interventionist movement of the early 1960s. Like Mills, he showed early support for the anti-HUAC protests, being personally drawn into the fracas over this controversial agency. Asked to testify in front of a Capitol hearing on HUAC, Williams played the role of intellectual rebel to a tee. As Paul Buhle and Edward Rice-Maximin document, Williams "charged that HUAC wasted money. . . . Asked what he taught his students, he answered, 'I teach people to think,' bringing down the house in a veritable explosion from the galleries." Taking on his role in earnest, Williams also threw himself into the teach-ins held against the Vietnam War at the University of Wisconsin in 1965 (in the wake of the first one at the University of Michigan—see Chap. 5). With his historical acumen and knowledge of foreign policy, he faced considerable demands on his time as a movement intellectual who could speak in a wide variety of public forums during the mid-to-late 1960s. Williams made sure to speak to a range of organizations—including more conservative ones like the Jaycees. Clearly, Williams underplayed his role in the New Left when he talked of signing a few letters in support of protesters. Indeed, he was made frantic by his commitment to

47. "Excerpts from a Conference to Honor William Appleman Williams," *Radical History Review* 50 (1991): 58; Jonathan Wiener, "Radical Historians and the Crisis in American History, 1959–1980," *Journal of American History* 76 (1989): 399–442. On this point, see also Buhle and Rice-Maximin, *William Appleman Williams,* 118–19.

intellectual activism. In 1968, he explained in a letter to his friend, Henry Berger: "I've been dashing around like a nuthead making speeches all over the damn country." Like his fellow New Left intellectuals, Williams took political commitment seriously—throwing himself into the challenge of building a democratic public capable of confronting the crisis of the Vietnam War and the American power elite.[48]

Clearly, his major activism revolved around the teach-in movement (see Chap. 5). In it, he found a way to engage as an academic in public deliberation about the Vietnam War and American foreign policy in general. Williams played a central role in the first Vietnam War teach-in held in Madison in 1965. As students gathered to discuss American intervention in Vietnam, Williams believed that he saw a budding democratic public. He claimed that in deliberative sessions, students showed the "makings of a community." They had come to "assemble as citizens" who wanted "to bring the government back into a dialogue with its own citizens." Here Williams started to define his flimsier conception of a community; it sounded more like the deliberative public that Mills had argued for earlier. Williams believed that the teach-in promised to rediscover the "reciprocal action of politics," by which he meant the dialogue between publics and political leaders that Mills had placed at the center of his vision of a New Left. As the teach-ins spread to other campuses and blossomed into protest movements, Williams saw a New Left forming (as the epigraph to this section suggests).[49]

In his thinking on teach-ins, Williams connected his own political theory with emerging movements. Not surprisingly, he liked the decentralized nature of the original teach-ins, which took place on individual college campuses through the initiative of local organizers. At the same time, these events added up to something more than random local occurrences. Williams argued against the movement going national—which, under the leadership of Arnold Kaufman, it did quite quickly in 1965 with the first

48. "Confessions of an Intransigent Revisionist" (1973), reprinted in *A William Appleman Williams Reader,* ed. Berger, 339; Buhle and Rice-Maximin, *William Appleman Williams,* 104; Williams to Henry Berger, April 4, 1968, William Appleman Williams Papers, folder of correspondence with Berger.

49. Williams quoted in Buhle and Rice-Maximin, *William Appleman Williams,* 158; Williams, "Our Leaders Are Following the Wrong Rainbow" (remarks at Wisconsin teach-in, April 1, 1965), reprinted in *Teach-Ins, U.S.A.: Reports, Opinions, Documents,* ed. Louis Menashe and Ronald Radosh (New York: Praeger, 1967), 47. On the first Wisconsin teach-in, see Tom Bates, *Rads: The 1970 Bombing of the Army Math Research Center at the University of Wisconsin and Its Aftermath* (New York: Harper Collins, 1992), 72–73.

National Teach-In held in Washington, D.C. Here government officials (including Arthur Schlesinger, who acted as a representative of the LBJ administration) debated leading academic critics of U.S. policy. Williams took this as a bastardization of the original local, decentralized teach-ins, such as the one he helped organize in Wisconsin. He argued, "The Washington affair carried [the teach-in movement] unfortunately far toward being institutionalized as a glorified faculty meeting of the Establishment." As I will show in the next chapter, much of Williams's critique was off-base. However, he at least offered an alternative to the National Teach-In. He wanted the movement to use the university as a civic resource rooted in its locale. The university, Williams argued, could enliven community debate. He wanted "the campus" to serve as "a base for reaching the community," transforming the university into "a center of serious intellectual activity dealing with the problems of the general society" in the process. He saw this spirit operating when, after leaving the University of Wisconsin, Williams landed at Oregon State University. As he saw it, teach-in and protest organizers "tried to involve the town (which is almost classic nineteenth century honest conservative)," as he explained in a letter. They even engaged local high schools and community groups, Williams pointed out. He believed that "it was the teach-ins rather than the marches that played the major role in generating the now widespread opposition to the Vietnam War." Locally organized, inspiring democratic debate, the teach-ins represented Williams's highest hopes for a New Left growing from below.[50]

As the teach-ins blossomed into a general protest movement, Williams encouraged participants to "speak American"—that is, appeal to American values even while criticizing America's actions abroad. In explaining his historical analysis of the Open Door to students gathered at the first teach-in at the University of Wisconsin, Williams argued that Americans should "honor our moral commitment to the principle of self-determination." Williams

50. William Appleman Williams: "Pseudo-Debate in the Teach-In: Criticism Contained" (1965; written for the *York Gazette and Daily* in York, Pa.), reprinted in *Teach-Ins, U.S.A.,* ed. Menashe and Radosh, 189; "How Can the Left Be Relevant?" *Current* (August 1969): 24; letter to Henry Berger, July 1970, William Appleman Williams Papers, folder of correspondence with Henry Berger (see also a letter he wrote to Henry Berger, dated October 1969, in the same folder); "How Can the Left Be Relevant?" 23. Williams's involvement in the National Teach-In can be gleaned from correspondence he had with his agent, Gerard McCauley. See a letter McCauley wrote Williams about getting transcripts of the National Teach-In: McCauley to Williams, May 21, 1965, William Appleman Williams Papers, folder of correspondence with Gerard McCauley.

believed that the New Left needed not only to speak American but also to act, fully aware that many Americans still disagreed with its aims. The goal had to be to convince conservatives that it was in their best interest to listen to the New Left's demands. Here again, his hope in a conservative power elite came to the fore. He argued that the "well-being of the U.S. depends upon the extent to which calm and confident and enlightened conservatives can see and bring themselves to act upon the validity of a radical analysis." When he confronted the repercussions from the Cuban Revolution, he argued, "There is the possibility that America's contemporary upper-class leaders can discipline themselves to recognize and adapt, and then act within, the tradition of responsible upper-class leadership provided by the Founding Fathers." Around Vietnam, he pressed this point further (even if it had failed during the Cuban catastrophe), telling his students in strident terms: "You have to split the ruling class!" Williams believed that the New Left could never entirely transform society, or so it seemed from remarks like these, but only push the conservative elite to take its demands seriously. He never explained how this position squared with his concern over co-optation.[51]

Aside from staying on the good side of the conservative power elite, Williams put two other demands on the New Left. First, it had to develop programs that focused its energy. Writing in 1967, Williams sounded like Paul Goodman during the early 1960s: "It is time radicalism [generated] a program that will attract human beings, offering them a reasoned way to achieve a more meaningful and creative life." "Radicals," Williams argued, needed to "devise workable plans and procedures for decentralization that will enable all of us to realize a more creative conception of freedom." Though Williams made this claim, he did not deliver the goods; his own writing suffered from an abstractness about programs and ways to obtain the ideals in which he believed. When he argued that the left needed to provide Americans with a "living conception of community," he exposed his own vagueness. He pointed out that the concept of community served as a useful corrective to the New Left's tendency toward libertarianism, highlighted by the late 1960s merger between the New Left and the counterculture: "A community," Williams wrote, "is not created, let alone maintained, by everyone simply doing their own thing." This was a fine point, but it did not

51. Williams, "Our Leaders Are Following," 52; "Cuba: Issues and Alternatives," 79; and quoted in Tom Bates, *Rads,* 98–99. For more on the point of educating the American oligarchy away from its expansion abroad, see Williams, "The Large Corporation," 104.

explain what a community actually *was* or how Americans were to acquire one. The term "community" was—and is—one of the fuzziest and emptiest terms in America's political language. Williams's use of it betrayed his own lack of program or sense of how the New Left was to transform American society.[52]

The "really existing" New Left continued to grow, and Madison, Wisconsin, served as one of its focal points. The University of Wisconsin's campus became notorious for conflict—culminating in the famous 1970 bombing of the Army Math Research Center as an angry protest against the university's complicity with the war machine. The tendency of the New Left toward this sort of confrontation, theatrics, and violence drove Williams to despair. Like Goodman, Williams became a vocal critic who remained connected to the movement. He argued (as Arnold Kaufman would more forcefully) that "confrontation politics are inherently and fundamentally limited." Confrontation showed off the New Left's tendency to pit itself against the mainstream—something that Williams opposed, due to its proclivity to generate "self-righteous arrogance." The New Left was becoming too obsessed with the short-term goal of stopping the Vietnam War and ignoring its long-range goal, which, Williams believed, should be decentralized, community-based socialism. He railed against "the assumption that we can have radical reform or a social revolution without the hard, dedicated, and effective work involved in building a social movement." The stern nature of these remarks made clear that Williams was becoming increasingly disillusioned with the New Left during the late 1960s.[53]

His disillusionment forced him to leave Madison once and for all; family troubles only made the decision easier. Right before leaving (and while drunk, unfortunately), he made one of his toughest, most mean-spirited attacks on the students within the New Left: "They are just the most selfish people I know. They just terrify me. They are acting out a society I'd like to live in as an orangutan. They have no experience of the way the world really works, or of coalition politics." This sounded like the complaints that neoconservatives would lob at the protesters who took over Columbia University—the sorts of complaints that Goodman both criticized and defended at

---

52. William Appleman Williams, review of *Senator Fulbright,* by Tristram Coffin, *Ramparts,* March 1967, 59; *Roots of the Modern American Empire,* 452; and "An American Socialist Community?" *Liberation,* June 1969, 9.

53. Williams, review of *Senator Fulbright,* 58; "An American Socialist Community?" 11; and "America II Continued," 78.

the same time. Unlike neoconservatives, Williams held out coalition politics as an alternative to New Left confrontationalism. Besides, Williams remained connected to the New Left as he transported himself to Oregon, where he lived out the rest of his life. In fact, he thought that the student protesters in Oregon had something to teach those at the University of Wisconsin—that is, common sense and a stronger link to the surrounding community. Though his drunken remark about New Left orangutanism might have sounded as though it signaled complete withdrawal, Williams remained connected to the hope of building a widespread movement, becoming an ambivalent movement intellectual. Here is how Henry Berger, a student of Williams, described him in 1971: "Unlike many on the New Left, Williams refuses to postulate a violent revolution as the only feasible means of social change. Such candor has alienated the more radical of the 'radicals,' and ironically enough has not altered the views of many in the academic establishment who have never forgiven Williams for his espousal of radicalism in the fifties before it was fashionable to express such ideas." Williams still thought of himself as part of the New Left. And yet, with his move to Oregon in 1968, he clearly receded, largely by his own design. The ambivalent movement intellectual became just a bit more ambivalent.[54]

At the same time that he became ambivalent and a bit crotchety about the New Left, he started to have doubts about the historian's role in relation to social and political change. This came out in his book, *The Roots of the Modern American Empire,* published in 1969—the same year that SDS was falling apart at the seams and breaking into factions *and* that Nixon escalated the war in Vietnam. An academic tome, the book's overall message reflected a leaning toward the "one-dimensional" society thesis of Marcuse. In it, Williams argued that the Open Door and free market *Weltanschauung* he had

54. Williams, quoted in *Sunday Oregonian* article, November 26, 1967, William Appleman Williams Papers; Henry Berger, in a press release announcing Williams's speech at Washington University, where Berger taught (found in the William Appleman Williams Papers, folder of correspondence between Williams and Berger). For the fact that Williams was drunk when he made the orangutan comment, I am indebted to Paul Buhle. In a letter to Henry Berger, dated May 3, 1967 (around the same time as the orangutan statement), Williams wrote, "The frenetic left at Madison seems to have screwed that situation up as bad as their buddies at Berkeley. I feel like Lewis, John L. that is: a plague on all your houses. Harrington's included." Harrington was the president of the University of Wisconsin (see William Appleman Williams Papers, folder of correspondence with Henry Berger). Williams's sense that things were different in Oregon is important. It made clear that the New Left had serious regional differences: Corvallis, Oregon, was not Madison, Wisconsin; was not Austin, Texas; was not New York City. This point is well made in Rossinow's *Politics of Authenticity.*

already explored in *The Tragedy of American Diplomacy* did not originate in the 1890s (which still served as a turning point in Williams's work) but in the thinking of nineteenth-century farmers. These farmers originally wanted to expand outward in order to find a market for their surplus goods; corporate industrialists simply jumped on board later. Even the populists—the first of America's modern radicals—wanted "farm businessmen" to "attain marketplace supremacy" through their famous subtreasury plan. Ironically, Williams made an argument here very much like those of the "consensus" school of historians—Richard Hofstadter, most prominently. *All* Americans, Hofstadter had argued in *The American Political Tradition,* seemed obsessed with private property and liberal entrepreneurialism. There seemed to be no possible way for Americans to conceive of any alternative to this system. Williams appeared to concur with Hofstadter in *The Roots of the Modern American Empire.* It was not just the present society that was one-dimensional, Williams suggested, but also the past. Radicals seemingly had no place—in the past, present, or future—to look for inspiration.[55]

At the end of the book, Williams asked what role the historian could play in relation to the left. The question can be broadened, though, to echo the one asked by Mills and Goodman: What is the role of the intellectual in social and political change? Unfortunately, Williams's answers were a bit rambling and unfocused, perhaps reflecting his confusion. His pessimism about historical possibilities led to a grim assessment of the contemporary intellectual's role in political change. Citizens wanted to know the "meaning" of the past, while historians could only "reconstruct what happened . . . and explain how and why it occurred." As both a citizen and historian, Williams suffered from "schizophrenia." He wrote, "The schizophrenic discipline of the historian is a harrowing way to stay sane. And of course very few men or women manage to master it. Certainly not I." A citizen wanted to know what could be done to change things in the present society; the historian made clear the limits placed upon the present by the past. The "meanings" that Williams offered "as a historian do not . . . tell me what to do as a citizen. Nor can they tell any other citizens what to do as a citizen." After all, the past that Williams was tracing out while he wrote *The Roots of the Modern American Empire* did not offer too many hopes. If anything, his-

---

55. Williams, *Roots of the Modern American Empire,* 400. For Hofstadter's historical analysis, I rely upon *The American Political Tradition* and Susan Stout Baker's interesting examination of his radical background and how it related to his pessimistic read on America's past. See Baker, *Radical Beginnings: Richard Hofstadter and the 1930s* (Westport, Conn.: Greenwood, 1985).

tory offered a "measure of humility and self-skepticism." But aside from these traits, the historian could offer very little to those interested in social and political change. Williams seemed to suggest here that the intellectual—in this case a practicing, academic historian—could not do much to help the New Left achieve political change. The intellectual and the movement needed to go their separate routes. The politics of truth severed itself from the politics of change.[56]

Conclusion: The Historian as Citizen-Activist?

Apparently, Williams resolved the New Left intellectual's dilemma by choosing truth telling over commitment (as witnessed in his move away from Madison in 1968 and his pessimistic analysis in *The Roots of the Modern American Empire*). At the same time, he remained engaged with the New Left, doing some political work in Oregon as much he could and staying active in history and politics until his death in 1990. Clearly, though, the tension between engagement and truth-telling—between the citizen and historian—marked Williams's work. For instance, at times, Williams argued for the New Left to influence, not overthrow, America's conservative elite; at other points, he warned about the potential danger of co-optation by the elite. He worried about the "willingness within the Establishment to reform and rationalize the corporate system according to its own adaptation of our criticisms." But at the same time, he suggested that this might not be so bad. Historically, he perceived almost all reform movements as limited: their approach to solving problems relied too heavily on the ideologies of private property and laissez-faire. For example, the Knights of Labor, a turn-of-the-century labor union, represented simply "the fulfillment of the laissez-faire labor movement." Williams argued, as Hofstadter had earlier, that "American reformers have been almost unique in the intensity of their commitment to private property." Seemingly, the dominant paradigm of American society—the free market and private property, later transmogrified into the corporate economy—sucked even reformers into its vortex. How could Williams believe in changing things for the better, when so much change looked like co-optation, and so many reformers mirrored the larger society?[57]

56. Williams, *Roots of the Modern American Empire,* 449, 450, 451.
57. Williams, "How Can the Left Be Relevant?" 20, and *Contours of American History,*

Williams's faith in an elite and his hope for decentralized, democratic socialism did not square too well either. Overall, his hope in community-based socialism suffered from tensions and weaknesses. Williams never explained how local communities would actually create socialist values, and he certainly had no examples of local communities that had already accomplished this feat. Generally, Williams's vision of a New Left was marked by a major tension—one manifested in all of the thinkers studied here. Williams had a gloomy analysis of American foreign expansion—the "tragedy of American diplomacy"—but simultaneously held to a certain optimism of the will, a hope for "community" and "commonwealth." Perhaps it is not surprising to find that in this book's grouping of intellectuals, the historian was the most pessimistic. After all, historians always discuss the limits placed upon the present by the past. But in the case of Williams, the tension between citizen and historian was that much more pronounced, if only because he himself identified it so consciously as his own "schizophrenia."

With this said, though, Williams offered a great deal to the New Left. His model of engaged scholarship would influence the editors of *Studies on the Left* and the next generation of intellectuals (see this book's final chapter). He showed the important role that historical awareness could play in the New Left's self-understanding. In his dissection of political thought as it related to historical changes, he argued that liberalism was too complicit with a corporate economic structure and therefore not conducive to participatory democracy. Williams also showed that intellectuals could actually aid the cause of participatory democracy through initiatives like local teach-ins. This sort of activism fit within his general faith in a communitarian form of socialism—one of his legacies to New Left thought. Perhaps most important of all, Williams showed that the New Left needed to deal with the fact that America's national identity was bound up with foreign expansion. He had done this even by the 1950s, before Cuba and Vietnam became major crises. He also showed that the New Left would have to allude to core American values when taking part in protest. Clearly, many New Leftists forgot this principle, but Williams's work shows that it was a philosophical argument that lay behind much protest of the time. Williams's connected criticism was central to the New Left's self-conceptualization, even if sometimes forgotten.

334, 373. Williams's arguments here influenced a great deal of New Left historiography—especially the interpretation of reform movements as limited by the strictures of America's corporate economy.

Finally, Williams showed that an intellectual could be both committed to and critical of the movement. His participation in the teach-in movement—and his philosophical thinking about its impact and significance—showed that he believed in intellectual engagement. At the same time, his fears about irrational tendencies within the New Left made him pull away. Though Williams seemed to resolve the dilemma of intellectual commitment in favor of withdrawal, he devoted himself to exploring that tension. It was a tension that could become a source of creativity and dialogue with a wider public. Such was the paradox of so much New Left thinking.

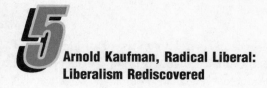

5 Arnold Kaufman, Radical Liberal: Liberalism Rediscovered

Liberalism is no insipid political brew. It is potentially the most radical doctrine in the modern world. Because, rightly interpreted, it cannot respect any arrangements—however firmly entrenched—which deny to every human being his full allotment of personal freedom. . . . A liberal hates that in man which seeks to accumulate power, prestige, and privileges at the expense of the rightful power, prestige, and privileges of others.
—Arnold Kaufman, review of *The New Class,* by Milovan Djlias, 1958

Radicalism without a coherent moral orientation is blind energy. The leftist must work out a social philosophy which combines social utility and justice.
—Arnold Kaufman, "A Philosophy for the American Left," 1963

Unlike the other intellectuals studied here, Arnold Kaufman is not always recognized as an intellectual who had significant influence on the New Left. Mention his name, and most historians of the New Left scratch their heads. And yet, more than others, Arnold Kaufman developed the idea of "participatory democracy" to its fullest extent, drawing the concept out from traditions within modern political theory. He inspired Tom Hayden, Robert Haber, and Carl Ogelsby of Students for a Democratic Society (SDS). At SDS's now-famous Port Huron conference, Kaufman gave a speech that found much of its way into the Port Huron Statement, perhaps the most sophisticated (if not the most significant) document in New Left history. Richard Flacks described the scene at one SDS conference: "Arnold spoke and people sat at his feet." Clearly, Kaufman had a captive audience among young New Leftists, and his own intellectual and political sympathies found a home here.[1]

---

1. Flacks quoted in James Miller, *"Democracy Is in the Streets,"* 111. See also the official invitation to Arnold Kaufman to speak at an SDS convention from June 11–15, 1962. Robert Haber and Sandra Hayden asked him to speak on "the intellectual foundations of the left": letter dated May 12, 1962, Arnold Kaufman Papers, Bentley Historical Library, University of Michigan, box 4, file on SDS.

During the 1960s, Kaufman became best known as an originator and spokesperson for the anti–Vietnam War teach-in, an event that defined the earlier and more intellectually oriented New Left. The teach-in, as we will see, created an audience—or democratic public—for academic and intellectual critics of the Vietnam War. By throwing his energy into organizing teach-ins (both local and national), Kaufman "solved," so to speak, the dilemma of the New Left intellectual. That is, he balanced a commitment to the politics of truth and deliberation with a respect for the politics of change and engagement. Jack Rothman, Kaufman's colleague at the University of Michigan, described him as an intellectual "in equal parts the academic-theorist and the politician-activist. The philosopher and the public man collided within him and demanded resolution." In the simplest terms, this was seen in the fact that Kaufman could never divorce his ideas from his activism. As he described his one and only book, *The Radical Liberal* (and the same could be said for his countless articles), "The inclination to write this book grew out of my participation in the teach-in movement and in the civil rights struggle." For Kaufman, ideas and a firm commitment to the politics of truth could never be divorced from activism and the politics of commitment.[2]

At the same time, Kaufman was a steadfast liberal. In his thinking and activism, we can see a dialogue between liberalism and radicalism—a dialogue important for the main themes of this book. The best radical critics at the time recognized the importance of Kaufman's insistence that radicalism and liberalism were deeply intertwined. Even a staunch critic of Kaufman's liberalism, Christopher Lasch, argued that the "emergence of dissident liberalism . . . is an important and heartening development." I will argue that Kaufman's intellectual and activist explorations show how the New Left, at its best, synthesized radicalism and liberalism, rather than rejecting liberalism altogether. As I have already shown, the relation between liberalism and radicalism in the work of most intellectuals studied here was, at the least, more complicated than typically thought. When pressed, these intellectuals often wound up defending liberalism, and for Kaufman such a defense came relatively naturally. By giving Kaufman his rightful standing in intellectual

---

2. Jack Rothman, "The Radical Liberal Strategy in Action: Arnold Kaufman and the First Teach-In," *Social Theory and Practice* 2 (1972): 42; Arnold Kaufman, *The Radical Liberal: New Man in American Politics* (New York: Atherton, 1968), xiv–xv.

history, I will argue that the vast chasm between liberalism and the New Left that many historians depict might not be such a hostile divide.[3]

Kaufman's position as a New Left intellectual can be discerned by placing him in the context developed here. He was clearly influenced by C. Wright Mills, who, as I will show, posed challenging intellectual problems for Kaufman to solve. Like Mills, Kaufman had an early (late 1950s to early 1960s) interest in England and in the New Left developing there at the time. Kaufman participated in the anti–civil defense protests of the 1960s—the sort that Paul Goodman supported in *The Society I Live in Is Mine*—and paid attention to ideas of human potentiality, autonomy, alienation, and participatory democracy. Like William Appleman Williams, Kaufman believed that protests against American foreign policy had to allude to American ideals while criticizing their misapplication. He corresponded with Williams, and the two men became allies in their shared criticisms of the peace movement, as we will see later. Due to these common intellectual traits (as well as his own ideas), Kaufman fits squarely within the post–World War II milieu of New Left intellectuals.[4]

Another "New York Immigrant Jew" Turned Leftist

Arnold Kaufman was born in 1927, and so, like Mills, was too young to be a full-fledged member of the New York Intellectual grouping and the "Old Left." But like Goodman, Kaufman was born a Jew in New York City. He attended Stuyvesant High School and then the City College of New York (CCNY)—the home of many New York Intellectuals during the Great Depression, a time that Kaufman was too young to remember. Nonetheless, Kaufman did absorb the art of spirited debate that the CCNY lunchrooms were still famous for in the 1940s. Like Williams, Kaufman entered the navy during World War II, but seemed to express little doubt about the war; he

3. Lasch, *Agony of the American Left,* 203; for interpretations of the New Left as inherently hostile toward liberalism, see Matusow, *Unraveling of America,* and some of the analysis of SDS found in Richard Ellis, *The Dark Side of the Left: Illiberal Egalitarianism in America* (Lawrence: University Press of Kansas, 1998).

4. With Goodman, Kaufman participated in a Wingspread Conference on October 26, 1966: see the Arnold Kaufman Papers, box 1. Kaufman's involvement in the anti–civil defense protests of the early 1960s can be seen in the archives, box 3, folder on the Peace Movement, Fall Out Shelters (I).

wound up participating in early civil rights protests. While Williams worked with the NAACP in Texas, Kaufman joined the Congress for Racial Equality (CORE), a civil rights organization active predominantly in northern states. At the young age of twenty-one, Kaufman participated in sit-ins against segregation in Palisades Park in New Jersey. This early experience with protest put him in touch with the radical pacifist tradition discussed in the pages of *politics*. It also made him particularly attuned to the causes of the New Left.[5]

Soon afterward, Kaufman went to Columbia University to pursue graduate work in philosophy. Here he studied with Charles Frankel, a liberal philosopher who taught a course with C. Wright Mills and with whom Kaufman had a good relationship. In choosing philosophy as a course of study, Kaufman ironically selected a profession whose mainstream attributes seemed antithetical to his own intellectual interests. By the late 1940s, American and British philosophy were both becoming increasingly influenced by logical positivism—a philosophical practice that, simply stated, saw "truth" as determined by the way in which written or spoken sentences were constructed. Philosophical inquiry became the equivalent of linguistic analysis; anything beyond analytically or empirically verifiable statements was dismissed as "metaphysics," something to be abhorred. Ethical statements, for instance, were "mere expressions of feeling," as A. J. Ayer, a logical positivist, wrote in a classic work. Logical positivism in philosophy shared much in common with the "abstracted empiricism" that C. Wright Mills hated in sociological inquiry. It limited philosophy to the analysis of language and steered it away from the larger questions of justice and politics.[6]

5. Kaufman described himself as a "New York immigrant Jew" in a letter to Branco and Natalia, June 3, 1960, Arnold Kaufman Papers, box 1; the CORE actions are documented in several résumés of Kaufman's found in the archives, as well as in a telephone interview I did with Elizabeth Kaufman, Arnold Kaufman's wife, on August 1, 2000. See also the letter from George Wiley, thanking Kaufman for lending money to CORE (January 25, 1966, Arnold Kaufman Papers, box 5, file on CORE). For more on CORE in the wider context of the civil rights movement, see August Meier and Elliot Rudwick, *CORE* (New York: Oxford University Press, 1973), and Morris, *Origins of the Civil Rights Movement,* 128–38. On 129, Morris describes CORE as an organization that "usually attracted middle-class white intellectuals" such as Kaufman.

6. A. J. Ayer, *Language, Truth, and Logic,* 2d ed. (New York: Dover, 1952), 112. For how logical positivism came to the United States, see Herbert Feigl, "The *Wiener Kreis* in America," *Perspectives in American History* 2 (1968): 630–73. On Charles Frankel, see his defense of liberalism and rationalism in *The Case for Modern Man* (New York: Harper and Brothers, 1955), and William Leuchtenburg, "Charles Frankel, 1917–1979," *South Atlantic Quarterly* 78

Kaufman made his feelings about logical positivism known, in part, by the company he kept. He met Ernest Gellner, a British philosopher and anthropologist, in 1954 when he traveled to England on a Fulbright Fellowship. The two of them talked about philosophy and the state of the left. In 1959, to much public acclaim, Gellner published *Words and Things,* a major polemic against linguistic philosophy and logical positivism. Gellner's book got inside the thinking and assumptions of this new philosophy in order to criticize it. Gellner thanked Kaufman for reading the manuscript, and Kaufman clearly lent his support. Nonetheless, Kaufman himself never took the time to write out a full-fledged criticism of logical positivism; instead, he simply defended what he thought had been left out by the new consensus in academic philosophy. Kaufman complained that linguistic philosophy had "abandoned one traditional function of philosophy—viz., the construction of social theories designed to guide individual and collective action." Because of this, logical positivism—and here Kaufman echoed a point made by Gellner—led to "political acquiescence." Rebelling against this philosophical tendency, Kaufman pledged himself to pursuing political theory, a practice that never abandoned larger questions of "collective action." A year after publishing *Words and Things,* Gellner wrote Kaufman to congratulate him on embracing a "conception of philosophy as something more than an idle pastime of a highly specialized coterie."[7]

In choosing political philosophy as his subdiscipline, Kaufman also chose pragmatism, to a large extent. In his first published essay, "The Nature and Function of Political Theory," Kaufman argued that political philosophy must have an "instrumental function"—that is, it had to measure its rele-

---

(1979): 419–27. Frankel eventually became Secretary of State for Educational and Cultural Affairs under President Johnson, but he grew disturbed over the Vietnam War, and he stayed in contact with Kaufman as the teach-in movement gained force. For Frankel's account of his brief political career, see his *High on Foggy Bottom* (New York: Harper and Row, 1968). Oddly enough, Frankel fails to receive attention even from intellectual historians working in the area of modern liberalism. On "abstracted empiricism," see Mills, *Sociological Imagination.*

7. Arnold Kaufman, review of *Philosophy, Politics, and Society,* by Peter Laslett, *Journal of Philosophy* 56 (1959): 288–89; Ernest Gellner to Arnold Kaufman, April 16, 1960, Arnold Kaufman Papers, box 1. Gellner himself complained that linguistic philosophy "refuses to undermine any accepted habits, but, on the contrary, concentrates on showing that the reasons underlying criticisms of accepted habits are in general mistaken." This is what made the philosophy "conservative." Ernest Gellner, *Words and Things* (1959; reprint, Harmondsworth: Penguin, 1968), 249. In 1965, Gellner wrote Kaufman, "I very much hope that 'technical' philosophers will or have ceased to be your reference group! They really are about as alienated from reality as anyone can be" (September 29, 1965, Arnold Kaufman Papers, box 1).

vance by certain applied practices rather than universal pronouncements. Indeed, Kaufman called for political theory to look at "consequences" and heed the teachings of "perpetual probing and testing." At the same time, though, he was wary of a philosophy wholly reliant on pragmatism. To a certain extent, he tried to stake out a middle ground between the two sides taken in an earlier debate between Dwight Macdonald, who defended universalistic ideals, and C. Wright Mills, who was a pragmatist comfortable with historical contingency (see Chaps. 1 and 2). For while expounding on the need for instrumentalism, Kaufman also embraced what he called "lofty principles" and "ultimate ideals." He explained, "Ultimate ideals, interpreted in terms of index values, can be used to evaluate conditions in a given society." As he would later explain, Kaufman did not believe that these ultimate ideals (i.e., justice, equity, democracy) needed to stand outside history or be fully justifiable. He argued that "to say that one cannot give reasons for [moral] beliefs is not the same as saying that they are *unreasoned* or *arbitrary*." Essentially, Kaufman steered a course between absolute relativism and universal absolutism (for instance, Platonic or Hegelian philosophy). He tried to marry pragmatism to a framework of democratic principles.[8]

Though not entirely at ease with the mainstream of his profession, Kaufman had no difficulty in finding a full-time teaching position after receiving his Ph.D., since academia was flush with students riding in on the benefits of the G.I. Bill. By 1955, he had moved (with his wife, Betty) to Ann Arbor, Michigan, to teach at the University of Michigan, a respectable institution that was growing at the time. Even with such a comfortable position, Kaufman never felt entirely settled in academia, however. He took a brief leave of absence and traveled to England, trying to stay up on politics with his friends from *Socialist Commentary* (a publication of democratic socialists) and Ernest Gellner, who had numerous contacts with the first rumblings of Britain's New Left. Kaufman wrote for a variety of publications—increasingly, popular and journalistic magazines rather than professional or academic journals. And he started to think of himself as more and more of an activist—someone who took seriously his own belief in "consequences" informing political theory. He threw himself into local struggles around Ann Arbor, especially those surrounding northern civil rights struggles, unemployment, and urban renewal. Just as Mills had during the 1940s, he assisted the educa-

8. Arnold Kaufman, "The Nature and Function of Political Theory," *Journal of Philosophy* 51 (1954): 5, 6, 7, 10, 22, and "Must Morality Be True?" *Quadrant* (Spring 1960): 72.

tional departments of certain labor unions. By the mid-to-late 1950s, Kaufman was well on his way to becoming an activist intellectual.[9]

Participatory Democracy as New Left Ideal: Kaufman's Intellectual Balancing Act, SDS, and the Port Huron Statement

Clearly Arnold Kaufman was a man associated with the left by the late 1950s, but *what* left? Part of the answer to this question can be discerned in the intellectual sources he started drawing upon and the targets of his political criticism. He was clearly influenced by C. Wright Mills, as Kaufman showed in a review essay that discussed *The Sociological Imagination*. Kaufman appreciated Mills's willingness to play the role of public and political intellectual within "these academic dog days of excessive caution and excessive jargon." Kaufman stressed Mills's penchant for rationally argued radicalism and his reliance upon John Dewey (who, Kaufman argued, informed Mills's critique of social scientists who never believed in citizens' capacities to practice democracy). This influence of Mills and Dewey would stay with Kaufman for years to come, as would other intellectual sources. In the same year that he pronounced Mills an intellectual hero, Kaufman condemned the Labor Party of England for being too tactical, too obsessed with holding power rather than "creating a new vision appropriate to the changing conditions of the modern Welfare State." Here Kaufman picked up on sentiments expressed by the British New Left—the sort of thinkers with whom Mills worked. Intellectuals like E. P. Thompson were making the same critique of the Labor Party and the limits of the welfare state as Kaufman had in the pages of *The Nation*. Kaufman was not content with welfare-state liberalism, and soon he was taking issue with the plight of "powerlessness" in modern society—the curse that Mills, Goodman, and Williams believed a New Left needed to overcome. And in calling for an "American Left" to confront powerlessness, Kaufman started to set out the principle of "participatory democracy."[10]

9. Most of this information comes from my interview with Betty Kaufman. By 1960, Arnold Kaufman had been active with numerous unions: see, for instance, his correspondence with Ben Segal, director of the Education Department with the International Union of Electrical, Radio, and Machine Workers (AFL-CIO), March 2, 1960, Arnold Kaufman Papers, box 1.

10. Arnold Kaufman, "The Irresponsibility of American Social Scientists," *Inquiry* 3

The idea of participatory democracy was the crux of Kaufman's New Left thinking. He came to the idea early. Reviewing Russell Kirk's book on conservative political thought in 1955, Kaufman pointed out that conservatives not only despised socialism but also *democracy*. Seeing human beings as fallen creatures—as touched by original sin—conservatives believed that humans were incapable of assuming the freedom and responsibility that democracy demanded. Criticizing this premise, Kaufman wrote that "few would deny that men can become better or worse through active participation in decision-making—precisely the sort of experience which enables human beings to act responsibly." To Kaufman, it seemed better to risk opening up opportunities for citizens to improve their individual standing and commitment to a public good than to lock them into a preordained status of depravity. By associating antidemocratic thought with the right, Kaufman made it clear that any future left would have to make democracy central to its political vision.[11]

Five years after writing this review, Kaufman noticed the same sort of antidemocratic position being taken by "end of ideology" thinkers—intellectuals more clearly "liberal" and to the left of Russell Kirk and those Kirk had discussed. Though Kaufman did not take on Daniel Bell, he did criticize another important political sociologist in the "end of ideology" school—namely, Seymour Martin Lipset. Kaufman was especially perturbed by Lipset's emphasis on working-class authoritarianism. It seemed that Lipset had used sociological findings about authoritarian attitudes among America's workers to construct an argument that ordinary citizens should not be trusted with democratic responsibilities. Kaufman argued back, "Lipset's priorities are fine for some parts of sociology. But when they are imported into moral discussion they are enervating and misleading." That is, sociological evidence could not disprove or invalidate a normative commitment to democratic participation. Slipping into a rare ironic tone, Kaufman wrote, "'Democracy' is not just another word, to be subjected to the sterilizing prescrip-

(1960): 102; "The Affluent Underdog," *The Nation*, November 5, 1960, 350; and "A Philosophy for the American Left," *Socialist Commentary*, November 1963, 14. For the British New Left critique of the welfare state, see Kenny, *The First New Left*, 144–46. In *The Radical Liberal*, Kaufman wrote, "One tendency of Mills's thought leads straight to what I have called the politics of radical pressure" (161). I will come back to this point; for now, suffice it to say that it shows Kaufman's continued reliance on Mills's thinking to inform his own political philosophy.

11. Review of *The Conservative Mind*, by Russell Kirk, *Journal of Philosophy* 52 (1955): 496.

tions of methodologically passionate social scientists." Rather, for Kaufman, democracy was one of the "lofty principles" that should guide the thinking of political theorists. Democracy was a "means of developing human potentialities," not something to be rejected due to the findings of academic social scientists. If people were found to be authoritarian, Kaufman seemed to suggest, than the political theorist should search for means (pragmatically tested, of course) to engage them and change their attitudes. Any solution to the problem of authoritarianism would have to include democratic participation—not abandon the principle.[12]

A future left needed to confront antidemocratic thinking. To begin buttressing the intellectual side of this effort, Kaufman recovered the political thinking of John Dewey, especially his classic work, *The Public and Its Problems* (1927). Like Dewey, Kaufman held democracy as a primary value to guide political theory. As any pragmatist would, Kaufman shied away from providing an absolutist grounding for democracy, any justification that stood outside the context of human history. His argument stemmed from a faith—or a "will to believe," a phrase William James once used and that Kaufman picked up on—in human potentiality. Knowingly or not, Kaufman borrowed a concept from the Gestalt therapy that Goodman had been practicing around that time. Kaufman declared, "The main justifying function of participation is development of man's essential powers—inducing human dignity and respect, and making men responsible, by developing their powers of deliberate action." Implicitly, Kaufman made a further attack on "end of ideology" thinkers here. He argued against those who believed that democracy's "main justifying function . . . has been . . . the extent to which it protects or stabilizes a community." Rather, Kaufman embraced the possibility of instability serving as a potential good. He argued that democracy was based not on a smoothly functioning social order, but on the "contribution it can make to the development of human powers of thought, feeling, and action."[13]

By emphasizing human potentiality, Kaufman risked sounding as though he were a blind optimist, one devoted to the idea that humans would always

12. "Evidence and Absolutes," *The Nation*, June 4, 1960, 496. Kaufman rightly showed that much of Lipset's antidemocratic thinking drew from the classical work of Joseph Schumpeter, *Capitalism, Socialism, and Democracy* (1942; reprint, New York: Harper and Row, 1976).

13. "Human Nature and Participatory Democracy" (1960), reprinted in *The Bias of Pluralism,* ed. William Connolly (New York: Atherton, 1969), 198, 184. For Kaufman's use of William James's "will to believe" idea, see 194.

act in accord with democratic principles. But such was not the case, for Kaufman heeded arguments about human evil. He simply argued that it was healthier for a political order to arrange itself with the *hope* that humans would act better than worse; besides, he argued, it seemed absurd to say that any individual had reached his or her potential, because people were constantly growing and changing. A political order should allow humans to discover their potential, rather than assume their depravity. Here Kaufman followed Dewey again. In *The Public and Its Problems,* Dewey had argued against his intellectual foe, Walter Lippmann, who believed that governing should be trusted only to elites informed by educated experts. Dewey wrote, "Popular government is educative as other modes of political regulation are not." The *potential* for education and enlightenment on the part of regular citizens became the major grounds of democracy, not any inherent goodness in humans. Similarly, Kaufman argued that only a democratic political order could provide opportunities for education that created citizens "able to judge men and policies with reasonable intelligence, and also to initiate policy in suitable spheres." Education and democracy were then synonymous; each justified the other, and each relied on a belief in human potentiality.[14]

Kaufman emphatically argued that participatory democracy required a "devolution of power." Since citizens needed to participate in public life in order to create a better society, they needed to have decision-making power within their reach. But for Kaufman, participatory democracy was not the equivalent of anarchism. Like Goodman, Kaufman wanted to decentralize decision making where possible and fruitful. At the same time, he argued that participatory democracy "must be achieved without dismantling that structure of laws and institutions which enables coherent planning." Instead of quickly decentralizing the welfare state, for instance, Kaufman followed the reasoning of the British New Left and of the social democrat Gunnar Myrdal. He wanted to "*enrich* the Welfare State by increasing the element of participatory democracy." That is, decentralization needed to be balanced

---

14. Dewey, *The Public and Its Problems,* 207; Arnold Kaufman, "Two Cheers for American Education," *Socialist Commentary,* November 1959, 23, and "Human Nature and Participatory Democracy." Kaufman pointed out that contemporary pragmatists forgot John Dewey's adamant defense of democracy. In a review of Sidney Hook's *The Paradoxes of Freedom,* Kaufman argued that Hook ignored "Dewey's stress on the developmental functions of responsible participation": review of *The Paradoxes of Freedom,* by Sidney Hook, *Journal of Philosophy* 62 (1965): 241. For more on the context in which John Dewey wrote *The Public and Its Problems,* see Westbrook, *John Dewey and American Democracy,* and Mattson, *Creating a Democratic Public,* chapters 3 through 6.

against a strong government capable of protecting individual rights and administering certain social provisions. This necessary balance made clear why Kaufman thought participatory democracy should be seen as a principle of the left. The good society the left needed to aim for was one that ensured not only economic, social, and civic equality but also participation as a means to realize each individual's highest potential.[15]

This idea captured the minds of the young activists gathered in Students for a Democratic Society, especially Tom Hayden, whose intellectual debt to Kaufman was enormous. As Kaufman recounted to a young historian writing a history of the New Left during the 1970s, Hayden "got turned on to the idea of a democracy of participation, and in any event, first started to think seriously about the theoretical dimensions of the topic, when he took one of my political philosophy courses." This was not a pretentious claim, for Hayden would later confirm in his autobiography that "a philosophy course taught by Professor Arnold Kaufman introduced me to the concept of 'participatory democracy.'" James Miller, writing on the intellectual sources of the Port Huron Statement, suggests that Hayden "closely followed his teacher," making it unclear where Hayden's thinking began and Kaufman's stopped within the Port Huron Statement. When Kaufman participated in the famous Port Huron conference, he felt proud of his student's political astuteness even as he retained "a healthy respect for" old leftists, such as Michael Harrington, who argued that Hayden was not being stringently anticommunist.[16]

In developing the idea of participatory democracy, Kaufman clearly gave SDS one of the intellectual building blocks that helped define the New Left against the Old. When SDS's Port Huron Statement actually came out, it manifested Kaufman's influence: the Statement lashed out at those who believed that an ordinary citizen was "inherently incapable of directing his own

15. Kaufman, "The Affluent Underdog," 350 (my italics), and "A Philosophy for the American Left," 15. Kaufman greatly admired Gunnar Myrdal's *Beyond the Welfare State* (1960). For this book's conception of participatory democracy and Myrdal's biography, see Walter Jackson, *Gunnar Myrdal and America's Conscience: Social Engineering and Racial Liberalism, 1938–1987* (Chapel Hill: University of North Carolina Press, 1990), 345.

16. Arnold Kaufman to George White, June 19, 1970, Arnold Kaufman Papers, box 4, SDS file; Hayden, *Reunion,* 42; James Miller, *"Democracy Is in the Streets,"* 95. On June 22, 1961, Tom Hayden formally wrote to Arnold Kaufman to ask him to "write a short essay on participatory democracy" for SDS (letter in Arnold Kaufman Papers, box 4, SDS file). On Harrington's relation to the New Left and his well-developed, left-wing, Trotskyist-inspired sectarianism, see Maurice Isserman, *The Other American: The Life of Michael Harrington* (New York: Public Affairs, 2000).

affairs"; and it argued for "participatory democracy" and for a federal program aimed at "the abolition of the structural circumstances of poverty" in
the same breath. Young enough to have evaded the sectarianism of the Old
Left—something that always drove the career and polemics of Michael Harrington—Kaufman helped provide the basic thinking that went into the
intellectual formulation of a New Left. In the Port Huron Statement, Tom
Hayden and his fellow SDS-ers tried to balance participatory democracy
with the Old Left (and modern liberal) concern for social justice.[17]

By 1962, the year of SDS's Port Huron conference, Kaufman had set out a
well-reasoned theory of participatory democracy as a concept that fueled a
New Left. He had already been engaged in the direct action activities of the
civil rights movement for quite some time. He traveled south to the Tuskegee
Institute in 1964–1965, where he cemented a relationship with SNCC and
other civil rights activists. As previously discussed, he had been involved in
anti–civil defense protests and other initiatives of the burgeoning peace movement. He even caught flak from fellow civil rights activists for his peace
activities, being told that he was spreading his energy too thin. (Kaufman
believed the civil rights and peace movements were symbiotic.) At the time
that Kaufman was writing on participatory democracy and engaging in activism (as well as helping raise his daughter and trying to acquire academic
tenure), the Vietnam War was heating up. Soon, Kaufman would take the next
step in becoming a New Left intellectual. He would help organize teach-ins at
both the local and national levels, and in so doing, he would start to resolve a
tension that always marked the work of New Left intellectuals.[18]

The Cultivation of an Engaged Intellectual Via the Teach-In

Democracy requires dissent. Dissent requires an effective and courageous opposition to Government policy.
—Arnold Kaufman, "Teach-Ins: New Force for the Times," 1965

17. Port Huron Statement, reprinted in James Miller, *"Democracy Is in the Streets,"* 333,
365. Today, some younger historians question the importance of the Port Huron Statement in
relation to the wider history of the New Left: see, for instance, Smith, "Present at the Creation and Other Myths." Clearly, the Statement was not as important as some other factors
(1940s pacifism, the civil rights movement, and so on) in relation to the activist New Left, but
in terms of intellectual history, I believe that the Statement's significance should not be
underplayed.

18. The information in this paragraph is drawn from my interview with Betty Kaufman.

While becoming active in the peace movement, Kaufman started to think about what role intellectuals and academics should play in politics. Though Kaufman never talked directly about the book, it would seem that C. Wright Mills's *The Causes of World War III* had an impact on his thinking. Mills placed intellectuals at the center of any future peace movement. They could build democratic publics capable of resisting government policy through intelligent deliberation and protest. Kaufman's own suggestions about the role of intellectuals in the peace movement seemed rooted even further back in Mills's biography: in the 1940s, Mills had called for alliances between labor unions and academics. In a letter Kaufman wrote to Dr. Benjamin Spock, noted child-care specialist and fellow member of the National Committee for a Sane Nuclear Policy (SANE), Kaufman suggested putting together "a research team of anti-war social scientists to do the much-needed investigations that might bring relevant evidence to bear on the interminable tactical debates that lead nowhere because no one really knows." Research could serve as a political weapon, Kaufman argued, and thereby establish a role for intellectuals in the movement. Though nothing seemed to come from this suggestion, Kaufman was clearly anxious to find a home for intellectuals and academics in social movements, to give content to Mills's earlier (and often vague) declarations about intellectual responsibility.[19]

The Vietnam War, of course, changed everything for America—especially for the peace movement. Suddenly, activists redirected their energy and attention from the nuclear arms race to an obscure and little-understood land war. In Ann Arbor, there were plenty of young professors and student activists engaged in both the civil rights and peace movements who were quickly growing critical of the Vietnam War. They wanted to find some way to express their anger at U.S. intervention. At the same time, they hoped to take advantage of their location within a university setting and their dedication to critical education. As Jack Rothman points out, many professors and students drew inspiration from the "Freedom Schools" that SNCC had instituted in the South during 1963. In these Freedom Schools, activists and regular citizens met to discuss not only the issues facing the movement but also wider questions of culture and politics. Freedom Schools established spaces in which ordinary citizens and educators could deliberate openly. They created a democratic public with which intellectuals could

19. Kaufman to Spock, undated, Arnold Kaufman Papers, box 3, Peace Movement file.

engage. Many activists believed that something similar was needed to open up questions about American foreign policy.[20]

At first, a set of professors at the University of Michigan wanted to have a moratorium on classes in order to hold a protest. The move would probably have been declared illegal, appearing to be a strike on the part of the faculty, which made some professors uncomfortable. Besides, this was prior to any of the big protests against the war that came later in the decade; most Americans knew little about the Vietnam imbroglio. As interested professors discussed the consequences of a moratorium, more of them expressed hesitation about the whole thing. In order not to lose momentum, a group of professors called for a meeting to resolve the debate. Held at Kaufman's home, participants stayed up practically all night debating what course of action should be taken. Debate was fierce, especially as one group adamantly defended the idea of a moratorium. It appears that Professors Marshall Sahlins and Eric Wolf, both anthropologists, came up with a compromise, however: instead of dismissing their classes, professors would hold a "teach-in" from 8:00 P.M. until 8:00 A.M. As one participant in the meeting recounted later, "We figured instead of canceling classes, we'd show just how much we *cared about* teaching—we'd teach all night!" Kaufman threw in with this position. At first, the moratorium believers stood their ground, but eventually (probably out of a combination of debate and sheer exhaustion) the group reached something of a consensus. It was agreed that an all-night teach-in would be a more productive way to express anger, since it would focus on nurturing discussion rather than pure protest and would therefore ensure wider participation among students and professors. Many of the participants at the meeting also understood that a teach-in ensured cooperation from the university administration. And so on March 24, 1965, the first teach-in against the Vietnam War was held at the University of Michigan.[21]

20. On the peace movement's shift from the nuclear arms race to Vietnam, see Paul Boyer, "From Activism to Apathy: The American People and Nuclear Weapons, 1963–1980," *Journal of American History* 70 (1984): 821–44. On the political culture of Ann Arbor, I rely upon my telephone interview with William Gamson, June 7, 2000. Jack Rothman makes the point about being inspired by Freedom Schools in his "Radical Liberal Strategy in Action," 35. For more on the Freedom Schools and their relation to the civil rights movement, see Clayborne Carson, *In Struggle: SNCC and the Black Awakening of the 1960s* (Cambridge: Harvard University Press, 1981), 109–10, 119–21. For how they related to democratic theory and engaged citizenship, see Sara Evans and Harry Boyte, *Free Spaces: The Sources of Democratic Change in America* (New York: Harper and Row, 1986), 65.

21. Jack Rothman, telephone interview with author, June 6, 2000. This account also

Arnold Kaufman became a leader of the Michigan teach-in. He handled the press relations and administrative details (e.g., finding a space for meetings, contacting speakers, and distributing publicity). And perhaps most important of all, he served as the culminating speaker—at the wee hour of 7:00 A.M. With so much thought and energy going into it, the teach-in was an enormous success. It garnered the support of two hundred faculty and drew three thousand students who listened to a number of speakers and presentations opposed to U.S. intervention in Vietnam. Plagued by three bomb threats (probably phoned in by right-wing students) and the anger of Governor George Romney, who accused its leaders of perpetrating "anarchy," the teach-in managed to gain national attention. (Enough attention that other teach-ins at a variety of colleges and universities quickly followed, a total of at least fifty in 1965.) Clearly, Kaufman and his fellow professors had started something of a movement.[22]

Most important in this context was how the teach-in provided some answers to Kaufman's question about the role intellectuals should play in the peace movement particularly and politics more broadly. Kaufman argued that the teach-in provided a democratic forum for intellectuals and counteracted the general "sense of powerlessness" that had plagued them in the post–World War II period. Kaufman explained, "If our government is to be restrained from pursuing its present hazardous course [in Vietnam], a significant portion of public opinion must be mobilized against its policies. We believe that the academic community has a *special responsibility* for accom-

---

draws from Rothman, "Radical Liberal Strategy in Action"; Gamson, interview; Tom Wells, *The War Within: America's Battle over Vietnam* (Berkeley and Los Angeles: University of California Press, 1994), 23–24; and materials throughout the University of Michigan Teach-In folder, Arnold Kaufman Papers. For an administrator's perspective, see William Haber, "The Birth of the Teach-In: Authority Without Freedom," *Michigan Quarterly Review* 7 (1968): 262–67. For the historical context of the teach-ins (including just how "lonely" antiwar sentiment was in 1965), see Nancy Zaroulis and Gerald Sullivan, *Who Spoke Up? American Protest Against the War in Vietnam, 1963–1975* (Garden City, N.J.: Doubleday, 1984), 37–38.

22. On the events of the teach-in, I rely upon the following: "A Short History of the University of Michigan Teach-In," Arnold Kaufman Papers, box 4, Peace Movement folder; Rothman, "Radical Liberal Strategy in Action"; notes found throughout the Kaufman Papers, box 4, University of Michigan Teach-In folder. On George Romney's attack on the "anarchy" of the teach-in, see Romney to Arnold Kaufman, Arnold Kaufman Papers, box 1. That Kaufman spoke at 7:00 A.M. is confirmed by Fritjhof Bergmann, a colleague of Arnold Kaufman, in a telephone interview on June 7, 2000. On the "fifty Teach-Ins at campuses across the land," I rely upon a document written by Kaufman, Arnold Kaufman Papers, box 4, folder on the National Teach-In.

plishing such mobilization. In view of the complexity of the problem and the difficulty in getting reliable information about Vietnam, our role as intellectuals is particularly crucial."

To a large extent, this special responsibility related to professors' ability to speak up with fewer repercussions than most people faced, due to the tenure system created in the wake of McCarthyism. Academics, Kaufman argued, had more freedom than other individuals, especially in relation to their work lives. Because of their self-proclaimed commitment to pursuing truth, academics also had a more profound responsibility to show their students and publics that "the life of reason need not be a life of endless, impotent deliberation." By making their arguments pertinent to a deliberating public considering live political options, academics would enliven democracy.[23]

Though intellectuals had a special responsibility, Kaufman made clear that they were no vanguard. After all, professors taking part in the teach-in "have in common with all persons a responsibility as citizens." That is, academics might have a specific role to play in providing information and interpretations of events, but they also had to listen to other citizens and take part in a general deliberative process. The intellectual was both responsible for creating a democratic public—as C. Wright Mills and Paul Goodman had argued—and listening to what this public had to say. In the end, the special role of the intellectual was "to build a society which is free because its citizens are thoughtful and informed." The intellectual helped create such a society and also *lived within it,* thus becoming an equal member with fellow citizens engaged in a mutual process of deliberation.[24]

This argument led Kaufman to criticize the modern university. Here he echoed ideas expounded by Mills, Goodman, and the leaders of the Free Speech Movement. First, Kaufman lambasted the notion that the university was neutral and should never become embroiled in political conflict. Kaufman rightfully pointed out that the university supported "the CIA," "military training," and "research for the Defense Department." Worse yet was the fact that "multiversities" had become, "after World War II . . . shopping centers for careerists." For Kaufman, these tendencies led to alienation on the part of students—most clearly witnessed in the events surrounding the Free Speech Movement at Berkeley that Paul Goodman had supported.

23. Kaufman, "Teach-Ins," 291; Kaufman in a letter and other statements found in the Kaufman Papers, box 4, University of Michigan Teach-In folder; and *The Radical Liberal,* 130.
24. Kaufman, "Teach-Ins," 287; and statement in the Kaufman Papers, box 4, University of Michigan Teach-In folder.

What students found at the modern multiversity, Kaufman argued, was a situation in which

> careerism is rampant; in which many of the most distinguished faculty members never teach undergraduates; in which conformist accommodation to power is rewarded, and authentic thought and action penalized; in which money talks—especially federal money; in which the gap between commencement rhetoric and educational practice is enormous; in which commitment to scholarship and research provides a rationale for political irresponsibility; in which, above all, basic decisions about educational processes and about the nonacademic lives of students are made by men who know little and care less about these things.

To counteract this cynical situation, Kaufman held up an alternative vision of education (inspired by Dewey and Goodman, it would seem) within which citizens "acquire the habit of reason and of Socratic self-examination" through a "lifelong educational experience" and a "liberal conception of education." In accord with this view of education and his idea of participatory democracy, Kaufman argued for more engagement on the part of students in making decisions about the future of their education—which included, not surprisingly, the ability to debate such things as the Vietnam War. Kaufman believed that "student participation" generated "excellent preparation for . . . assuming the roles of citizen [and] leader." Though this principle was already developed by the Free Speech Movement and Paul Goodman, Kaufman gave it concrete form in his thinking on the teach-in. Students essentially had an opportunity to create a deliberating public about issues with civic consequences. Participatory democracy, Kaufman suggested, needed to live within *and* without academia's walls.[25]

The Michigan teach-in provided a solution to the dilemma of the New Left intellectual. By engaging in it, intellectuals on the left could commit themselves to deliberation and the collective quest for truth. Indeed, intellectuals became directly responsible for nurturing these processes. At the same time, the intellectual could pledge him or herself to certain substantive goals—namely, ending an unjust war and seeking out an alternative foreign policy. By taking part in a teach-in, intellectuals would try to convince

25. *The Radical Liberal,* 127, 106, 124, 42. (In the notes to follow, *The Radical Liberal* will be abbreviated *RL*.)

fellow citizens that they were right (using facts as well as the arts of rational and passionate persuasion), but they had to confront a deliberating public that could very easily disagree with them. The intellectual both contributed and was held accountable to a democratic public. The teach-in created an opportunity for intellectuals to be heard but also to be challenged, for regular citizens to be educated but also to educate. By organizing and thinking about the teach-in, Kaufman found a resolution to the tension of New Left intellectuals. He seemed to think that perhaps the "powerless" intellectual was now a figure of the past.

Building a National Peace Movement: The Risks of an Engaged Intellectual

The National Teach-In is conceived as a rebellion of the intellectuals against the ideology of the Cold War, and especially its manifestation in Vietnam; against the impotence of the public, and particularly the intellectual, in determining government policy . . .
—National Teach-In Flyer, 1965

As we have seen, William Appleman Williams was content with the proliferation of teach-ins at college campuses across America in 1965. Williams thought that teach-ins should remain local in nature and that any attempt to go national would inherently damage their core principles of conversation and face-to-face dialogue. Arnold Kaufman understood this sentiment (or at least his own belief in decentralization and participatory democracy would suggest so). Nonetheless, Kaufman worried that teach-ins could become insular, walled off to the peculiar world of academia and thus incapable of transforming American politics. A desire to counteract this possibility led Kaufman to help organize a national teach-in in the wake of the heralded success at Michigan.

Recognized for his central role in planning and managing the Michigan teach-in, Kaufman was encouraged to take a lead in organizing the National Teach-In on Vietnam. Held on May 15, 1965 (fewer than two months after the Michigan teach-in), in Washington, D.C., this event had spokespeople from the Johnson administration confront and debate intellectual and academic critics of U.S. foreign policy. Kaufman's responsibilities grew in proportion to the requirements of this high-profile national event. He helped choose the speakers (no easy matter, because he needed to maintain a bal-

ance between pro- and antiwar sentiments, while bracketing his own feelings on the issue). Kaufman also dealt with journalists; this task was made
even more difficult by journalists who took the views of certain participants
as representative of the entire event. Kaufman and his colleagues also tried to
get the networks to broadcast the affair and, in so doing, attempted to retain
control over what C. Wright Mills had called the "cultural apparatus." Organizers wanted the media to treat the proceedings as fairly and rationally as
possible, making sure that the intellectual participants did not lose control
over the event. They set rules and tried their best to prevent media misrep-
resentation. Essentially, Kaufman wanted to reproduce the deliberative processes captured in local teach-ins at a national level.[26]

Perhaps the biggest coup for the National Teach-In organizers was getting McGeorge (Mac) Bundy, national security adviser to the Kennedy and
Johnson administrations as well as an astute intellectual, to participate (for
more on Bundy, see Chap. 3). In committing to the event, Bundy made
certain demands, such as a balance between spokespeople for and against the
current U.S. foreign policy. Bundy advocated the participation of Arthur
Schlesinger Jr., a liberal intellectual who started his career in government
consulting with the Kennedy administration and then, like Bundy, moved
on to the Johnson administration (the same Schlesinger that C. Wright
Mills, Paul Goodman, and William Appleman Williams had criticized).
These two high-profile figures generated more attention from the press.
With national networks promising to cover the teach-in, Kaufman and other
organizers had to find a bigger place to hold the event, landing eventually
on the Sheraton Park Hotel. Not surprisingly, Kaufman's workload now
included nights without sleep. A colleague who worked on this event with
him described the entire experience and Kaufman's perception of it as
"thrilling."[27]

On the day of the event, Bundy failed to show (he supposedly had to take
care of other pressing foreign policy matters in the Dominican Republic),
and Schlesinger gave a muddled defense of the Johnson administration's position on Vietnam. Despite this, the event received excellent coverage, and it
broadcasted the thinking of those who opposed the Vietnam War to a much

---

26. On the National Teach-In, see Max Frankel, "Vietnam Debate Heard on 100 Campuses," *New York Times,* May 16, 1965, A1; Meg Greenfield, "After the Washington Teach-
In," *The Reporter,* June 3, 1965, 16–19; and the materials in the Kaufman Papers, box 4, folder
on the National Teach-In.

27. Gamson, interview.

wider audience than ever before. In addition to receiving coverage on all major networks, the National Teach-In was broadcast live to over one hundred college campuses. Kaufman believed that the event served as "a means of vitalizing the process of discussion and debate without which democracy lacks significance. A free society requires that its citizens not only express their will, but that they do so in a reasoned manner." It also provided a stage on which intellectuals could find a wider audience while balancing a commitment to truth and political engagement. Observing the event, Jack Gould, a journalist for the *New York Times,* gushed about its significance. It was, he explained, "as if the intellectual campus community suddenly had come out of hiding to serve as an exciting new catalyst of national thought and opinion." Though critics like William Appleman Williams (who, it should be pointed out, actually participated in the event) thought that the national teach-in corrupted the local nature of previous teach-ins, Kaufman held that it was worth the risk to try to take the democratic debate and deliberation that had worked locally to a national level. The only thing to be lost was academic insularity; the return was the exposure of more and more American citizens to dissent and debate.[28]

Kaufman's optimism, though, may not have been appropriate. A warning came from Steve Weissman, a young student activist and writer. Weissman believed that after the event, the "teach-in professors" would "perform" like all other academics. They would simply "write for little magazines, publish books, go to meetings where the same people continually meet each other." Weissman wrote, "Talking amongst themselves becomes the whole of action [for professors] rather than a necessary background for action." He would go on to make the same argument in an article published in *The New Leader.* Whatever their general merit, these arguments certainly did not apply to Kaufman, who had found his preferred role in being an activist intellectual committed to re-creating a democratic public. Accepting that his own writing and intellectual work might suffer, Kaufman threw himself into even more activist work than before.[29]

Kaufman started by assisting academics on other campuses who wanted to

28. Materials found in the Kaufman Papers, box 4, folder on the National Teach-In; Jack Gould's editorial appeared in the *New York Times,* May 17, 1965 (article found in the Kaufman Papers, box 4, National Teach-In folder).

29. Steve Weissman to Arnold Kaufman, November 15, 1966, Arnold Kaufman Papers, box 1; Steve Weissman, "Lament for the Teach-Ins," *The New Leader,* March 27, 1967, 14–19.

organize teach-ins and public events aimed at confronting the Vietnam War. He helped form and then served on the board (as Vice President of Public Relations) of the Inter-University Committee for a Hearing on Vietnam (IUC). On June 21, 1965, the group successfully set up a televised debate, moderated by Eric Sevareid, between McGeorge Bundy and Hans Morgenthau, making up for the former's absence at the National Teach-In. Kaufman served as the point person for the press on this event. Then in 1966, the IUC formed "The National Dialogue," which provided "seminar and conference packets for local or regional groups which contain films, tapes, and written material from all points of view" on Vietnam. The goal was to make it easier for local activists to organize teach-ins and debates. The IUC also set up a network for speakers on the war, including those who had traveled from Vietnam. Kaufman saw the benefit in having a national network that grounded itself in local discussion. In fact, he believed that the best "technique" to follow was "the political coffee hour to which neighborhood groups are invited by some local sympathizer." National networks and assistance would aid local deliberation.[30]

But Kaufman's hope for the IUC and the organization's direction started to clash one year after the organization formed. Increasingly, the organization's staff started pressing to support protests (including things like draft card burnings and more theatrical tactics) rather than educational and discussion-based events. Kaufman believed that the IUC's "appropriate function is that of making the scholarship and dissenting commitments of academic people relevant to the discussion and debate of foreign policy generally, and of Vietnam in particular." Once the organization threw in with the International Days of Protest (IDP), started in 1965 by organizers in Berkeley, California (including the notorious soon-to-be-Yippie, Jerry Rubin), and the National Coordinating Committee to End the War in Vietnam (NCC), debate within the IUC took a new turn. Kaufman called the endorsement of IDP a "strategic disaster," because confrontational protest would alienate undecided Americans more than it would win them over. Though William Appleman Williams and Kaufman differed on the National Teach-In, they reached consensus on this point. Williams wrote Kaufman about his "strategic disaster" interpretation: "I agree with your analysis for the most part; and, in fact, wrote newspaper columns to these points right after the Wash-

---

30. Leaflet in Arnold Kaufman Papers, box 4, folder on IUC; Kaufman to the IUC Board, letter dated November 16, 1965, Arnold Kaufman Papers, box 4, IDP folder. All the other information about the IUC comes from the IUC folder in the Arnold Kaufman Papers.

ington teach-in, and further refused, after finding out what was planned here, to participate actively in the Madison part of the IDP. Anticipating just what happened, I spent the following week talking with the Jaycees, Wisconsin newspaper people, etc. in an effort to repair some of the damage." But Williams and Kaufman were in the minority as more and more IUC members—feeling an understandable sense of urgency about the war and a need to make their anger known—wanted to get involved in direct protest. On May 9, 1967, Kaufman decided that there was nothing else to do but resign, complaining that the group had focused too much on protest and that Robert Greenblatt, IUC's vice president, was "authoritarian, arbitrary, reckless, and intolerable." Not surprisingly, the IUC dissolved soon afterward, merging into the general protest movement building in America at the time.[31]

Kaufman's complaints about the IUC reflected his penchant for strategic thinking—for *applied* political theory that examined the consequences of certain decisions. His essay, "The International Days of Protest: A Strategic Disaster," which circulated among the IUC's membership, was a prime example of this. The general message of this polemical essay was that confrontational protests often did more to make protesters feel good about themselves than to change things for the better. The culmination of this therapeutic tendency, Kaufman argued, was Norman Mailer, known for appearing at protests drunk, loud, and confrontational. Kaufman argued that Mailer "seems to think that foul-mouthed abuse is the moral equivalent of civil disobedience." Mailer served as an easy target, but one that made Kaufman's larger point for him: the peace movement was starting to alienate itself from the American public. For Kaufman, the teach-in—which was deliberative in nature, rather than confrontational—served as a counterexample to Mailer's narcissism. Interestingly enough, Kaufman started the IDP essay off by quoting C. Wright Mills's essay on intellectuals and powerlessness written for *politics* back in the 1940s. Mills had cautioned that the intellectual must be "aware of the sphere of strategy that is really open to his influence." Kaufman believed that his critique did what Mills had demanded of intellec-

---

31. Kaufman in a statement to the IUC, undated, Arnold Kaufman Papers, box 4, folder on IUC; Kaufman, "International Days of Protest: A Strategic Disaster," essay forwarded to IUC members, Arnold Kaufman Papers, box 4, IDP folder; Williams to Kaufman, undated letter ("Saturday night" written on top), box 4, IDP folder. For more on the history of the IDP and IUC, see Zaroulis and Sullivan, *Who Spoke Up?* and Wells, *The War Within*, 51.

tuals engaging in political change. It asked them to balance a politics of telling the truth with a critical analysis of strategic effectiveness.[32]

When Kaufman quit the IUC, he was joined by an old comrade (and later, enemy) of C. Wright Mills, Irving Howe. Howe was becoming increasingly vocal in his criticism of the New Left, and Kaufman was drawn to his critique. It must have surprised Howe, then, when Kaufman started to distance himself from Howe's increasingly strident and dismissive attitude toward the New Left. Indeed, one year after leaving the IUC together, Kaufman defended Tom Hayden against Howe's attacks. In a letter to Kaufman, Howe turned their debate into the sort of question any good editor asks: "Would you want to write that more sympathetic account of the New Left about which you speak?" What Howe perceived (correctly) as identification with or at least sympathy for the New Left came out in Kaufman's complaint that *Dissent*'s editors were alienating New Left writers and readers. Though still sympathetic to some of Howe's critique, Kaufman remained closer to the New Left. In order to clarify just where he stood on all of this, Kaufman decided to write *The Radical Liberal*—a book that, not surprisingly, was printed first as an entire issue of *Dissent*. Kaufman had responded to Howe's editorial query by setting out a political philosophy that tried to synthesize radicalism and liberalism.[33]

Radical Liberalism: A Political Philosophy in Dialogue with the New Left

The liberal tradition possesses moral and intellectual resources richer than those of any competing tradition.
—Arnold Kaufman, *The Radical Liberal: New Man in American Politics*, 1968

The intellectuals studied in the previous chapters clearly differed in their attitudes toward liberalism. Mills had suggested the need to preserve certain

32. Kaufman, "International Days of Protest," 14, Arnold Kaufman Papers, box 4, IDP folder. Mailer's style of political engagement can be picked up from reading the opening pages of *The Armies of the Night: History as a Novel, the Novel as History* (New York: Signet, 1968).

33. Howe to Kaufman, October 4, 1968, Arnold Kaufman Papers, box 3, *Dissent* folder (2). The debates between Kaufman and Howe concerning the New Left and SDS are found here as well. Kaufman eventually became totally frustrated with *Dissent* when it refused to break with the League for Industrial Democracy (LID)—the organization that spawned SDS but was still endorsing Hubert Humphrey in 1968. See Kaufman's plea to the editors of *Dissent* to stay open to the New Left and break from LID (letter dated April 3, 1969, Arnold Kaufman Papers, box 3, *Dissent* folder [1]). On Howe's thought, see *Beyond the New Left*, ed. Howe, and Alexander, *Irving Howe*, chapter 6.

elements within the tradition, while William Appleman Williams seemed willing to scrap most of it. Arnold Kaufman was the most forthright about the need to preserve what he saw as a crucial political tradition. In his defense of liberalism, we begin to perceive that New Left radicalism and modern liberalism were not necessarily as conflicted as so many believe.

Until 1965, Kaufman's greatest gift to the New Left was a nuanced and well-developed articulation of participatory democracy. As the peace movement and civil rights movement intensified and changed course after 1965, Arnold Kaufman started to rethink the idea of participatory democracy. Leaders within SDS were doing the same. In 1967, Greg Calvert, national secretary of SDS, criticized the idea of participatory democracy for ignoring the need for strong (i.e., Marxist-Leninist) leadership. Kaufman's rethinking did not take this authoritarian path; instead, he started to identify more and more with the liberal tradition. While Paul Goodman wound up invoking liberal values out of necessity—for instance, his spirited defense of "bourgeois civil liberties" against SDS's Leninist arguments—Kaufman directly articulated what was good about liberalism and set this out against what he called "the venomous liberal-baiting so fashionable among the enragés." As he saw it, what was "at issue" was "the very integrity of the liberal ideal that has guided the more progressive factions within American political life since the inception of the American experiment." A part of his liberal defense came out in his criticism of participatory democracy.[34]

Kaufman questioned the concept of participatory democracy for a few reasons. First (and most simply), it could not solve all the problems of American politics. Obviously, the practices of participatory democracy could do little to establish a "comprehensive federal health insurance act" or redistribute income. For these things to take place, a strong, centralized state was needed. Secondly, Kaufman could not square his own activist experience—including that within the civil rights movement—with the principle of participatory democracy. Here he parted company with Paul Goodman, who constantly used the civil rights movement as a shining example of decentralized action. Kaufman agreed that the civil rights movement had a participatory and decentralized element to it. But he also argued, with history on his side, that it showed the need for a strong federal government—with power at "higher levels"—capable of doing battle with local and "municipal tyr-

---

34. Arnold Kaufman, "Wants, Needs, and Liberalism," *Inquiry* 14 (1971): 193, and "Radicalism and Conventional Politics," *Dissent* 14 (1967): 439. Calvert's turn against participatory democracy is discussed in Ellis, *The Dark Side of the Left,* 187.

anny." *Both* local participation and a strong government were needed. Finally, Kaufman started to doubt the concept of participatory democracy because it "has become, not a definite idea of how to make decisions, but a ritual expression." Participatory democracy, Kaufman argued, was marked by "uncritical exuberance" rather than thoughtful application.[35]

For Kaufman, this was not simply a movement problem but a political theory problem. Democratic theorists had to find ways to balance two different demands on a political system: the demand for order and stability, and the demand for participation and spontaneity. By 1965, Kaufman had already set out this challenge: "As we are a morally underdeveloped nation in important political respects, we need checks—even if they are creaky ones—on our tendencies to sacrifice justice to what we perceive as utility. On the other hand, these checks ought to be continued as to encourage the growth both of respect for freedom and a capacity for responsible participation in the political process." In *The Radical Liberal,* Kaufman traced out these two principles and then associated them with two thinkers he admired—James Madison and Jean-Jacques Rousseau. Oversimplifying these political philosophers for a general audience, Kaufman made Madison stand for political order and representative institutions, and Rousseau, for participatory democracy and a politics of civic engagement. Furthermore, he proposed two aims for social movements: first, to build coalitions capable of transforming national politics, and second, to engage participants in local and spontaneous activities. The first, with its reliance on leadership and representative institutions, was Madisonian, the second Rousseauan. Then, Kaufman argued,

> The fundamental opposition between . . . the Madisonian and the Rousseauan may arrive at limited agreement. The latter claims that coalition politics without participatory democracy tends to be irresponsible, manipulative, and class dominated. The former claims that participatory democracy without coalition politics tends to be provincial, factional, and lacking in necessary political and material props— i.e., stability, welfare, and a framework of protected rights. They are both right. In the final analysis, the two institutional processes are essential to one another because in important respects they comple-

35. Arnold Kaufman, "Participatory Democracy: Ten Years Later" (1968), in *The Bias of Pluralism,* ed. Connolly, 204, 205, 206, and "A Politics of Dignity," *Engage,* January 1–15, 1969, 14–15.

ment and reinforce one another. This is so even though in other respects there is, and always must be, unresolved tension between them.

Essentially, for the New Left to be effective, it had to balance participatory democracy with coalition building—the spontaneity of citizens acting locally and conjointly with the transformation of representative political institutions. Only such a vision and practice could improve the quality of public life and politics while being effective.[36]

Kaufman believed that this balanced vision stemmed from the liberal tradition, but a liberal tradition of his own making. When Kaufman set out the lineage of his tradition, he made little use of Adam Smith or John Locke—two figures typically taken to lay the groundwork for modern liberalism. Rather, all the liberal thinkers Kaufman cited came *after* Karl Marx; they were knowledgeable of the damage capitalist inequality could do to democratic values and institutions. Kaufman set out three major founding fathers, so to speak, for his intellectual tradition: John Stuart Mill, Leonard Hobhouse, and John Dewey. All of these political theorists believed in individual rights (i.e., those set out in Mill's *On Liberty*), a common good, a certain amount of state intervention to protect the public interest (weaker in Mill's case, but very strong in those of Hobhouse and Dewey), and political participation as a means of educating citizens for the responsibilities of a democracy. This last trait might have surprised some political critics. It was commonly accepted that liberals respected individual rights (both economic and political) and that during the Progressive Era and Great Depression, liberals hoped government would intervene in the economy to protect social and economic equality. But by embracing an interventionist and activist government, liberals also became associated with bureaucratic, top-down power, and they were thus negligent of local participation or democracy. Kaufman claimed just the opposite: "The need to deepen and enrich the quality of the democratic process, to make it both more deliberative and more participatory, flows directly from the central doctrines of liberalism." He further argued, "Intimately related to the right of participation is the liberal concern that the virtues of responsible citizenship be developed in the largest possible

36. Kaufman, review of *The Paradoxes of Freedom,* 245, and *RL,* 67. Kaufman also wrote, "Rousseau, it is true, was wrong to claim that once representative institutions are permitted, the state is lost. Nevertheless, unless a system of coalition politics is invigorated by participatory institutions, important values are needlessly forfeited, the prospect of urgently needed radical reform is destroyed and equally important, the prospect of improving the quality of the processes of coalition politics is severely limited" (*RL,* 61).

number of people." By emphasizing Mill, Hobhouse, and Dewey—all liberals who wrote about the need for participation and democratic citizenship—Kaufman made a strong case. It might not have been *the* liberal tradition, as he thought, but certainly *a* liberal tradition—one that married rights, welfare, and community-based participation.[37]

Kaufman's liberal tradition still placed a great deal of emphasis on individualism, but not an economic, entrepreneurial, or purely self-interested sort of individualism. If anything, it was a type of individualism that was more romantic or expressive in its content, and certainly more attuned to the need for individuals to take part in communal participation (the sort of "positive freedoms" that the British political philosopher T. H. Green had expounded on earlier: see Chap. 2). Kaufman wrote that liberalism as a "political theory" rested upon "the protection and promotion of each person's equal opportunity to develop his potentialities as fully as possible" within the "constraints of civility." Potentiality, as used here, was remarkably similar to Paul Goodman's thinking on self-realization within Gestalt therapy. For Kaufman, this concept made liberalism *radical* because it implied "an obligation to remove, not only obstructions due to human interference, but any chronic obstructions" to full self-realization. The goal for liberals was, then, to create a "society in which each individual has a roughly equal opportunity to carve out a destiny in conformity with his own nature and deliberative choice." This might have sounded abstract to some readers, but for Kaufman, the "strategy for radical liberals" was straightforward and required no small set of goals. Radical liberals needed to eliminate poverty and racism, guarantee full employment, provide decent housing and medical care, preserve the environment, and grant equal access to higher education. While ensuring these things, radical liberals also needed to nurture opportunities for participatory democracy. They had to balance a strong government against local participation. This balance was necessary because only it could assure full self-realization for all citizens.[38]

37. Kaufman, *RL,* 7, 59; he cites Mill, Hobhouse, and Dewey on xiv of *RL.* Dewey's standing as a participatory democrat is confirmed in *RL* and in Westbrook, *John Dewey and American Democracy.* For Hobhouse's beliefs, see the comments made about Mill in his *Liberalism* (1911; reprint, New York: Oxford University Press, 1964), 61. On Mill's thinking regarding participation and democracy, see Carole Pateman, *Participation and Democratic Theory* (Cambridge: Cambridge University Press, 1970), 28–35, and David Held, *Models of Democracy* (Stanford: Stanford University Press, 1987), chapter 3.

38. Arnold Kaufman, *RL,* 4; "A Sketch of Liberal Theory of Fundamental Human Rights," *Monist* 52 (1968): 610, 611; and "A Strategy for Radical Liberals," *Dissent* 18 (1971):

The philosophy of radical liberalism pushed Kaufman to stake out a critical relation to the New Left in 1967. Beyond reviving participatory democracy, Kaufman believed that the New Left had historically forced liberals to consider issues and concerns that might otherwise have been left off the table. After all, the civil rights movement made liberals within the Democratic Party take the issue of racial oppression seriously. And the peace movement was pressing liberals to rethink foreign policy. But by 1967, Kaufman was convinced that the New Left was allowing participatory democracy to trump political effectiveness. Some young activists seemed more concerned about "the state of their souls" than the state of politics. Much in the same vein as Paul Goodman, Irving Howe, and Michael Harrington, Kaufman saw moralism creeping into New Left political activism. Activists allowed purity to override compromise. He saw this most powerfully in the increasing talk about "cooptation" among young New Left thinkers who discussed the welfare state (see Chap. 6). Kaufman agreed that the welfare state could often turn poor people into degraded clients lacking political power. He also believed that the War on Poverty was "financially skimpy and politically hamstrung from the start." Nonetheless, he was careful not to allow this line of thinking to result in a rejection of the welfare state altogether. All along, he had made clear that the welfare state should—as the British New Left originally argued—be *supplemented by* participatory democracy and an infused sense of justice. The idea developing among the latter New Left—that the welfare state was *solely* about co-optation—undermined this position. Kaufman explained that "conservatives exaggerate the virtues of the welfare state; some in the New Left underestimate its accomplishments and its potentials." He then polemicized, "Fear that welfarism is cooptative is morally arrogant and politically senseless from the point of view of genuine radicalism." In the end, Kaufman defended the welfare state's original premise of *reform* as the basis of political change and held this up against the New Left's growing fear of co-optation, which

---

382–93. In writing on young activists, Kaufman appreciated the younger generation's penchant for an "individualism" that "has moral, not entrepreneurial meaning"; Kaufman, "Party Reform or Mounting Disorder" (1969), Arnold Kaufman Papers, box 1, Correspondence folder. On T. H. Green and his influence on modern liberal thinking, see Kloppenberg, *Uncertain Victory,* 30–32, 130–32. For an interesting attempt to show a potential synthesis between liberalism and romanticism (one that Kaufman would probably have embraced), see Nancy Rosenblum, *Another Liberalism: Romanticism and the Reconstruction of Liberal Thought* (Cambridge: Harvard University Press, 1987).

seemed to veer toward revolutionary politics or moral purity substituting for any politics whatsoever. He pointed out that "peripheral movement," his term for reform, could become "substantial social change" if there was enough of it. If the New Left lost sight of this fact, it would consign itself to ineffectiveness and marginality based upon an out-of-touch theory of revolution.[39]

A tendency toward moral purity and self-indulgence seemed apparent to Kaufman in the rise of the counterculture during the late 1960s and the ideas of social critics who tried to speak in its name—spokespeople like Theodore Roszak, Philip Slater, and Charles Reich. The counterculture's emphasis on youthful "authenticity," Kaufman argued, was not a sound basis for politics. The thinkers who tried to expound on the values of the counterculture seemed "naïve and politically muddled." Kaufman essentially repeated the concerns that Mills and Goodman had expressed about earlier forms of counterculture protest—that these lifestyle rebellions could do little to alter political or socioeconomic relations, let alone the mainstream culture. But now, with the development of the New Left, there seemed higher stakes. By 1968, as one historian points out, "the line separating the antiwar movement and the counterculture had blurred." Kaufman complained, "The counterculture threatens the very qualities upon which our best hope for a brighter future depends—a disciplined ability to reason and a morally passionate commitment to a politics that is both rational and relatively independent of the quest for personal salvation." Essentially, the "drop-outs" in the counterculture represented the final steps of the New Left's dangerous dance with the idea of authenticity. That the two were now merging during the late 1960s only confirmed Kaufman's suspicions. As he saw it, Rousseau (in the guise of the counterculture) was now trumping Madison (the hope for coalition building), and progressive politics suffered because of it.[40]

39. Kaufman, *RL,* 51, 12–13, 9, and "A Strategy for Radical Liberals," 387.

40. Arnold Kaufman, "Youth and Politics," *The Progressive,* October 1968, 44, and "A Strategy for Radical Liberals," 385; Farber, *The Age of Great Dreams,* 220; Kaufman, "Beyond Alienation," *The Progressive,* February 1970, 45. These attitudes toward the counterculture carried over into Kaufman's criticism of Herbert Marcuse. Kaufman respected Marcuse's arguments about co-optation and "repressive tolerance" much more than many Old Leftists would: see Kaufman's essay, "Democracy and the Paradox of Want-Satisfaction," *The Personalist* 52 (1971), especially 187–88. At the same time, he drew upon his liberal faith to argue that Marcuse's "One-Dimensional" thesis made political change seem impossible—a belief that should be anathema to the New Left, Kaufman argued. See *RL,* 162, and William Connolly and Arnold Kaufman, "Between Exaltation and Despair," *Dissent* 15 (1968): 373.

Kaufman's critique was not entirely original. Others were saying the same thing at the same time. Paul Goodman, Irving Howe, Michael Harrington, and Christopher Lasch sounded these arguments; later historians, such as James Miller, and historian–participants, such as Todd Gitlin, would reiterate them. Kaufman, however, couched his critique within his wider vision of radical liberalism. This vision respected individual rights, grounding them in the idea of human potentiality. At the same time, rights were to be balanced against the need for decentralized and democratic participation as a means of political education for citizens. Additionally, rights could not trump the need for governmental action in the name of racial or economic justice. Radical liberalism seemed the best political option precisely *because* of this mixture of values. It could be made to support a great deal of the New Left's political activities and thinking, but could also criticize its shortcomings. Kaufman did not simply critique the actually existing New Left. He offered what seemed to be a viable and coherent political philosophy of his own.

What a New Left and Liberals Should Do: The Political Strategy of Radical Pressure

As we have already seen, Arnold Kaufman was deeply committed to political practice as well as to developing ideas. Indeed, Kaufman stuck with his original 1955 argument that political theorists had a special responsibility to pay attention to consequences. Like Goodman, Kaufman was intent on making "practical proposals," but unlike Goodman, Kaufman believed that he had to show how *proposals* could be transformed into *politics*—that is, into effective change. Here again was the New Left intellectual's charge to marry a politics of truth with a politics of impact. Kaufman never separated the two.

Against what he perceived to be the growing utopian aspirations of the New Left, Kaufman saw himself as a realist who began with an assessment of what the left could actually accomplish. Here was his starting point: "Radical liberals are not and for the foreseeable future will not be a majority of the population or the voting public." Because of this, radicals had to realize that they were reliant upon the efforts and the atmosphere created by more center-leaning liberals. New Leftists, he argued, "rely for support on the 'finks' they abuse." Hence, confrontation politics on the part of the New Left needed to be put to careful scrutiny, for it could easily prompt a *backlash* against the victories of liberalism and the New Left, a backlash that Kaufman recognized before the idea became a more popular term in American political discussions (associated most clearly with Nixon's call for a "silent majority" to take back American politics from hippies and liberals). For instance, Kaufman followed quite seriously the political career of George Wallace. He believed that Wallace exemplified the possibility of a reactionary response to the New Left and liberalism. (Wallace was famous for criticizing "pseudo-intellectuals" on the left.) What made the Wallace movement significant was how deeply rooted it was in the concerns of a vast sector of America's voting population. Kaufman warned that "[t]oo many reply" to Wallace supporters, "especially within the liberal and left communities, 'You are the forces of right-wing fascist reaction.'" Against this dismissive response, Kaufman argued that liberals and New Leftists needed to consider the "millions of Americans, many responsive to Wallace's siren song, who have real discontents, legitimate complaints." What Wallace's insurgent candidacy in 1968 showed was just how much opposition to the New Left was evident in America and how much the New Left needed to take this into account while crafting its political vision.[41]

Kaufman called his political strategy "radical pressure." Its distinctiveness stemmed from a sense of realism and a synthesis of different types of political practice. Radical liberals needed to combine a "more deliberative process of coalition politics, the growth of participatory institutions, and the completion of the welfare state." Kaufman warned that "when one of these three vital components of a total liberal strategy is formally absent or defective, everything, short of rebellion, required to provide informal substitutes for them ought to be done—but done *effectively*." Radical liberals needed to practice civil disobedience and confrontation—both as a means to capture public attention and to ensure that politics remained in touch with local activists—but had to be careful about the overuse of these tactics. Kaufman explained, "The judicious use of unconventional tactics [i.e., civil disobedience] can drive wedges into established structures; and these initial gains can be converted by conventional political action into more substantial accomplishments." The overall strategy that resulted from this would include "community organization in combination with radical political education and conventional political organization." In the electoral realm, radical lib-

---

41. Kaufman, "A Strategy for Radical Liberals," 382; *RL,* 53–54; notes in Arnold Kaufman Papers, box 2, Miscellaneous Political Papers folder; and "A Politics of Dignity," 16. For more on Wallace as a symbol of backlash, see Matusow, *Unraveling of America,* 422–39.

erals needed to try to drag the Democratic Party to the left by making clear the importance of the coalition it was putting together. Kaufman assured, "The new coalition from among the poor, militant blacks, Hispanics, American Indians, liberal intellectuals, young radicals, radicalized businessmen and professional people, artists and writers, militant—often newly organized— trade unionists, disaffected veterans, and even retired bankers and generals provide a solid base for a new program of radical liberalism." This coalition could make clear why the Democratic Party needed to consider the arguments of radical liberals.[42]

Based upon this strategic vision, Kaufman threw himself into a wide range of activities from 1967 to 1969. Having argued against those who wanted to form a left-wing third party, Kaufman made good on his word by trying to pull the Democratic Party to the left. Having "chosen to work within the Democratic Party," he helped with the Coalition for an Open Convention (COC), an organization that opposed the election of Humphrey to the candidacy of the Democratic Party and instead endorsed Eugene McCarthy and George McGovern. This group fought the Democratic Party machine—including that of Chicago's Mayor Daley—to get antiwar candidates onto the ballot. After this initiative failed, Kaufman embarked on another project: an organization called the National Conference of Concerned Democrats (1967–1968). Kaufman's activity here merged with the more well-known activism of Allard Lowenstein, who helped manage the "Dump Johnson" movement within the Democratic Party at this time (an action that Kaufman supported). As the historian William Chafe makes clear, the "Dump Johnson" movement was based upon a merger of strong conscience and political strategy. In many ways, Kaufman's political thought became something of an elaboration of Lowenstein's activism at this time. Both Kaufman's and Lowenstein's efforts coalesced into the New Democratic Coalition (NDC), a group of activists and intellectuals who tried to pull the Democratic Party to the left throughout the late 1960s, after Humphrey had been defeated (Lowenstein himself decided to run for office soon afterward). Kaufman insisted that Democrats needed to attract the "alienated" sectors of

42. Kaufman, *RL,* 72; Connolly and Kaufman, "Between Exaltation and Despair," 374; Kaufman, "A Future for Dissidents," *Commonweal,* November 29, 1968, 316; "Between Exaltation and Despair," 375. For more on these points, see also "A Politics of Dignity" and "A Strategy for Radical Liberals." Kaufman was critical of those who believed that the civil rights movement's reliance upon civil disobedience could be generalized to all types of political engagement: see *RL,* 50.

the American population—African Americans, young people, and others—
to the Democratic Party. Once these groups were "convinced that political
ambitions are subordinate to values and programs, then they will hopefully
be more willing to organize as a constituency of conscience within the electoral process." Kaufman believed that while pulling the Democrats left, the
NDC needed to make the party into an organization that cared about more
than just winning elections. Here, he was willing to gamble with some
pretty high stakes. In a set of cryptic notes, Kaufman spelled out his own
hope for the NDC: "Radical reconstruction without abandoning or repu-
diating established political processes. Issues not candidates. Political education—principal task." Instead of being obsessed with electoral victories, the
party should focus on the "education of publics" and "issue development."
The NDC's coalition would form a "constituency of conscience" that could
make clear why politicians should at least listen to more radical arguments.
Only such a coalition could prevent the Democrats from rushing to the
center in order to counteract right-wing backlash. Kaufman argued, "Power,
not trust, must be our principal aim within the New Democratic Coalition. . . . But power without trust corrupts our cause and debases our people." Once again, the NDC would have to balance effectiveness and conscience—that peculiar balance that Mills had originally counseled New Left
intellectuals to embrace.[43]

Kaufman was painfully aware that a constituency of conscience within the
Democratic Party might fail to transform it. After all, he had lived through
the 1964 attempt of the Mississippi Freedom Democratic Party (MFDP) to
rid the Democrats of southern white racists—an internal protest that made

43. Arnold Kaufman: "Draft Manifesto for the Coalition for an Open Convention," Arnold Kaufman Papers, box 1, folder on Coalition for an Open Convention; for Kaufman's
argument against a progressive Third Party run, see "New Party or New Democratic Coalition?" *Dissent* 16 (1969): 13; "New Politics," unpublished essay, Arnold Kaufman Papers, box
1; notes on the Michigan Democratic Reform Commission, Arnold Kaufman Papers, box 2,
Miscellaneous Papers; "Party Reform or Mounting Disorder"; "Milwaukee Speech," Arnold
Kaufman Papers, box 1, NDC folder; "A Politics of Dignity," 17. On Allard Lowenstein, see
William Chafe, *Never Stop Running: Allard Lowenstein and the Struggle to Save American Liberalism* (New York: Basic, 1993), especially 262. For the National Conference of Concerned
Democrats, see the Arnold Kaufman Papers, box 1, folder on National Conference of Concerned Democrats. The NDC gets little attention among historians, even though it seemed to
play a role in transforming the Democratic Party during the tumultuous times of 1968. For a
brief treatment, see Herbert Parmet, *The Democrats: The Years After FDR* (New York: Macmillan, 1976), 290–91; on the general transformation of the Democratic Party at this time, see
William Crotty, *Decision for the Democrats: Reforming the Party Structure* (Baltimore: Johns Hopkins University Press, 1978).

many civil rights workers wary of any future coalition. Therefore, Kaufman continued to support initiatives outside the party as well, in much the same way that Allard Lowenstein had struggled to decide how much he wanted to work within the Democratic Party or with forces outside it. In his own way, Kaufman tried to balance civil disobedience and movement organizing with electoral politics. During the period between 1967 and 1969, this took the form of supporting the Poor People's Campaign (PPC), an organization that grew out of Martin Luther King Jr.'s attempt to make the civil rights movement address issues of economic inequality in both the South and the North. This group of activists would try to force the Democratic Party to address issues of poor and working-class people—some organized, some not, some white, some people of color—and thus push the country to the left. In 1967, this seemed to be a live political option; it had the dedication of Martin Luther King Jr. and many others behind it, and it eventually spilled over into the short-lived presidential campaign of Robert Kennedy. By supporting the PPC, Kaufman made clear that he wanted a multitiered strategy beyond simply winning elections.[44]

Kaufman's arguments about "radical pressure" also came out in his continued support of the peace movement—a movement that Martin Luther King Jr. started throwing his support behind just before he was assassinated in 1968. As we have seen, Kaufman was deeply concerned with the strategy of the peace movement from the beginning. How leaders framed their arguments, he claimed, would largely determine their success. Following this principle, Kaufman argued in 1965 for America to cease bombing North Vietnam, nurture a democratic government in South Vietnam, and then start bargaining and negotiating with the North. Though a radical proposition for its time, it did not *embrace* the Vietcong, as certain portions of the New Left would start doing in years to come. It was difficult to hold to his original position, but Kaufman stuck to the idea that a critic of American foreign policy did not have to embrace America's enemy. Kaufman wrote, "One does not have to romanticize the rebel cause to oppose an American military onslaught." Kaufman believed—as he had in domestic policy—that

44. On Kaufman's involvement in the Poor People's Campaign, see box 5 of the Arnold Kaufman Papers. For more on the PPC, see Gerald McKnight, *The Last Crusade: Martin Luther King, Jr., the FBI, and the Poor People's Campaign* (Boulder: Westview, 1998). On Allard Lowenstein's struggle, which is remarkably similar to Arnold Kaufman's, see Richard Cummings, *The Pied Piper: Allard K. Lowenstein and the Liberal Dream* (New York: Grove, 1985), 357.

the left had to appeal to American values of democracy and freedom while showing how these ideals conflicted with realities. Sounding like William Appleman Williams, with whom he had found agreement on these points, Kaufman pressed the left to use "moral argument and appeal to self-interest" at the same time in opposing the Vietnam War. For Kaufman, the war was both morally questionable and unwinnable. In opposing it, he argued, the American left also needed to put forth an alternative, and here he set Vietnam within a wider context of American foreign policy, contending that "the Cold War did not endow the West with the powers of Divine Agency." Instead of acting as if it did possess these powers, America should craft an anticommunist (antiauthoritarian, in Kaufman's mind) foreign policy that relied upon economic and political aid more than military suppression of so-called enemies. Kaufman argued that by going back to the inception of the Cold War—which, for him, was right in the wake of World War II—radical liberals could rediscover the potential of the Marshall Plan that balanced "a creative, constructive, and responsible application of American resources to the problems of European reconstruction." In the context of the Third World, Kaufman counseled a new foreign policy that would stress "economic, political, cultural, and educational assistance" rather than military suppression of communists. Such an alternative policy could challenge those liberals in office who seemed focused solely on military solutions to foreign crises. It also challenged any New Left espousal of the Vietcong.[45]

Kaufman believed that the politics of "radical pressure" could keep the New Left in contact with America's political realities while it tried to push the country to the left. He helped create institutional power—in the form of organizations within the Democratic Party—that could make good on this promise. When he thought polemics against those in the New Left were needed, he wrote or spoke them. At every point, he tried to balance a number of different political strategies, values, and arguments—forging an

45. Arnold Kaufman: "An American Speaks," *Socialist Commentary,* September 1965, 18–19; "The Cold War in Retrospect," in *A Dissenter's Guide to Foreign Policy,* ed. Irving Howe (New York: Praeger, 1966), 85; *RL,* 166; "An American Speaks," 19; "The Cold War in Retrospect," 70; *RL,* 156–57. Kaufman was also active in the Peace Research Group, which tried to figure out why Americans might support Vietnam and what sort of argument could be crafted to dissuade them. See the communiqué from Kaufman dated May 20, 1967, in which he writes, "We [of Peace Research Group] are action-oriented and wish to apply our knowledge to reducing tensions which lead to war. We are interested in why people support the war in Vietnam and what arguments will be effective in convincing people to oppose the war" (Arnold Kaufman Papers, box 5, folder on Peace Research Group).

effective coalition politics, respecting the value of participatory democracy, accepting the limits of what radical liberals could accomplish while not becoming cynical, being tough-minded while not becoming interested in winning at all costs, arguing against American policies while not sounding anti-American, and facing one's enemies with respect and seriousness. In all of these ways, Kaufman attempted to show just what liberals could accomplish within the limits set by American politics. He also made clear that radical liberals had a history of ideas that they could defend with intellectual integrity.

The Final Days and the Beginnings of Backlash: The Personal Is Political

It is clear that Kaufman's life from 1967 to 1969 was hectic. These were years of frenzied activism not only in his own life, but also for most liberals. It is remarkable to note just how much Kaufman's intellectual and activist biography meshes with what was happening to liberals and leftists during the late 1960s. After the Chicago Convention of 1968, liberalism started to "unravel," as Allen Matusow has shown. So too did Kaufman's life. Spending so much time away from home in meetings of national organizations, Kaufman became estranged from his family. Additionally, his increased fame and stature created jealousies among other faculty members at the University of Michigan. Kaufman's relations with his colleagues were marked increasingly by bickering and fights, petty academic politics heightened by the tensions of the time. Recognizing this personal crisis, Kaufman decided to take up an offer that came his way from Donald Kalish, chair of the Philosophy Department at the University of California, Los Angeles (UCLA). He and his family moved to Los Angeles in the fall of 1969. Clearly, Kaufman saw this move as an attempt to salvage both his family and intellectual life. As he wrote in a letter one year after moving to Los Angeles, "I came to UCLA in order to have more time to write, read, think." Not surprisingly, he had "engaged in political action since my arrival." Though the move clearly succeeded in improving his family life, Kaufman was to remain a politically engaged intellectual.[46]

46. Kaufman to George White, June 19, 1970, Arnold Kaufman Papers, box 4, folder on SDS. The information related here comes from my interview with Betty Kaufman. I also thank Daniel Millstone for providing a sense of the University of Michigan during the late 1960s (Millstone was then a graduate student in philosophy).

His activism, though, changed significantly. It seemed increasingly obsessed with the backlash that had set in against liberals and the New Left after 1968 (the sort of backlash that Kaufman had earlier associated with George Wallace). One of the first political activities Kaufman engaged in was the Angela Davis case. Davis was a philosophy professor who, even more important, was an African American member of the Communist Party (and a student of Herbert Marcuse). She found herself under threat of having her UCLA teaching contract nullified. Of course, Kaufman was no communist, nor was he a rigid anticommunist. For him, the case centered on the issue of "academic freedom, the right of militants to be free of repressive action, the integrity of the university as a milieu within which criticism of society is fostered, and Miss Davis's right to have contracts observed." Essentially, Kaufman, like anyone concerned with civil rights, tried to defend someone with whom he did not agree politically. Kaufman ironically found himself in a dispute with SDS over the Davis case, however; SDS, instead of defending Davis, attacked her for not being radical enough and for being "too bourgeois," as its leaders explained. Like Goodman's more humorous critique of SDS's increasingly Leninist rhetoric (the sort that flayed "bourgeois civil rights"), Kaufman argued that "well-established bourgeois institutions like the judicial system, academic tenure, the Bill of Rights" needed to be defended adamantly. Of course, Kaufman had an easier time in making the defense, since it was in sync with his overall political philosophy. He also discovered new political enemies, not only in the regents of the University of California, but also in the governor of California—Ronald Reagan, a one-time liberal who recrafted himself as a conservative by attacking liberals and New Leftists within the state university system.[47]

In Reagan, Kaufman faced a new kind of backlash. To counteract it, he helped form (in 1970) Citizens for the Survival of Higher Education, a group that defended academics against increasing attacks made on the university and that tried to ensure more funding for the university. Kaufman found himself speaking in public and writing articles—all of them in defense

47. Arnold Kaufman, "Political Strife at UCLA," unpublished essay, Arnold Kaufman Papers, box 5, folder on Angela Davis; "The Communist and the Governor," *The New Republic,* January 3, 1970, 24. For Davis's account, see her *Angela Davis: An Autobiography* (New York: Random House, 1974), 216–17. On Reagan, see Matthew Dallek, *The Right Moment: Ronald Reagan's First Victory and the Decisive Turning Point in American Politics* (New York: Free, 2000).

of academic freedom. Additionally, Kaufman became president of Local 1990, the American Federation of Teachers union representing UCLA faculty. In setting out the purpose of this academic union, Kaufman focused once again on the issue of "academic freedom." He made clear that union leaders needed to do what "educators are presumably best suited to do—educate publics about the meaning of a university." As they had during the teach-in, university-based intellectuals would have to reach out and engage in public deliberation. More and more, though, this deliberation would be aimed at defending a beleaguered set of values, such as intellectual freedom and democracy. After all, Reagan's policies were extremely popular with the electorate. Kaufman was painfully aware of the increasingly defensive nature of his own work.[48]

Perhaps this is most evident in Kaufman's writings while he was at UCLA. His discussion of democracy became increasingly abstract, and absent from the writings were the clear, strategic arguments that could be found only a few years before. One of Kaufman's primary arguments in 1970 was that democracy required a certain amount of disorder. He had made this point earlier, suggesting that the best justification for participatory democracy was not stability but human development. But in 1970, this position seemed framed by a growing number of urban riots and unruly protests on America's campuses (this was the year of the famous Kent State incident, in which trigger-happy National Guardsmen fired on protesters). Kaufman argued that conservatives—such as Reagan and Nixon—wanted citizens in a democracy to feel "gratitude" about their government. He maintained that this was a paltry and empty defense of democracy, and he pointed out that democracy demanded dissent. Besides, as far as Kaufman could discern, the historical record was clear: violence had been necessary in the past to acquire more social justice. This was not—Kaufman made known—an argument in favor of politically motivated violence. He explained, "More than any alternative political system, democracy does increase the likelihood that social advance can be brought about peacefully. Therefore . . . , within democracies we do have a special reason to suppose that a peaceful route to some desirable change can be discovered." Nonetheless, Kaufman argued, "even if all good things will come about peacefully in the long run, it does not establish that it is better to wait for opportunities to develop than to practice disorder."[49]

48. "Union: An Essential Condition of a Great University," unpublished essay, Arnold Kaufman Papers, box 6, UCLA Faculty folder. For Citizens for the Survival of Higher Education, see the folder on the organization within the Arnold Kaufman Papers, box 6.

49. "Democracy and Disorder," unpublished essay, Arnold Kaufman Papers, box 5, Hope College Visiting Philosopher Program folder, 7, 9, 10, 11, 15.

These arguments made a certain amount of sense, as Kaufman had always defended the use of civil disobedience as a means to achieve political goals. But there was something abstract about the line of reasoning now. No longer was Kaufman setting his arguments in the context of other strategic options, as he had in his writings on the New Democratic Coalition. Instead, the argument in favor of disorder was more philosophical in nature; it was as if Kaufman was speaking more of *fate* rather than *political choice*. Perhaps his relocation to Los Angeles took him out of the context of activism that had informed his ideas. Perhaps his new efforts in support of academic freedom against the likes of Ronald Reagan gave him a more defensive attitude. Or more worrisome still, perhaps with the NDC's national disarray in 1970 (as Paul Wieck recounted in a story for the *New Republic*), Kaufman's increasingly abstract arguments related to the fact that his own political strategies were falling apart. Whatever the reason, Kaufman's statements suffered from a lack of strategic thinking that was out of character.[50]

Unfortunately, soon after writing down his thoughts on democracy and disorder, Kaufman died in an airplane crash on June 6, 1971. He was a casualty of America's military: an Air Force pilot had flown off course, and after he ejected, his plane collided into the passenger plane on which Kaufman was traveling. Not only did Kaufman leave behind his family (including a newly born son), but he also left behind numerous questions about where his activism and thinking would go next. As American liberalism crashed and burned from 1970–1971, Kaufman admitted confusion about where the left should go. He wanted to develop his ideas about democracy more fully in some sort of book, and he even thought of writing a historical account of the New Left and liberalism. We will never know what this work would have been.[51]

Conclusion: Kaufman's Legacy

Arnold Kaufman ranks as an important figure in the history of New Left political thought. He was clearly influenced by C. Wright Mills's vision of the engaged intellectual who was both committed to the politics of truth and the politics of change. Kaufman's thinking on participatory democracy

50. Paul Wieck, "What Happened to the New Politics?" *The New Republic,* February 28, 1970, 12–13.
51. The information from this paragraph is drawn from my interviews with Jack Rothman and Betty Kaufman.

had a major impact on early thinkers within SDS and, to a lesser extent, on the New Left as a whole. Kaufman himself found a home within SDS and within the civil rights and peace movements of the 1960s. He believed that political thinking needed to connect to movements and to address issues of concern for political publics. In his efforts as an intellectual and an activist, Kaufman found a resolution to the tension between commitment and truth that had always stamped the work of New Left intellectuals. He discovered a balance between activism and ideas, best seen in his work on the teach-in and his arguments for a politically effective peace movement. As he set it out, the intellectual's role here was to nurture deliberative practices that could directly oppose the government's foreign policy. The intellectual would thus remain engaged in the collective pursuit of truth without losing sight of political relevance.

Kaufman also provided a political and philosophical vision for the New Left—one that matched participatory democracy with larger structures capable of protecting individual rights and social justice. His idea of "radical liberalism" articulated this vision and set it within a wider context of intellectual history and political theory. He insisted that the New Left needed to have intellectual integrity as well as a commitment to effective activism. (He himself performed this balancing act by articulating a "strategy" for radical liberals.) Kaufman's work—like that of Allard Lowenstein—with the New Democratic Coalition showed young activists that they need not bolt from the home of liberalism in order to be politically effective. At the same time, his arguments with *Dissent*'s editors made clear that the Old Left—and liberals—needed to make room for those committed to participatory democracy.

All of these ideas showed signs of weakness as well as strength. For instance, it was never clear whether the coalition in which Kaufman believed could really transform American politics. After all, the young and minority groups Kaufman wanted to include in his coalition were often so alienated from politics that they did not vote (his own writings about the counterculture captured this). Besides, the NDC itself collapsed, and thus the institutional practices Kaufman took as a secure grounding for radical liberalism were weaker than he had originally hoped. Additionally, Kaufman tried to balance certain principles—most important, a strong state and participatory democracy—without recognizing that sometimes they might be difficult to synthesize easily. Often his call for such synthesis reflected his lack of ideas on how exactly to do this.

Even so, Kaufman's thinking on radical liberalism deserves a stronger hearing today. It certainly died away with the frenetic conflict of the late 1960s and early 1970s—a time of tragedy and of great hope—but it remains an inspiration to those willing to revisit that period. His political theory protected the important gains of modern liberalism, respecting individual rights and protecting social justice. It recognized the importance of participatory democracy as a means by which to educate citizens. For these reasons, Kaufman believed that radical liberalism held out answers and alternatives to New Leftists increasingly prone to embracing revolutionary or utopian aspirations or to dropping out of politics altogether. Though his ideas were marked by the time in which they emerged (as all ideas are), they also lived on as a vision of radical democracy offset by the checks and balances of constitutional liberalism. That Kaufman's thinking was enmeshed in real, active debates within the New Left only heightens his importance in this context. In recognizing this, we also recognize that the tensions between radicalism and liberalism might not have needed to exist.

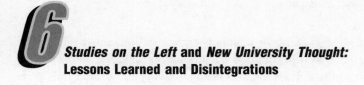

Studies on the Left and New University Thought: Lessons Learned and Disintegrations

[The New Left] found a home in the burgeoning student publications such as *Studies on the Left* and *New University Thought*. These magazines are the closest we have to a new movement. This creation of magazines rather than organizations is the confession of ideological uncertainty and political weakness, but given the position of the left in American society, it is perhaps the only honest response to be made.
—Robert Scheer, "Notes on the New Left," 1964

The most consistent failing of intellectual and radical thinking and activity in this country has been its inability to form any kind of lasting and necessary identification as part of the American scene.
—Editorial, *New University Thought,* 1961

At best a New Left may only be able to define a new intellectual creed at home which permits honest men to save their consciences and integrity even when they cannot save or transform politics.
—Gabriel Kolko, "The Decline of American Radicalism," 1966

While C. Wright Mills, Paul Goodman, William Appleman Williams, and Arnold Kaufman wrote books and essays describing what a New Left should look like, a younger generation of activists and scholars was coming of age. Developing their own voices while relying upon a critical intellectual heritage, young intellectuals began forming small magazines in which they both drew upon and went beyond the ideas developed by previous thinkers. Taken independently, these young writers—Staughton Lynd, Tom Hayden, James Weinstein, Otto Feinstein—never produced an individual opus like that of Mills or Goodman, but the magazines they formed certainly carried a great deal of collective weight. At this point, we have come full circle: in the first chapter, we saw the central role that a small magazine, *politics,* played in providing the seedbed for New Left political thought. In the case of *Studies on the Left* and *New University Thought,* magazines became a place in which ideas could be drawn into dialogue with social movements. Both in the magazine articles and the internal debates among editors, we can glean where New Left political thinking was headed during the tumultuous years of the 1960s. These publications tell us a great deal about the consequences of previous attempts to create and sustain a New Left movement—and how a new generation crafted its own ideas in dialogue with changing historical developments.[1]

I will organize this chapter much more tightly than the previous ones, returning to the themes set out in the introduction—the role of the intellectual in social change, the relation between radicalism and liberalism, and the possibility of left-wing politics within American history. In stating these themes more boldly and tying together some of the looser strands in the book, I will start to sketch out my conclusions about New Left political thinking. I will also provide some coherence to magazines that, like all magazines, explored a variety of ideas. Obviously, I cannot focus on every subject discussed in each publication (for instance, in the case of *Studies on the Left,* I will pay little attention to the theories of Brechtian drama or debates within Western Marxism that certain editors examined in depth). Nonetheless, I believe that the ideas highlighted here—questions about liberalism and radicalism, in particular—were central to the thought behind both publications in the changing context of the 1960s.

Different Magazines, Similar Trajectories

Studies on the Left and *New University Thought* were very different publications, but they were remarkably similar in method and style. Unlike *politics,* which had a single chief of staff, these magazines were collectively edited. They were also much more academic in tone, breaking with the tradition of "literary journalism" developed at *politics* and carried on within the pages of *Dissent* (and, to a lesser extent, *Liberation*) throughout the 1950s and 1960s. Richard Chase, writing for *Harper's,* described *Studies on the Left* and *New University Thought* as "literate but seldom literary." Both publications ex-

---

1. On the importance of small magazines in the history of intellectual radicalism, see James Gilbert, *Writers and Partisans: A History of the Literary Radical in America* (New York: John Wiley, 1968), 1–9. In order to get at the dialogue among editors, I have consulted the *Studies on the Left* Archives, Wisconsin State Historical Society, Madison, Wisconsin; unfortunately, no archive exists for *New University Thought*.

plored and took on the tone of recent research in the university-based social sciences and humanities. After all, these journals were put out by graduate students and recently minted Ph.D.'s. For instance, *Studies on the Left* began through the efforts of graduate students at the University of Wisconsin at Madison. Situated within a comfortable midwestern university town, the editors perceived an advantage: "The isolation from the large metropolitan centers provided the opportunity to develop our own conceptions of the necessity for radical scholarship." As Eleanor Hakim, managing editor of *Studies on the Left* during its early years, explained to a friend, "A journal like Studies could never have originated on either the east or west coast where there are so many splits and factions—most of which are at least 25 years behind the times." *New University Thought* began at the University of Chicago and then eventually moved to Detroit, Michigan, as the editors became faculty members at Wayne State University. Both publications were therefore capable of avoiding the sectarianism of such places as New York City (where *Dissent,* for instance, was located).[2]

Midwestern locations also drew these publications in contact with many of their rightful forefathers. At the University of Wisconsin at Madison, the editors of *Studies on the Left* drew support and assistance from William Appleman Williams. Because James Weinstein, probably the most prominent editor, was a graduate student at Columbia University, he did not know Williams very well (even when he lived in Madison). But Martin Sklar was Williams's graduate student and helped him in developing the idea of "corporate liberalism." Other students of Williams, such as Lloyd Gardner, played a role in the journal as well. (Much to its detriment—or so Eleanor Hakim thought, only one year into the journal's existence. Hakim wrote to Martin Sklar that one editor was "very sensitive to the fact that our reader-

2. Richard Chase, "The New Campus Magazines," *Harper's,* October 1961, 168; "A Note from the Editors," *Studies on the Left* 3 (1962): 3; Eleanor Hakim to Helene Brewer, no date, *Studies on the Left* Records, 1959–1967, Wisconsin State Historical Society, Madison, Wisconsin, box 1. For more on the origins of *Studies on the Left,* see the introduction to *For a New America: Essays in History and Politics from* Studies on the Left, *1959–1967,* ed. James Weinstein and David Eakins (New York: Vintage, 1970), especially 6, and James Weinstein, "Studies on the Left," in *History and the New Left,* ed. Buhle. Andrew Hacker argued that *Studies on the Left* came out of a long tradition of progressive thinking at the University of Wisconsin. Though partially true, this claim fails to note the breaks that the editors of *Studies* made with the progressive tradition: see Andrew Hacker, "The Rebelling Young Scholars," *Commentary,* November 1960, 405. On literary journalism, see Howe, *The Decline of the New,* 240–42. In the notes to follow, *Studies on the Left* will be abbreviated *SoL,* and *New University Thought, NUT.*

ship is getting a bit irritated by the Williams–crowd American history" found in "articles in *Studies.*") Another editor at *Studies on the Left* had a strong connection with C. Wright Mills. Saul Landau traveled with Mills throughout Europe in 1960 and believed that the journal should take this thinker's ideas seriously. Mills, in fact, joined the editorial board for a brief period right before his death, even though he had earlier written the editors at *Studies on the Left* urging them to merge with *New University Thought,* a journal he praised. This might have been because the chief editor at *New University Thought,* Otto Feinstein, had been Mills's first choice to accompany him on his travels to Europe. When Feinstein was at the University of Chicago in the late 1940s (where he also met Marc Raskin), he took a course with Mills that became a defining intellectual experience. Feinstein also collaborated with Arnold Kaufman, whom he described as a "friend." Finally, both *Studies on the Left* and *New University Thought* drew a great deal of inspiration from Paul Goodman, though less directly. These journals clearly recognized their intellectual debt.[3]

Partially due to their youthfulness, the magazine editors drew much closer to New Left movements and organizations than Mills, Goodman, Williams, or Kaufman ever could. Especially important was the leading intellectual organization of young activists, Students for a Democratic Society (SDS), seen by both publications as an ally and source of political hope. The feelings were mutual. As Tom Hayden explained it in 1963, "The editors of NUT are quite interested supporters of SDS, and I for one support them wholeheartedly." In the same year, Todd Gitlin, an important leader in SDS, joined the editorial board of *New University Thought* while Hayden wrote two significant articles for the publication. Their sympathies were shared by *Studies on the Left.* Weinstein attended the 1962 Pine Hill convention of SDS, where he spoke on the legacy of the left (Kaufman and Goodman

---

3. Eleanor Hakim to Martin Sklar, October 4, 1960, *SoL* Records, box 9; Martin Sklar described Landau's travels with Mills in a letter to Steven Ambrose, July 27, 1961, *SoL* Records, box 1; C. Wright Mills in a letter to *Studies,* no date, suggesting that they merge with *NUT,* *SoL* Records, box 6; correspondence between Mills and Feinstein in the C. Wright Mills Papers, box 4B398; Otto Feinstein, telephone interview by author, July 16, 1999, for both points about Mills and Kaufman. The interest in Paul Goodman can be seen in early attempts to get a review of *Growing Up Absurd,* which was taken as a very important book by the editors: see Morgan Gibson to "Mr. Weiner," September 13, 1959, *SoL* Records, box 3, and Eleanor Hakim to Saul Landau, October 20, 1961, *SoL* Records, box 5. Showing off his sense of humor, Mills claimed to Feinstein that he came to love *New University Thought* when he realized that its abbreviation read "NUT": Feinstein, interview.

were also present). In the same year that Hayden expressed interest in *New University Thought,* James Weinstein tried to affiliate his journal more closely with SDS, urging C. Clark Kissinger, the national secretary at the time, to join with him. Hayden himself did join up with the editors of *Studies on the Left,* but the relationship, as we will see, became conflict-ridden and quickly ended in ideological and personal disputes.[4]

Because these publications drew close to movements, they traveled the same bumpy roads as those movements. In 1959 and 1960, the years in which they formed, *Studies on the Left* and *New University Thought* witnessed the entrance of students into the civil rights movement with the founding of the Student Non-Violent Coordinating Committee (SNCC), protests against HUAC, and the spread of the peace movement. Even so, both sets of editors saw themselves writing within a fairly apathetic context. In 1960, *Studies on the Left* was busy building its subscriber base and finding some minor foundation support, while *New University Thought* did the same without assistance from a foundation. Soon, though, both publications witnessed the increased popularity of social movements and, following this, larger numbers of subscribers. In 1965, James Weinstein provided a nice synopsis of the history of his publication to a potential funder:

> From 1959 through 1964 Studies was read primarilly [*sic*] by graduate students and young faculty members in the social sciences. Our main emphasis was on the reexamination of recent American history and sociology in order to help lay the theoretical basis for the emergence of a new radical politics in the United States. Since the movements have blossomed we have been reorienting the journal toward a more active and immediate concern with existing practice. In addition to continuing our interest in history, sociology, and political science, our purpose is to provide critical information and analysis about the movements. The new section on the movementss [*sic*] has been very well received, especially in SDS, and our readership has increased steadily among student activists in the last year.

4. Tom Hayden to Steve Johnson, May 10, 1963, in Students for a Democratic Society Records, 1958–1970, Wisconsin State Historical Society, Madison, Wisconsin, folder entitled Presidential Correspondence; James Weinstein to C. Clark Kissinger, May 25, 1963, *SoL* Records, box 5; Weinstein, telephone interview with author, June 1, 1999; see also *For a New America,* ed. Weinstein and Eakins, 14, for the connection between *SoL* and SDS.

The same could have been said about *New University Thought*. For only a year after Weinstein wrote his synopsis of *Studies on the Left,* the editors at *New University Thought* wrote, "Civil rights activity, campus protests, heightened activity and consciousness in religious and professional circles, and an increased tendency to apply academic analysis to relevant problems may indicate that in some sense the community that NUT had hoped to identify has become real; that there is a role to be played by a publication providing reportage, communication, analysis, and theory." That year, *Studies on the Left* changed from a quarterly to a bimonthly, attempting to become more timely for the movements. Ironically, only one year later, the journal collapsed, due largely to ideological differences, exhaustion on the part of editors, and a growing sense that SDS—its strongest gateway to the activist New Left—was falling into chaos and factionalization. Though *New University Thought* lasted until 1970, its last three years were marked by disarray. It sometimes appeared to be an adjunct of SANE, but at other times became dominated by academic anthropologists and seemed to lose its broader mission. Essentially, by 1968, both journals had either literally or figuratively left the scene.[5]

During their heyday, both magazines explored comparable themes. Most centrally, they concerned themselves with the meaning of American liberalism and its relation to radicalism. They came to different conclusions—making clear the varieties of political thought inherited and developed within the New Left. But their intellectual trajectories also uncovered some very similar ideas (or at least important parallel tracks) that tell us where New Left political thought was heading during the 1960s.

Intellectuals or Academics?

The academicism one finds in [*New University Thought* and *Studies on the Left*]—the long articles on Senator Borah, Woodrow Wilson, chapters extracted from Ph.D. dissertations, and so on—must be attributed in part to the uncertainty of the young rebels about themselves and their place in society.
—Richard Chase, "The New Campus Magazines," 1961

5. Marty Sklar explained *Studies on the Left's* funding and subscriber base in a letter to Herb Gans, June 14, 1960, *SoL* Records, box 3; James Weinstein to Mrs. Ann Farnsworth, August 3, 1965, *SoL* Records, box 3; editorial, *NUT* 4 (1966).

Because both journals were produced within the university, it is not surprising to find their tone more academic than that of previous small magazines (the words "Studies" and "University" were displayed prominently in their titles). But it is a bit more remarkable to find the editors not simply drawing upon academic thought but also being deeply concerned about their career standing within the institution (something missing from the writings of C. Wright Mills or Paul Goodman, for instance). The editors spoke apprehensively about their hopes for future careers in opening editorials. The first words of the inaugural issue of *Studies on the Left* sounded somewhat self-absorbed: "As graduate students anticipating academic careers, we feel a very personal stake in academic life, and we feel that, as radicals, we are hampered in our work by the intrusion of prevailing standards of scholarship." The opening editorial of *New University Thought* echoed this sentiment: "We look forward to academic and professional careers," the editors explained, while claiming that they wanted to create a "community of intellectuals" and a society free of "alienation." The desire to become tenured academics did not necessarily exclude what has been called "radical scholarship." Warren Susman, a cultural historian, saw *Studies on the Left* promising "to make scholarship activist without making it vulgar." On the other hand, gaining academic standing took a great deal of time and energy away from less scholarly and political pursuits. Staughton Lynd—who wound up being denied tenure at Yale due, in part, to his political activism—argued in 1961 that "Radicals should enter the mainstream of scholarly discussion," as if this move had high political stakes. The assumption, it would seem, was that by changing academia, a scholar changed society. As Robert Scheer pointed out in a short-lived, small left magazine of the 1960s, *Root and Branch,* the editors of both *Studies on the Left* and *New University Thought* were "caught up in the myth that the university intellectuals have power." This assumption about academia also colored the content of both journals, since both favored specialized articles difficult to understand or follow by general readers. The public intellectual seemed to give way to the specialist. Even some of the editors themselves were bored by the mission. Saul Landau, while traveling with Mills, wrote his fellow editors in 1961, "You know what everyone thinks about Studies? (By everyone, I mean four or five people.) They think it is very professional and very dull." Academic careerism was not simply a neutral thing, Landau seemed to argue, since it demanded specialization and engagement in academic rather than public life.

Both publications symbolized a shift within American intellectual history—from "public intellectuals" toward academic radicals.[6]

There were some good reasons for working within academia. Most important, these young scholars followed the criticism of their forefathers—C. Wright Mills and Paul Goodman—who argued that the New York Intellectuals (the most prominent set of American public intellectuals) had become increasingly conservative, leaving behind few intellectual tools for young radicals. With the abnegation of these thinkers, there seemed fewer and fewer places to look for the development of ideas. Editors at *New University Thought* explained, "Our generation has been accused of being 'silent' because it has not provided any ideological and political movements. . . . An important reason for this lack is that we cannot find the kind of sound thinking from which to develop a consistent political and social program." Feinstein and his fellow editors recognized the withdrawal both of intellectuals and professionals more broadly: "In a world facing enormous problems, including threatened nuclear death, American intellectuals, students, and professionals have withdrawn from participation in public life. Valuable knowledge and training, which could be directed toward solving social and intellectual problems, becomes increasingly overspecialized; professions and disciplines are isolated from one another and from society." This, of course, was worrisome, for the same thing that drew them to academia—the decline of left-wing public intellectuals—led them to work with an institution that was admittedly specialized and divorced from public engagement, sometimes engaging in scientific research to benefit the very same warfare state these editors protested. There seemed no other place to go, even though the place they were going deserved only partial loyalty.[7]

The editors at *Studies on the Left* more squarely blamed McCarthyism for stifling political debate and radical intellectuals in America. The blame

6. "The Radicalism of Disclosure" (editorial), *SoL* 1 (1959): 3; opening editorial, *NUT* 1 (1960): 1; Warren Susman, "Smoking Room of History," in *History and the New Left,* ed. Buhle, 45; Staughton Lynd to Eleanor Hakim, March 13, 1961, *SoL* Records, box 6 (for Lynd, I also relied upon the Staughton Lynd Papers, 1938–1977, Wisconsin State Historical Society, Madison, Wisconsin); Robert Scheer, "Notes on the New Left," *Root and Branch,* no. 2 (1963–64): 19; Saul Landau to fellow editors (dated 1961), *SoL* Records, box 5. The term "public intellectual" was made famous by Russell Jacoby in *The Last Intellectuals.* Though many complained that Jacoby's work was more polemical than scholarly in its arguments, his belief that the New Left became increasingly academic in nature certainly bears itself out in the historical research that I have done, even if some of Jacoby's own heroes had already skulked off into academia by this time.

7. Opening editorial, *NUT* 1 (1960): 1.

spread out from here to liberals who, the editors argued, had become so anticommunist in tone that they actually conspired unwittingly with the likes of Joseph McCarthy. While blaming liberals, they also explained their rejection of journalism as an intellectual practice; they saw it as too superficial, lacking the analytical power necessary to understand current issues. For instance, in rejecting a poet's submissions, Eleanor Hakim explained that *Studies on the Left* was now going to "limit itself to high-level scholarly and speculative analyses and think pieces." Because the public intellectuals of yore had become so complicit with anticommunism—one need only think of Sidney Hook—and had changed the terms of wider public debate so successfully, the editors at *Studies on the Left* seemed to see the ivory tower as a place partially (though by no means entirely) protected from rabid anticommunism.[8]

None of this means that these journals were entirely comfortable with academia. They inherited a deep suspicion about academia that ran throughout the course of radical intellectual history, from Thorstein Veblen to Mills. First, both journals expressed concern about academia's obsession with "objective" knowledge, noting the disconnection of academic work from political engagement. In 1965, *New University Thought*'s editors complained about "over-specialization of knowledge, the decreasing social relevance of facts and training in college, the unparalleled growth of universities' facilities and submergence of the individual students in dehumanized learning and living experiences." John Weiss followed Thorstein Veblen's famous critique of the modern university, arguing that trustees held too much power. College life, from Weiss's perspective, was overly bureaucratic and inhuman. Students became "clients." Ralph Nicholas had already made this point before the Free Speech Movement emerged, arguing that college was no "community" full of "idealism," as might be expected, but a place that fell prey to "the pressures of business and industry (including the military)." It would therefore seem counterintuitive that radicals could ever find a satisfying home within the ivory tower.[9]

This discomfort with academia meant that some young writers tried, if

---

8. Eleanor Hakim to Charles Anderson, November 29, 1961, *SoL* Records, box 1; for the argument about McCarthyism, see John Steinke and James Weinstein, "McCarthy and the Liberals," reprinted in *For a New America,* ed. Weinstein and Eakins.

9. "Vietnam: The Bar Mitzvah of American Intellectuals," *NUT* 4 (1965): 3; John Weiss, "The University as Corporation," *NUT* 4 (1965): 38; Ralph Nicholas, "Higher Education: A View of the Problem," *NUT* 1 (1961): 40–41.

only briefly, to find an alternative role to that of the academic scholar. In fact, Martin Sklar had been doing labor organizing on the West Coast while finishing his graduate studies. There he found another model of engaged scholarship—quite akin to the conception of the labor intellectual that C. Wright Mills embraced in the late 1940s. Sklar wrote his fellow editors that he liked "scholarship outside the academic community and inside the labor movement." Around the same time, Saul Landau joined forces with C. Wright Mills who, as we know, was fast becoming *the* public intellectual of the New Left, or as Landau called him, a "pamphleteer, the Tom Paine of the New Left." At *New University Thought,* there was optimism about a new experiment called the "Committees of Correspondence" and the aforementioned "Liberal Project," which engaged intellectuals like David Riesman, Erich Fromm, H. Stuart Hughes (of SANE), and A. J. Muste in dialogue with politicians. As Marc Raskin—later a founder of the Institute for Policy Studies—explained, these experiments were "the first real attempt in recent years to combine the intellectual and political liberals as a cohesive power group" with the hope of having "influence on the direction of national policy." Clearly, the idea that intellectuals could address issues of public concern and have an impact on national policy still informed both journals. In reviewing *Growing Up Absurd* for *New University Thought,* one young writer urged the sort of political course—the "practical proposals" and engagement with the Free Speech Movement—that Goodman's career was about to take: "Goodman does not distinguish those forms of dissidence which lead to viable political action and institutional change. Nor does he evaluate the possibilities for development of such movements within the contemporary scene." In these criticisms could be seen a waning hope among these young academics to become public intellectuals. C. Wright Mills's conception of the engaged intellectual haunted the pages of *Studies on the Left* and *New University Thought,* even as each publication seemed to accept the new terrain of academia.[10]

Perhaps the most compelling reason for the academic nature of both magazines was that, as they originated, there were few political movements to engage in dialogue. Eleanor Hakim took issue with Richard Chase's characterization of *Studies on the Left* as an overly academic journal, largely by

---

10. Sklar to editors, July 3, 1960, *SoL* Records, box 9; Marcus Raskin, "Issues Versus Institutions," *NUT* 1 (1961): 37; Saul Landau, "From the Labor Youth League to the Cuban Revolution," in *History and the New Left,* ed. Buhle, 112; Paul Mandell, review of *Growing Up Absurd, NUT* 1 (1961): 72.

agreeing with him. She compared her fellow Wisconsin scholars with those at the *New Left Review* of England (i.e., E. P. Thompson and the other intellectual comrades of C. Wright Mills): "The New Left Review people have a student movement and a political party to work within. We have no such institutions of this sort yet. Given this dismal reality, we are much more limited to the scholarly radicalism of disclosure rather than being able to take directly programmatic political stands in our journal." Hakim was right to suggest that once movements emerged, the editors would be willing to engage with them: this is precisely what happened to *Studies on the Left* when it created a new section entitled "On the Movements" in 1965. Thus, in the case of these journals, movements on the ground became the key instigators of politically engaged thinking. Without the movements, the journals might have remained more academic. Indeed, once the movements emerged, both magazines became more optimistic about the dawn of a newly engaged political intellectual. In 1965—the year of the teach-ins—the editors of *New University Thought* wrote, "American academics have begun to feel that they have the competence and the right to pass judgement upon our policy, to express this judgement and to work actively in a variety of ways to make this judgement felt." This optimism was still in evidence two years later, when the editors wrote, "At this time people are yearning for . . . discussions if they are factual and not propagandist—in the best academic tradition—showing the realities and the options rather than arguing for one point of view. By promoting a national discussion out of which a new orientation might arise we would be making by far the greatest contribution that can be made at this time." This perspective was shared by the editors at *Studies on the Left,* even though, as we will see, they were deeply critical of the teach-in movement. They believed that by debating and making suggestions to movement participants, young intellectuals might help push the growing movement against the Vietnam War to broaden itself beyond simply ending the war.[11]

Even with this newfound engagement with movements, some editors wondered whether they were comfortable with the idea of a politically engaged intellectual. These thinkers pressed the question: Just how committed to writing for movements should radical intellectuals be? Debates raged among the editors of *Studies on the Left.* For instance, Helen Kramer (an

---

11. Eleanor Hakim to Richard Chase, July 7, 1961, *SoL* Records, box 2; "Vietnam: The Bar Mitzvah," 2; back-page editorial, *NUT* 5 (1966–67).

academic) wrote to James Weinstein (who was never a full-time academic) and complained: "A fundraising letter was sent out by the New York officer in which it is stated that Studies increasingly was to take an ideological position as the leader of the New Left. . . . It would be a serious error for Studies to adopt an editorial line, since inevitably it would restrict the scope and freshness of discussion in our pages." Essentially, Kramer suggested that there might be some validity behind the ideas of objectivity and neutrality (concepts the editors had originally criticized in their first issue), especially if the alternative was ideological commitment to specific movements. Two years later, Evan Stark objected as well, noting that *Studies on the Left* had become too connected to movements and needed to return to its older pursuits of scholarship and "theory," as he called it. Stark echoed the complaint of one reader who argued that "there is a tendency in Studies to make it more like a newspaper." Other editors expressed growing concern over the pressures of academic life, hinting that they could no longer dedicate all their time to political causes. In 1965, the editors wrote, "Classes have to be prepared; papers and books have to be written in an academic world of 'publish or perish'; administrative duties have to be fulfilled." This explained the intent behind the "Socialist Scholars' Conference" that editors were organizing at the time. Editors hoped to grapple with the admittedly "peripheral scholarly work being done now in various fields" and create "socialist political scholarship," a term that could sound slightly oxymoronic. The fact that this meant the editors were increasingly making a pact with academia— something that would draw their attention away from political engagement—was not lost on them.[12]

One year after *Studies on the Left* collapsed, Otto Feinstein was still hopeful that academics could play a role in social and political change. He counseled his colleagues to "prepare papers on the issues, on potential solutions, and on political variables that must be dealt with in order to realize the solutions." But his own journal was fast being taken over by anthropology students who had a tendency to write about specialized, academic topics in a specialized, academic way. Though Feinstein may have wanted more, it was not clear that his publication could live up to the promise. He himself stopped participating in *New University Thought* after about 1969. Seemingly, the academic institution—with its increased demand for scholarship and re-

12. Helen Kramer to James Weinstein, June 13, 1963, *SoL* Records, box 5; Evan Stark, "Theory on the Left," *SoL* 5 (1965): 82–83; Mike Lebowitz to James Weinstein, undated, *SoL* Records, box 6; "From the Editors," *SoL* 5 (1965): 7.

search—was swallowing up the possibility of political engagement on the part of these scholars. The project of engaged intellectuals originally set out by Mills now seemed to be perishing.[13]

Liberalism Versus Radicalism or Liberalism *and* Radicalism?

The younger thinkers at *Studies on the Left* and *New University Thought* inherited a variety of ideas about the meaning of contemporary liberalism in American political culture. There was hostility expressed by Paul Goodman at times (and then retracted at other times) and by William Appleman Williams. There were those who were both critical and reliant upon some liberal intellectual traditions—C. Wright Mills to a lesser extent, and Arnold Kaufman to the fullest. The tensions among these approaches played themselves out in the pages of the two publications, showing the changing parameters of New Left political thinking during the 1960s.

From the outset, *New University Thought* seemed much more favorable toward liberalism. This might have been due to the influence of Arnold Kaufman or perhaps to the thinking of C. Wright Mills. Whatever the reason, editors here described liberals in 1960 as "confused and disorganized." This was a far cry from the idea that liberalism was the overarching ideology of American life; it admitted weakness and conflict where most—including New York Intellectuals such as Richard Hofstadter and Lionel Trilling—saw hegemony. The editors also suggested that there was a potentially radical outcome in liberal political thinking. They threw themselves behind the early "Liberal Project," organized by Marcus Raskin, and behind other initiatives as well, hoping that more radical politicians could actually win power through electoral politics. Perhaps the most important reason for their willingness to work within the framework of liberalism was their recognition that a serious right-wing alternative was lurking on the stage of history, even at the time that liberals seemed in the forefront. The editors described their self-conceived role in 1964: "The function of our community at this time is to block the Right and help the American people—and that includes us— to discover the realities of power, the problematics of immediate issues, and the general trends of the coming social change." The editors feared the possibility of driving liberalism off the political map, and so they hoped, as

13. See Otto Feinstein's brief statement found in *NUT* 6 (1968): 12.

Tom Hayden put it, to "spur liberalism" into drawing more radical conclusions. For instance, writers in *New University Thought* called for building on the accomplishments of the War on Poverty, trying to create more participatory forms of governance within the welfare state. Robb Burlage criticized the limits of the War on Poverty by calling for an even stronger welfare state, combined with worker representation carried out through democratic unions within the private sector. This was an in-house critique, not an utter rejection of really existing liberalism. Even as late as 1968, when the publication supported the McCarthy campaign, it argued for functioning "within . . . the existing institutional framework of American politics" and offered "reasonable solutions to our greatest domestic and foreign crisis." Arnold Kaufman's idea of "radical liberalism" and "radical pressure" seemed both to rely on and to influence many of the political positions found in *New University Thought*.[14]

The *New University Thought* perspective contrasted with that of *Studies on the Left*. The latter publication expressed little concern about right-wing politics. Liberalism appeared to the editors as the dominant ideology of American life. In calling the "ultra-right" a fringe, the editors argued, "If the left hopes to begin to play a meaningful role in American life, it must cut itself free from the stifling framework of liberal rhetoric and recognize that at heart the leaders of the United States are committed to the warfare state as the last defense of the large-scale corporate system." This passage captured the editors' overall conception of modern liberalism. They saw the tradition growing out of the social and political reform movements of the Progressive Era, then consolidating during the New Deal (a vision propounded by William Appleman Williams: see Chap. 4). Martin Sklar described the origins of modern liberalism this way: "These movements—what are known as the Progressive reform movements (and they were reforms)—were movements led by and consisting of large corporate interests and political and intellectual leaders affirming the large corporate industrial capitalist system, and convinced of the necessity of institutionalized reforms, legal and otherwise, to accommodate the nation's laws and habits, and the people's thinking, to the new corporate business structure and its requirements, domestic and foreign." Historically, then, liberalism reconciled

14. Opening editorial, *NUT* 1 (1960); for an interesting perspective on the "Liberal Project," see Peter Jacobson and Earl Medlinsky, "The Meyer Campaigns," *NUT* 1 (1961); editorial, *NUT* 3 (1964): 6; Eugene Feingold and Tom Hayden, "What Happened to Democracy," *NUT* 4 (1964): 48; editorial, *NUT* 6 (1968): 2.

Americans to the large corporate structure growing up at the turn of the century—an argument hinted at by Mills and Williams.[15]

At its simplest, the editors' historical interpretation could lead to a reductionist reading of contemporary liberalism. One *Studies on the Left* editorial read, "Twentieth century liberalism, in so far as it is not purely rhetorical, is a system of political ideas consciously developed to strengthen the system of large-scale corporate capitalism." In setting out their political vision, Martin Sklar and James Weinstein argued that activists and intellectuals should be "assuming that liberalism will remain the dominant political ideology of the large corporations—that is, the basic commitment to formal democracy will be maintained and the socially disruptive programs of the ultra-right will continue to be rejected." As history would prove two years later—with Richard Nixon's political victory, based upon a call for the "silent majority" to rise up against dirty hippies, student activists, and liberal elites (akin to George Wallace's earlier arguments)—this assumption was false. Just as important, Sklar and Weinstein's reasoning here suggested that liberal reform (of the sort that *New University Thought* embraced) would only prop up a corrupt corporate system of power. Reform, therefore, operated as a rearguard and protective action on the part of the powerful. In a letter to Staughton Lynd, James Weinstein explained that the "liberal administration [of LBJ] will do whatever is deemed by the wisest and most powerful of our financial and corporate leaders. . . . At present, it appears they see an advantage in moving 'left'—that is in espousing a program against poverty, supporting 'disarmament,' all considered steps in the direction of liberalism. . . . Of course, none of these programs are designed to solve the problems, or, rather, the Administration cannot and does not want to go far enough to effectuate these programs, but they are a good pose, and thus must take token steps." Following this line of reasoning, reformist efforts and coalition-building initiatives with liberals were merely smoke screens, nothing else.[16]

Weinstein's and Sklar's views predominated within *Studies on the Left*. But when the editors invited in representatives from the New Left—especially

15. "The Ultra-Right and Cold War Liberalism," *SoL* 3 (1962): 6; Martin Sklar, "Woodrow Wilson and the Political Economy of Modern U.S. Liberalism" (1960), in *For a New America,* ed. Weinstein and Eakins, 86. This interpretation was thoroughly developed much later in Martin Sklar, *The Corporate Reconstruction of American Capitalism, 1890–1916* (Cambridge: Cambridge University Press, 1988).

16. "The Ultra-Right," 8; Martin Sklar and James Weinstein, "Socialism and the New Left," *SoL* 6 (1966): 70; Weinstein to Lynd, April 29, 1964, *SoL* Records, box 6.

Tom Hayden and Norm Fruchter—some challenges were posed. For instance, Hayden and Fruchter wanted the liberal and left-wing elements of the civil rights movement to join together, since "the radical and moderate wings of the civil rights movement are mutually dependent." This related back to Hayden's arguments in *New University Thought* for radicals to "spur liberalism." The editors at *Studies on the Left* even invited radical liberals into their pages, such as Herbert Gans, who argued against driving a wedge between liberals and radicals—precisely the sort of argument that Arnold Kaufman was making. The inclusion of these voices suggested that debate was never completely closed down in the pages of *Studies on the Left,* even if one voice seemed to predominate.[17]

As we will see later, James Weinstein himself could sound like a radical liberal when he spelled out his own vision of coalition politics, though he coupled this understanding with a fear of co-optation and a criticism of actually existing liberals. Nonetheless, Weinstein's argument would come to parallel those of Arnold Kaufman and Herbert Gans. For now, it is important to note that, at the least, Helen Kramer's fear of an "ideological position" taking over the pages of *Studies on the Left* was unfounded. Radical liberals could still voice their opinions in a publication that was prone to dismissing corporate liberalism. The diversity of debate found here suggested that the case was not closed on the radical potential of liberalism coming out New Left political thinking—even if it seemed a dimmer alternative during the mid-to-late 1960s among editors at *Studies on the Left.*

Possibilities for an Effective Left

The attitude editors expressed toward liberalism related directly to their hope (or lack thereof) in the possibilities of political change in America. In facing what the editors of *New University Thought* took as a "disorganized" ideology and what *Studies on the Left* believed was a dominant form of political thought, they had to ask themselves what could be *done* with liberalism. Even if liberalism was not absolutely dominant, it certainly played a crucial

17. Tom Hayden, Norman Fruchter, and Robert Cheuse, "Up from Irrelevance," *SoL* 5 (1965): 4. The three New Left representatives went on to argue that the radicals should not be counseled to break from the liberals, because they did not have "something to break *towards.*" Herbert Gans, "Rational Approach to Radicalism," *SoL* 6 (1966): 45, and "The New Radicalism: Sect or Action Movement," *SoL* 5 (1965): 127. For another defense of liberalism, see James O'Connor's remarks in *SoL* 3 (1962): 61.

role in American political culture by the mid-1960s. In 1964–65, whether the "vital center" that Arthur Schlesinger had articulated only ten or fifteen years before could be pushed to the left was a live question. Could one "spur liberals" to become more radical, as Tom Hayden had hoped? Or was any reformist movement destined to be co-opted by systemic forces and the ideology of corporate liberalism? In what could radicals place their fragile hope? Such questions burned in the minds of those who edited these two journals.[18]

In assessing the future of radicalism, both publications agreed that cultural rebellion had little to provide. The Beats—still the most popular cultural radicals of the late 1950s and early 1960s—faced major criticisms from writers in *New University Thought* and *Studies on the Left*. Like Paul Goodman, Lawrence La Fave described the Beats as "conforming non-conformists" in the pages of *New University Thought*. He explained, "By furnishing Squares with clowns to laugh at, Beats increase the smug complacency of the Squares; like the king's jester, Beats entertain the Squares and flatter, thereby, the status quo." Robert White argued that the penchant Beats had for cultural liberation from mainstream values made them libertarians—akin to the egoistic heroes of Ayn Rand's right-wing novels. Paul Breslow echoed these sentiments in his reflections on the Beats for *Studies on the Left*. He criticized the "mystical salvation" sought out by Allen Ginsberg and Jack Kerouac as leading down dead-end roads of political withdrawal. Both publications took seriously the cultural alienation and conformity that the Beats had dissected in their poems and novels. But they believed that *this-worldly* politics was the appropriate salvation, not *other-worldly* withdrawal. As John Flaherty put it in *New University Thought,* "Many decent men [*sic*] are finding the comfortable life of the middle class boring and ethically unsatisfying. Young people see their lives threatened by the arms race and feel driven to political protest." Such was the more effective resolution for cultural alienation, *New University Thought* and *Studies on the Left* argued.[19]

18. Schlesinger's *The Vital Center* stands as a classic text in the intellectual history of liberalism.

19. Lawrence La Fave, "Any Glory in the Beat Way to Satori?" *NUT* 1 (1961): 14; Robert White, "Ayn Rand—Hipster on the Right," *NUT* 2 (1962): 61; Paul Breslow, "The Support of the Mysteries," *SoL* 1 (1959): 16, and see his later critique of Mailer's thinking in his review of *Advertisements for Myself, SoL* 1 (1959): 78; John Flaherty, "The Case of the County Seat," *NUT* 1 (1961): 10. It is interesting to note that *Liberation*—a publication of older pacifists and anarchist political thinkers—seemed to have a more favorable reaction to the Beats, a group of literary rebels they saw as reacting to the senselessness of the bomb. See,

If the Beats were not the answer, both publications were more hopeful about the early activities of the civil rights movement (especially the students who formed SNCC), the anti-HUAC protests, and the peace movement. But they also took note of these movements' limits. The editors of *New University Thought* wrote in their second issue, "We hope to see the development of the present politics of protest, which has the danger of being single-issued, limited, and temporary, into a politics *for* as well as *against.* Short and long-run proposals must be put forward, debated, and enacted." Just a year later, though, Philip Altbach complained that the student movement was still limited and failed "to think things through with deliberation and conscientiousness; their actions remain superficial." And Otto Feinstein criticized the student movement in particular for failing to address economic issues. The same critique was heard at *Studies on the Left.* Martin Sklar expressed some tentative optimism about the new movements in 1960: "What we are witnessing in the student and Negro movements . . . is a process that contains the seeds of a new American left capable of becoming a politically viable movement nationally, a process in which the new left is learning those forms of struggle which will make a radical movement relevant to the American body politic. As such it requires close study; it requires that leftists participate in these struggles as fully as possible, and learning from it, help give the movement sources of intelligent leadership." But in response to Sklar's take, Eleanor Hakim expressed the sort of pessimism that prevailed among the editors of *Studies on the Left:* "The big student movements; the sit-ins; the anti-capital punishment; anti-HUAC; pro-Cuba's right to make her own revolution as well as that of the emerging nations of Latin America, Africa, and Asia; the disarmament and peace movements, etc., are, it seems to me, not political movements per se. Rather, they are issue-oriented protest movements, they are radical dissenting movements, but they are not yet, by and large, left-wing political movements." Hakim described those who took

---

for instance, Jeanne Bagby, "Behind the Scene with the Beats," *Liberation,* May 1959, and "After the Beat Generation" symposium, *Liberation,* June 1959. It is also important to note that Mailer's original defense of hipsterism (an outgrowth of the Beat movement) originally appeared in *Dissent,* something that Irving Howe never lived down (on this point, see Alexander, *Irving Howe,* 258 n. 53). Of course, *Dissent* did publish good debunkings of the Beats: see, for instance, Neil Friedman, "Geist, Guise, and Guitar," *Dissent* 7 (1960): 151–52. It would seem that *Studies on the Left* and *New University Thought* were a bit more astute and showed more foresight than their elders on the apolitical quality of Beat culture. For the only defense of the Beats within *New University Thought,* see Bill Smith, "Three Men on a Horse," *NUT* 2 (1962): 73.

part in these movements as "idealistic young 'liberals' who do not have any overall left-wing orientation." Hakim's suspicion seemed to capture the spirit of *Studies on the Left,* for editors would continue to express her doubt even after she left the publication in 1963.[20]

Both magazines hoped to articulate the bigger—if sometimes only implicit—visions of what they perceived to be restricted social movements. By the mid-1960s, it seemed that the intellectual's primary role was to analyze the limits of certain movements and then draw fuller connections between different issues for participating members. For instance, as the civil rights movement came to the North, the editors articulated how it could become most effective by addressing economic inequality caused by overexpenditures on the war in Vietnam—thus linking the peace movement to community organizing initiatives. By engaging in these discussions, academic scholars could come out of hiding and once again find a balance between the politics of truth and the politics of engagement that Mills thought so central to intellectual work. At the same time, both sets of editors worried that they might be incapable of seriously influencing movements on the ground. In 1963, Tom Hayden noticed an "uncertainty" at *New University Thought* and described its editors as "glum . . . , feeling apparently that their original strategy—of organizing students around a magazine—is not working out as they'd hoped." James Weinstein, looking back on *Studies on the Left,* recently remarked that it was "hard to say who read *Studies on the Left* outside Madison or what its influence was." Coming after the optimism of 1960, such statements symbolized a growing sense of limits—that is, a belief that ideas might only play a marginal role in the world of politics. These young thinkers doubted whether activists should pay any attention to detached scholars. The intellectual was concerned with truth and other lofty ideals,

20. Opening editorial, *NUT* 1 (1960): 1; Philip Altbach, "The Need for Leadership and Ideology," *NUT* 2 (1961): 14; Otto Feinstein, "Is There a Student Movement?" *NUT* 1 (1961): 27; Martin Sklar to "Board Members," November 19, 1960, *SoL* Records, box 9; Eleanor Hakim in response to Martin Sklar, no date, *SoL* Records, box 9. In 1960, George Cunningham, an editor of *Studies on the Left,* made clear that the journal was already reconsidering its role in political change. He wrote, "Studies does not ordinarily publish reportage type articles, but so important do we regard the present Negro student movement in the South that we think it is not only appropriate but obligatory to run something" (undated letter in *SoL* Records, box 2). It should also be noted that in 1968, Arthur Waskow continued to articulate *New University Thought's* critique of the peace movement, complaining that it lacked a "vision of an end" or a sense of "what was legitimate." It only acted on "revulsion," and "action out of pure revulsion is not, in the long run, likely to build a decent society." See Waskow, "Looking Forward," 38.

but activists hoped to have an impact in an imperfect world. Paul Goodman and Arnold Kaufman had tried to find ways to bridge this gap (perceived or real), but the gap did not disappear. The apparent failure of the editors' work in this area made clear that their self-conceived role was held with a certain amount of trepidation.[21]

New University Thought tried to move beyond intellectual detachment by literally lending research aid to the peace movement—something that Arnold Kaufman had counseled. They formed the New University Peace Research Committee in 1961, providing "student peace groups" with information that would make their arguments and activism more effective. It follows that the editors of *New University Thought* would be optimistic about the teach-in movement that took off four years later (see Chap. 5). The editors believed that there were ways in which intellectuals could lend themselves to pushing American politics to the left and increasing the deliberative capacities of ordinary citizens. At the same time, they accepted some of the limits of these new movements, even while hoping for more from them. The intellectual, after all, could not expect to control the movements, which did not hold out any grand ideological transformation of America. Rather, they drew from the long national tradition of "citizen action"—an ethic that would always ebb and flow throughout history. The processes these movements tried to engender, not necessarily their substantive goals, were most important for some of the writers at *New University Thought*. These processes often tried to transcend the limits placed on American politics by the conservative atmosphere of the 1950s. Writing on the early student movements at the University of California at Berkeley (long before the Free Speech Movement), Herb Mills explained, "The most basic desire and hope which lies behind the political action of both the liberal and 'radical' student is that by raising and acting on certain basic issues he can do something to create an atmosphere where political debate and discussion is again possible. Reacting against a period during which political debate was suffocated by an all-pervasive McCarthyism and complacency, the student has an urgent desire to make politics—almost *any* kind of politics—legitimate once more." The last phrase—"almost any kind of politics"—was key; it symbolized an awareness that the New Left might be limited in its scope, and that this was

21. Tom Hayden to Steve Johnson; Weinstein, "Studies on the Left," 116; and Weinstein, interview.

both necessary and acceptable, especially considering the wider historical context and the generally conservative nature of American politics.[22]

This is why the editors of *New University Thought* were especially attuned to the idea of participatory democracy. Instead of articulating a socialist vision, one editor, Gabriel Breton, set out the idea of "radical humanism" representing the implicit philosophy of young student activists. He cautioned that "we have not yet evolved an all-encompassing ideology" for the movement—and seemed to offer this thought with few apologies. Then he explained, lifting a page from Albert Camus's philosophy: "But we have no doubt regarding what is for us the ultimate and most irreducible value, and that is the person, the human being—not aspects, or parts of capacities of the human being, not systems or institutions, not any particular creation of man, not his beliefs or his ideas—but the person, in his totality, in his freedom, in his originality and in his essential dignity." This individualism did not lead to withdrawal for Breton but to participation in collective, public life. Like Kaufman and Goodman, Breton believed in democratic participation justified by a faith in the potentiality of all humans. He drew from an ancient tradition of political thought that saw human interaction as the basis of the good life: "The recognition of the right of every member in the society to participate in the affairs of society is not based merely on some attitude of democratic fair play, but on the knowledge that every individual bears the burden of the problems of society and of mankind, and that his own responsibility as a moral agent commits him to work towards their solution." Again, it was not a single substantive goal or ideology that drove students to engage in politics, but the hope of building a vibrant public life more broadly construed.[23]

Breton's moral philosophy of politics had its political consequences elaborated by Tom Hayden in the pages of *New University Thought*. First, the idea of participatory democracy was to be taken as both radical and reformist—as a clear suggestion for serious restructuring of the American political system.

22. "Student Peace Groups," *NUT* 1 (1961): 52–53; Raskin, "Issues Versus Institutions," 38; Herb Mills, "In Defense of the Student Movement," *NUT* 2 (1961): 10. Charles Jones restated some of these arguments in his analysis of SNCC. See "SNCC: Non-Violence and Revolution," *NUT* 3 (1963). This sort of philosophy of the student movement could also be found in one of the few books written about young students at the University of California at Berkeley: see David Horowitz, *Student* (New York: Ballantine, 1962).

23. Gabriel Breton, "The Ideology of the Person," *NUT* 2 (1962): 9, 11. This sort of political philosophy could also be gleaned from Arendt, *The Human Condition*.

Hayden (with his co-author, Eugene Feingold) wrote, "The idea of democratic participation . . . implies massive and continuous involvement of the people in whatever decisions affect them in all their working and living conditions." As a principle, it could be used as what Arnold Kaufman would have called an "indicator" of political health. If social policy was to gain political legitimacy, it needed to ensure citizen engagement. Following this line of reasoning, writers at *New University Thought* called for decentralized and democratic planning in the economy—the sort that Paul Goodman was encouraging.[24]

While setting out the principles of radical humanism and participatory democracy, the editors also took note that the civil rights movement was moving north by 1963. The movement wound up appearing in the editors' home city at this time, and they were eager for it to merge with Detroit's strong union movement. For instance, the editors expressed sympathy for the Trade Union Leadership Council, which had started to build a community organization focusing on education, welfare, and economic equality. They also believed that once the civil rights movement came north, it would have to focus on economic issues, most likely embracing social democracy (precisely what Martin Luther King Jr. did during the later 1960s). Feinstein and Breton called for activists to focus on a "shift from arms expenditures to social investments (such as schools), on the inclusion of people from the lower third of the economy into the market, the control of monopoly, and a general increase in economic activity." In making this argument, they fully embraced the sort of radical liberalism Arnold Kaufman was articulating—a combination of participatory democracy and social justice protected by a stronger welfare state. Four years later, Arthur Waskow argued that only a coalition politics based on bringing together "the Kennedys, the Reform Democrats, SDS, and Watts" activists (i.e., inner-city community organizers) could create the change that Feinstein and Hayden wanted. Waskow's contribution completed the radical liberal vision of *New University Thought*. Participatory democracy, grounded in radical humanism, plus a strong sense of social justice protected by an activist welfare state— such was the dream of these young radicals.[25]

24. Feingold and Hayden, "What Happened to Democracy," 40; Robb Burlage, "The American Planned Economy," *NUT* 4 (1965): 14.

25. Robert Battle III and Horace Sheffield, "Trade Union Leadership Council: Experiment in Community Action," *NUT* 3 (1963); Otto Feinstein and Gabriel Breton, "Civil Rights: A Political Strategy," *NUT* 3 (1963–64): 5; Waskow, "Looking Forward," 50.

This vision contrasted with that of *Studies on the Left*. While *New University Thought*'s editors were expressing hope about the potential for a New Left, James Weinstein and his colleagues were still gloomy in 1965—continuing to draw out the dismissive tone that Eleanor Hakim had expressed to Martin Sklar about the newly emerging movements of 1960. They described the state of the New Left as "isolated groups of radicals, with individual radicals within innumerable single-issue and protest organizations" facing off against "the gigantic Johnson combine." For the editors, the New Left was not committed enough to socialist politics for it to make any real dent in American politics. They continued, "Radicalism has firm roots in no party, no movement, no class, and has no continuing and influential body and experience." The editors concluded that one of the major reasons for radicalism's lack of success—not surprisingly—was the "genius for cooptation" of the American political system.[26]

A bleak picture, indeed. Other editors at *Studies on the Left,* though, were a bit more optimistic about political possibilities, and seemed more akin to the hopeful members of *New University Thought*'s editorial board. Take Staughton Lynd, for instance, a radical historian who came out of the radical pacifist movement of the 1940s and 1950s (the same one that Goodman knew so well), having lived at the Macedonia Community before becoming a scholar. Now at Yale University, he was deeply engaged in the civil rights movement (directing the Freedom Schools sprouting up around the South) and the peace movement. He knew his radical history, as Weinstein and Sklar did, and set out to develop a political philosophy the New Left could embrace. In *Studies on the Left,* he published a poorly titled article, "Socialism, the Forbidden Word." Any reader who expected a call for the New Left to embrace Marxian socialism was deeply disappointed. Instead, Lynd argued for contemporary radicals to be aware of predecessors like Henry George, Edward Bellamy, and Henry Demarest Lloyd. None of these activist-thinkers were Marxists; indeed, George was a steadfast critic of socialism. Lynd knew this and called for contemporary radicals to embrace their "older vocabulary in which America was seen as a house divided between economic aristocracy and an endangered political democracy." This was no picture of capitalist society riddled with the objective class conflict between the proletariat and the bourgeoisie. Combined with his calls for participatory

26. "After the Election," *SoL* 5 (1965): 3–4.

democracy, Lynd sounded much more like a radical republican (small *r* intended) or a turn-of-the-century populist than a socialist.[27]

Lynd's comfort with populism and participatory democracy was felt by Tom Hayden and Norm Fruchter as well. Fruchter, for instance, embraced the democratic decision making he saw within SNCC and argued that it was much more radical than socialist planning. Hayden had the same things to say about SNCC in a review of Howard Zinn's *The New Abolitionists*— drawing out the organization's ideas of direct action, participatory democracy, and popular education. From the viewpoint of Lynd, Hayden, and Fruchter, the New Left had a burgeoning ideology, not one grounded in socialism but in participatory democracy and populism. They saw this political philosophy as sensible and deeply American—certainly not a limitation.[28]

This contrasted with the view of James Weinstein, who allied with Eugene Genovese and Stanley Aronowitz in 1965. These editors believed that the New Left needed to embrace socialism if it wanted to transform American society. Participatory democracy, though important, was not enough. Hayden had argued that using terms like "socialism" would simply alienate too many Americans (and, as Lynd suggested, there were better American ideals that could be alluded to). The debate between Weinstein and Hayden was played out both in the pages of *Studies on the Left* and in private. While Hayden argued that socialism was inappropriate, Weinstein accused Hayden of "redbaiting." Even with this deep ideological and personal divide, Hayden and Weinstein could agree on one thing: the power of co-optation threatened their ideals. After thrashing one another's political visions in an editorial debate, the combative editors pointed out, "Our editorial board agreed on a description of this society as 'the most flexible of totalitarianisms,' in which nearly all human activity is paralyzed in dependence on welfare-capitalism and the Cold War."[29]

Co-optation became perhaps the single most important term of political

27. Staughton Lynd, "Socialism, the Forbidden Word," *SoL* 3 (1963): 17, 19–20. For Lynd's biography, I rely upon the Staughton Lynd Papers. On Macedonia, see Orser, *Searching for a Viable Alternative.*

28. Norm Fruchter, "Mississippi: Notes on SNCC," *SoL* 5 (1965): 77–78; Tom Hayden, review of *The New Abolitionists,* by Howard Zinn, *SoL* 5 (1965): 114, 120. For a fairly thoughtless critique of participatory democracy, see Ronald Aronson, "The Movement and Its Critics," *SoL* 6 (1966): 4.

29. James Weinstein to Staughton Lynd, April 24, 1966, *SoL* Records, box 6; for Weinstein's complaint about Hayden, see his letter to Robin Brooks, July 13, 1965, *SoL* Records, box 1; Hayden, Fruchter, and Cheuse, "Up from Irrelevance," 3.

analysis at *Studies on the Left,* far more important than participatory democracy or socialist alternatives. Before Herbert Marcuse developed his theory of a "one-dimensional society," James Weinstein and Martin Sklar thought through the political implications behind their corporate liberalism thesis and foresaw some of Marcuse's later conclusions. By 1962, for instance, Eleanor Hakim was connecting the historical work done by Martin Sklar on corporate liberalism to the idea that American society co-opted almost all opposition. She wrote to Barton Bernstein, another historian associated with the New Left:

> Surely the double-think and totalitarianism by dissent of corporate capitalist liberalism is much more subtle and smooth than the bludgeoning techniques of fascism! And then there is the added advantage of neutralizing and making impotant [*sic*] any protest movement—radicals and dissenters need not be persecuted too much since they are made harmless. Thus, the illusion of tolerance and democracy can be maintained. Such techniques are much more effective then out and out fascism, and in fact, render it superfluous.

Only two years later, Herbert Marcuse would speak of a "comfortable, smooth, reasonable democratic unfreedom . . . in advanced industrial civilization" that sounded remarkably close to Hakim's judgment. Weinstein used this line of reasoning to argue against radical liberals and those like Hayden who believed that the New Left could "spur liberalism." Such hopes seemed foolish. Weinstein wrote, "My understanding of recent American history is that 'victories' for reform within the system have never been more than partial and almost invariably have been intended to blunt the effect of, or break up, movements for serious social change." Liberal reform seemed, to Weinstein, a weak palliative.[30]

30. Eleanor Hakim to Bart Bernstein, December 6, 1962, *SoL* Records, box 1; Marcuse, *One-Dimensional Man,* 1 (see also 3 for his use of the word "totalitarian" to describe advanced societies); James Weinstein, response to Gans and Hayden, *SoL* 5 (1965): 138. The editors of *Studies on the Left* kept trying, unsuccessfully, to get Herbert Marcuse to write for their journal: see the correspondence in *SoL* Records, box 6. Ironically, after failing, they dismissed Marcuse for his "static and monolithic model of American society," never explaining how the ideas of co-optation and corporate liberalism differed from Marcuse's conception of a one-dimensional society built upon "repressive tolerance." See "Beyond Protest," *SoL* 7 (1967): 10. It is also not surprising to find that the historians at *Studies on the Left* followed the teachings of consensus history developed by Richard Hofstadter and Louis Hartz during the

Co-optation as a political theory seemed only to build up steam as the editors moved beyond the study of history to assess contemporary political struggles. In analyzing the teach-in, for instance, the thinking of William Appleman Williams once again came to the fore. James Gilbert embraced *local* teach-ins, because they were more protest-oriented. The National Teach-In, in contrast, was too neutral and hence co-opted by the phony terms of liberal debate. Joan Scott went further than Gilbert, claiming that the professors who participated in the National Teach-In formed a "loyal opposition." These professors "were bound to lose; for in the context of expertise a policy maker's words automatically carry greater authority than an intellectual's ideas." Essentially, debate was pointless. Peter Lathrop drew this conclusion out more fully. He argued that Kaufman's efforts during the National Teach-In were clearly co-opted, for "the powerful and their representatives cannot be expected to submit themselves to the test of Reason." Of course, Lathrop never offered an *alternative* to reason (was he suggesting revolution?). He and other writers at *Studies on the Left* simply argued that public deliberation and reform were futile.[31]

Community organizing also seemed hopeless to many. After Port Huron, SDS had declared that members should throw in with the Economic Research and Action Project (ERAP), moving to poorer urban communities to organize citizens, just as Saul Alinsky had done earlier. This new form of politics received a great deal of attention from editors at *Studies on the Left*. In fact, some of the best writing done on it appeared in the journal's pages. The most engaging pieces were sympathetic but realistic about the challenges of doing community organizing. For instance, William Miller explained that the participatory democratic vision that motivated community organizers was not so easy to put into practice. He spoke honestly about conflicts "between the need for action based on defined issues and the unwillingness or inability of many people to make decisions . . . and between the levels of political development of organizers and most community people." Often community organizing projects seemed to result in fairly meager victories—such as keeping a small day-care center open in a neighborhood—that paled in contrast with the numbers of socioeconomic problems

---

1950s. For an example of this, see Gabriel Kolko, "The Decline of American Radicalism" (1966), in *For a New America,* ed. Weinstein and Eakins, 209.

31. James Gilbert, "The Teach-In: Protest or Cooptation," *SoL* 5 (1965): 75–81; Joan Scott, "The Teach-In: A National Movement or the End of an Affair," *SoL* 5 (1965): 86; Peter Lathrop, "Teach-Ins: New Force or Isolated Phenomenon?" *SoL* 5 (1965): 52.

faced by community residents. Stanley Aronowitz argued that these piece-meal efforts were incapable of sustaining a "permanent movement." But Norm Fruchter and Robert Kramer defended the idea by arguing that community organizing made politics real for disenfranchised citizens in poorer neighborhoods—moving them from immediate concerns (a day-care center) to a wider sense of politics (federal policy surrounding inner-city programs). For this reason, Fruchter and Kramer argued, community organizing should play a central role in the New Left. Whether it served "as the foundation for a national radical movement" was a question they left open to debate.[32]

These balanced accounts, though, were swiftly denounced. James Weinstein and Martin Sklar argued that community organizing relied upon a "pluralist" model of politics—the sort that C. Wright Mills had criticized. It had no conception of the way in which power worked, and simply placed a naive faith in the noble—but powerless—initiatives of poorer citizens. Worse yet, they argued, community organizing led to a "crude" co-optation of local leaders into an urban elite. It was Danny Schechter, a young journalist based in Syracuse, New York, who had the harshest take on community organizing—in this case, the efforts of Saul Alinsky, who was trying to engage poor African Americans in local political action. Schechter saw Alinsky's efforts as potentially apolitical and futile. He wrote, "Kept simple and self-interest-oriented, with organizers playing a passive role which does not help people draw connections between their own lives and the national political and economic system, social action could be an intelligent, updated method of social control rather than social change." The term "social control" could be read here as co-optation. Once again, even a practice that appeared to be "radically democratic"—the mobilization of poor citizens for social justice—could become just another way of strengthening the status quo.[33]

This seemed a gloomy predicament. Taken to its furthest extent, the po-

32. William Miller, "New Brunswick: Community Action Project," *SoL* 5 (1965): 77; Stanley Aronowitz, "Poverty, Politics, and Community Organizations," *SoL* 3 (1964): 104, and "New York City: After the Rent Strikes," *SoL* 5 (1965): 87; Norm Fruchter and Robert Kramer, "An Approach to Community Organizing Projects," *SoL* 6 (1966): 40. For the day-care example, see "Chicago: Join Project," *SoL* 5 (1965): 125. For more on ERAP generally, see James Miller, *"Democracy Is in the Streets,"* 188–211.

33. Weinstein and Sklar, "Socialism and the New Left," 62; "After the Election," 11; Danny Schechter, "Reveille for Reformers II," *SoL* 6 (1966): 27; see also "Reveille for Reformers: Report from Syracuse," *SoL* 5 (1965): 86; Jesse Allen, "Newark: Community Union," *SoL* 5 (1965): 80–84 (on radical democracy).

litical thinking found in *Studies on the Left* seemed utterly depressing. That is what makes James Weinstein's waffling on the issue of co-optation so important. Very often, Weinstein was pressed on this matter by other editors, precisely because his ideas seemed to close out political alternatives. Yet while making his pessimistic prognostications, Weinstein was also discovering his own reformist heroes in American history—the Socialist Party that dominated left politics before the onslaught of Bolshevism in 1919. This party won mayoral positions in America's cities as well as some Congressional seats. Weinstein believed that it was "democratic and decentralized," but also radical. So what assured it of not being co-opted? Here is where Weinstein seemed to fudge. Writing to Saul Landau, he explained: "I don't think the SP played into [Theodore Roosevelt's] hand by advocating reform any more than I think the [Communist Party] played into FDR's hand by advocating, let's say, the FEPC. To say so is to say that any demand other than socialism now! is reformism. If anything, in 1912, it was the socialists who forced TR's hand—made him advocate reform more strenuously. This is the effect of any vigorous socialist movement on wise capitalist politicians." Essentially, reform could be effective, not just softened through co-optation. In fact, in a later letter, Weinstein argued that the reform carried out by the Socialist Party was "genuinely progressive," a far cry from describing it as co-optation.[34]

Weinstein's admission here showed how he might give ground on the debates surrounding co-optation and liberalism. In 1964, Weinstein and his fellow editors called for a coalition politics aimed at achieving "secure jobs, decent schools, comfortable housing, urban transport and, soon, an end to the holy war against colonial peoples and the fear of nuclear cataclysm." The coalition would have to be built out of northern ghetto activists (community organizers), the more radical elements of labor unions, and the student movement. It seemed difficult to distinguish between this vision and that of Bayard Rustin, who was arguing for the civil rights movement to start focusing on issues of economic inequality as it moved north. But there *were* some important differences. First, Rustin had made too much of a pact with LBJ on the Vietnam War (which, it should be pointed out, made Martin

---

34. Editorial, *SoL* 5 (1965): 12; James Weinstein to Saul Landau, December 6, 1958, *SoL* Records, box 5; James Weinstein to Lawrence Goldman, October 11, 1962, *SoL* Records, box 4. For Weinstein's positive view of the Socialist Party, see his "Socialism's Hidden Heritage" (1963), in *For a New America,* ed. Weinstein and Eakins. These arguments would eventually find their way into his book, *The Decline of Socialism in America.*

Luther King Jr.'s decision to denounce the war so important). Second, as Weinstein saw it, Rustin's coalition politics was simply not radical enough: "The Rustin approach, which we reject, is based on an assumption that independent radical politics is meaningless and that 'coalition' must mean hooking up with the existing political power structure, or with those bureaucratic sections of the trade union leadership, religious organizations, etc., which are on the fringes of power." How this made Weinstein's vision different, say, from Arnold Kaufman's was still not clear.[35]

Weinstein's call for the New Left to turn to electoral politics did little to clarify what made his vision distinct. Once again, he sounded remarkably similar to some liberals whom he chastised, arguing against the New Left's narrow focus on protest politics and its avoidance of long-term electoral work. *Studies on the Left* published a piece by Julian Bond, a onetime SNCC activist turned politician. Bond explained that fears of co-optation seemed misplaced: "I found that my own fears about controlling people or manipulating them blurred in the give-and-take dialogue (which implies give-and-take of decision-making and ideas) with the community." Taking this sort of lesson to heart, Weinstein decided to experiment with electoral politics, running for Congress in 1966 on the Upper West Side of Manhattan (perhaps the most liberal district in America). Forming the Committee for Independent Political Action (CIPA), which was something of a third party, Weinstein dove into the murky world of politics. He explained CIPA to Saul Landau: "Our perspective is to build a popular socialist movement. . . . There is no such thing, of course, and we make it plain that there won't be for some years (5–20), but that all activity must build toward this or go play golf. We use the old Debs party [SP] as our loose model." Here Weinstein set out his own political vision. With radical liberals, he shared an embrace of electoral politics and building coalitions, meshed with participatory democracy. The key difference, though, was that Weinstein saw third parties as the right place to do this.[36]

Weinstein lost the election, and there seemed something a bit unrealistic in retrospect (and, according to critics like Arnold Kaufman, at the time) in

35. "Civil Rights and the Northern Ghetto," *SoL* 4 (1964): 10; "After the Election," 4; James Weinstein to Louis Goldberg, June 23, 1965, *SoL* Records, box 3. On Rustin's coalition politics, see Jervis Anderson, *Bayard Rustin: Troubles I've Seen (A Biography)* (New York: Harper Collins, 1997), 284–85, and 294 for his pact with LBJ on the Vietnam War.

36. Sklar and Weinstein, "Socialism and the New Left," 70; Julian Bond, "Atlanta: The Bond Campaign," *SoL* 5 (1965): 82; James Weinstein to Saul Landau, May 3, 1966, *SoL* Records, box 5.

his assessment that a socialist movement might emerge five to twenty years after 1966. During the late 1960s, even Kaufman's vision of a radical liberal and left-of-center Democratic Party had a hard time sustaining itself. What seems remarkable in looking back is the parallel between what Weinstein and Kaufman wanted, even though the former might never have admitted to sharing much of anything with the latter. Both wanted to draw on the energy behind the New Left's activism and the idea of participatory democracy, but they wanted to match this with a sustained commitment to electoral politics and the building of coalitions. The difference was that one wanted to work within the Democratic Party, and the other, to break with it. This seemed more a matter of strategy and political estimation than of core ideological vision. Nonetheless, neither Weinstein's nor Kaufman's strategy made an impact on American politics for long.

Conclusion: The Death of the Magazines—and the Death of the New Left Intellectual?

Studies on the Left moved to New York. There, activism, not debate, or even the historical revisionism of the earlier generation, was the order of the day. The positions that many of the older generation of students had arrived at, painfully and with a great deal of hesitation and qualification, were the beginning assumptions of the new student generation. They believed us when we declared that liberalism was a corrupt tradition and that American socialism and communism had deeply flawed and troubled pasts. But they believed these things too literally.
—James Gilbert, "Intellectuals and the First New Left," 1990

During the 1960s, *Studies on the Left* and *New University Thought* found themselves facing questions of political possibilities through the lens of new social movements arising in America in those years. The editors at both publications were quick to take note of the inherent limits of these movements, seeing them as single-issue movements oriented toward protest, not transformation. As we have seen, *New University Thought* seemed more willing to accept some of these limits, believing that participatory democracy and radical humanism were fine ideals, especially when coupled with building a stronger welfare state (which included, they believed, vibrant citizen participation), community organizing, and democratic unions. Some editors at *Studies on the Left* also seemed attuned to these possibilities, articulating a radical republican, populist vision grounded in community organizing. This model probably aligned nicely with those of midwestern or southwestern

SDS members who, in the words of Doug Rossinow, "mixed Jeffersonian democracy, agrarian radicalism, and New Deal liberalism." It was really the socialist critique of these movements—articulated by James Weinstein, Martin Sklar, Eugene Genovese, and Stanley Aronowitz—that seemed the most dismissive. And even these critics seemed to recognize that participatory democracy would have to inform any strategy of independent third-party coalition politics.[37]

These conflicting views stemmed from the editors' analyses of liberalism. Here we see variety and strain, rather than any single interpretation. *New University Thought,* of course, seemed more sympathetic to the radicalizing potential of liberal politics and worried that radicals might threaten to push liberalism off the map if they were not careful. Those at *Studies on the Left,* in contrast, were more willing to make the break with the "corporate liberalism" they had traced out in American history. (As actually existing liberals continued to pursue the war in Vietnam, the break came more easily.) Nonetheless, there was always something more of a tension here than an absolute fissure. Even when they criticized the Vietnam War, the editors at *New University Thought* still held up the radical potential of liberalism. And even when some editors at *Studies on the Left* attacked liberals, their own vision of coalition politics and electoral work seemed remarkably parallel to the strategic thinking of Arnold Kaufman. Both *Studies on the Left* and *New University Thought* inherited a conflict-ridden vision of liberalism, a conflict that remained unresolved in the minds of these young intellectuals.

The editors at both publications also fell heir to a challenging model of intellectual life in the career and thinking of previous New Left intellectuals. As we have seen in this chapter, the hope for an engaged public intellectual came smack up against the pressures of academia. Because the editors were young and starting professional careers, they worried openly about how the desire to be politically engaged clashed with the pressure to be academically successful. As movements emerged, some saw a possibility of inheriting the mantle left by C. Wright Mills. The engaged intellectual still seemed a possibility, even if just for a moment. The teach-ins provided hope for the editors at *New University Thought;* serious discussions about community organizing and other political alternatives alleviated some of the gloomier sentiments at *Studies on the Left.* But perhaps the mid-1960s was their last gasp. Soon thereafter, both publications started to disintegrate.

What caused the destruction of *Studies on the Left* can be debated. But

37. Rossinow, *Politics of Authenticity,* 12.

undoubtedly, when Tom Hayden, Norm Fruchter, and Staughton Lynd bolted from the editorial board, things radically changed. The debate between Hayden and Weinstein seemed too difficult to overcome. Weinstein felt that Hayden misled other editors about his political views and thus made it difficult to work together. As Weinstein wrote to Robin Brooks, "The problem with Tom has nothing to do with where he stands (that changes constantly in any case) but with his refusal to participate honestly in theoretical discussion. To Tom, theory is something you use to rationalize where you're at." Hayden, as Weinstein saw it, would go to *Dissent* meetings and bad-mouth the editors at *Studies on the Left,* and then turn around and become chummy with those very same editors. Staughton Lynd came to Hayden's defense. He wrote Weinstein, "The fact seems to me that in Tom you have encountered the only representative of the new generation of student leaders who has taken a major part in the magazine and have not merely failed to enlist his energies permanently but have contributed (for surely it cannot all be Tom's fault) to the present bitterness." This personal debate, in any event, should simply be taken for what it was—the sign of a journal about to come to an end out of both political and personal conflict. Soon after the debate cooled off, editors scattered into different academic posts (participating in the occasional "Socialist Scholars' Conference"), except for Weinstein, who tried to experiment with a string of other publications after dismantling *Studies on the Left.* But as he himself explained to Paul Buhle in 1967: "The universities are obviously the best place we have to work." Perhaps this symbolized the discomfort or uncertainty of acting as publicly engaged intellectuals. There seemed no place to go.[38]

New University Thought did not witness such harsh ideological or personal breaks (perhaps because it was never wedded to ideological self-definition in

38. James Weinstein to Robin Brooks, July 13, 1965, *SoL* Records, box 1 (I also rely upon my interview with James Weinstein to understand the Hayden-Weinstein conflict); Staughton Lynd to James Weinstein, May 9, 1966, *SoL* Records, box 6; James Weinstein to Paul Buhle, April 12, 1967, *Radical America* Archives, Wisconsin State Historical Society, box 4. *Radical America,* it should be noted, began in 1967 and modeled itself slightly on *Studies on the Left.* For more on the experiment, see John McMillian, "Love Letters to the Future: REP, *Radical America,* and New Left History," *Radical History Review* 77 (2000): 20–59. Here is how Lee Baxandall, an editor at *Studies on the Left,* explained the journal's breakup to Paul Buhle: "The background involves STUDIES' move to New York, the strengthening of its editorial board, then the disastrous move to get rid of 'mindless activists' Hayden and Lynd, and Weinstein's megalomaniac maneuvers to dominate content and policy, the erosion of both the magazine's relevance and its internal democracy and efficiency, etc." (letter dated February 8, 1969, *Radical America* Archives, box 1).

the way that *Studies on the Left* was). Rather, the journal simply seemed to lose direction by 1969. Even by 1968, there were entire issues that were really just books published by peace movement writers. The publication came out only once from 1969 to 1970. In 1971, a new set of editors appeared on the masthead, and they decided to publish work being done in radical anthropology. Otto Feinstein seemed nowhere in sight; wherever he was, the magazine petered out. The 1971 anthropology issue was the last issue of *New University Thought*.

The loss of these publications was significant. New Left movements would continue to press on—indeed, the protests against the Vietnam War were just heating up when *Studies on the Left* collapsed—but they lost two places in which ideas could be exchanged about the deeper issues that these movements provoked. The critique of liberalism, as James Gilbert pointed out, turned less intellectual and more emotional as the New Left became more apocalyptic in tone. And identity politics—especially in the guise of black power—posed new divisions and conflicts within the movements. Many of the young intellectuals working with these publications burrowed further into academia. It was not clear whether C. Wright Mills's vision of engaged intellectuals could ever reemerge. Though it might border on hyperbole to suggest that the end of these two magazines entailed the death of the New Left intellectual, a certain chapter in American intellectual history seemed to come to an end at this point. Unresolved tensions between radicalism and liberalism, intellectual commitment and truth telling in an academic world, and political change and co-optation—all of these tensions remained, but without younger thinkers to address them in effective ways, as they had before.

Conclusion:
Lost Causes, Radical Liberalism, and the Future

Any new left in America must be, in large measure, a left with real intellectual skills committed to deliberativeness, honesty, reflection as working tools.
—Port Huron Statement, 1962

Lost causes have a way of shrinking in importance in the memory of later generations, and the historian must go back to the days before their overthrow, and view them in the light of their hopes. Time is not always a just winnower; it is partial to success and its verdict too often inclines to the side of the biggest cannon or the noisiest *claque*. The exhuming of buried reputations and the revivifying of dead causes is the familiar business of the historian, in whose eyes forgotten men may assume as great significance as others with whom posterity has dealt more generously.
—Vernon Parrington, *Main Currents in American Thought*, 1927

It might seem ironic that a book telling a tale of decline would wind up, in the end, arguing for something salvageable from that same story of decline. But so it is with this book. Writing about "lost causes," as the historian Vernon Parrington called them, is not an easy task, either from the standpoint of getting at those lost causes or explaining why they should matter to contemporary readers. Some explanation of the significance of this story is required. So here is my conclusion, starkly stated: For those interested in contemporary American intellectual life and politics, there is something in this story that can help us consider the future of democratic political thought. Nonetheless, this act of salvaging the past requires a forthright admission that the present story is one of defeat—the tough lesson of history.

Indeed, to tell the story of politics and intellectual life from 1970 onward is to tell a story of *conservative* ascendancy. Though conservative intellectuals were a conflicted and minority voice in 1945, by the mid-1950s, they had an important institutional presence in *National Review* magazine (edited by William F. Buckley, a leading conservative intellectual). Some conservative thinkers found themselves floundering, not entirely comfortable with political spokespeople like Barry Goldwater or with the centrist (Eisenhower) wing of the Republican Party. Still, during the tumultuous decade of the 1960s, when intellectuals like Paul Goodman and Arnold Kaufman steered a rocky and conflicted course, many of those within the New York Intellectual grouping shifted hard to the right. Reacting against the excesses of the counterculture (what some of them called the "adversary culture") and liberalism, which became increasingly defined as the pursuit of an elitist "New Class" bent on questionable causes, these "neoconservatives" flooded the broader ranks of conservative thinkers throughout the late 1960s and into the early 1970s. At this time, conservative CEOs and business leaders, many of them interested in pushing through deregulation as a public policy, took notice of this intellectual reorientation and funded a slew of think tanks that hosted and promoted the work of right-wing intellectuals. With these institutions in place, the right won the war of ideas during the 1970s—and wound up fueling the intellectual and political revolution that catapulted Ronald Reagan to presidential victory in 1980 and moved American political discourse to the right for some time to come.[1]

The New Left—as an idea, but more so as a *stereotype*—became a fixture in neoconservative arguments. In fact, if the New Left had not existed, neoconservatives would have invented it. Though marked by idiosyncrasies and conflicts, neoconservative political thought has certainly developed a few key features related to New Left ideas. First, neoconservatives have tried to portray radical student confrontations, such as those at Columbia University, as representative of the *entire* New Left. Confrontationalism, neoconservatives argue, symbolized not only a direct assault on legitimate authority but also an underlying pathology among New Leftists and even left-leaning liberals. There was absolutely no legitimacy in such confrontations—*pace* the more nuanced criticisms of Paul Goodman and Arnold Kaufman. As Peter Steinfels explains, "In 1971, [Norman] Podhoretz [a leading neoconservative who had originally helped publish Paul Goodman's *Growing Up Absurd*] was willing to describe not only the New Left but virtually the entire middle-class New Politics movement—Senator Eugene McCarthy excepted but not

---

1. This history has been told in many fine sources. See, for instance, George Nash, *The Conservative Intellectual Movement in America, Since 1945* (New York: Basic, 1976); John Judis, *William F. Buckley: Patron Saint of the Conservatives* (New York: Simon and Schuster, 1988); Steinfels, *The Neoconservatives;* and Sidney Blumenthal, *The Rise of the Counter-Establishment: From Conservative Ideology to Political Power* (New York: Harper and Row, 1988).

his followers—as 'Stalinist' and 'anti-American.'" Neoconservatives began associating liberalism with a New Class of highly educated professionals who tried to impose their views on the rest of society. No longer agents of democracy or of noble causes, liberals and leftists were turned into *elitists*. Add to all this the fact that the counterculture—something that neoconservatives equated with the New Left—is to blame for a general moral breakdown in American society, and you have the primary features of neoconservative thought as they relate to the New Left and the 1960s. In the minds of neoconservatives, the New Left is best understood as loony, confrontational, elitist, and all about cultural rebellion and breakdown.[2]

The tradition that I have traced out in this book suggests a very different picture. If anything, the New Left thinkers studied here seem firmly rooted in Enlightenment rationality. They were reform-minded, not confrontational or crazy—or elitist. They did not pursue the self-interests of a New Class, but had a firm commitment to democracy. Certainly, intellectuals could help take a lead in social and political reform, as Mills, Goodman, and Kaufman argued, but their work was to be rooted in processes of citizen dialogue, rather than direct advice to those in power. These thinkers varied in terms of how much governmental action was necessary to improve the lives of Americans, but none of them should be seen as statist or anti-democratic. And as far as cultural rebellion goes, these intellectuals constantly criticized the *limits* of countercultural rebellion, seeing it as inherently restricted in a consumer, capitalist society that encouraged and relied upon the ethic of self-expression. They did not see the Beats, the Angry Young Men, or the hippies as revolutionary or subversive, the way neoconservatives did, but as apolitical, unthreatening, and easily co-opted.

The neoconservative take on the New Left helps highlight the general features of the thinkers I have studied here. We can now get a better sense of what these thinkers on the left had in common and what their convictions tell us today about ideas and politics. In so doing, we need to recognize strengths and weaknesses within New Left thought. Far be it from me to flip the neoconservative picture around, however: there *were* certainly weaknesses and paradoxes among the thinkers I have studied. Nonetheless, the neoconservative version seems to present only a part of the story about the New Left. By pushing beyond it and focusing on certain themes that I have

2. Steinfels, *The Neoconservatives*, 48.

emphasized here, we can get at what really matters about this history for the present.

Clearly, these thinkers shared a number of traits that require some restating. First, there was the shared fate of history and biography. C. Wright Mills and Paul Goodman were both unwilling to go along with the "drift" of many intellectuals during the Cold War—a drift that ended in Dwight Macdonald's decision to short-circuit his search for a new radicalism in order to "choose the West" in 1952. In opposing Macdonald's course, Mills and Goodman were not soft on communism, as some might think, but rather concerned with where anticommunism led in terms of domestic questions about democracy and an increasingly rigid foreign policy. Mills's and Goodman's biographies failed to fit into a general pattern of the time: communist origins leading to centrist and conservative endings—the primary path taken by the New York Intellectuals, many of whom became neoconservatives. Moreover, Kaufman was simply too young to take this route, and Williams was too midwestern to start off as a New York sectarian Marxist. Without the baggage of Old Leftism, these thinkers were free to travel their own paths toward a new set of ideas. In this way, they were out of what some intellectual historians see as mainstream developments in American political and social thought.

In other ways, though, these intellectuals fit squarely within certain trends of their times. For instance, all of them were influenced by the flowering of social criticism during the 1950s. Mills and Goodman picked up on and helped develop the cultural criticism for which the decade became known, seeing it as a sign that all was not necessarily well in America—that, in fact, prosperity and world power could never smother anxieties. At the same time, they *politicized* cultural criticism, showing how it opened up the possibilities for public debate on issues of great importance. They did this while criticizing the limitations of cultural rebels—the "Beats" for Goodman, the Angry Young Men for Mills, the countercultural hippies for Williams and Kaufman—who had mistaken self-expression for effective social and political change. In so doing, the thinkers studied here showed that a New Left needed to be rational and committed to serious political restructuring rather than cultural rebellion.

In pursuing their own work as intellectuals, these thinkers tried to balance the pursuit of truth telling with political engagement. At their best, they struck a careful balance between what could at first appear to be conflicting values. Arnold Kaufman's activism in the teach-in movement showed how an intellectual could remain committed to the search for truth with fellow citizens while engaging in the messy world of political change. None-theless, this balancing act could never resolve all the conflicts in left debates. For instance, the editors at *Studies on the Left* deliberated over whether they should engage directly in social movements or draw back from political commitment in order to pursue "theory," as some of them called it. This tension also appeared in William Appleman Williams's thinking during the late 1960s. Williams pondered whether the historian and the citizen-activist existed in a permanent state of schizophrenia, the former pursuing a sort of knowledge that challenged the latter's desire to transform the world for the better. And yet, even with this recurrent struggle, the hope that intellectuals could join the pursuit of truth (with no pretense toward objectivity or final-ity) to political relevance served as the most basic assumption undergirding this New Left intellectual project.

This assumption required a special responsibility on the part of the intel-lectuals working toward a New Left. They had to resist the temptation to speak directly to those who held power; rather, they had to help create what C. Wright Mills called "self-cultivating publics." These publics, comprised of citizens, intellectuals, and activists, would hold those in power account-able to democratic demands. Goodman came to this vision by pondering his frustration in writing under-read poetry and fiction; Williams saw the solu-tion operating in local teach-ins. Even a thinker like Arnold Kaufman, who had the greatest amount of faith in electoral politics, believed that political parties should engage in processes of open-ended education—deliberation, debate, discussion—as much as they should try to win elections. The idea of a democratic public was central to all of these thinkers' visions of political reform.

To help create democratic publics, intellectuals had to take part in certain practices of institution building. Engaged citizens who formed a public would have to be able to resist the power of the "cultural apparatus," the term Mills used to describe the mass media and other means of communica-tion. Intellectuals, therefore, had to conceive of themselves as cultural *workers* ("craftspeople" was Mills's preferred term), responsible not solely for gener-ating ideas but also for ensuring that those ideas wound up in the minds and arguments of a thoughtful audience and public. That is why I have spent so much time describing the practices of these intellectuals: how C. Wright Mills renewed the tradition of writing political pamphlets; how Paul Good-man worked with the Institute for Policy Studies to create a space in which

thinkers, activists, and politicians could gather to discuss the future of politics; how William Appleman Williams and Arnold Kaufman helped organize
teach-ins through which the resources of academia nurtured deliberating
publics; how small magazines gave movement activists a forum in which to
discuss the wider implications of their work. None of these practices suggested that intellectuals served as a vanguard. For though scholars and intellectuals had a special responsibility to share research and thinking with other
citizens, they also *belonged to* the "self-cultivating publics" they helped nurture. Essentially, the New Left intellectual had to share democratic power
with fellow citizens—*pace* neoconservative arguments about any sort of educated, elitist New Class seizing power.

The idea that the intellectual was part of a democratic process goes to the
heart of these thinkers' political theory—the idea of participatory democracy. Mills spoke of radical democracy, Goodman of populism and decentralization, Williams of communitarianism, and Kaufman most directly of participatory democracy. But these ideas often collided with an Old Left faith
in social justice, best protected by an activist government that could transcend local arenas of participation and thus help address inequalities. The
civil rights movement served as a historical example of this balanced demand, for here a group of citizens used local civic institutions to press the
federal government to help ensure equality for an oppressed minority. Neither local action nor governmental power was enough in itself. The puzzle
of how to balance justice and democracy emerged not only in the civil
rights movement but also within the history of political theory. The thinkers
studied here, at their best, recognized this.[3]

In drawing upon the tradition of civic republicanism, these intellectuals'
arguments for localism and democracy could often become confusing. For
instance, at times, Williams wrote what seemed to be moralistic and overly
vague jeremiads. Mills and Goodman could also sound as if they were pining
for a past golden age, one in which all citizens were fiercely independent
property owners and problems were solved through town meetings in local
communities. It was difficult to see what these ideas had to teach citizens
who happened to live in a modern world, with its much greater centralization of economic and political power (as Mills and Goodman never failed to
mention). But at other times, these thinkers believed that their democratic

---

3. For a contemporary statement that explores the difficulties of squaring democracy and
justice, see Ian Shapiro, *Democratic Justice* (New Haven: Yale University Press, 1999).

values could inspire constructive suggestions for the present. Goodman, for instance, moved away from the more individualist and personalist anarchism he developed during the 1940s—a philosophy that grew out of his resistance to World War II—to a belief in pragmatic decentralization. By the mid-1960s, he set out a none-too-rigid principle: "We ought to adopt a political maxim: to decentralize where, how, and how much is expedient. But where, how, and how much are empirical questions; they require research and experiment." Kaufman's political thinking also captured this balance; he always saw democracy as a guiding value, but one that needed to be justified in light of the pragmatic explorations of political theory and experimentation. Where participatory democracy did not square with social justice or equality, then the principle needed to be rethought, Kaufman argued. These thinkers seemed to suggest that when the New Left got down to political reform, it would need to balance out values that could conflict with one another *or* serve as the basis of creative political thinking.

All of these arguments related to the liberal tradition in a critical way. As American liberalism moved into the period of the Cold War, New Left intellectuals asked serious questions about its political future. Many of these thinkers saw the ideology of liberalism as outdated, living on past assumptions no longer relevant for current socioeconomic or political realities. But I have also argued that the critique of liberalism launched here was much more nuanced than previously thought. These thinkers drew a number of their own ideas straight from the liberal tradition: civil rights (such as the right to free speech that Mills, for instance, thought needed to be put into practice rather than simply celebrated), democratic publics, and political and social reform within a constitutional and representative democracy. Perhaps this is best captured in the idea of radical liberalism, a concept hinted at by Mills and fully developed by Kaufman. This was no apology for liberalism as it presently existed; rather, Kaufman believed that liberals needed radicals to press them on difficult matters, such as race relations, abusive foreign policy practices, and the persistence of socioeconomic inequality. Nonetheless, Kaufman asserted, liberalism had the intellectual resources to grapple with these problems. It also possessed a rich and varied tradition that could help get radicals out of the intellectual and political quandaries they often faced.

Today, the teachings of radical liberalism hold more appeal than might at first be thought. Americans have clearly recognized that democratic and civic participation among ordinary citizens has continued to decline since the 1960s. Not only are citizens "bowling alone," as the political scientist

Robert Putnam points out, but they are voting less and engaging in meaningful political debate less. The need for more participatory democracy to enliven our political culture seems obvious. But we need this participation to be balanced with institutions capable of monitoring social justice; conservatives would rather leave everything to the market or to local religious institutions. Radical liberalism teaches us the need for both local participation *and* government strong enough to ensure equality. (Economic inequality, it should be pointed out, has only continued to rise since the 1960s.) In order to get closer to this vision in American politics, we certainly need healthier political debate, discussions that bring in alternative viewpoints about political change. For intellectuals, this requires the sort of activity in which New Left thinkers believed: the combating of an increasingly superficial treatment of political issues by the "cultural apparatus." Mills and Goodman could not have foreseen the rise of the Internet or what Eric Alterman has called the "punditocracy," but they knew that the intellectual's primary responsibility was to create thoughtful and deliberative publics capable of holding leaders accountable. This need only seems more urgent today.[4]

Another teaching of radical liberalism deserves attention. One of Kaufman's most important assertions during the 1960s—and here he differed greatly from Paul Goodman and the editors at *Studies on the Left*—was that the left had to take the radical right very seriously. He took early note of George Wallace, for instance, and argued that radical liberals needed to be chastened about any utopian hopes for political transformation. As he put it in 1971, "Radical liberals are not and for the foreseeable future will not be a majority of the population or the voting public." He argued that New Leftists needed to recognize that they relied "for support on the 'finks' they abuse," that is, centrist liberals. Kaufman's argument seems poignant in our current political context, one in which neither welfare-state liberalism nor the New Left predominates in America. Radical liberalism—with its goal to strike the right balance between participatory democracy and social justice, its faith in public deliberation, its call for coalition politics—seems crucial today for any reinvention of an effective left. But we can no longer believe that liberalism is a dominant ideology or that the right is unworthy of recognition. Only someone blind to current political realities could think this. On the other hand, we should not allow these political facts to lead us to scoff at

4. Robert Putnam, *Bowling Alone: The Collapse and Revival of American Community* (New York: Simon and Schuster, 2000); Eric Alterman, *Sound and Fury: The Making of the Punditocracy* (Ithaca: Cornell, 1999).

(or misread) the political hope that informed New Left political thinking. What this book suggests is the need for a chastened sort of radical liberalism today. This would be a political vision that recognizes what Kaufman already saw in 1971: radical liberalism is not a majoritarian view, and there are those who oppose it. But this need not prevent us from pledging ourselves to the idea of political reform that is committed to creating a participatory and deliberative democracy while nurturing social justice.[5]

Perhaps it is best to think of radical liberalism as forever being a force of *conscience*—a minority voice that tries its best to remind all Americans of higher ideals, such as democracy and equality. When leftists speak of building a "majoritarian" movement, I am reminded of Kaufman's warning about the left's minority status. Certainly, coalition building is necessary (as Kaufman and Williams argued), but the idea that this can produce some sort of massive transformation or realignment seems quite unlikely, especially considering how far to the right the political spectrum has moved. I am entirely comfortable with the idea that radical liberalism will remain a minority voice in American politics and intellectual life. That it cannot be effective as a minority voice—this I would contest.[6]

All of this brings us back to questions of decline and the recent conservative ascendancy—that is, to questions of the present. In the end, I am not arguing that the tradition set out here has died, although I do see it as crowded out by the events of the late 1960s and by the more recent conser-

5. Interestingly enough, SDS recognized its minority status in the Port Huron Statement: "We are a minority—the vast majority of our people regard the temporary equilibriums of our society and world as eternally functional parts" (see James Miller, *"Democracy Is in the Streets,"* 330). For two recent statements that are slightly akin to what I am arguing for here, see William Julius Wilson, *The Bridge Over the Racial Divide,* and Richard Rorty, *Achieving Our Country: Leftist Thought in Twentieth-Century America* (Cambridge: Harvard University Press, 1998). See also my review of Richard Rorty, "Having His Cake and Eating It Too: Richard Rorty on the Revitalization of the Left," *Negations,* no. 3 (1998): 78–83. Unfortunately, Wilson's arguments suffer from a lack of range in describing political examples of what he is aiming for (he simply alludes to the Industrial Areas Foundation, not enough to warrant his overall argument). Rorty, on the other hand, simply gets his history wrong, projecting his own wishful thinking onto the past, as I have shown in my review of his book. For more on the vision set out here, see my "Remember Liberalism?"

6. The most recent example of majoritarianism in American progressive thought is Stanley Greenberg and Theda Skocpol, eds., *The New Majority: Toward a Popular Progressive Politics* (New Haven: Yale University Press, 1997). I should point out that I agree with a number of points raised in this book. I am also indebted to Mark Schmitt for conversations regarding the left and majoritarian politics and to much of the thinking found in Jeffrey Isaac, *Democracy in Dark Times* (Ithaca: Cornell University Press, 1998).

vative ascendancy. But I have always found narratives of decline somewhat suspect. If a tradition like the one explored here was so intertwined with central features of American intellectual history, then how could it simply pass away so easily and quickly? I believe that the New Left intellectual spirit did live on. As many have argued, it certainly found its way into academic historical explorations pursued during the 1970s and 1980s by Herbert Gutman, Eugene Genovese, Jesse Lemisch, and others. But precisely because of their academic nature, these works were cut off from social movements or wider public debates. We have already seen how editors at *Studies on the Left* and *New University Thought* were preparing themselves for academic careers. We know now that this led to political acquiescence, or at least a withdrawal from public debate (getting tenure, let alone finding an academic job in the first place, has only gotten more difficult and time-consuming). We also know that there were few left-leaning think tanks set up after the Institute for Policy Studies was founded in the mid-1960s. Certainly, we can name some public intellectuals on the left today, but we have a harder time naming institutions (aside from large corporate book publishers) or institutional practices that allow those intellectuals to take a leading role in public deliberation about America's future. Teach-ins might still take place in this day and age, but at the same time, the academic institutions that typically host them seem that much more detached from public life. Though I do not believe that the set of ideas discussed here has disappeared, the institutional practices and movements in which those ideas were enmeshed have clearly fallen into decline.[7]

What we still have are the central concepts presented here: participatory democracy, social justice, public deliberation, and the idea of an engaged intellectual. What we need, in addition to these ideas, is a serious attempt to rethink how they fit into our current situation—and perhaps even more important, we need the energy to act upon them. Since 1970, American politics has shifted hard (and quickly) to the right. The historical reconstruction of a radical liberal and democratic tradition of thought—the purpose of this book—may help improve our current situation. But it is not enough. Here I echo the sentiment of William Appleman Williams, who wrote, "History does not offer any answers. Men and women of the present must provide the answers. Hence the historian must return to his own society as a

7. On New Left history, see McMillian, "Love Letters to the Future," 20–59. See also Wiener, "Radical Historians" (and Christopher Lasch's astute response to this piece in the following pages), as well as my "Where Are the Young Left Intellectuals?"

citizen and, with no quarter asked or given, engage other citizens in a dialogue to determine the best answers to these questions." History can only begin a process of thinking about a viable democratic left in this country. The rest will take a great deal more work. America, though, will become a better place if we discover how we can start down this path.

Selected Bibliography

Manuscripts

Goodman, Paul. Papers. Houghton Library, Harvard University.

Kaufman, Arnold. Papers. Bentley Historical Library, University of Michigan.

Lynd, Staughton. Papers, 1938–1977. Wisconsin State Historical Society, Madison, Wisconsin.

Macdonald, Dwight. Papers. Sterling Library, Yale University, Division of Manuscripts and Archives.

Mills, C. Wright. Papers, 1934–1965. Center for American History, University of Texas, Austin, Texas.

Radical America Archives, 1966–1975. Wisconsin State Historical Society, Madison, Wisconsin.

Students for a Democratic Society. Records, 1958–1970. Wisconsin State Historical Society, Madison, Wisconsin.

Studies on the Left Records, 1959–1967. Wisconsin State Historical Society, Madison, Wisconsin.

Williams, William Appleman. Papers. Ava Helen and Linus Pauling Papers, The Valley Library, Oregon State University, Corvallis, Oregon.

Interviews

Bergmann, Fritjhof. Telephone interview with author. June 7, 2000.

Feinstein, Otto. Telephone interview with author. July 16, 1999.

Gamson, William. Telephone interview with author. June 7, 2000.

Gettleman, Marvin. Telephone interview with author. January 8, 2001.

Kaufman, Elizabeth. Telephone interview with author. August 1, 2000.

Landau, Saul. Telephone interview with author. December 15, 1999.

Raskin, Marc. Telephone interview with author. December 8, 1999.

Rothman, Jack. Telephone interview with author. June 6, 2000.

Waskow, Arthur. Telephone interview with author. November 8, 1999.

Weinstein, James. Telephone interview with author. June 1, 1999.

Magazines

The Activist [student publication, Oberlin, Ohio], 1961–1962.

The American Socialist, 1954–1959.

Freedomways, 1961–1968.
Liberation, 1956–1968.
New University Thought, 1960–1971.
Partisan Review, 1940–1945.
politics, February 1944–Winter 1949.
Studies on the Left, 1959–1967.
Venture [Student League for Industrial Democracy publication], 1959–1960.

Books and Articles

Abel, Lionel. "Seven Heroes of the New Left." *New York Times Magazine,* May 5, 1968, 30–31.

Abrahams, Edward. *The Lyrical Left.* Charlottesville: University Press of Virginia, 1986.

Agee, James, and Walker Evans. *Let Us Now Praise Famous Men.* Boston: Houghton-Mifflin, 1939.

Allsop, Kenneth. *The Angry Decade: A Survey of the Cultural Revolt of the 1950s.* New York: British Book Centre, 1958.

Alperovitz, Gar. *Atomic Diplomacy: Hiroshima and Potsdam.* New York: Simon and Schuster, 1965.

Alt, John. "Reclaiming C. Wright Mills." *Telos* 18 (1985): 6–43.

"America II: A Symposium on the Work of William Appleman Williams." *Partisan Review* 37 (1970): 498–527.

Anderson, Jervis. *Bayard Rustin: Troubles I've Seen (A Biography).* New York: Harper Collins, 1997.

Baker, Susan Stout. *Radical Beginnings: Richard Hofstadter and the 1930s.* Westport, Conn.: Greenwood, 1985.

Barrett, William. *The Truants: Adventures Among the Intellectuals.* Garden City, N.J.: Anchor, 1982.

Bates, Tom. *Rads: The 1970 Bombing of the Army Math Research Center at the University of Wisconsin and Its Aftermath.* New York: Harper Collins, 1992.

Bell, Daniel. *The End of Ideology: On the Exhaustion of Political Ideas in the Fifties.* New York: Free, 1960.

———. "Notes on the Monopoly State." *The New Leader,* October 30, 1943, 2.

Bender, Thomas. *Intellect and Public Life: Essays on the Social History of Academic Intellectuals in the United States.* Baltimore: Johns Hopkins University Press, 1993.

Berger, Henry, ed. *A William Appleman Williams Reader.* Chicago: Ivan R. Dee, 1992.

Bergreen, Lawrence. *Agee: A Life.* New York: Penguin, 1985.

Berman, Paul. *A Tale of Two Utopias.* New York: Norton, 1996.

Bess, Michael. "E. P. Thompson: The Historian as Activist." *American Historical Review* 98 (1993): 19–38.

Bingham, Alfred. *Insurgent America: Revolt of the Middle Classes.* New York: Harper and Brothers, 1935.

Bird, Kai. *The Color of Truth: McGeorge Bundy and William Bundy, Brothers in Arms.* New York: Simon and Schuster, 1998.

Blake, Casey Nelson. *Beloved Community: The Cultural Criticism of Randolph Bourne, Van*

Wyck Brooks, Waldo Frank, and Lewis Mumford. Chapel Hill: University of North Carolina Press, 1990.

Bloom, Alexander. *Prodigal Sons: The New York Intellectuals and Their World.* New York: Oxford University Press, 1986.

Blum, John Morton. *V Was for Victory: Politics and American Culture During World War II.* New York: Harcourt Brace Jovanovich, 1976.

Blumenthal, Sidney. *The Rise of the Counter-Establishment: From Conservative Ideology to Political Power.* New York: Harper and Row, 1988.

Boggs, Carl. *Intellectuals and the Crisis of Modernity.* Albany: State University of New York Press, 1993.

Bogue, Allan, and Robert Taylor, eds. *The University of Wisconsin: One Hundred and Twenty-Five Years.* Madison: University of Wisconsin Press, 1975.

Bourne, Randolph. *The Radical Will: Selected Writings, 1911–1918.* New York: Urizen, 1977.

Boyer, Paul. "From Activism to Apathy: The American People and Nuclear Weapons, 1963–1980." *Journal of American History* 70 (1984): 821–44.

Boyle, Kevin. *The UAW and the Heyday of American Liberalism, 1945–1968.* Ithaca: Cornell University Press, 1995.

Branch, Taylor. *Parting the Waters.* New York: Simon and Schuster, 1988.

———. *Pillar of Fire.* New York: Simon and Schuster, 1998.

Breines, Wini. *Community and Organization in the New Left: 1962–1968 (The Great Refusal).* New York: Praeger, 1982.

———. "Whose New Left?" *Journal of American History* 75 (1988): 528–45.

Brick, Howard. *Age of Contradiction: American Thought and Culture in the 1960s.* New York: Twayne, 1998.

———. *Daniel Bell and the Decline of Intellectual Radicalism.* Madison: University of Wisconsin Press, 1986.

Brinkley, Alan. *The End of Reform.* New York: Knopf, 1995.

———. *Liberalism and Its Discontents.* Cambridge: Harvard University Press, 1998.

Buhle, Paul. *Marxism in the United States.* New York: Verso, 1987.

———, ed. *History and the New Left: Madison, Wisconsin, 1950–1970.* Philadelphia: Temple University Press, 1990.

Buhle, Paul, and Edward Rice-Maximin. *William Appleman Williams: The Tragedy of Empire.* New York: Routledge, 1995.

Burner, David. *Making Peace with the Sixties.* Princeton: Princeton University Press, 1996.

Burnham, James. *The Machiavellians.* New York: John Day, 1943.

———. *The Managerial Revolution: What Is Happening in the World.* New York: John Day, 1941.

Carmichael, Stokely, and Charles Hamilton. *Black Power: The Politics of Liberation in America.* New York: Random House, 1967.

Carson, Clayborne. *In Struggle: SNCC and the Black Awakening of the 1960s.* Cambridge: Harvard University Press, 1981.

Cavallo, Dominick. *A Fiction of the Past: The Sixties in American History.* New York: St. Martin's, 1999.

Chafe, William. *Never Stop Running: Allard Lowenstein and the Struggle to Save American Liberalism.* New York: Basic, 1993.

Chase, Richard. "The New Campus Magazines." *Harper's,* October 1961, 168–72.

Chomsky, Noam. *American Power and the New Mandarins.* New York: Pantheon, 1967.

Chun, Lin. *The British New Left.* Edinburgh: Edinburgh University Press, 1993.

Clecak, Peter. *Radical Paradoxes: Dilemmas of the American Left, 1945–1970.* New York: Harper and Row, 1973.

Coleman, Peter. *The Liberal Conspiracy: The Congress for Cultural Freedom and the Struggle for the Mind of Postwar Europe.* New York: Free, 1989.

Connolly, William, and Arnold Kaufman. "Between Exaltation and Despair." *Dissent* 15 (1968): 373–76.

Cooney, Terry. *The Rise of the New York Intellectuals:* Partisan Review *and Its Circle.* Madison: University of Wisconsin Press, 1986.

Corey, Lewis. *The Decline of American Capitalism.* New York: Covici, Friede, 1934.

Cotkin, George. *William James, Public Philosopher.* Baltimore: Johns Hopkins University Press, 1990.

Cottrell, Robert. *Izzy: A Biography of I. F. Stone.* New Brunswick: Rutgers University Press, 1992.

Crotty, William. *Decision for the Democrats: Reforming the Party Structure.* Baltimore: Johns Hopkins University Press, 1978.

Cruse, Harold. *The Crisis of the Negro Intellectual.* New York: William Morrow, 1967.

Cummings, Richard. *The Pied Piper: Allard K. Lowenstein and the Liberal Dream.* New York: Grove, 1985.

Cummings, Robert. "Dwight Macdonald in the 1940s." *New Politics* 1 (1986): 213–32.

Dallek, Matthew. *The Right Moment: Ronald Reagan's First Victory and the Decisive Turning Point in American Politics.* New York: Free, 2000.

Dellinger, David. *From Yale to Jail.* New York: Pantheon, 1993.

Dennison, George. "In Memory of Paul Goodman." *New York Review of Books,* December 13, 1973, 5–53.

Dewey, John. *The Public and Its Problems.* Denver: Swallow, 1927.

Dickstein, Morris. *Gates of Eden: American Culture in the Sixties.* New York: Basic, 1977.

Diggins, John Patrick. *The Proud Decades: America in War and Peace, 1941–1960.* New York: Norton, 1989.

———. *The Rise and Fall of the American Left.* New York: Norton, 1992.

———. *Up from Communism: Conservative Odysseys in American Intellectual History.* New York: Harper and Row, 1975.

———, ed. *The Liberal Persuasion: Arthur Schlesinger, Jr., and the Challenge of the American Past.* Princeton: Princeton University Press, 1997.

Dionne, E. J. *Why Americans Hate Politics.* New York: Simon and Schuster, 1992.

Dittberner, Job. *The End of Ideology and American Social Thought, 1930–1960.* Ann Arbor: UMI Press, 1979.

"Editorial." *Universities and Left Review* 1 (1957): ii.

Eisen, Jonathan, and David Steinberg. "The Student Revolt Against Liberalism." *Annals of American Academy of Political and Social Science* 323 (March 1969): 83–94.

Eldridge, John. *C. Wright Mills.* London: Tavistock, 1983.

Ellis, Richard. *The Dark Side of the Left: Illiberal Egalitarianism in America.* Lawrence: University Press of Kansas, 1998.

Epstein, Barbara. *Political Protest and Cultural Revolution: Nonviolent Direct Action in the 1970s and 1980s.* Berkeley and Los Angeles: University of California Press, 1991.

Epstein, Joseph. "Paul Goodman in Retrospect." *Commentary,* February 1978, 70–73.

Evans, Richard William. "In Quest of a Usable Past: Young Leftist Historians in the 1960s." Ph.D. diss., Case Western Reserve University, 1979.

"Excerpts from a Conference to Honor William Appleman Williams." *Radical History Review* 50 (1991): 39–70.

Farber, David. *The Age of Great Dreams: America in the 1960s.* New York: Hill and Wang, 1994.

———, ed. *The Sixties: From Memory to History.* Chapel Hill: University of North Carolina Press, 1994.

Farrell, James. *The Spirit of the Sixties: Making Postwar Radicalism.* New York: Routledge, 1997.

Feldman, Gene, and Max Gartenberg, eds. *The Beat Generation and the Angry Young Men.* New York: Citadel, 1958.

Fiedler, Leslie. *An End to Innocence: Essays on Culture and Politics.* Boston: Beacon, 1952.

Flacks, Richard. *Making History: The American Left and the American Mind.* New York: Columbia University Press, 1988.

"Foreign Policy and the American Mind." *Commentary,* February 1962, 155–60.

Frankel, Max. "Vietnam Debate Heard on 100 Campuses." *New York Times,* May 16, 1965, A1.

Fraser, Steve, and Gary Gerstle, eds. *The Rise and Fall of the New Deal Order, 1930–1980.* Princeton: Princeton University Press, 1989.

Fried, Richard. *Nightmare in Red: The McCarthy Era in Perspective.* New York: Oxford University Press, 1990.

Friedman, John, ed. *First Harvest: The Institute for Policy Studies, 1963–1983.* New York: Grove, 1983.

Friedman, Neil. "Geist, Guise, and Guitar." *Dissent* 7 (1960): 151–52.

Gaddis, John Lewis. *The United States and the Origins of the Cold War, 1941–1947.* New York: Columbia University Press, 1972.

Galbraith, John Kenneth. *The Affluent Society.* New York: Mentor, 1958.

Gamson, William. "Commitment and Agency in Social Movements." *Sociological Forum* 6 (1991): 27–50.

Gardner, Geoffrey. "Citizen of the World, Animal of Nowhere." *New Letters* 42 (1976): 216–27.

Gardner, Lloyd, ed. *Redefining the Past: Essays in Diplomatic History in Honor of William Appleman Williams.* Corvallis: Oregon State University Press, 1986.

Garrow, David. *Bearing the Cross: Martin Luther King and the Southern Christian Leadership Conference.* New York: Vintage, 1988.

Genovese, Eugene. *The Political Economy of Slavery.* New York: Pantheon, 1965.

Gerth, Hans. "C. Wright Mills, 1916–1962." *Studies on the Left* 2 (1962): 7–11.

Gilbert, James. *A Cycle of Outrage: America's Reaction to the Juvenile Delinquent in the 1950s.* New York: Oxford University Press, 1986.

———. *Writers and Partisans: A History of the Literary Radical in America.* New York: John Wiley, 1968.

Gillam, Richard. "C. Wright Mills, 1916–1948: An Intellectual Biography." Ph.D. diss., Stanford University, 1972.

———. "C. Wright Mills and the Politics of Truth: *The Power Elite* Revisited." *American Quarterly* 26 (1975): 461–79.

———. "The Intellectual as Rebel: C. Wright Mills, 1916–1948." Master's thesis, Columbia University, 1966.

———. "Intellectuals and Power." *Center Magazine,* May–June 1977, 15–29.

———. "Richard Hofstadter, C. Wright Mills, and 'the Critical Ideal.'" *American Scholar* (Winter 1977–78): 69–85.

———. "*White Collar* from Start to Finish." *Theory and Society* 10 (1981): 2–32.

Gillon, Steven. *Politics and Vision: The ADA and American Liberalism, 1947–1985.* New York: Oxford University Press, 1987.

Gitlin, Todd. *The Sixties: Years of Hope, Days of Rage.* New York: Bantam, 1987.

Glazer, Penina Migdal. "From the Old Left to the New: Radical Criticism in the 1940s." *American Quarterly* 24 (1972): 584–603.

Goldberg, Harvey, and William Appleman Williams. "Thoughts About American Radicalism." In *American Radicals: Some Problems and Personalities,* edited by Harvey Goldberg. New York: Monthly Review, 1957.

Goodman, Paul. "Abolishing the Grading System." In *1945–1970: Twenty-Five Years.* San Francisco: Jossey-Bass, 1970.

———. "The American Writer and His Americanism." *Kenyon Review* 21 (1959): 478–82.

———. An Apology for Literature." In *Creator Spirit Come! The Literary Essays of Paul Goodman,* edited by Taylor Stoehr. New York: Dutton, 1977.

———. "The Art of Hollywood." *The New Leader,* August 23, 1947, 11, 15.

———. "The Attempt to Invent an American Style." *politics,* February 1944, 17–18.

———. "Bentley on Theater." *Kenyon Review* 15 (1953): 662–68.

———. "Berkeley in February." In *Revolution at Berkeley,* edited by Michael Miller and Susan Gilmore. New York: Dial, 1965.

———. "Better Judgment and Public Conscience." *Partisan Review* (July–August 1942): 348–51.

———. "Biography Going to Be Great." *Kenyon Review* 16 (1954): 154–63.

———. "The Black Flag of Anarchism." *New York Times Magazine,* July 14, 1968, 10–11, 15–16, 20, 22.

———. "Children and Psychology." *Liberation,* September 1956, 19–21.

———. "The Children of Birmingham." *Commentary,* September 1963, 242–44.

———. "City Crowds." *politics,* December 1946, 390–91.

———. "Classical Draft Dodgers." *The New Leader,* September 20, 1947, 11.

———. "Comment." *Dissent* 14 (1967): 251–52.

———. "Comment." In *The Law School of Tomorrow,* edited by David Haber and Julius Cohen. New Brunswick: Rutgers University Press, 1968.

———. "Comment." *Liberation,* November 1965, 25–26.

———. *Compulsory Mis-Education and The Community of Scholars.* New York: Vintage, 1964.

———. "A Conjecture in American History, 1783–1815." *politics,* Winter 1949, 11–12.

———. "The Continuing Disaster." *The New Republic,* January 26, 1963, 24–26.

——. "Corny." *New York Times,* November 29, 1970, sec. 2, 7.

——. *Creator Spirit Come! The Literary Essays of Paul Goodman.* Edited by Taylor Stoehr. New York: Dutton, 1977.

——. *Decentralizing Power: Paul Goodman's Social Criticism.* Edited by Taylor Stoehr. Montreal: Black Rose, 1994.

——. "Declaring Peace Against the Government." In *Drawing the Line: The Political Essays of Paul Goodman,* edited by Taylor Stoehr. New York: Dutton, 1977.

——. "The Devolution of Democracy." *Dissent* 9 (1962): 6–22.

——. "The Diggers in 1984: A Fantasy." In *Conversations with the New Reality,* edited by the editors of *Ramparts.* San Francisco: Canfield Colophon, 1971.

——. "Don't Disturb the Children." *The New Republic,* March 16, 1963, 28–30.

——. *Drawing the Line: The Political Essays of Paul Goodman.* Edited by Taylor Stoehr. New York: Dutton, 1977.

——. "The Duty of Professionals." *Liberation,* November 1967, 36–39.

——. *Empire City.* New York: Bobbs-Merrill, 1959.

——. "English Education Today." *The New Republic,* January 8, 1945, 57.

——. "Essay." In *Freedom and Order in the University,* edited by Samuel Gorovitz. Cleveland: Press of Western Reserve University, 1967.

——. "Essay on John Dewey." Paul Goodman Papers. Houghton Library, Harvard University.

——. "Essays by Rosenberg." *Dissent* 6 (1959): 305–7.

——. "Fifty Years Have Passed." *Resistance* (March–April 1948).

——. *Five Years: Thoughts During a Useless Time.* 1966. Reprint, New York: Vintage, 1969.

——. "The Freedom to Be Academic." In *Identity and Anxiety: Survival of the Person in Mass Society,* edited by Maurice Stein. Glencoe: Free, 1960.

——. "French Uncle." *Kenyon Review* 9 (1947): 477–80.

——. "Freudian Journalism." *The New Leader,* December 20, 1947, 11.

——. "The Great Society." *New York Review of Books,* October 14, 1965, 8–12.

——. *Growing Up Absurd.* New York: Vintage, 1960.

——. "Human Nature and the Anthropology of Neurosis." In *Recognitions in Gestalt Therapy,* edited by Paul David Pursglove. New York: Funk and Wagnalls, 1968.

——. "In Praise of Populism." *Commentary,* June 1968, 25–30.

——. Introduction to *"Never Trust a God Over 30": New Styles in Campus Ministry,* edited by Albert H. Friedlander. New York: McGraw-Hill, 1967.

——. "Judaism of a Man of Letters." *Commentary,* September 1948, 242–43.

——. "Leisure and Work." In *Automation: Implications for the Future,* edited by Morris Philipson. New York: Vintage, 1962.

——. Letter. *Harper's,* May 1966, 83.

——. Letter. *Liberation,* November 1965, 31.

——. Letter. *New York Times Magazine,* February 23, 1969, 12–13.

——. "A Letter to John Lindsay." *New York Review of Books,* December 23, 1965, 8–10.

——. "The Liberal Victory." *New York Review of Books,* December 3, 1964, 7.

——. *Little Prayers and Finite Experience.* New York: Harper and Row, 1972.

——. "The Moral Idea of Money." *Journal of Philosophy* 32 (1935): 126–31.

————. *Nature Heals: The Psychological Essays of Paul Goodman.* Edited by Taylor Stoehr. New York: Dutton, 1977.

————. "Neo-Classicism, Platonism, and Romanticism." *Journal of Philosophy* 31 (1934): 148–63.

————. *New Reformation: Notes of a Neolithic Conservative.* New York: Vintage, 1969.

————. "New Theater and the Unions." *Dissent* 6 (1959): 370, 474–76.

————. "Non-Commercial Channels." *The New Republic,* April 13, 1963, 32–34.

————. "No Processing Whatsoever." In *Radical School Reform,* edited by Beatrice Gross and Ronald Gross. New York: Simon and Schuster, 1969.

————. "Notes on Decentralization." *Dissent* 11 (1964): 389–403.

————. "Nothing but Ads." *The New Republic,* February 9, 1963, 28–30.

————. "Objective Values." In *To Free a Generation: The Dialectics of Liberation,* edited by David Cooper. New York: Collier, 1968.

————. "Occasional Poetry." *politics,* March–April 1947, 58–60.

————. "On Gandhi." *politics,* Winter 1948, 4–5.

————. "On Liberal Anti-Communism." *Commentary,* September 1967, 41–42.

————. "On the Brink of Action." *Liberation,* March 1967, 6.

————. "On the Massacre at Kent State." *New York Review of Books,* June 4, 1970, 43.

————. "Our Best Journalist." *Dissent* 5 (1958): 82–86.

————. *People or Personnel and Like a Conquered Province.* New York: Vintage, 1968.

————. "A Platform for Radicals." *Liberation,* February 1968, 5–7.

————. "Plea for a Hesiod." *politics,* January 1947, 19–20.

————. "The Political Meaning of Some Recent Revisions of Freud." *politics,* July 1945, 197–203.

————. "Power Struggles." Interview with Paul Goodman. In *Drawing the Line: The Political Essays of Paul Goodman,* edited by Taylor Stoehr. New York: Dutton, 1977.

————. "A Rationalistic Architecture." *Symposium* 3 (1932): 283–304.

————. "Reflections on Civil Disobedience." *Liberation,* July–August 1968, 11–15.

————. "Reflections on Racism, Spite, Guilt, and Non-Violence." *New York Review of Books,* May 23, 1968, 18–23.

————. Review of *Education and the Cult of Efficiency,* by Raymond Callahan. *Harvard Educational Review* 33 (1963): 533–36.

————. Review of *Let Us Now Praise Famous Men,* by James Agee and Walker Evans. *Partisan Review* 9 (1942): 86–87.

————. "A Romantic Architecture." *Symposium* 2 (1931): 514–24.

————. "Socialism." *Commentary,* April 1970, 35.

————. "Society and the Writer." *Washington Post Book Week,* June 12, 1966, 1, 13.

————. *The Society I Live in Is Mine.* New York: Horizon, 1962.

————. "A Southern Conceit." *Dissent* 4 (1957): 204–8.

————. "Stale Marxism." *Kenyon Review* 9 (1947): 608–12.

————. "Student Draft Deferments." *Liberation,* May–June 1966, 3.

————. "Susskind and Sevareid." *The New Republic,* February 23, 1963, 24–26.

————. "Tardy and Partial Recognition." *Kenyon Review* 10 (1948): 340–46.

————. "Ten Letters on Free Speech." *Liberation,* March 1965, 33–37.

————. "Thoughts on Berkeley." In *The Berkeley Student Revolt,* edited by Seymour Martin Lipset and Sheldon Wolin. Garden City, N.J.: Anchor, 1965.

————. "Toward a 'Duplex' Society." *The New Leader,* February 8, 1947, 13.

————. "Two Issues in Planning." *Commentary,* August 1967, 75–77.

————. "Two Little Essays on Democracy." *Liberation,* May–June 1966, 38–39.

————. "The Unalienated Intellectual." *politics,* November 1944, 318–19.

————. "Urbanization and Rural Reconstruction." *Liberation,* November 1966, 6–11.

————. *Utopian Essays and Practical Proposals.* New York: Vintage, 1964.

Goodman, Percival, and Paul Goodman. *Communitas: Means of Livelihood and Ways of Life.* New York: Vintage, 1960.

Gorman, Robert. *Michael Harrington: Speaking American.* New York: Routledge, 1995.

————. *Yankee Red: Nonorthodox Marxism in Liberal America.* New York: Praeger, 1989.

Gosse, Van. *Where the Boys Are: Cuba, Cold War America, and the Making of a New Left.* New York: Verso, 1993.

Graebner, William. *The Age of Doubt: American Thought and Culture in the 1940s.* Boston: Twayne, 1991.

Greenfield, Meg. "After the Washington Teach-In." *The Reporter,* June 3, 1965, 16–19.

Griffin, Leland. "The Rhetorical Structure of the 'New Left' Movement." *Quarterly Journal of Speech* 50 (1964): 113–35.

Guilbaut, Serge. *How New York Stole the Idea of Modern Art.* Chicago: University of Chicago Press, 1983.

Haber, William. "The Birth of the Teach-In: Authority Without Freedom." *Michigan Quarterly Review* 7 (1968): 262–67.

Hacker, Andrew. "The Rebelling Young Scholars." *Commentary,* November 1960, 404–12.

Hamby, Alonzo. *Beyond the New Deal: Harry S. Truman and American Liberalism.* New York: Columbia University Press, 1973.

Harrington, Michael. "Is There a New Radicalism?" *Partisan Review* (Spring 1964): 194–205.

————. "On Paul Goodman." *Atlantic,* August 1965, 88–91.

Hayden, Tom. *Reunion: A Memoir.* New York: Random House, 1988.

Heineman, Kenneth. *Campus Wars: The Peace Movement at American State Universities in the Vietnam Era.* New York: New York University Press, 1993.

Hentoff, Nat. "Is There a New Radicalism?" *Partisan Review* (Spring 1964): 183–93.

Hobhouse, Leonard. *Liberalism.* 1911. Reprint, New York: Oxford University Press, 1964.

Hofstadter, Richard. *The Age of Reform.* New York: Vintage, 1955.

————. *The American Political Tradition.* New York: Vintage, 1948.

————. *The Progressive Historians: Turner, Beard, Parrington.* New York: Vintage, 1970.

Hollinger, David. *Morris R. Cohen and the Scientific Ideal.* Cambridge: MIT Press, 1975.

Horkheimer, Max. *The Eclipse of Reason.* New York: Oxford University Press, 1947.

Horowitz, Daniel. *Betty Friedan and the Making of* The Feminine Mystique: *The American Left, the Cold War, and Modern Feminism.* Amherst: University of Massachusetts Press, 1998.

————. *Vance Packard and American Social Criticism.* Chapel Hill: University of North Carolina Press, 1994.

Horowitz, David. *Student.* New York: Ballantine, 1962.

Horowitz, Irving Louis. *C. Wright Mills: An American Utopian.* New York: Free, 1983.

————. "The Unfinished Writings of C. Wright Mills: The Last Phase." *Studies on the Left* 3 (1963): 3–23.

Howe, Irving. "The ADA: Vision and Myopia." *Dissent* 2 (1955): 107–13.

———. *The Decline of the New.* New York: Harcourt, Brace, and World, 1970.

———. *A Margin of Hope: An Intellectual Autobiography.* New York: Harcourt Brace Jovanovich, 1982.

———. "Possibilities for Politics." *Partisan Review* (December 1948): 1356–59.

———. *Steady Work: Essays in the Politics of Democratic Radicalism, 1953–1966.* New York: Harcourt, Brace, and World, 1966.

———, ed. *Beyond the New Left.* New York: McCall, 1970.

Howe, Irving, and B. J. Widwick. *The UAW and Walter Reuther.* New York: Random House, 1949.

Howe, Irving, and Lewis Coser. *The American Communist Party: A Critical History.* 1957. Reprint, New York: Praeger, 1962.

Hughes, H. Stuart. *An Approach to Peace and Other Essays.* New York: Atheneum, 1962.

———. "A Politics of Peace." *Commentary,* February 1959, 118–26.

Hunt, Andrew. "When Did the Sixties Happen?" *Journal of Social History* (Fall 1999): 147–61.

Institute for Policy Studies. *The First Three Years: 1963–1966.* Washington, D.C.: IPS, 1966.

"An Interview with William Appleman Williams." *Radical History Review* 22 (1979–80): 65–91.

Isaac, Jeffrey. *Arendt, Camus, and Modern Rebellion.* New Haven: Yale University Press, 1992.

———. *Democracy in Dark Times.* Ithaca: Cornell University Press, 1998.

Isaac, Rael. "The Institute for Policy Studies: Empire on the Left." *Midstream* (June–July 1980): 7–18.

Isserman, Maurice. *If I Had a Hammer: The Death of the Old Left and the Birth of the New.* New York: Basic, 1987.

———. *The Other American: The Life of Michael Harrington.* New York: Public Affairs, 2000.

Isserman, Maurice, and Michael Kazin. *America Divided: The Civil War of the 1960s.* New York: Oxford University Press, 2000.

Jackson, Walter. *Gunnar Myrdal and America's Conscience: Social Engineering and Racial Liberalism, 1938–1987.* Chapel Hill: University of North Carolina Press, 1990.

Jacobs, Paul, and Saul Landau. *The New Radicals.* New York: Random House, 1966.

Jacoby, Russell. *The Last Intellectuals: American Culture in an Age of Academe.* New York: Basic, 1987.

———. *The Repression of Psychoanalysis: Otto Fenichel and the Political Freudians.* New York: Basic, 1983.

———. *Social Amnesia: A Critique of Conformist Psychology from Adler to Laing.* Boston: Beacon, 1975.

Jamison, Andrew, and Ron Eyerman. *Seeds of the Sixties.* Berkeley and Los Angeles: University of California Press, 1994.

Jay, Martin. *The Dialectical Imagination: A History of the Frankfurt School and the Institute of Social Research, 1923–1950.* Boston: Little, Brown, 1973.

Jordan, J. P. Letter. *New York Times Magazine,* August 25, 1968, 21.

Judis, John. *William F. Buckley: Patron Saint of the Conservatives.* New York: Simon and Schuster, 1988.

Judt, Tony. *The Burden of Responsibility: Blum, Camus, Aron, and the French Twentieth Century.* Chicago: University of Chicago Press, 1998.

Jumonville, Neil. *Henry Steele Commager: Midcentury Liberalism and the History of the Present.* Chapel Hill: University of North Carolina Press, 1999.

———. "The New York Intellectuals: Defense of the Intellect." *Queen's Quarterly* 97 (1990): 290–304.

Kant, Immanuel. *Fundamental Principles of the Metaphysics of Morals.* Indianapolis: Bobbs-Merrill, 1949.

———. *The Philosophy of Immanuel Kant.* Edited by Carl Friedrich. New York: Modern Library, 1949.

Kaufman, Arnold. "Ability." In *The Nature of Human Action,* edited by Myles Brand. Glenview, Ill.: Scott, Foresman, 1970.

———. "The Affluent Underdog." *The Nation,* November 5, 1960, 349–50.

———. "An American Speaks." *Socialist Commentary,* September 1965, 18–19.

———. "Beyond Alienation." *The Progressive,* February 1970, 44–46.

———. "Black Reparations." *Dissent* (July–August 1969): 318–20.

———. "The Cold War in Retrospect." In *A Dissenter's Guide to Foreign Policy,* edited by Irving Howe. New York: Praeger, 1966.

———. "Comments." In *Educational Judgments,* edited by James Doyle. London: Routledge, 1973.

———. "The Communist and the Governor." *The New Republic,* January 3, 1970, 21–24.

———. "The Complete Cold Warrior." *The Nation,* February 21, 1966, 214–16.

———. "Democracy and Disorder." In *Society: Revolution and Reform: Proceedings of the 1969 Oberlin Colloquium in Philosophy.* Cleveland: Case Western Reserve University, 1971.

———. "Democracy and the Paradox of Want-Satisfaction." *The Personalist* 52 (1971): 186–215.

———. "Evidence and Absolutes." *The Nation,* June 4, 1960, 496–97.

———. "A Future for Dissidents." *Commonweal,* November 29, 1968, 314–17.

———. "Human Nature and Participatory Democracy." In *The Bias of Pluralism,* edited by William Connolly. New York: Atherton, 1969.

———. "The Irresponsibility of American Social Scientists." *Inquiry* 3 (1960): 102–17.

———. "Moral Responsibility and the Use of 'Could Have.'" *Philosophical Quarterly* 12 (1962): 120–28.

———. "Murder in Tuskegee: Day of Wrath in the Model Town." *The Nation,* January 31, 1966, 118–25.

———. "Must Morality Be True?" *Quadrant* (Spring 1960): 67–73.

———. "The Nature and Function of Political Theory." *Journal of Philosophy* 51 (1954): 5–22.

———. "New Party or New Democratic Coalition?" *Dissent* 16 (1969): 13–18.

———. "On Alienation." *Inquiry* 8 (1965): 141–65.

———. "Participatory Democracy: Ten Years Later." In *The Bias of Pluralism,* edited by William Connolly. New York: Atherton, 1969.

———. "A Philosophy for the American Left." *Socialist Commentary,* November 1963, 3–15.

——— [Joseph Hill, pseud.]. "Plight of American Unions." *Socialist Commentary,* September 1960, 21–23.

————. "A Politics of Dignity." *Engage,* January 1–15, 1969, 14–17.

————. "Radicalism and Conventional Politics." *Dissent* 14 (1967): 432–39.

————. *The Radical Liberal: New Man in American Politics.* New York: Atherton, 1968.

————. "The Reform Theory of Punishment." *Ethics* 71 (1960): 49–53.

————. Review of *The Conservative Mind,* by Russell Kirk. *Journal of Philosophy* 52 (1955): 493–99.

————. Review of *The Democratic Prospect,* by Charles Frankel. *Harvard Educational Review* 33 (1963): 530–33.

————. Review of *The New Class,* by Milovan Djilas. *Ethics* 68 (1958): 144–47.

————. Review of *The Paradoxes of Freedom,* by Sidney Hook. *Journal of Philosophy* 62 (1965): 241–46.

————. Review of *Philosophy, Politics, and Society,* by Peter Laslett. *Journal of Philosophy* 56 (1959): 284–89.

————. "A Sketch of Liberal Theory of Fundamental Human Rights." *Monist* 52 (1968): 595–615.

————. "Some Comments on Chapter Five of the Pastoral Constitution of Vatican Council II." In *The Church in the Modern World,* edited by Charles O'Donnell. Milwaukee: Bruce, 1967.

————. "A Strategy for Radical Liberals." *Dissent* 18 (1971): 382–93.

————. "Teach-Ins: New Force for the Times." In *Teach-Ins, U.S.A.: Reports, Opinions, Documents,* edited by Louis Menashe and Ronald Radosh. New York: Praeger, 1967.

————. "Two Cheers for American Education." *Socialist Commentary,* November 1959, 21–23.

————. "Wants, Needs, and Liberalism." *Inquiry* 14 (1971): 191–212.

————. "Youth and Politics." *The Progressive,* October 1968, 44–45.

Kazin, Alfred. *Starting Out in the Thirties.* Boston: Little, Brown, 1965.

Kelly, Frank. *Court of Reason: Robert Hutchins and the Fund for the Republic.* New York: Free, 1981.

Kelman, Steven. "The Feud Among the Radicals." *Harper's,* June 1966.

Kenny, Michael. *The First New Left: British Intellectuals After Stalin.* London: Lawrence and Wishart, 1995.

Kerr, Clark. *The Uses of the University.* Cambridge: Harvard University Press, 1964.

King, Martin Luther, Jr. *Testament of Hope.* Edited by James Melvin Washington. New York: Harper and Row, 1986.

King, Mary. *Freedom Song: A Personal Story of the 1960s Civil Rights Movement.* New York: William Morrow, 1987.

King, Richard. *The Party of Eros: Radical Social Thought and the Realm of Freedom.* Chapel Hill: University of North Carolina Press, 1972.

Kostelanetz, Richard. "Paul Goodman: Persistence and Prevalence." In *Masterminds.* New York: Macmillan, 1969.

————. "The Prevalence of Paul Goodman." *New York Times Magazine,* April 3, 1966, 70–71, 91, 93, 96.

Kutulas, Judy. *The Long War: The Intellectual People's Front and Anti-Stalinism, 1930–1940.* Durham: Duke University Press, 1995.

LaFeber, Walter. *America, Russia, and the Cold War, 1945–1966.* New York: John Wiley and Sons, 1967.

Landau, Saul. "C. Wright Mills—The Last Six Months." *Root and Branch,* no. 2 (1963–64): 2–15.

Lasch, Christopher. *The Agony of the American Left.* New York: Vintage, 1969.

———. *The Culture of Narcissism.* New York: Warner, 1979.

———. "Getting Out of Power." *Commentary,* November 1965, 116–18.

———. *The New Radicalism in America, 1889–1963: The Intellectual as a Social Type.* New York: Norton, 1965.

———. "On Richard Hofstadter." *New York Review of Books,* March 8, 1973, 7–13.

———. *The True and Only Heaven: Progress and Its Critics.* New York: Norton, 1991.

———. "A Typology of Intellectuals." *Salmagundi* 70–71 (1986): 102–6.

———. "William Appleman Williams on American History." *Marxist Perspectives* 1 (1978): 118–26.

———. *Women and the Common Life: Love, Marriage, and Feminism.* Edited by Elisabeth Lasch-Quinn. New York: Norton, 1997.

Lawson, Alan. *The Failure of Independent Liberalism, 1930–1941.* New York: G. P. Putnam's and Sons, 1971.

"The Legacy of Paul Goodman." *Change* 4 (1972): 38–47.

"Legend of the Left." *Newsweek,* May 11, 1964, 91–92.

Leuchtenburg, William. "Charles Frankel, 1917–1979." *South Atlantic Quarterly* 78 (1979): 419–27.

Levine, George. "Paul Goodman, Outsider, Looking In." *New York Times Book Review,* February 18, 1973, 4–6.

Levy, Peter. *The New Left and Labor in the 1960s.* Urbana: University of Illinois Press, 1994.

Liben, Meyer. "View of Paul in a Room." *New Letters* 42 (1976): 213–15.

Lichtenstein, Nelson. *The Most Dangerous Man in Detroit: Walter Reuther and the Fate of American Labor.* New York: Basic, 1995.

Longstaff, Stephen A. "The New York Family." *Queen's Quarterly* 83 (1976): 556–72.

———. "*Partisan Review* and the Second World War." *Salmagundi* (Winter 1979): 108–29.

Luce, Phillip Abbott. *The New Left.* New York: David McKay, 1966.

Lynd, Robert. *Knowledge for What? The Place of Social Science in American Culture.* 1948. Reprint, Princeton: Princeton University Press, 1970.

Lynd, Staughton. *The Intellectual Origins of American Radicalism.* New York: Pantheon, 1968.

———. "Toward a History of the New Left." In *The New Left,* edited by Priscilla Long. Boston: Extending Horizons, 1969.

Macdonald, Dwight. *Discriminations: Essays and Afterthoughts, 1938–1974.* New York: Grossman, 1974.

———. *Memoirs of a Revolutionist.* New York: Farrar, Straus, and Cudahy, 1957.

———. *Politics Past: Essays in Political Criticism.* New York: Viking, 1957.

———. "The Question of Kitsch." *Dissent* 5 (1958): 397–99.

———. "The Root Is Man." *politics,* April 1946, 97–115.

———. "The Root Is Man (II)." *politics,* July 1946, 194–214.

Macedo, Stephen, ed. *Reassessing the Sixties: Debating the Political and Cultural Legacy.* New York: Norton, 1997.

Mailer, Norman. *The Armies of the Night: History as a Novel, the Novel as History.* New York: Signet, 1968.

Marcuse, Herbert. *One-Dimensional Man.* Boston: Beacon, 1964.
———. *Reason and Revolution: Hegel and the Rise of Social Theory.* Boston: Beacon, 1960.
———. "Repressive Tolerance." In *A Critique of Pure Tolerance,* edited by Robert Paul Wolff et al. Boston: Beacon, 1969.
MARHO: The Radical Historians' Organization. *Visions of History.* Edited by Henry Abelove. New York: Pantheon, 1983.
Markowitz, Norman. *The Rise and Fall of the People's Century: Henry A. Wallace and American Liberalism, 1941–1948.* New York: Free, 1973.
Mattson, Kevin. *Creating a Democratic Public: The Struggle for Urban Participatory Democracy During the Progressive Era.* University Park: The Pennsylvania State University Press, 1998.
———. "Having His Cake and Eating It Too: Richard Rorty on the Revitalization of the Left." *Negations,* no. 3 (1998): 78–83.
———. "Remember Liberalism?" *Social Theory and Practice* (forthcoming).
———. "Talking About My Generation (and the Left)." *Dissent* (Fall 1999): 58–63.
———. "Where Are the Young Left Intellectuals?" *Social Policy* (Spring 1999): 53–58.
Matusow, Allen. *The Unraveling of America: A History of Liberalism in the 1960s.* New York: Harper and Row, 1984.
May, Lary, ed. *Recasting America: Culture and Politics in the Age of the Cold War.* Chicago: University of Chicago Press, 1989.
McAuliffe, Mary Sperling. *Crisis on the Left: Cold War Politics and American Liberals, 1947–1954.* Amherst: University of Massachusetts Press, 1978.
McKnight, Gerald. *The Last Crusade: Martin Luther King, Jr., the FBI, and the Poor People's Campaign.* Boulder: Westview, 1998.
McMillian, John. "Love Letters to the Future: REP, *Radical America,* and New Left History." *Radical History Review* 77 (2000): 20–59.
Meeropol, Michael. "William Appleman Williams's Historiography." *Radical America* 6 (1970): 29–53.
Meier, August, and Elliot Rudwick. *CORE.* New York: Oxford University Press, 1973.
Melanson, Richard. "The Social and Political Thought of William Appleman Williams." *Western Political Quarterly* 31 (1978): 392–409.
Menashe, Louis, and Ronald Radosh, eds. *Teach-Ins, U.S.A.: Reports, Opinions, Documents.* New York: Praeger, 1967.
Mendel-Reyes, Meta. *Reclaiming Democracy: The Sixties in Politics and Memory.* New York: Routledge, 1995.
Michels, Robert. *Political Parties.* New York: Free, 1962.
Miller, Donald. *The New American Radicalism: Alfred M. Bingham and Non-Marxian Insurgency in the New Deal Era.* Port Washington, N.Y.: Kennikat, 1979.
Miller, James. "Democracy and the Intellectual: C. Wright Mills Reconsidered." *Salmagundi* 70–71 (1986): 82–101.
———. *"Democracy Is in the Streets": From Port Huron to the Siege of Chicago.* New York: Simon and Schuster, 1987.
Miller, William. *Dorothy Day: A Biography.* New York: Harper and Row, 1982.
Mills, C. Wright. "The Balance of Blame." *The Nation,* June 18, 1960, 523–31.
———. "A Bibliography of War." *Partisan Review* 10 (1943): 301–2.
———. "The Case for the Coal Miners." *The New Republic,* May 24, 1943, 695–98.

———. *The Causes of World War III.* New York: Simon and Schuster, 1958.

———. "Commentary on Our Country, Our Culture." *Partisan Review* 19 (1952): 446–50.

———. "The Conscription of America." *Common Sense,* April 1945, 15–17.

———. "The Conservative Mood." *Dissent* 1 (1954): 22–31.

———. "Crackpot Realism." *Fellowship,* January 1, 1959, 3–8.

———. "Dogmatic Indecision." *Labor Zionist,* April 15, 1949, 3.

———. "Five 'Publics' the Polls Don't Catch." *Labor and Nation,* May–June 1947, 22–27.

———. "For Ought?" C. Wright Mills Papers, 1934–1965, box 4B390. Barker Texas History Center, Center for American History, University of Texas at Austin.

———. "La Gauche Americaine: Savoir Attendre." *Esprit,* November 1952, 693–99.

———. "'Grass-Roots' Union with Ideas: The Auto Workers—Something New in American Labor." *Commentary,* March 1948, 240–47.

———. "The History Makers." *Social Progress* (October 1959): 5–16.

———. "Intellectuals and Russia." *Dissent* 6 (1959): 295–301.

———. "The Intellectuals' Last Chance." *Esquire,* October 1959, 101–2.

———. Introduction to *The Theory of the Leisure Class,* by Thorstein Veblen. New York: Mentor, 1953.

———. *Listen, Yankee: The Revolution in Cuba.* New York: Ballantine, 1960.

———. *The Marxists.* New York: Dell, 1962.

———. *The New Men of Power: America's Labor Leaders.* New York: Harcourt, Brace, 1948.

———. "No Mean Sized Opportunity." In *The House of Labor: Internal Operations of American Unions,* edited by J. B. S. Hardman and Maurice Neufeld. New York: Prentice-Hall, 1951.

———. "Notes on White Collar Unionism." *Labor and Nation,* March–April 1949, 17–21, 42.

———. "On Latin America, the Left, and the U.S." Interview with C. Wright Mills. *Evergreen Review* 5 (1961): 110–22.

———. "The People in the Unions." *Labor and Nation,* January–February 1947, 28–31.

———. "The Politics of Skill." *Labor and Nation,* June–July 1946, 35.

———. *The Power Elite.* New York: Oxford University Press, 1956.

———. "'The Power Elite': Comment and Criticism." *Dissent* 4 (1957): 22–34.

———. "The Power Elite: Military, Economic, and Political." In *Problems of Power in American Democracy,* edited by Arthur Kornhauser. Detroit: Wayne State University Press, 1957.

———. "The Powerless People: The Role of the Intellectual in Society." *politics,* April 1944, 68–72.

———. *Power, Politics, and People: The Collected Essays of C. Wright Mills.* Edited by Irving Louis Horowitz. New York: Oxford University Press, 1963.

———. "Probing the Two Party System." *The New Leader,* October 30, 1943, 3, 7.

———. "A Program for Peace." *The Nation,* December 7, 1957, 419–24.

———. Review of *The Academic Man,* by Logan Wilson. *American Sociological Review* 7 (1942): 444–46.

———. *The Sociological Imagination.* New York: Oxford University Press, 1959.

———. *Sociology and Pragmatism: The Higher Learning in America.* New York: Oxford University Press, 1969.

————. "What Research Can Do for Labor." *Labor and Nation,* June–July 1946, 17–20.

————. "What the People Think." *Labor and Nation,* March–April 1947, 258.

————. "What the People Think: Review of Selected Opinion Polls." *Labor and Nation,* November–December 1946, 11–13.

————. *White Collar: The American Middle Classes.* New York: Oxford University Press, 1951.

————. "White Collar Unionism." *Labor and Nation,* May–June 1949, 17–23.

————. "A Who's What of Union Leadership." *Labor and Nation,* December 1945, 33–36.

Mills, C. Wright, and Hans Gerth. *Character and Social Structure.* New York: Harcourt, Brace, and World, 1953.

————. *From Max Weber: Essays in Sociology.* New York: Oxford University Press, 1946.

Mills, C. Wright, and Patricia Salter. "The Barricade and the Bedroom." *politics,* October 1945, 313–15.

Mills, C. Wright, and Saul Landau. "Modest Proposals for Patriotic Americans." *Tribune* (London), May 19, 1961, 5.

Mills, Hilary. *Mailer: A Biography.* New York: Empire, 1982.

Mills, Kate, ed. *C. Wright Mills: Letters and Autobiographical Writings.* Berkeley and Los Angeles: University of California Press, 2000.

Miroff, Bruce. *Pragmatic Illusions: The Presidential Politics of John F. Kennedy.* New York: McKay, 1976.

Morris, Aldon. *The Origins of the Civil Rights Movement.* New York: Free, 1984.

Mumford, Lewis. *The City in History.* New York: Harcourt, Brace, Jovanovich, 1961.

————. *My Works and Days: A Personal Chronicle.* New York: Harcourt, Brace, Jovanovich, 1979.

Myers, R. David, ed. *Toward a History of the New Left: Essays from Within the Movement.* Brooklyn: Carlson, 1989.

Nash, George. *The Conservative Intellectual Movement in America, Since 1945.* New York: Basic, 1976.

Neumann, Franz. *Behemoth: The Structure and Practice of National Socialism, 1933–1944.* New York: Harper Torchbooks, 1966.

Newfield, Jack. *A Prophetic Minority.* New York: New American, 1970.

Noble, David. *The End of American History: Democracy, Capitalism, and the Metaphor of Two Worlds in Anglo-American Historical Writings, 1880–1980.* Minneapolis: University of Minnesota Press, 1985.

Novick, Peter. *That Noble Dream: The 'Objectivity Question' and the American Historical Profession.* Cambridge: Cambridge University Press, 1988.

Oakes, Guy, and Arthur Vidich. *Collaboration, Reputation, and Ethics in American Academic Life: Hans H. Gerth and C. Wright Mills.* Urbana: University of Illinois Press, 1999.

Orser, W. Edward. *Searching for a Viable Alternative: The Macedonia Community Cooperative, 1937–1958.* New York: Burt Franklin, 1981.

Ostriker, Alicia. "Paul Goodman." *Partisan Review* 43 (1976): 286–95.

Pareto, Vilfredo. *Sociological Writings.* London: Pall Mall, 1966.

Parisi, Peter, ed. *Artist of the Actual: Essays on Paul Goodman.* Metuchen, N.J.: Scarecrow, 1986.

Parmet, Herbert. *The Democrats: The Years After FDR.* New York: Macmillan, 1976.

Parrington, Vernon. *Main Currents in American Thought.* Vol. 2, *1800–1860: The Romantic Revolution in America.* New York: Harcourt, Brace, and World, 1927.

Patner, Andrew. *I. F. Stone: A Portrait.* New York: Pantheon, 1988.

Pells, Richard. *The Liberal Mind in a Conservative Age: American Intellectuals in the 1940s and 1950s.* Middletown: Wesleyan University Press, 1989.

———. *Radical Visions and American Dreams.* New York: Harper Torchbooks, 1973.

Perkins, Bradford. "*The Tragedy of American Diplomacy,* Twenty-Five Years Later." *Reviews in American History* 12 (1984): 1–18.

Perls, Frederick S., Ralph Hefferline, and Paul Goodman. *Gestalt Therapy: Excitement and Growth in the Human Personality.* New York: Julian, 1951.

Person, James. *Russell Kirk: A Critical Biography of a Conservative Mind.* Lanham, Md.: Madison, 1999.

Pfeffer, Paula. *A. Philip Randolph: Pioneer of the Civil Rights Movement.* Baton Rouge: Louisiana State University Press, 1990.

Podhoretz, Norman. "The Know-Nothing Bohemians." *Partisan Review* (Spring 1958): 305–18.

Rader, Dotson. *Blood Dues.* New York: Knopf, 1973.

Radita, Leo. "On Paul Goodman—and Goodmanism." *Iowa Review* 5 (1973): 62–79.

Reeves, Richard. *President Kennedy: Profile of Power.* New York: Simon and Schuster, 1993.

Riesman, David. "The Intellectuals and Discontented Classes." *Partisan Review* (Spring 1962): 250–62.

Riesman, David, et al. *The Lonely Crowd.* New York: Doubleday, 1955.

Robinson, Jo Ann. *Abraham Went Out: A Biography of A. J. Muste.* Philadelphia: Temple University Press, 1981.

Rodewald, Richard, and Richard Wasserstrom. "The Political Philosophy of Arnold Kaufman." *Social Theory and Practice* 2 (1972): 5–31.

Rossinow, Doug. *The Politics of Authenticity: Liberalism, Christianity, and the New Left in America.* New York: Columbia University Press, 1998.

Rossman, Michael. *The Wedding Within the War.* Garden City, N.J.: Doubleday, 1971.

Rothman, Jack. "The Radical Liberal Strategy in Action: Arnold Kaufman and the First Teach-In." *Social Theory and Practice* 2 (1972): 33–45.

Rudd, Mark. Letter. *New York Times Magazine,* August 4, 1968, 56.

Sale, Kirkpatrick. *SDS.* New York: Vintage, 1974.

Saloff, Stephen. "Cyrus Easton." *Queen's Quarterly* 90 (1983): 379–86.

Sandel, Michael. *Democracy's Discontent.* Cambridge: Harvard University Press, 1996.

Saunders, Frances Stonor. *The Cultural Cold War: The CIA and the World of Arts and Letters.* New York: Free, 1999.

Scheer, Robert. "Notes on the New Left." *Root and Branch,* no. 2 (1963–64): 16–22.

Schlesinger, Arthur. *The Vital Center: The Politics of Freedom.* 1949. Reprint, New York: Da Capo, 1988.

Schluchter, Wolfgang. *The Rise of Western Rationalism.* Berkeley and Los Angeles: University of California Press, 1981.

Schwarz, Jordan. *Liberal: Adolf A. Berle and the Vision of an American Era.* New York: Free, 1987.

Seidman, Steven. *Liberalism and the Origins of European Social Theory.* Berkeley and Los Angeles: University of California Press, 1983.

Selvin, David. "Carey McWilliams: Reformer as Historian." *California Historical Quarterly* 53 (1974): 173–80.

Shannon, Christopher. *Conspicuous Criticism: Tradition, the Individual, and Culture in American Social Thought, from Veblen to Mills.* Baltimore: Johns Hopkins University Press, 1996.

Singal, Daniel. "Beyond Consensus: Richard Hofstadter and American Historiography." *American Historical Review* 89 (1984): 976–1004.

Smith, Allen. "Present at the Creation and Other Myths: The Port Huron Statement and the Origins of the New Left." *Socialist Review* 27 (1999): 1–27.

Sontag, Susan. "On Paul Goodman." In *Under the Sign of Saturn.* New York: Farrar, Straus, Giroux, 1980.

Soper, Kate. "Socialist Humanism." In *E. P. Thompson: Critical Perspectives,* edited by Harvey Kaye and Keith McClelland. Philadelphia: Temple University Press, 1990.

Starr, Mark. "Labor Through the Polls." *Labor Zionist,* March 18, 1949, 2.

Steel, Ronald. *Walter Lippmann and the American Century.* New York: Vintage, 1980.

Steigerwald, David. *The Sixties and the End of Modern America.* New York: St. Martin's, 1995.

Steiner, George. "On Paul Goodman." *Commentary,* August 1963, 199.

Steinfels, Peter. *The Neoconservatives.* New York: Simon and Schuster, 1979.

Stoehr, Taylor. "Growing Up Absurd—Again." *Dissent* (Fall 1990): 486–94.

———. *Here, Now, Next: Paul Goodman and the Origins of Gestalt Therapy.* San Francisco: Jossey-Bass, 1994.

———. "Paul Goodman and the New York Jews." *Salmagundi* 66 (1985): 50–103.

Stone, I. F. *The Haunted Fifties.* New York: Vintage, 1963.

Sumner, Gregory. *Dwight Macdonald and the* politics *Circle: The Challenge of Cosmopolitan Democracy.* Ithaca: Cornell University Press, 1996.

Swados, Harvey. "C. Wright Mills: A Personal Memoir." *Dissent* 10 (1963): 35–42.

Teodori, Massimo, ed. *The New Left: A Documentary History.* Indianapolis: Bobbs-Merrill, 1969.

Thomas, John. *Alternative America: Henry George, Edward Bellamy, Henry Demarest Lloyd, and the Adversary Tradition.* Cambridge: Belknap Press, 1983.

Thompson, E. P. "C. Wright Mills: The Responsible Craftsman." *Radical America* (July–August 1979): 61–73.

———. "The New Left." *New Reasoner,* Summer 1959, 1–17.

———. *William Morris: Romantic to Revolutionary.* London: Lawrence and Wishart, 1955.

———, ed. *Out of Apathy.* London: Stevens and Sons, 1960.

Tilman, Rick. *C. Wright Mills: A Native Radical and His American Intellectual Roots.* University Park: The Pennsylvania State University Press, 1984.

Tobin, Eugene. *Organize or Perish: America's Independent Progressives, 1913–1933.* New York: Greenwood, 1986.

Trilling, Diana. "An Interview with Dwight Macdonald." *Partisan Review* 51 (1984): 799–819.

Trilling, Lionel. *The Liberal Imagination: Essays on Literature and Society.* Garden City, N.J.: Anchor, 1950.

True, Michael. "Paul Goodman and the Triumph of American Prose Style." *New Letters* 42 (1976): 228–36.

Unger, Irwin. *The Movement: A History of the American New Left, 1959–1972.* New York: Dodd, Mead, 1974.

Veblen, Thorstein. *The Engineers and the Price System.* New York: Viking, 1921.

Vickers, George. *The Formation of the New Left.* Lexington: Lexington, 1975.

Wainwright, Hilary. *Arguments for a New Left: Answering the Free Market Right.* Oxford: Blackwell, 1994.

Wakefield, Dan. *New York in the Fifties.* Boston: Houghton Mifflin, 1992.

———. "Taking It Big: A Memoir of C. Wright Mills." *Atlantic Monthly,* September 1971.

Wald, Alan. *The New York Intellectuals: The Rise and Decline of the Anti-Stalinist Left from the 1930s to the 1980s.* Chapel Hill: University of North Carolina Press, 1987.

Walzer, Michael. *The Company of Critics: Social Criticism and Political Commitment in the Twentieth Century.* New York: Basic, 1988.

———. "Paul Goodman's Community of Scholars." *Dissent* 11 (1964): 21–27.

Ward, Colin. "The Anarchist as Citizen." *New Letters* 42 (1976): 237–45.

Waskow, Arthur. *The Limits of Defense.* Garden City, N.J.: Doubleday, 1962.

———. "Marc Raskin." *Social Policy* (Winter 1999): 59–63.

Watson, Steven. *The Birth of the Beat Generation.* New York: Pantheon, 1995.

Weber, Max. *Economy and Society.* 3 vols. New York: Bedminster, 1968.

———. *The Protestant Ethic and the Spirit of Capitalism.* New York: Scribner, 1958.

Wechsler, James. *Reflections of an Angry Middle-Aged Editor.* New York: Random House, 1960.

Weinstein, James. *Ambiguous Legacy: The Left in American Politics.* New York: New Viewpoints, 1975.

———. *The Corporate Ideal in the Liberal State, 1900–1918.* Boston: Beacon, 1968.

———. *The Decline of Socialism in America, 1912–1925.* New York: Vintage, 1967.

Weinstein, James, and David Eakins, eds. *For a New America: Essays in History and Politics from Studies on the Left, 1959–1967.* New York: Vintage, 1970.

Weisberg, Jacob. "Cold War Without End." *New York Times Magazine,* November 29, 1999, 116–23, 155–58.

Weissman, Steve. "Lament for the Teach-Ins." *The New Leader,* March 27, 1967, 14–19.

Wells, Tom. *The War Within: America's Battle over Vietnam.* Berkeley and Los Angeles: University of California Press, 1994.

West, Cornel. *The American Evasion of Philosophy: A Genealogy of Pragmatism.* Madison: University of Wisconsin Press, 1989.

Westbrook, Robert. "Christopher Lasch, *The New Radicalism,* and the Vocation of Intellectuals." *Reviews in American History* 23 (1995): 176–91.

———. "Horrors—Theirs and Ours: The *politics* Circle and the Good War." *Radical History Review* 36 (1986): 9–25.

———. *John Dewey and American Democracy.* Ithaca: Cornell University Press, 1991.

———. "The Responsibility of Peoples: Dwight Macdonald and the Holocaust." In *America and the Holocaust,* edited by Sanford Pinsker and Jack Fischel. Greenwood, Fla.: Penkevill, 1983.

Whitfield, Stephen. *A Critical American: The Politics of Dwight Macdonald.* Guilford, Conn.: Archon, 1984.

———. *The Culture of the Cold War.* Baltimore: Johns Hopkins University Press, 1991.

Whyte, William. *Organization Man*. Garden City, N.J.: Anchor, 1956.

Widmer, Kingsley. *Paul Goodman*. Boston: Twayne, 1980.

Wieck, David. Review of *Drawing the Line*. *Telos*, no. 35 (1978): 199–214.

Wieck, Paul. "What Happened to the New Politics?" *The New Republic*, February 28, 1970, 12–13.

Wiener, Jonathan. "Radical Historians and the Crisis in American History, 1959–1980." *Journal of American History* 76 (1989): 399–442.

Wilford, Hugh. *The New York Intellectuals: From Vanguard to Institution*. Manchester: Manchester University Press, 1995.

Williams, William Appleman. "The Age of Re-Forming History." *The Nation*, June 30, 1956, 552–54.

———. "America II Continued." *Partisan Review* 38 (1971): 67–78.

———. *America and the Middle East: Open Door Imperialism or Enlightened Leadership?* New York: Rinehart, 1958.

———. "American Century: 1941–1957." *The Nation*, November 2, 1957, 297–301.

———. *American-Russian Relations, 1781–1947*. New York: Rinehart, 1952.

———. "An American Socialist Community?" *Liberation*, June 1969, 8–11.

———. "Babbitt's New Fables." *The Nation*, January 7, 1956, 3–6.

———. "Brooks Adams and American Expansion." *New England Quarterly* 25 (1952): 217–32.

———. "Charles Austin Beard: The Intellectual as Tory Radical." In *American Radicals: Some Problems and Personalities*, edited by Harvey Goldberg. New York: Monthly Review, 1957.

———. "China and Japan: A Challenge and a Choice of the 1920s." *Pacific Historical Review* 26 (1957): 259–79.

———. "Cold War Perspectives." *The Nation*, May 28, 1955, 458–61.

———. "The Cold War Revisionists." *The Nation*, November 13, 1967, 492–95.

———. *The Contours of American History*. New York: New Viewpoints, 1973.

———. "The Convenience of History." *The Nation*, September 15, 1956, 274–79.

———. "The Crown on Clio's Head." *The Nation*, March 9, 1970, 279–80.

———. "Cuba: Issues and Alternatives." *Annals of the American Academy of Political and Social Science*, no. 351 (January 1964): 72–80.

———. "Fire in the Ashes of Scientific History." *William and Mary Quarterly* 19 (1962): 274–87.

———. "Go Left or Go Under." *Liberation*, April 1957, 14–17.

———. *The Great Evasion*. Chicago: Quadrangle, 1964.

———. "How Can the Left Be Relevant?" *Current* (August 1969): 20–24.

———. "The Irony of Containment." *The Nation*, May 5, 1956, 376–79.

———. "The Irony of the Bomb." *The Centennial Review* 4 (1961): 373–84.

———. "The Large Corporation and American Foreign Policy." In *Corporations and the Cold War*, edited by David Horowitz. New York: Monthly Review, 1969.

———. "Last Chance for Democracy." *The Nation*, January 2, 1967, 23–25.

———. "Latin America: Laboratory of American Foreign Policy in the 1920s." *Inter-American Economic Affairs* 11 (1957): 3–30.

———. "The 'Logic' of Imperialism." *The Nation*, July 6, 1957, 14–15.

———. "Moscow Peace Drive: Victory for Containment?" *The Nation,* July 11, 1953, 28–30.

———. "Needed: Production for Peace." *The Nation,* February 21, 1959, 149–53.

———. "A Note on American Foreign Policy in Europe in the 1920s." *Science and Society* 22 (1958): 1–20.

———. "A Note on Charles Austin Beard's Search for a General Theory of Causation." *American Historical Review* 62 (1956): 59–80.

———. "A Note on the Isolationism of Senator William E. Borah." *Pacific Historical Review* 22 (1953): 391–92.

———. "The Origin of the Cold War." *Commentary,* February 1962, 142–59.

———. "The Outdoor Mind." *The Nation,* October 30, 1954, 384–85.

———. "The President and His Critics." *The Nation,* March 16, 1963, 226–28, 236.

———. "A Proposal to Put the American Back into American Socialism." *New Politics* (Spring 1962): 40–45.

———. "Protecting Overseas Investors." *The Nation,* August 26, 1961, 100–101.

———. "Pseudo-Debate in the Teach-In: Criticism Contained." In *Teach-Ins, U.S.A.: Reports, Opinions, Documents,* ed. Louis Menashe and Ronald Radosh. New York: Praeger, 1967.

———. Review of *Russia: A History and Interpretation,* by Michael Florinsky. *Science and Society* 19 (1955): 345–50.

———. Review of *Senator Fulbright,* by Tristram Coffin. *Ramparts,* March 1967, 57–59.

———. Review of *Woodrow Wilson,* by Arthur Link. *Science and Society* 18 (1954): 348–51.

———. "Rise of an American World Power Complex." In *Struggle Against History: U.S. Foreign Policy in an Age of Revolution,* edited by Neal Houghton. New York: Washington Square, 1968.

———. *The Roots of the Modern American Empire.* New York: Random House, 1969.

———. "Schlesinger: Right Crisis—Wrong Order." *The Nation,* March 23, 1957, 257–60.

———. "Take a New Look at Russia." *Foreign Policy Bulletin,* April 15, 1959, 118, 120.

———. "Taxing for Peace." *The Nation,* January 19, 1957, 53.

———. *The Tragedy of American Diplomacy.* 1959. Reprint, New York: Delta, 1962.

———. *The United States, Cuba, and Castro.* New York: Monthly Review, 1962.

———. "The Vicious Circle of American Imperialism." *New Politics* 4 (1965): 48–55.

Wittner, Lawrence. *Rebels Against War: The American Peace Movement, 1933–1983.* Philadelphia: Temple University Press, 1984.

Wreszin, Michael. *A Rebel in Defense of Tradition: The Life and Politics of Dwight Macdonald.* New York: Basic, 1994.

Zaroulis, Nancy, and Gerald Sullivan. *Who Spoke Up? American Protest Against the War in Vietnam, 1963–1975.* Garden City, N.J.: Doubleday, 1984.

Zieger, Robert. *American Workers, American Unions, 1920–1985.* Baltimore: Johns Hopkins University Press, 1986.

Index